WORD ON FIRE
Classics

CATHOLIC SOCIAL TEACHING COLLECTION

FOREWORD BY BISHOP ROBERT BARRON

CATHOLIC
SOCIAL TEACHING
COLLECTION

Unless otherwise indicated, Church Father quotes from *Nicene and Post-Nicene Fathers*,
Second Series, edited by Philip Schaff and Henry Wace (Buffalo, NY: Christian Literature
Publishing Co., 1894). Revised and edited for NewAdvent.org by Kevin Knight,
adapted in some places for this book. Used by permission. All rights reserved.

Church documents excerpted from Vatican.va with permission. All rights reserved.
© Libreria Editrice Vaticana.

Excerpt from *A Prophetic Bishop Speaks to His People: The Complete Homilies of Archbishop
Óscar Romero* (Convivium, 2017) © Óscar Romero. Used with permission.

Old Testament and New Testament quotations are from the
New Revised Standard Version, Catholic Edition (NRSV-CE) ©1989, 1993.

Word on Fire, Park Ridge, IL 60068
©2020 by Word on Fire Catholic Ministries
Printed in the United States of America
All rights reserved.

22 21 20 19   1 2 3 4
ISBN: 978-1-943243-66-2

Library of Congress Control Number: 2020942560
Barron, Robert E., 1959–

www.wordonfire.org

CONTENTS

❖

PART II

SCRIPTURE, SAINTS, AND SCHOLARS 335

FOREWORD

by Bishop Robert Barron

❖

Catholic social teaching—when it is not distorted or misrepresented—is famously confounding to the pundits and politicos, both left and right. How can the Catholic Church simultaneously advocate against abortion and assisted suicide but for immigration reform and attention to the poor? How can it stand against the abuse of the environment and for the free market, against the death penalty and for the family?

This unique collection for our *Word on Fire Classics* series aims to bring the both/and of the Church's social teaching into sharp relief. That teaching comes roaring out of the Old Testament prophets and the New Testament, into the writings of the Church Fathers, and down through the Church's encyclicals and in the lives of the saints. This collection encompasses all of these different dimensions of the Church's history. But its purpose if not just to reveal the ethical and historical breadth of Catholic social teaching; it is to reveal its metaphysical heart—namely, God. With God out of the picture, it is indeed hard to make sense of the array of opinions the Church holds. But with God at the heart of things, the positions fall into harmony, much like the medallions in a rose window. If God exists, then every individual person is a subject of rights, freedom, and dignity. If God exists, then no one is expendable and everyone is equally worthy of respect.

Why? Because Scripture teaches us that every human being is an *imago Dei*—a creature made in the image and likeness of God (cf. Gen. 1:26).

There is no philosophy, no religion, no social theory, no ideology that has ever proposed a more thoroughgoing affirmation of the human being than the Bible has. Neither ancient programs of perfectibility, nor Renaissance humanism, nor modern progressivism, nor Marxism, nor the contemporary valorization of freedom have come close to holding up the human person as high as do the Scriptures. For the biblical authors' claim is that the human being is marked, in every aspect of his existence, by a likeness unto God, that he has been endowed with a distinctive mission from God, and that he is ultimately destined for life on high in union with God.

Many philosophers and social theorists have tried to ground a sense of human dignity in something other than God, but these attempts have all proven fruitless. For instance, if human worth is a function of a person's intelligence or creativity or imagination, or her capacity to enter into friendship, then why not say that this worth disappears the moment those powers are underdeveloped, weakened, or eliminated altogether? Or if respect for human dignity is related to the strength of one's feelings for another person, then who is to say that that dignity doesn't vanish once one's sentiments change or dry up? For the past two hundred years, atheists have been loudly asserting that the dismissal of God will lead to human liberation. I would strenuously argue precisely the contrary. Once the human being is untethered from God, he becomes, in very short order, an object among objects, and hence susceptible to the grossest manipulation by the powerful and the self-interested. In the measure that people still speak of the irreducible dignity of the individual, they are, whether they know it or not, standing upon biblical foundations. When those foundations are shaken—as they increasingly are today—a culture of death will follow just as surely as night follows day.

The first part of this book offers a summary of magisterial statements articulating the Church's social teaching. Economics, and the ways in which it can be harnessed either to elevate or denigrate human dignity, is a key preoccupation of those statements. In 1891, Pope Leo XIII, one of the really great popes in Church history, wrote an encyclical called *Rerum Novarum*, Latin for "About the New Things" (reproduced in full in this collection). The "new things" were the economic and political realities of that turning century: a largely unbridled, unregulated, undisciplined capitalism, which was producing a crisis in the West and giving rise to socialist and communist reactions and a great deal of upheaval. In response, Pope Leo XIII gave us this fountainhead of the modern Catholic social teaching tradition, which is a very clear judgment against socialist options, and a mitigated and carefully nuanced affirmation of capitalism, or what the Church tends to call "the market economy." Several other documents built on the foundation of *Rerum Novarum*, from Pope Pius XI's *Quadragesimo Anno* (Latin for "On the Fortieth Year," written forty years after *Rerum Novarum*) to Pope John XXIII's *Mater et Magistra* and *Pacem in Terris*. John Paul II also wrote a number of significant letters, including *Sollicitudo Rei Socialis* in 1987, but if you're going to read one document in the Church's social teaching tradition, read John Paul II's *Centesimus Annus* (also reproduced here in full). This encyclical letter, written to mark the one hundredth anniversary of *Rerum Novarum*, sums up Catholic social teaching better than any other document.

In the midst of *Centesimus Annus*, John Paul responds to the question whether, after the collapse of communism, capitalism should be embraced as the optimal economic system. He says:

> If by "capitalism" is meant an economic system which recognizes the fundamental and positive role of business, the market, private property . . . as well as free human creativity in the economic sector, then the answer is certainly in the affirmative. . . . But if by "capitalism" is meant a system in which freedom in the economic sector is not circumscribed within a strong juridical framework which places it at the service of human freedom in its totality . . . the core of which is ethical and religious, then the reply is certainly negative.

In this subtle, nuanced, and balanced answer, John Paul gives voice to the major principles of Catholic social teaching on the economy, and endeavors to show the way in which Jesus Christ can exercise his lordship in this arena of life.

The second part of this collection looks at the origins of Catholic social teaching in the biblical and patristic writings, and its flowering in the lives of its saints and scholars, from St. Thomas Aquinas, who wrote about the image of God in man; to St. Damien of Molokai, who ministered to a colony of lepers and inevitably contracted the disease himself; to St. Teresa of Kolkata, who led her Missionaries of Charity in serving the poorest of the poor. It also includes writings from Bartolomé de las Casas, the final figure featured in Word on Fire's *Pivotal Players* film series, who fiercely advocated for the Indians of the newly discovered Americas, and anticipated, by four centuries, many of the key features of Catholic social teaching—especially human dignity. His writings in this collection are from his *Short Account of the Destruction of the Indies*, written in 1542, shortly after the first papal document in this collection, Pope Paul III's *Sublimus Deus: On the Enslavement and Evangelization of the Indians*. When many of the leaders of both Church and state were more than content to countenance the oppression of the Indians, Las Casas, in the name of Jesus, said no. When so many in Europe were more than willing to see the conquered Indians as little more than pack animals to be exploited and enslaved, he insisted that the rights of the Indians be respected and their dignity upheld. In his passion to set things right, Las Casas is a worthy successor of the Israelite prophets and justice-minded Church Fathers, as well as a precursor of Oscar Romero and John Paul II. He shows, as vividly as any figure in the great Christian tradition, that a commitment to justice is an essential dimension of Christian discipleship. You simply cannot claim to be a follower of Jesus and remain indifferent to suffering and injustice.

Some argue that the Church has no business talking about social issues in the first place. Shouldn't the teaching authority of the Church be focusing instead on religious questions? But the idea that the Church shouldn't have a social teaching is simply repugnant to the Catholic view of God. If God is merely a distant supreme being, as many of the American founding fathers thought, then what emerges indeed is a purely secular world that's only at best obliquely related to God. But God is not a distant supreme being; rather, he is the creative ground of all existence, which is here and now giving rise to the whole of creation. Thomas Aquinas calls God *ipsum esse*, which means the act of "to be" itself, through which all things come to be. Therefore, there is no purely independent secular realm untouched by God; rather, God impinges upon all of reality—including social realties.

But Catholic social teaching is, necessarily, very deep and broad, one to which countless saints and documents in the history of the Church bear witness. This collection is not intended as an exhaustive academic treatment of that tradition but as a prolegomenon for further study—and action. God is a God of justice, and my hope is that this collection will inspire people—especially young people who may have wandered away from the faith—and draw them into the Church's fight for justice.

PART I

CHURCH TEACHING

CHAPTER I

Sublimis Deus:
On the Enslavement and Evangelization of the Indians

(Full Text)

Pope Paul III
June 2, 1537

Issued by Pope Paul III in 1537, the encyclical affirms the full personhood of the indigenous people of the Americas, condemns their enslavement or the taking of their property, and calls for the evangelization of all people into the Catholic faith.

✷

To all faithful Christians to whom this writing may come, health in Christ our Lord and the apostolic benediction.

The sublime God so loved the human race that He created man in such wise that he might participate, not only in the good that other creatures enjoy, but endowed him with capacity to attain to the inaccessible and invisible Supreme Good and behold it face to face; and since man, according to the testimony of the sacred scriptures, has been created to enjoy eternal life and happiness, which none may obtain save through faith in our Lord Jesus Christ, it is necessary that he should possess the nature and faculties enabling him to receive that faith; and that whoever is thus endowed should be capable of receiving that same faith. Nor is it credible that any one should possess so little understanding as to desire the faith and yet be destitute of the most necessary faculty to enable him to receive it. Hence Christ, who is the Truth itself, that has never failed and can never fail, said to the preachers of the faith whom He chose for that office "Go ye and teach all nations." He said all, without exception, for all are capable of receiving the doctrines of the faith.

The enemy of the human race, who opposes all good deeds in order to bring men to destruction, beholding and envying this, invented a means never before heard of, by which he might hinder the preaching of God's word of Salvation to the people: he inspired his satellites who, to please him, have not hesitated to publish abroad that the Indians of the West and the South, and other people of whom We have recent knowledge should be treated as dumb brutes created for our service, pretending that they are incapable of receiving the Catholic Faith.

We, who, though unworthy, exercise on earth the power of our Lord and seek with all our might to bring those sheep of His flock who are outside into the fold committed to our charge, consider, however, that the Indians are truly men and that they are not only capable of understanding the Catholic Faith but, according to our information, they desire exceedingly to receive it. Desiring to provide ample remedy for these evils, We define and declare by these Our letters, or by any translation thereof signed by any notary public and sealed with the seal of any ecclesiastical dignitary, to which the same credit shall be given as to the originals, that, notwithstanding whatever may have been or may be said to the contrary, the said Indians and all other people who may later be discovered by Christians, are by no means to be deprived of their liberty or the possession of their property, even though they be outside the faith of Jesus Christ; and that they may and should, freely and legitimately, enjoy their liberty and the possession of their property; nor should they be in any way enslaved; should the contrary happen, it shall be null and have no effect.

By virtue of Our apostolic authority We define and declare by these present letters, or by any translation thereof signed by any notary public and sealed with the seal of any ecclesiastical dignitary, which shall thus command the same obedience as the originals, that the said Indians and other peoples should be converted to the faith of Jesus Christ by preaching the word of God and by the example of good and holy living.

CHAPTER 2

Rerum Novarum: The Rights and Duties of Capital and Labor

(Full Text)

Pope Leo XIII

May 15, 1891

This encyclical on capital and labor by Pope Leo XIII is often considered the foundational text of modern Catholic social teaching.

To Our Venerable Brethren the Patriarchs, Primates, Archbishops, Bishops, and other ordinaries of places having Peace and Communion with the Apostolic See.

That the spirit of revolutionary change, which has long been disturbing the nations of the world, should have passed beyond the sphere of politics and made its influence felt in the cognate sphere of practical economics is not surprising. The elements of the conflict now raging are unmistakable, in the vast expansion of industrial pursuits and the marvellous discoveries of science; in the changed relations between masters and workmen; in the enormous fortunes of some few individuals, and the utter poverty of the masses; the increased self reliance and closer mutual combination of the working classes; as also, finally, in the prevailing moral degeneracy. The momentous gravity of the state of things now obtaining fills every mind with painful apprehension; wise men are discussing it; practical men are proposing schemes; popular meetings, legislatures, and rulers of nations are all busied with it—actually there is no question which has taken deeper hold on the public mind.

2. Therefore, venerable brethren, as on former occasions when it seemed opportune to refute false teaching, We have addressed you in the interests of the Church and of the common weal, and have issued letters bearing on political power, human liberty, the Christian constitution of the State, and like matters, so have We thought it expedient now to speak on the condition of the working classes.[1] It is a subject on which We have already touched more than once, incidentally. But in the present letter, the responsibility of the apostolic office urges Us to treat the question of set purpose and in detail, in order that no misapprehension may exist as to the principles which truth and justice dictate for its settlement. The discussion is not easy, nor is it void of danger. It is no easy matter to define the relative rights and mutual duties of the rich and of the poor, of capital and of labor. And the danger lies in this, that crafty agitators are intent on making use of these differences of opinion to pervert men's judgments and to stir up the people to revolt.

3. In any case we clearly see, and on this there is general agreement, that some opportune remedy must be found quickly for the misery and wretchedness pressing so unjustly on the majority of the working class: for the ancient workingmen's guilds were abolished in the last century, and no other protective organization took their place. Public institutions and the laws set aside the ancient religion. Hence, by degrees it has come to pass that working men have been surrendered, isolated and helpless, to the hardheartedness of employers and the greed of unchecked competition. The mischief has been increased by rapacious usury, which, although more than once condemned by the Church, is nevertheless, under a different guise, but with like injustice, still practiced by covetous and grasping men. To this must be added that the

---

1. The title sometimes given to this encyclical, *On the Condition of the Working Classes*, is therefore perfectly justified. A few lines after this sentence, the Pope gives a more comprehensive definition of the subject of *Rerum novarum*. We are using it as a title.

The authority of the divine law adds its sanction, forbidding us in severest terms even to covet that which is another's: "Thou shalt not covet thy neighbour's wife; nor his house, nor his field, nor his man-servant, nor his maid-servant, nor his ox, nor his ass, nor anything that is his."[2]

12. The rights here spoken of, belonging to each individual man, are seen in much stronger light when considered in relation to man's social and domestic obligations. In choosing a state of life, it is indisputable that all are at full liberty to follow the counsel of Jesus Christ as to observing virginity, or to bind themselves by the marriage tie. No human law can abolish the natural and original right of marriage, nor in any way limit the chief and principal purpose of marriage ordained by God's authority from the beginning: "Increase and multiply."[3] Hence we have the family, the "society" of a man's house—a society very small, one must admit, but none the less a true society, and one older than any State. Consequently, it has rights and duties peculiar to itself which are quite independent of the State.

13. That right to property, therefore, which has been proved to belong naturally to individual persons, must in like wise belong to a man in his capacity of head of a family; nay, that right is all the stronger in proportion as the human person receives a wider extension in the family group. It is a most sacred law of nature that a father should provide food and all necessaries for those whom he has begotten; and, similarly, it is natural that he should wish that his children, who carry on, so to speak, and continue his personality, should be by him provided with all that is needful to enable them to keep themselves decently from want and misery amid the uncertainties of this mortal life. Now, in no other way can a father effect this except by the ownership of productive property, which he can transmit to his children by inheritance. A family, no less than a State, is, as We have said, a true society, governed by an authority peculiar to itself, that is to say, by the authority of the father.

2. Deut. 5:21.
3. Gen. 1:28.

Provided, therefore, the limits which are prescribed by the very purposes for which it exists be not transgressed, the family has at least equal rights with the State in the choice and pursuit of the things needful to its preservation and its just liberty. We say, "at least equal rights"; for, inasmuch as the domestic household is antecedent, as well in idea as in fact, to the gathering of men into a community, the family must necessarily have rights and duties which are prior to those of the community, and founded more immediately in nature. If the citizens, if the families on entering into association and fellowship, were to experience hindrance in a commonwealth instead of help, and were to find their rights attacked instead of being upheld, society would rightly be an object of detestation rather than of desire.

14. The contention, then, that the civil government should at its option intrude into and exercise intimate control over the family and the household is a great and pernicious error. True, if a family finds itself in exceeding distress, utterly deprived of the counsel of friends, and without any prospect of extricating itself, it is right that extreme necessity be met by public aid, since each family is a part of the commonwealth. In like manner, if within the precincts of the household there occur grave disturbance of mutual rights, public authority should intervene to force each party to yield to the other its proper due; for this is not to deprive citizens of their rights, but justly and properly to safeguard and strengthen them. But the rulers of the commonwealth must go no further; here, nature bids them stop. Paternal authority can be neither abolished nor absorbed by the State; for it has the same source as human life itself. "The child belongs to the father," and is, as it were, the continuation of the father's personality; and speaking strictly, the child takes its place in civil society, not of its own right, but in its quality as member of the family in which it is born. And for the very reason that "the child belongs to the father" it is, as St. Thomas Aquinas says, "before it attains the use of free will, under the power and the charge of its parents."[4] The socialists, therefore, in setting aside the parent and

---

4. *Summa theologiae*, IIa-IIae, q. x, art. 12, Answer.

setting up a State supervision, act against natural justice, and destroy the structure of the home.

15. And in addition to injustice, it is only too evident what an upset and disturbance there would be in all classes, and to how intolerable and hateful a slavery citizens would be subjected. The door would be thrown open to envy, to mutual invective, and to discord; the sources of wealth themselves would run dry, for no one would have any interest in exerting his talents or his industry; and that ideal equality about which they entertain pleasant dreams would be in reality the levelling down of all to a like condition of misery and degradation. Hence, it is clear that the main tenet of socialism, community of goods, must be utterly rejected, since it only injures those whom it would seem meant to benefit, is directly contrary to the natural rights of mankind, and would introduce confusion and disorder into the commonweal. The first and most fundamental principle, therefore, if one would undertake to alleviate the condition of the masses, must be the inviolability of private property. This being established, we proceed to show where the remedy sought for must be found.

16. We approach the subject with confidence, and in the exercise of the rights which manifestly appertain to Us, for no practical solution of this question will be found apart from the intervention of religion and of the Church. It is We who are the chief guardian of religion and the chief dispenser of what pertains to the Church; and by keeping silence we would seem to neglect the duty incumbent on us. Doubtless, this most serious question demands the attention and the efforts of others besides ourselves—to wit, of the rulers of States, of employers of labor, of the wealthy, aye, of the working classes themselves, for whom We are pleading. But We affirm without hesitation that all the striving of men will be vain if they leave out the Church. It is the Church that insists, on the authority of the Gospel, upon those teachings whereby the conflict can be brought to an end, or rendered, at least, far less bitter; the Church uses her efforts not only to enlighten the mind, but to direct by her

precepts the life and conduct of each and all; the Church improves and betters the condition of the working man by means of numerous organizations; does her best to enlist the services of all classes in discussing and endeavoring to further in the most practical way, the interests of the working classes; and considers that for this purpose recourse should be had, in due measure and degree, to the intervention of the law and of State authority.

17. It must be first of all recognized that the condition of things inherent in human affairs must be borne with, for it is impossible to reduce civil society to one dead level. Socialists may in that intent do their utmost, but all striving against nature is in vain. There naturally exist among mankind manifold differences of the most important kind; people differ in capacity, skill, health, strength; and unequal fortune is a necessary result of unequal condition. Such inequality is far from being disadvantageous either to individuals or to the community. Social and public life can only be maintained by means of various kinds of capacity for business and the playing of many parts; and each man, as a rule, chooses the part which suits his own peculiar domestic condition. As regards bodily labor, even had man never fallen from the state of innocence, he would not have remained wholly idle; but that which would then have been his free choice and his delight became afterwards compulsory, and the painful expiation for his disobedience. "Cursed be the earth in thy work; in thy labor thou shalt eat of it all the days of thy life."[5]

18. In like manner, the other pains and hardships of life will have no end or cessation on earth; for the consequences of sin are bitter and hard to bear, and they must accompany man so long as life lasts. To suffer and to endure, therefore, is the lot of humanity; let them strive as they may, no strength and no artifice will ever succeed in banishing from human life the ills and troubles which beset it. If any there are who pretend differently—who hold out to a hard-pressed people the boon of freedom from pain and trouble, an undisturbed repose, and constant enjoyment—they delude the people and impose upon them, and their

5. Gen. 3:17.

lying promises will only one day bring forth evils worse than the present. Nothing is more useful than to look upon the world as it really is, and at the same time to seek elsewhere, as We have said, for the solace to its troubles.

19. The great mistake made in regard to the matter now under consideration is to take up with the notion that class is naturally hostile to class, and that the wealthy and the working men are intended by nature to live in mutual conflict. So irrational and so false is this view that the direct contrary is the truth. Just as the symmetry of the human frame is the result of the suitable arrangement of the different parts of the body, so in a State is it ordained by nature that these two classes should dwell in harmony and agreement, so as to maintain the balance of the body politic. Each needs the other: capital cannot do without labor, nor labor without capital. Mutual agreement results in the beauty of good order, while perpetual conflict necessarily produces confusion and savage barbarity. Now, in preventing such strife as this, and in uprooting it, the efficacy of Christian institutions is marvellous and manifold. First of all, there is no intermediary more powerful than religion (whereof the Church is the interpreter and guardian) in drawing the rich and the working class together, by reminding each of its duties to the other, and especially of the obligations of justice.

20. Of these duties, the following bind the proletarian and the worker: fully and faithfully to perform the work which has been freely and equitably agreed upon; never to injure the property, nor to outrage the person, of an employer; never to resort to violence in defending their own cause, nor to engage in riot or disorder; and to have nothing to do with men of evil principles, who work upon the people with artful promises of great results, and excite foolish hopes which usually end in useless regrets and grievous loss. The following duties bind the wealthy owner and the employer: not to look upon their work people as their bondsmen, but to respect in every man his dignity as a person ennobled by Christian character. They are reminded that, according to natural

reason and Christian philosophy, working for gain is creditable, not shameful, to a man, since it enables him to earn an honorable livelihood; but to misuse men as though they were things in the pursuit of gain, or to value them solely for their physical powers—that is truly shameful and inhuman. Again justice demands that, in dealing with the working man, religion and the good of his soul must be kept in mind. Hence, the employer is bound to see that the worker has time for his religious duties; that he be not exposed to corrupting influences and dangerous occasions; and that he be not led away to neglect his home and family, or to squander his earnings. Furthermore, the employer must never tax his work people beyond their strength, or employ them in work unsuited to their sex and age. His great and principal duty is to give every one what is just. Doubtless, before deciding whether wages are fair, many things have to be considered; but wealthy owners and all masters of labor should be mindful of this—that to exercise pressure upon the indigent and the destitute for the sake of gain, and to gather one's profit out of the need of another, is condemned by all laws, human and divine. To defraud any one of wages that are his due is a great crime which cries to the avenging anger of Heaven. "Behold, the hire of the laborers . . . which by fraud has been kept back by you, crieth; and the cry of them hath entered into the ears of the Lord of Sabaoth."[6] Lastly, the rich must religiously refrain from cutting down the workmen's earnings, whether by force, by fraud, or by usurious dealing; and with all the greater reason because the laboring man is, as a rule, weak and unprotected, and because his slender means should in proportion to their scantiness be accounted sacred. Were these precepts carefully obeyed and followed out, would they not be sufficient of themselves to keep under all strife and all its causes?

21. But the Church, with Jesus Christ as her Master and Guide, aims higher still. She lays down precepts yet more perfect, and tries to bind class to class in friendliness and good feeling. The things of earth cannot be understood or valued aright without taking into consideration

---

6. James 5:4.

the life to come, the life that will know no death. Exclude the idea of futurity, and forthwith the very notion of what is good and right would perish; nay, the whole scheme of the universe would become a dark and unfathomable mystery. The great truth which we learn from nature herself is also the grand Christian dogma on which religion rests as on its foundation—that, when we have given up this present life, then shall we really begin to live. God has not created us for the perishable and transitory things of earth, but for things heavenly and everlasting; He has given us this world as a place of exile, and not as our abiding place. As for riches and the other things which men call good and desirable, whether we have them in abundance, or are lacking in them—so far as eternal happiness is concerned—it makes no difference; the only important thing is to use them aright. Jesus Christ, when He redeemed us with plentiful redemption, took not away the pains and sorrows which in such large proportion are woven together in the web of our mortal life. He transformed them into motives of virtue and occasions of merit; and no man can hope for eternal reward unless he follow in the blood-stained footprints of his Saviour. "If we suffer with Him, we shall also reign with Him."[7] Christ's labors and sufferings, accepted of His own free will, have marvellously sweetened all suffering and all labor. And not only by His example, but by His grace and by the hope held forth of everlasting recompense, has He made pain and grief more easy to endure; "for that which is at present momentary and light of our tribulation, worketh for us above measure exceedingly an eternal weight of glory."[8]

22. Therefore, those whom fortune favors are warned that riches do not bring freedom from sorrow and are of no avail for eternal happiness, but rather are obstacles;[9] that the rich should tremble at the threatenings of Jesus Christ—threatenings so unwonted in the mouth of our Lord[10]—and that a most strict account must be given to the Supreme

---

7. 2 Tim. 2:12.
8. 2 Cor. 4:17.
9. Matt. 19:23–24.
10. Luke 6:24–25.

Judge for all we possess. The chief and most excellent rule for the right use of money is one the heathen philosophers hinted at, but which the Church has traced out clearly, and has not only made known to men's minds, but has impressed upon their lives. It rests on the principle that it is one thing to have a right to the possession of money and another to have a right to use money as one wills. Private ownership, as we have seen, is the natural right of man, and to exercise that right, especially as members of society, is not only lawful, but absolutely necessary. "It is lawful," says St. Thomas Aquinas, "for a man to hold private property; and it is also necessary for the carrying on of human existence."[11] But if the question be asked: How must one's possessions be used?—the Church replies without hesitation in the words of the same holy Doctor: "Man should not consider his material possessions as his own, but as common to all, so as to share them without hesitation when others are in need. Whence the Apostle with, 'Command the rich of this world . . . to offer with no stint, to apportion largely.'"[12] True, no one is commanded to distribute to others that which is required for his own needs and those of his household; nor even to give away what is reasonably required to keep up becomingly his condition in life, "for no one ought to live other than becomingly."[13] But, when what necessity demands has been supplied, and one's standing fairly taken thought for, it becomes a duty to give to the indigent out of what remains over. "Of that which remaineth, give alms."[14] It is a duty, not of justice (save in extreme cases), but of Christian charity—a duty not enforced by human law. But the laws and judgments of men must yield place to the laws and judgments of Christ the true God, who in many ways urges on His followers the practice of almsgiving—"It is more blessed to give than to receive";[15] and who will count a kindness done or refused to the poor as done or refused to Himself—"As long as you did it to one of My least brethren you did it to Me."[16] To sum up, then, what has been said:

---

11. *Summa theologiae*, IIa-IIae, q. lxvi, art. 2, Answer.
12. *Ibid.*
13. *Ibid.*, q. xxxii, art. 6, Answer.
14. Luke 11:41.
15. Acts 20:35.
16. Matt. 25:40.

PART I: CHURCH TEACHING

Whoever has received from the divine bounty a large share of temporal blessings, whether they be external and material, or gifts of the mind, has received them for the purpose of using them for the perfecting of his own nature, and, at the same time, that he may employ them, as the steward of God's providence, for the benefit of others. "He that hath a talent," said St. Gregory the Great, "let him see that he hide it not; he that hath abundance, let him quicken himself to mercy and generosity; he that hath art and skill, let him do his best to share the use and the utility hereof with his neighbor."[17]

23. As for those who possess not the gifts of fortune, they are taught by the Church that in God's sight poverty is no disgrace, and that there is nothing to be ashamed of in earning their bread by labor. This is enforced by what we see in Christ Himself, who, "whereas He was rich, for our sakes became poor";[18] and who, being the Son of God, and God Himself, chose to seem and to be considered the son of a carpenter—nay, did not disdain to spend a great part of His life as a carpenter Himself. "Is not this the carpenter, the son of Mary?"[19]

24. From contemplation of this divine Model, it is more easy to understand that the true worth and nobility of man lie in his moral qualities, that is, in virtue; that virtue is, moreover, the common inheritance of men, equally within the reach of high and low, rich and poor; and that virtue, and virtue alone, wherever found, will be followed by the rewards of everlasting happiness. Nay, God Himself seems to incline rather to those who suffer misfortune; for Jesus Christ calls the poor "blessed";[20] He lovingly invites those in labor and grief to come to Him for solace;[21] and He displays the tenderest charity toward the lowly and the oppressed. These reflections cannot fail to keep down the pride of the well-to-do, and to give heart to the unfortunate; to move the former to be generous and the latter to be moderate in their desires. Thus, the

---

17. *Hom. in Evang.*, 9, n. 7 (PL 76, 1109B).
18. 2 Cor. 8:9.
19. Mark 6:3.
20. Matt. 5:3.
21. Matt. 11:28.

separation which pride would set up tends to disappear, nor will it be difficult to make rich and poor join hands in friendly concord.

25. But, if Christian precepts prevail, the respective classes will not only be united in the bonds of friendship, but also in those of brotherly love. For they will understand and feel that all men are children of the same common Father, who is God; that all have alike the same last end, which is God Himself, who alone can make either men or angels absolutely and perfectly happy; that each and all are redeemed and made sons of God, by Jesus Christ, "the first-born among many brethren"; that the blessings of nature and the gifts of grace belong to the whole human race in common, and that from none except the unworthy is withheld the inheritance of the kingdom of Heaven. "If sons, heirs also; heirs indeed of God, and co-heirs with Christ."[22] Such is the scheme of duties and of rights which is shown forth to the world by the Gospel. Would it not seem that, were society penetrated with ideas like these, strife must quickly cease?

26. But the Church, not content with pointing out the remedy, also applies it. For the Church does her utmost to teach and to train men, and to educate them and by the intermediary of her bishops and clergy diffuses her salutary teachings far and wide. She strives to influence the mind and the heart so that all may willingly yield themselves to be formed and guided by the commandments of God. It is precisely in this fundamental and momentous matter, on which everything depends that the Church possesses a power peculiarly her own. The instruments which she employs are given to her by Jesus Christ Himself for the very purpose of reaching the hearts of men, and derive their efficiency from God. They alone can reach the innermost heart and conscience, and bring men to act from a motive of duty, to control their passions and appetites, to love God and their fellow men with a love that is outstanding and of the highest degree and to break down courageously every barrier which blocks the way to virtue.

---

22. Rom. 8:17.

27. On this subject we need but recall for one moment the examples recorded in history. Of these facts there cannot be any shadow of doubt: for instance, that civil society was renovated in every part by Christian institutions; that in the strength of that renewal the human race was lifted up to better things—nay, that it was brought back from death to life, and to so excellent a life that nothing more perfect had been known before, or will come to be known in the ages that have yet to be. Of this beneficent transformation Jesus Christ was at once the first cause and the final end; as from Him all came, so to Him was all to be brought back. For, when the human race, by the light of the Gospel message, came to know the grand mystery of the Incarnation of the Word and the redemption of man, at once the life of Jesus Christ, God and Man, pervaded every race and nation, and interpenetrated them with His faith, His precepts, and His laws. And if human society is to be healed now, in no other way can it be healed save by a return to Christian life and Christian institutions. When a society is perishing, the wholesome advice to give to those who would restore it is to call it to the principles from which it sprang; for the purpose and perfection of an association is to aim at and to attain that for which it is formed, and its efforts should be put in motion and inspired by the end and object which originally gave it being. Hence, to fall away from its primal constitution implies disease; to go back to it, recovery. And this may be asserted with utmost truth both of the whole body of the commonwealth and of that class of its citizens—by far the great majority—who get their living by their labor.

28. Neither must it be supposed that the solicitude of the Church is so preoccupied with the spiritual concerns of her children as to neglect their temporal and earthly interests. Her desire is that the poor, for example, should rise above poverty and wretchedness, and better their condition in life; and for this she makes a strong endeavor. By the fact that she calls men to virtue and forms them to its practice she promotes this in no slight degree. Christian morality, when adequately and

completely practiced, leads of itself to temporal prosperity, for it merits the blessing of that God who is the source of all blessings; it powerfully restrains the greed of possession and the thirst for pleasure—twin plagues, which too often make a man who is void of self-restraint miserable in the midst of abundance;[23] it makes men supply for the lack of means through economy, teaching them to be content with frugal living, and further, keeping them out of the reach of those vices which devour not small incomes merely, but large fortunes, and dissipate many a goodly inheritance.

29. The Church, moreover, intervenes directly in behalf of the poor, by setting on foot and maintaining many associations which she knows to be efficient for the relief of poverty. Herein, again, she has always succeeded so well as to have even extorted the praise of her enemies. Such was the ardor of brotherly love among the earliest Christians that numbers of those who were in better circumstances despoiled themselves of their possessions in order to relieve their brethren; whence "neither was there any one needy among them."[24] To the order of deacons, instituted in that very intent, was committed by the Apostles the charge of the daily doles; and the Apostle Paul, though burdened with the solicitude of all the churches, hesitated not to undertake laborious journeys in order to carry the alms of the faithful to the poorer Christians. Tertullian calls these contributions, given voluntarily by Christians in their assemblies, deposits of piety, because, to cite his own words, they were employed "in feeding the needy, in burying them, in support of youths and maidens destitute of means and deprived of their parents, in the care of the aged, and the relief of the shipwrecked."[25]

30. Thus, by degrees, came into existence the patrimony which the Church has guarded with religious care as the inheritance of the poor. Nay, in order to spare them the shame of begging, the Church has provided aid for the needy. The common Mother of rich and poor has

---

23. 1 Tim. 6:10.
24. Acts 4:34.
25. *Apologia secunda*, 39 (*Apologeticus*, cap. 39; PL1, 533A).

aroused everywhere the heroism of charity, and has established congregations of religious and many other useful institutions for help and mercy, so that hardly any kind of suffering could exist which was not afforded relief. At the present day many there are who, like the heathen of old, seek to blame and condemn the Church for such eminent charity. They would substitute in its stead a system of relief organized by the State. But no human expedients will ever make up for the devotedness and self sacrifice of Christian charity. Charity, as a virtue, pertains to the Church; for virtue it is not, unless it be drawn from the Most Sacred Heart of Jesus Christ; and whosoever turns his back on the Church cannot be near to Christ.

31. It cannot, however, be doubted that to attain the purpose we are treating of, not only the Church, but all human agencies, must concur. All who are concerned in the matter should be of one mind and according to their ability act together. It is with this, as with providence that governs the world; the results of causes do not usually take place save where all the causes cooperate. It is sufficient, therefore, to inquire what part the State should play in the work of remedy and relief.

32. By the State we here understand, not the particular form of government prevailing in this or that nation, but the State as rightly apprehended; that is to say, any government conformable in its institutions to right reason and natural law, and to those dictates of the divine wisdom which we have expounded in the encyclical *On the Christian Constitution of the State.*[26] The foremost duty, therefore, of the rulers of the State should be to make sure that the laws and institutions, the general character and administration of the commonwealth, shall be such as of themselves to realize public well-being and private prosperity. This is the proper scope of wise statesmanship and is the work of the rulers. Now a State chiefly prospers and thrives through moral rule, well-regulated family life, respect for religion and justice, the moderation and fair imposing of public taxes, the progress of the arts and of trade, the

---

26. See above, pp. 161–184.

abundant yield of the land—through everything, in fact, which makes the citizens better and happier. Hereby, then, it lies in the power of a ruler to benefit every class in the State, and amongst the rest to promote to the utmost the interests of the poor; and this in virtue of his office, and without being open to suspicion of undue interference—since it is the province of the commonwealth to serve the common good. And the more that is done for the benefit of the working classes by the general laws of the country, the less need will there be to seek for special means to relieve them.

33. There is another and deeper consideration which must not be lost sight of. As regards the State, the interests of all, whether high or low, are equal. The members of the working classes are citizens by nature and by the same right as the rich; they are real parts, living the life which makes up, through the family, the body of the commonwealth; and it need hardly be said that they are in every city very largely in the majority. It would be irrational to neglect one portion of the citizens and favor another, and therefore the public administration must duly and solicitously provide for the welfare and the comfort of the working classes; otherwise, that law of justice will be violated which ordains that each man shall have his due. To cite the wise words of St. Thomas Aquinas: "As the part and the whole are in a certain sense identical, so that which belongs to the whole in a sense belongs to the part."[27] Among the many and grave duties of rulers who would do their best for the people, the first and chief is to act with strict justice—with that justice which is called *distributive*—toward each and every class alike.

34. But although all citizens, without exception, can and ought to contribute to that common good in which individuals share so advantageously to themselves, yet it should not be supposed that all can contribute in the like way and to the same extent. No matter what changes may occur in forms of government, there will ever be differences and inequalities of condition in the State. Society cannot exist

---

27. *Summa theologiae*, IIa-IIae, q. lxi, art. l, ad 2m.

PART I: CHURCH TEACHING

or be conceived of without them. Some there must be who devote themselves to the work of the commonwealth, who make the laws or administer justice, or whose advice and authority govern the nation in times of peace, and defend it in war. Such men clearly occupy the foremost place in the State, and should be held in highest estimation, for their work concerns most nearly and effectively the general interests of the community. Those who labor at a trade or calling do not promote the general welfare in such measure as this, but they benefit the nation, if less directly, in a most important manner. We have insisted, it is true, that, since the end of society is to make men better, the chief good that society can possess is virtue. Nevertheless, it is the business of a well-constituted body politic to see to the provision of those material and external helps "the use of which is necessary to virtuous action."[28] Now, for the provision of such commodities, the labor of the working class— the exercise of their skill, and the employment of their strength, in the cultivation of the land, and in the workshops of trade—is especially responsible and quite indispensable. Indeed, their co-operation is in this respect so important that it may be truly said that it is only by the labor of working men that States grow rich. Justice, therefore, demands that the interests of the working classes should be carefully watched over by the administration, so that they who contribute so largely to the advantage of the community may themselves share in the benefits which they create—that being housed, clothed, and bodily fit, they may find their life less hard and more endurable. It follows that whatever shall appear to prove conducive to the well-being of those who work should obtain favorable consideration. There is no fear that solicitude of this kind will be harmful to any interest; on the contrary, it will be to the advantage of all, for it cannot but be good for the commonwealth to shield from misery those on whom it so largely depends for the things that it needs.

35. We have said that the State must not absorb the individual or the family; both should be allowed free and untrammelled action so far as

---

28. Thomas Aquinas, *On the Governance of Rulers*, 1, 15 (*Opera omnia*, ed. *Vives*, Vol. 27, p. 356).

is consistent with the common good and the interest of others. Rulers should, nevertheless, anxiously safeguard the community and all its members; the community, because the conservation thereof is so emphatically the business of the supreme power, that the safety of the commonwealth is not only the first law, but it is a government's whole reason of existence; and the members, because both philosophy and the Gospel concur in laying down that the object of the government of the State should be, not the advantage of the ruler, but the benefit of those over whom he is placed. As the power to rule comes from God, and is, as it were, a participation in His, the highest of all sovereignties, it should be exercised as the power of God is exercised—with a fatherly solicitude which not only guides the whole, but reaches also individuals.

36. Whenever the general interest or any particular class suffers, or is threatened with harm, which can in no other way be met or prevented, the public authority must step in to deal with it. Now, it is to the interest of the community, as well as of the individual, that peace and good order should be maintained; that all things should be carried on in accordance with God's laws and those of nature; that the discipline of family life should be observed and that religion should be obeyed; that a high standard of morality should prevail, both in public and private life; that justice should be held sacred and that no one should injure another with impunity; that the members of the commonwealth should grow up to man's estate strong and robust, and capable, if need be, of guarding and defending their country. If by a strike of workers or concerted interruption of work there should be imminent danger of disturbance to the public peace; or if circumstances were such as that among the working class the ties of family life were relaxed; if religion were found to suffer through the workers not having time and opportunity afforded them to practice its duties; if in workshops and factories there were danger to morals through the mixing of the sexes or from other harmful occasions of evil; or if employers laid burdens upon their workmen which were unjust, or degraded them with conditions repugnant to their dignity as

human beings; finally, if health were endangered by excessive labor, or by work unsuited to sex or age—in such cases, there can be no question but that, within certain limits, it would be right to invoke the aid and authority of the law. The limits must be determined by the nature of the occasion which calls for the law's interference—the principle being that the law must not undertake more, nor proceed further, than is required for the remedy of the evil or the removal of the mischief.

37. Rights must be religiously respected wherever they exist, and it is the duty of the public authority to prevent and to punish injury, and to protect every one in the possession of his own. Still, when there is question of defending the rights of individuals, the poor and badly off have a claim to especial consideration. The richer class have many ways of shielding themselves, and stand less in need of help from the State; whereas the mass of the poor have no resources of their own to fall back upon, and must chiefly depend upon the assistance of the State. And it is for this reason that wage-earners, since they mostly belong in the mass of the needy, should be specially cared for and protected by the government.

38. Here, however, it is expedient to bring under special notice certain matters of moment. First of all, there is the duty of safeguarding private property by legal enactment and protection. Most of all it is essential, where the passion of greed is so strong, to keep the populace within the line of duty; for, if all may justly strive to better their condition, neither justice nor the common good allows any individual to seize upon that which belongs to another, or, under the futile and shallow pretext of equality, to lay violent hands on other people's possessions. Most true it is that by far the larger part of the workers prefer to better themselves by honest labor rather than by doing any wrong to others. But there are not a few who are imbued with evil principles and eager for revolutionary change, whose main purpose is to stir up disorder and incite their fellows to acts of violence. The authority of the law should intervene to put restraint upon such firebrands, to save the working classes

from being led astray by their maneuvers, and to protect lawful owners from spoliation.

39. When work people have recourse to a strike and become voluntarily idle, it is frequently because the hours of labor are too long, or the work too hard, or because they consider their wages insufficient. The grave inconvenience of this not uncommon occurrence should be obviated by public remedial measures; for such paralysing of labor not only affects the masters and their work people alike, but is extremely injurious to trade and to the general interests of the public; moreover, on such occasions, violence and disorder are generally not far distant, and thus it frequently happens that the public peace is imperiled. The laws should forestall and prevent such troubles from arising; they should lend their influence and authority to the removal in good time of the causes which lead to conflicts between employers and employed.

40. The working man, too, has interests in which he should be protected by the State; and first of all, there are the interests of his soul. Life on earth, however good and desirable in itself, is not the final purpose for which man is created; it is only the way and the means to that attainment of truth and that love of goodness in which the full life of the soul consists. It is the soul which is made after the image and likeness of God; it is in the soul that the sovereignty resides in virtue whereof man is commanded to rule the creatures below him and to use all the earth and the ocean for his profit and advantage. "Fill the earth and subdue it; and rule over the fishes of the sea, and the fowls of the air, and all living creatures that move upon the earth."[29] In this respect all men are equal; there is here no difference between rich and poor, master and servant, ruler and ruled, "for the same is Lord over all."[30] No man may with impunity outrage that human dignity which God Himself treats with great reverence, nor stand in the way of that higher life which is the preparation of the eternal life of heaven. Nay, more; no man has in

---

29. Gen. 1:28.
30. Rom. 10:12.

PART I: CHURCH TEACHING

this matter power over himself. To consent to any treatment which is calculated to defeat the end and purpose of his being is beyond his right; he cannot give up his soul to servitude, for it is not man's own rights which are here in question, but the rights of God, the most sacred and inviolable of rights.

41. From this follows the obligation of the cessation from work and labor on Sundays and certain holy days. The rest from labor is not to be understood as mere giving way to idleness; much less must it be an occasion for spending money and for vicious indulgence, as many would have it to be; but it should be rest from labor, hallowed by religion. Rest (combined with religious observances) disposes man to forget for a while the business of his everyday life, to turn his thoughts to things heavenly, and to the worship which he so strictly owes to the eternal Godhead. It is this, above all, which is the reason and motive of Sunday rest; a rest sanctioned by God's great law of the Ancient Covenant—"Remember thou keep holy the Sabbath day,"[31] and taught to the world by His own mysterious "rest" after the creation of man: "He rested on the seventh day from all His work which He had done."[32]

42. If we turn not to things external and material, the first thing of all to secure is to save unfortunate working people from the cruelty of men of greed, who use human beings as mere instruments for money-making. It is neither just nor human so to grind men down with excessive labor as to stupefy their minds and wear out their bodies. Man's powers, like his general nature, are limited, and beyond these limits he cannot go. His strength is developed and increased by use and exercise, but only on condition of due intermission and proper rest. Daily labor, therefore, should be so regulated as not to be protracted over longer hours than strength admits. How many and how long the intervals of rest should be must depend on the nature of the work, on circumstances of time and place, and on the health and strength of the workman. Those who work

---

31. Exod. 20:8.
32. Gen. 2:2.

in mines and quarries, and extract coal, stone and metals from the bowels of the earth, should have shorter hours in proportion as their labor is more severe and trying to health. Then, again, the season of the year should be taken into account; for not unfrequently a kind of labor is easy at one time which at another is intolerable or exceedingly difficult. Finally, work which is quite suitable for a strong man cannot rightly be required from a woman or a child. And, in regard to children, great care should be taken not to place them in workshops and factories until their bodies and minds are sufficiently developed. For, just as very rough weather destroys the buds of spring, so does too early an experience of life's hard toil blight the young promise of a child's faculties, and render any true education impossible. Women, again, are not suited for certain occupations; a woman is by nature fitted for home-work, and it is that which is best adapted at once to preserve her modesty and to promote the good bringing up of children and the well-being of the family. As a general principle it may be laid down that a workman ought to have leisure and rest proportionate to the wear and tear of his strength, for waste of strength must be repaired by cessation from hard work.

In all agreements between masters and work people there is always the condition expressed or understood that there should be allowed proper rest for soul and body. To agree in any other sense would be against what is right and just; for it can never be just or right to require on the one side, or to promise on the other, the giving up of those duties which a man owes to his God and to himself.

43. We now approach a subject of great importance, and one in respect of which, if extremes are to be avoided, right notions are absolutely necessary. Wages, as we are told, are regulated by free consent, and therefore the employer, when he pays what was agreed upon, has done his part and seemingly is not called upon to do anything beyond. The only way, it is said, in which injustice might occur would be if the master refused to pay the whole of the wages, or if the workman should

not complete the work undertaken; in such cases the public authority should intervene, to see that each obtains his due, but not under any other circumstances.

44. To this kind of argument a fair-minded man will not easily or entirely assent; it is not complete, for there are important considerations which it leaves out of account altogether. To labor is to exert oneself for the sake of procuring what is necessary for the various purposes of life, and chief of all for self preservation. "In the sweat of thy face thou shalt eat bread."[33] Hence, a man's labor necessarily bears two notes or characters. First of all, it is personal, inasmuch as the force which acts is bound up with the personality and is the exclusive property of him who acts, and, further, was given to him for his advantage. Secondly, man's labor is necessary; for without the result of labor a man cannot live, and self-preservation is a law of nature, which it is wrong to disobey. Now, were we to consider labor merely in so far as it is personal, doubtless it would be within the workman's right to accept any rate of wages whatsoever; for in the same way as he is free to work or not, so is he free to accept a small wage or even none at all. But our conclusion must be very different if, together with the personal element in a man's work, we consider the fact that work is also necessary for him to live: these two aspects of his work are separable in thought, but not in reality. The preservation of life is the bounden duty of one and all, and to be wanting therein is a crime. It necessarily follows that each one has a natural right to procure what is required in order to live, and the poor can procure that in no other way than by what they can earn through their work.

45. Let the working man and the employer make free agreements, and in particular let them agree freely as to the wages; nevertheless, there underlies a dictate of natural justice more imperious and ancient than any bargain between man and man, namely, that wages ought not to be insufficient to support a frugal and well-behaved wage-earner. If

---

33. Gen. 3:19.

through necessity or fear of a worse evil the workman accept harder conditions because an employer or contractor will afford him no better, he is made the victim of force and injustice. In these and similar questions, however—such as, for example, the hours of labor in different trades, the sanitary precautions to be observed in factories and workshops, etc.—in order to supersede undue interference on the part of the State, especially as circumstances, times, and localities differ so widely, it is advisable that recourse be had to societies or boards such as We shall mention presently, or to some other mode of safeguarding the interests of the wage-earners; the State being appealed to, should circumstances require, for its sanction and protection.

46. If a workman's wages be sufficient to enable him comfortably to support himself, his wife, and his children, he will find it easy, if he be a sensible man, to practice thrift, and he will not fail, by cutting down expenses, to put by some little savings and thus secure a modest source of income. Nature itself would urge him to this. We have seen that this great labor question cannot be solved save by assuming as a principle that private ownership must be held sacred and inviolable. The law, therefore, should favor ownership, and its policy should be to induce as many as possible of the people to become owners.

47. Many excellent results will follow from this; and, first of all, property will certainly become more equitably divided. For, the result of civil change and revolution has been to divide cities into two classes separated by a wide chasm. On the one side there is the party which holds power because it holds wealth; which has in its grasp the whole of labor and trade; which manipulates for its own benefit and its own purposes all the sources of supply, and which is not without influence even in the administration of the commonwealth. On the other side there is the needy and powerless multitude, sick and sore in spirit and ever ready for disturbance. If working people can be encouraged to look forward to obtaining a share in the land, the consequence will be that the gulf between vast wealth and sheer poverty will be bridged over,

and the respective classes will be brought nearer to one another. A further consequence will result in the great abundance of the fruits of the earth. Men always work harder and more readily when they work on that which belongs to them; nay, they learn to love the very soil that yields in response to the labor of their hands, not only food to eat, but an abundance of good things for themselves and those that are dear to them. That such a spirit of willing labor would add to the produce of the earth and to the wealth of the community is self evident. And a third advantage would spring from this: men would cling to the country in which they were born, for no one would exchange his country for a foreign land if his own afforded him the means of living a decent and happy life. These three important benefits, however, can be reckoned on only provided that a man's means be not drained and exhausted by excessive taxation. The right to possess private property is derived from nature, not from man; and the State has the right to control its use in the interests of the public good alone, but by no means to absorb it altogether. The State would therefore be unjust and cruel if under the name of taxation it were to deprive the private owner of more than is fair.

48. In the last place, employers and workmen may of themselves effect much, in the matter We are treating, by means of such associations and organizations as afford opportune aid to those who are in distress, and which draw the two classes more closely together. Among these may be enumerated societies for mutual help; various benevolent foundations established by private persons to provide for the workman, and for his widow or his orphans, in case of sudden calamity, in sickness, and in the event of death; and institutions for the welfare of boys and girls, young people, and those more advanced in years.

49. The most important of all are workingmen's unions, for these virtually include all the rest. History attests what excellent results were brought about by the artificers' guilds of olden times. They were the means of affording not only many advantages to the workmen, but in no small degree of promoting the advancement of art, as numerous

monuments remain to bear witness. Such unions should be suited to the requirements of this our age—an age of wider education, of different habits, and of far more numerous requirements in daily life. It is gratifying to know that there are actually in existence not a few associations of this nature, consisting either of workmen alone, or of workmen and employers together, but it were greatly to be desired that they should become more numerous and more efficient. We have spoken of them more than once, yet it will be well to explain here how notably they are needed, to show that they exist of their own right, and what should be their organization and their mode of action.

50. The consciousness of his own weakness urges man to call in aid from without. We read in the pages of holy Writ: "It is better that two should be together than one; for they have the advantage of their society. If one fall he shall be supported by the other. Woe to him that is alone, for when he falleth he hath none to lift him up."[34] And further: "A brother that is helped by his brother is like a strong city."[35] It is this natural impulse which binds men together in civil society; and it is likewise this which leads them to join together in associations which are, it is true, lesser and not independent societies, but, nevertheless, real societies.

51. These lesser societies and the larger society differ in many respects, because their immediate purpose and aim are different. Civil society exists for the common good, and hence is concerned with the interests of all in general, albeit with individual interests also in their due place and degree. It is therefore called a public society, because by its agency, as St. Thomas of Aquinas says, "Men establish relations in common with one another in the setting up of a commonwealth."[36] But societies which are formed in the bosom of the commonwealth are styled *private*, and rightly so, since their immediate purpose is the private advantage of the associates. "Now, a private society," says St. Thomas again, "is

---

34. Eccles. 4:9–10.
35. Prov. 18:19.
36. *Contra impugnantes Dei cultum et religionem*, Part 2, ch. 8 (*Opera omnia*, ed. Vives, Vol. 29, p. 16).

one which is formed for the purpose of carrying out private objects; as when two or three enter into partnership with the view of trading in common."[37] Private societies, then, although they exist within the body politic, and are severally part of the commonwealth, cannot nevertheless be absolutely, and as such, prohibited by public authority. For, to enter into a "society" of this kind is the natural right of man; and the State has for its office to protect natural rights, not to destroy them; and, if it forbid its citizens to form associations, it contradicts the very principle of its own existence, for both they and it exist in virtue of the like principle, namely, the natural tendency of man to dwell in society.

52. There are occasions, doubtless, when it is fitting that the law should intervene to prevent certain associations, as when men join together for purposes which are evidently bad, unlawful, or dangerous to the State. In such cases, public authority may justly forbid the formation of such associations, and may dissolve them if they already exist. But every precaution should be taken not to violate the rights of individuals and not to impose unreasonable regulations under pretense of public benefit. For laws only bind when they are in accordance with right reason, and, hence, with the eternal law of God.[38]

53. And here we are reminded of the confraternities, societies, and religious orders which have arisen by the Church's authority and the piety of Christian men. The annals of every nation down to our own days bear witness to what they have accomplished for the human race. It is indisputable that on grounds of reason alone such associations, being perfectly blameless in their objects, possess the sanction of the law of nature. In their religious aspect they claim rightly to be responsible to the Church alone. The rulers of the State accordingly have no rights over them, nor can they claim any share in their control; on the contrary,

---

37. *Ibid.*

38. "Human law is law only by virtue of its accordance with right reason; and thus it is manifest that it flows from the eternal law. And in so far as it deviates from right reason it is called an unjust law; in such case it is no law at all, but rather a species of violence." Thomas Aquinas, *Summa theologiae*, Ia-IIae, q. xciii, art. 3, ad 2m.

it is the duty of the State to respect and cherish them, and, if need be, to defend them from attack. It is notorious that a very different course has been followed, more especially in our own times. In many places the State authorities have laid violent hands on these communities, and committed manifold injustice against them; it has placed them under control of the civil law, taken away their rights as corporate bodies, and despoiled them of their property, in such property the Church had her rights, each member of the body had his or her rights, and there were also the rights of those who had founded or endowed these communities for a definite purpose, and, furthermore, of those for whose benefit and assistance they had their being. Therefore We cannot refrain from complaining of such spoliation as unjust and fraught with evil results; and with all the more reason do We complain because, at the very time when the law proclaims that association is free to all, We see that Catholic societies, however peaceful and useful, are hampered in every way, whereas the utmost liberty is conceded to individuals whose purposes are at once hurtful to religion and dangerous to the commonwealth.

54. Associations of every kind, and especially those of working men, are now far more common than heretofore. As regards many of these there is no need at present to inquire whence they spring, what are their objects, or what the means they imply. Now, there is a good deal of evidence in favor of the opinion that many of these societies are in the hands of secret leaders, and are managed on principles ill-according with Christianity and the public well-being; and that they do their utmost to get within their grasp the whole field of labor, and force working men either to join them or to starve. Under these circumstances Christian working men must do one of two things: either join associations in which their religion will be exposed to peril, or form associations among themselves and unite their forces so as to shake off courageously the yoke of so unrighteous and intolerable an oppression. No one who does not wish to expose man's chief good to extreme risk will for a moment hesitate to say that the second alternative should by all means be adopted.

55. Those Catholics are worthy of all praise—and they are not a few—who, understanding what the times require, have striven, by various undertakings and endeavors, to better the condition of the working class by rightful means. They have taken up the cause of the working man, and have spared no efforts to better the condition both of families and individuals; to infuse a spirit of equity into the mutual relations of employers and employed; to keep before the eyes of both classes the precepts of duty and the laws of the Gospel—that Gospel which, by inculcating self restraint, keeps men within the bounds of moderation, and tends to establish harmony among the divergent interests and the various classes which compose the body politic. It is with such ends in view that we see men of eminence, meeting together for discussion, for the promotion of concerted action, and for practical work. Others, again, strive to unite working men of various grades into associations, help them with their advice and means, and enable them to obtain fitting and profitable employment. The bishops, on their part, bestow their ready good will and support; and with their approval and guidance many members of the clergy, both secular and regular, labor assiduously in behalf of the spiritual interest of the members of such associations. And there are not wanting Catholics blessed with affluence, who have, as it were, cast in their lot with the wage-earners, and who have spent large sums in founding and widely spreading benefit and insurance societies, by means of which the working man may without difficulty acquire through his labor not only many present advantages, but also the certainty of honorable support in days to come. How greatly such manifold and earnest activity has benefited the community at large is too well known to require Us to dwell upon it. We find therein grounds for most cheering hope in the future, provided always that the associations We have described continue to grow and spread, and are well and wisely administered. The State should watch over these societies of citizens banded together in accordance with their rights, but it should not thrust itself into their peculiar concerns and their organization, for

things move and live by the spirit inspiring them, and may be killed by the rough grasp of a hand from without.

56. In order that an association may be carried on with unity of purpose and harmony of action, its administration and government should be firm and wise. All such societies, being free to exist, have the further right to adopt such rules and organization as may best conduce to the attainment of their respective objects. We do not judge it possible to enter into minute particulars touching the subject of organization; this must depend on national character, on practice and experience, on the nature and aim of the work to be done, on the scope of the various trades and employments, and on other circumstances of fact and of time—all of which should be carefully considered.

57. To sum up, then, We may lay it down as a general and lasting law that working men's associations should be so organized and governed as to furnish the best and most suitable means for attaining what is aimed at, that is to say, for helping each individual member to better his condition to the utmost in body, soul, and property. It is clear that they must pay special and chief attention to the duties of religion and morality, and that social betterment should have this chiefly in view; otherwise they would lose wholly their special character, and end by becoming little better than those societies which take no account whatever of religion. What advantage can it be to a working man to obtain by means of a society material well-being, if he endangers his soul for lack of spiritual food? "What doth it profit a man, if he gain the whole world and suffer the loss of his soul?"[39] This, as our Lord teaches, is the mark or character that distinguishes the Christian from the heathen. "After all these things do the heathen seek . . . Seek ye first the Kingdom of God and His justice: and all these things shall be added unto you."[40] Let our associations, then, look first and before all things to God; let religious instruction have therein the foremost place, each one

---

39. Matt. 16:26.
40. Matt. 6:32–33.

being carefully taught what is his duty to God, what he has to believe, what to hope for, and how he is to work out his salvation; and let all be warned and strengthened with special care against wrong principles and false teaching. Let the working man be urged and led to the worship of God, to the earnest practice of religion, and, among other things, to the keeping holy of Sundays and holy days. Let him learn to reverence and love holy Church, the common Mother of us all; and hence to obey the precepts of the Church, and to frequent the sacraments, since they are the means ordained by God for obtaining forgiveness of sin and for leading a holy life.

58. The foundations of the organization being thus laid in religion, We next proceed to make clear the relations of the members one to another, in order that they may live together in concord and go forward prosperously and with good results. The offices and charges of the society should be apportioned for the good of the society itself, and in such mode that difference in degree or standing should not interfere with unanimity and good-will. It is most important that office bearers be appointed with due prudence and discretion, and each one's charge carefully mapped out, in order that no members may suffer harm. The common funds must be administered with strict honesty, in such a way that a member may receive assistance in proportion to his necessities. The rights and duties of the employers, as compared with the rights and duties of the employed, ought to be the subject of careful consideration. Should it happen that either a master or a workman believes himself injured, nothing would be more desirable than that a committee should be appointed, composed of reliable and capable members of the association, whose duty would be, conformably with the rules of the association, to settle the dispute. Among the several purposes of a society, one should be to try to arrange for a continuous supply of work at all times and seasons; as well as to create a fund out of which the members may be effectually helped in their needs, not only in the cases of accident, but also in sickness, old age, and distress.

59. Such rules and regulations, if willingly obeyed by all, will sufficiently ensure the well being of the less well-to-do; whilst such mutual associations among Catholics are certain to be productive in no small degree of prosperity to the State. Is it not rash to conjecture the future from the past. Age gives way to age, but the events of one century are wonderfully like those of another, for they are directed by the providence of God, who overrules the course of history in accordance with His purposes in creating the race of man. We are told that it was cast as a reproach on the Christians in the early ages of the Church that the greater number among them had to live by begging or by labor. Yet, destitute though they were of wealth and influence, they ended by winning over to their side the favor of the rich and the good-will of the powerful. They showed themselves industrious, hard-working, assiduous, and peaceful, ruled by justice, and, above all, bound together in brotherly love. In presence of such mode of life and such example, prejudice gave way, the tongue of malevolence was silenced, and the lying legends of ancient superstition little by little yielded to Christian truth.

60. At the time being, the condition of the working classes is the pressing question of the hour, and nothing can be of higher interest to all classes of the State than that it should be rightly and reasonably settled. But it will be easy for Christian working men to solve it aright if they will form associations, choose wise guides, and follow on the path which with so much advantage to themselves and the common weal was trodden by their fathers before them. Prejudice, it is true, is mighty, and so is the greed of money; but if the sense of what is just and rightful be not deliberately stifled, their fellow citizens are sure to be won over to a kindly feeling towards men whom they see to be in earnest as regards their work and who prefer so unmistakably right dealing to mere lucre, and the sacredness of duty to every other consideration.

61. And further great advantage would result from the state of things We are describing; there would exist so much more ground for hope, and likelihood, even, of recalling to a sense of their duty those working

men who have either given up their faith altogether, or whose lives are at variance with its precepts. Such men feel in most cases that they have been fooled by empty promises and deceived by false pretexts. They cannot but perceive that their grasping employers too often treat them with great inhumanity and hardly care for them outside the profit their labor brings; and if they belong to any union, it is probably one in which there exists, instead of charity and love, that intestine strife which ever accompanies poverty when unresigned and unsustained by religion. Broken in spirit and worn down in body, how many of them would gladly free themselves from such galling bondage! But human respect, or the dread of starvation, makes them tremble to take the step. To such as these Catholic associations are of incalculable service, by helping them out of their difficulties, inviting them to companionship and receiving the returning wanderers to a haven where they may securely find repose.

62. We have now laid before you, venerable brethren, both who are the persons and what are the means whereby this most arduous question must be solved. Every one should put his hand to the work which falls to his share, and that at once and straightway, lest the evil which is already so great become through delay absolutely beyond remedy. Those who rule the commonwealths should avail themselves of the laws and institutions of the country; masters and wealthy owners must be mindful of their duty; the working class, whose interests are at stake, should make every lawful and proper effort; and since religion alone, as We said at the beginning, can avail to destroy the evil at its root, all men should rest persuaded that [the] main thing needful is to re-establish Christian morals, apart from which all the plans and devices of the wisest will prove of little avail.

63. In regard to the Church, her cooperation will never be found lacking, be the time or the occasion what it may; and she will intervene with all the greater effect in proportion as her liberty of action is the more unfettered. Let this be carefully taken to heart by those whose

office it is to safeguard the public welfare. Every minister of holy religion must bring to the struggle the full energy of his mind and all his power of endurance. Moved by your authority, venerable brethren, and quickened by your example, they should never cease to urge upon men of every class, upon the high-placed as well as the lowly, the Gospel doctrines of Christian life; by every means in their power they must strive to secure the good of the people; and above all must earnestly cherish in themselves, and try to arouse in others, charity, the mistress and the queen of virtues. For, the happy results we all long for must be chiefly brought about by the plenteous outpouring of charity; of that true Christian charity which is the fulfilling of the whole Gospel law, which is always ready to sacrifice itself for others' sake, and is man's surest antidote against worldly pride and immoderate love of self; that charity whose office is described and whose Godlike features are outlined by the Apostle St. Paul in these words: "Charity is patient, is kind, . . . seeketh not her own, . . . suffereth all things, . . . endureth all things."[41]

64. On each of you, venerable brethren, and on your clergy and people, as an earnest of God's mercy and a mark of Our affection, we lovingly in the Lord bestow the apostolic benediction.

Given at St. Peter's in Rome, the fifteenth day of May, 1891, the fourteenth year of Our pontificate.

LEO XIII

---

41. 1 Cor. 13:4–7.

CHAPTER 3

Quadragesimo Anno: On Reconstruction of the Social Order

(Excerpt)

Pope Pius XI

May 15, 1931

Written by Pope Pius XI on the fortieth anniversary of Rerum Novarum, *the encyclical supports Pope Leo XIII's condemnation of socialism and communism and highlights the need for Christianity to shape the social and political realms.*

127. Preceding this ardently desired social restoration, there must be a renewal of the Christian spirit, from which so many immersed in economic life have, far and wide, unhappily fallen away, lest all our efforts be wasted and our house be builded not on a rock but on shifting sand.[1]

128. And so, Venerable Brethren and Beloved Sons, having surveyed the present economic system, We have found it laboring under the gravest of evils. We have also summoned Communism and Socialism again to judgment and have found all their forms, even the most modified, to wander far from the precepts of the Gospel.

1. Cf. Matt. 7:24ff.

129. "Wherefore," to use the words of Our Predecessor, "if human society is to be healed, only a return to Christian life and institutions will heal it."[2] For this alone can provide effective remedy for that excessive care for passing things that is the origin of all vices; and this alone can draw away men's eyes, fascinated by and wholly fixed on the changing things of the world, and raise them toward Heaven. Who would deny that human society is in most urgent need of this cure now?

130. Minds of all, it is true, are affected almost solely by temporal upheavals, disasters, and calamities. But if we examine things critically with Christian eyes, as we should, what are all these compared with the loss of souls? Yet it is not rash by any means to say that the whole scheme of social and economic life is now such as to put in the way of vast numbers of mankind most serious obstacles which prevent them from caring for the one thing necessary; namely, their eternal salvation.

131. We, made Shepherd and Protector by the Prince of Shepherds, Who Redeemed them by His Blood, of a truly innumerable flock, cannot hold back Our tears when contemplating this greatest of their dangers. Nay rather, fully mindful of Our pastoral office and with paternal solicitude, We are continually meditating on how We can help them; and We have summoned to Our aid the untiring zeal of others who are concerned on grounds of justice or charity. For what will it profit men to become expert in more wisely using their wealth, even to gaining the whole world, if thereby they suffer the loss of their souls?[3] What will it profit to teach them sound principles of economic life if in unbridled and sordid greed they let themselves be swept away by their passion for property, so that "hearing the commandments of the Lord they do all things contrary."[4]

132. The root and font of this defection in economic and social life from the Christian law, and of the consequent apostasy of great numbers

---

2. Encyclical, *On the Condition of Workers*, 41.
3. Cf. Matt. 16:26.
4. Cf. Judg. 2:17.

of workers from the Catholic faith, are the disordered passions of the soul, the sad result of original sin which has so destroyed the wonderful harmony of man's faculties that, easily led astray by his evil desires, he is strongly incited to prefer the passing goods of this world to the lasting goods of Heaven. Hence arises that unquenchable thirst for riches and temporal goods, which has at all times impelled men to break God's laws and trample upon the rights of their neighbors, but which, on account of the present system of economic life, is laying far more numerous snares for human frailty. Since the instability of economic life, and especially of its structure, exacts of those engaged in it most intense and unceasing effort, some have become so hardened to the stings of conscience as to hold that they are allowed, in any manner whatsoever, to increase their profits and use means, fair or foul, to protect their hard-won wealth against sudden changes of fortune. The easy gains that a market unrestricted by any law opens to everybody attracts large numbers to buying and selling goods, and they, their one aim being to make quick profits with the least expenditure of work, raise or lower prices by their uncontrolled business dealings so rapidly according to their own caprice and greed that they nullify the wisest forecasts of producers. The laws passed to promote corporate business, while dividing and limiting the risk of business, have given occasion to the most sordid license. For We observe that consciences are little affected by this reduced obligation of accountability; that furthermore, by hiding under the shelter of a joint name, the worst of injustices and frauds are penetrated; and that, too, directors of business companies, forgetful of their trust, betray the rights of those whose savings they have undertaken to administer. Lastly, We must not omit to mention those crafty men who, wholly unconcerned about any honest usefulness of their work, do not scruple to stimulate the baser human desires and, when they are aroused, use them for their own profit.

133. Strict and watchful moral restraint enforced vigorously by governmental authority could have banished these enormous evils and even

forestalled them; this restraint, however, has too often been sadly lacking. For since the seeds of a new form of economy were bursting forth just when the principles of rationalism had been implanted and rooted in many minds, there quickly developed a body of economic teaching far removed from the true moral law, and, as a result, completely free rein was given to human passions.

134. Thus it came to pass that many, much more than ever before, were solely concerned with increasing their wealth by any means whatsoever, and that in seeking their own selfish interests before everything else they had no conscience about committing even the gravest of crimes against others. Those first entering upon this broad way that leads to destruction[5] easily found numerous imitators of their iniquity by the example of their manifest success, by their insolent display of wealth, by their ridiculing the conscience of others, who, as they said, were troubled by silly scruples, or lastly by crushing more conscientious competitors.

135. With the rulers of economic life abandoning the right road, it was easy for the rank and file of workers everywhere to rush headlong also into the same chasm; and all the more so, because very many managements treated their workers like mere tools, with no concern at all for their souls, without indeed even the least thought of spiritual things. Truly the mind shudders at the thought of the grave dangers to which the morals of workers (particularly younger workers) and the modesty of girls and women are exposed in modern factories; when we recall how often the present economic scheme, and particularly the shameful housing conditions, create obstacles to the family bond and normal family life; when we remember how many obstacles are put in the way of the proper observance of Sundays and Holy Days; and when we reflect upon the universal weakening of that truly Christian sense through which even rude and unlettered men were wont to value higher things, and upon its substitution by the single preoccupation of getting in any way whatsoever one's daily bread. And thus bodily labor, which Divine

---

5. Cf. Matt. 7:13.

Providence decreed to be performed, even after original sin, for the good at once of man's body and soul, is being everywhere changed into an instrument of perversion; for dead matter comes forth from the factory ennobled, while men there are corrupted and degraded.

136. No genuine cure can be furnished for this lamentable ruin of souls, which, so long as it continues, will frustrate all efforts to regenerate society, unless men return openly and sincerely to the teaching of the Gospel, to the precepts of Him Who alone has the words of everlasting life,[6] words which will never pass away, even if Heaven and earth will pass away.[7] All experts in social problems are seeking eagerly a structure so fashioned in accordance with the norms of reason that it can lead economic life back to sound and right order. But this order, which We Ourselves ardently long for and with all Our efforts promote, will be wholly defective and incomplete unless all the activities of men harmoniously unite to imitate and attain, in so far as it lies within human strength, the marvelous unity of the Divine plan. We mean that perfect order which the Church with great force and power preaches and which right human reason itself demands, that all things be directed to God as the first and supreme end of all created activity, and that all created good under God be considered as mere instruments to be used only in so far as they conduce to the attainment of the supreme end. Nor is it to be thought that gainful occupations are thereby belittled or judged less consonant with human dignity; on the contrary, we are taught to recognize in them with reverence the manifest will of the Divine Creator Who placed man upon the earth to work it and use it in a multitude of ways for his needs. Those who are engaged in producing goods, therefore, are not forbidden to increase their fortune in a just and lawful manner; for it is only fair that he who renders service to the community and makes it richer should also, through the increased wealth of the community, be made richer himself according to his position, provided that all these things be sought with due respect for the

---

6. Cf. John 6:69.
7. Cf. Matt. 24:35.

laws of God and without impairing the rights of others and that they be employed in accordance with faith and right reason. If these principles are observed by everyone, everywhere, and always, not only the production and acquisition of goods but also the use of wealth, which now is seen to be so often contrary to right order, will be brought back soon within the bounds of equity and just distribution. The sordid love of wealth, which is the shame and great sin of our age, will be opposed in actual fact by the gentle yet effective law of Christian moderation which commands man to seek first the Kingdom of God and His justice, with the assurance that, by virtue of God's kindness and unfailing promise, temporal goods also, in so far as he has need of them, shall be given him besides.[8]

137. But in effecting all this, the law of charity, "which is the bond of perfection,"[9] must always take a leading role. How completely deceived, therefore, are those rash reformers who concern themselves with the enforcement of justice alone—and this, commutative justice—and in their pride reject the assistance of charity! Admittedly, no vicarious charity can substitute for justice which is due as an obligation and is wrongfully denied. Yet even supposing that everyone should finally receive all that is due him, the widest field for charity will always remain open. For justice alone can, if faithfully observed, remove the causes of social conflict but can never bring about union of minds and hearts. Indeed all the institutions for the establishment of peace and the promotion of mutual help among men, however perfect these may seem, have the principal foundation of their stability in the mutual bond of minds and hearts whereby the members are united with one another. If this bond is lacking, the best of regulations come to naught, as we have learned by too frequent experience. And so, then only will true cooperation be possible for a single common good when the constituent parts of society deeply feel themselves members of one great family and children of the same Heavenly Father; nay, that they are one body in

8. Cf. Matt. 6:33.
9. Col. 3:14.

Christ, "but severally members one of another,"[10] so that "if one member suffers anything, all the members suffer with it."[11] For then the rich and others in positions of power will change their former indifference toward their poorer brothers into a solicitous and active love, listen with kindliness to their just demands, and freely forgive their possible mistakes and faults. And the workers, sincerely putting aside every feeling of hatred or envy which the promoters of social conflict so cunningly exploit, will not only accept without rancor the place in human society assigned them by Divine Providence, but rather will hold it in esteem, knowing well that everyone according to his function and duty is toiling usefully and honorably for the common good and is following closely in the footsteps of Him Who, being in the form of God, willed to be a carpenter among men and be known as the son of a carpenter.

138. Therefore, out of this new diffusion throughout the world of the spirit of the Gospel, which is the spirit of Christian moderation and universal charity, We are confident there will come that longed-for and full restoration of human society in Christ, and that "Peace of Christ in the Kingdom of Christ," to accomplish which, from the very beginning of Our Pontificate, We firmly determined and resolved within Our heart to devote all Our care and all Our pastoral solicitude,[12] and toward this same highly important and most necessary end now, you also, Venerable Brethren, who with Us rule the Church of God under the mandate of the Holy Ghost,[13] are earnestly toiling with wholly praiseworthy zeal in all parts of the world, even in the regions of the holy missions to the infidels. Let well-merited acclamations of praise be bestowed upon you and at the same time upon all those, both clergy and laity, who We rejoice to see, are daily participating and valiantly helping in this same great work, Our beloved sons engaged in Catholic Action, who with a singular zeal are undertaking with Us the solution of the social problems in so far as by virtue of her divine institution this is proper to and

10. Rom. 12:5.
11. 1 Cor. 12:26. 12. Encyclical, *Ubi Arcano*, Dec. 23, 1922.
12. Encyclical, *Ubi Arcano*, Dec. 23, 1922.
13. Cf. Acts 20:28.

devolves upon the Church. All these We urge in the Lord, again and again, to spare no labors and let no difficulties conquer them, but rather to become day by day more courageous and more valiant.[14] Arduous indeed is the task which We propose to them, for We know well that on both sides, both among the upper and the lower classes of society, there are many obstacles and barriers to be overcome. Let them not, however, lose heart; to face bitter combats is a mark of Christians, and to endure grave labors to the end is a mark of them who, as good soldiers of Christ,[15] follow Him closely.

139. Relying therefore solely on the all-powerful aid of Him "Who wishes all men to be saved,"[16] let us strive with all our strength to help those unhappy souls who have turned from God and, drawing them away from the temporal cares in which they are too deeply immersed, let us teach them to aspire with confidence to the things that are eternal. Sometimes this will be achieved much more easily than seems possible at first sight to expect. For if wonderful spiritual forces lie hidden, like sparks beneath ashes, within the secret recesses of even the most aban-doned man—certain proof that his soul is naturally Christian—how much the more in the hearts of those many upon many who have been led into error rather through ignorance or environment.

140. Moreover, the ranks of the workers themselves are already giving happy and promising signs of a social reconstruction. To Our soul's great joy, We see in these ranks also the massed companies of young workers, who are receiving the counsel of Divine Grace with willing ears and striving with marvelous zeal to gain their comrades for Christ. No less praise must be accorded to the leaders of workers' organizations who, disregarding their own personal advantage and concerned solely about the good of their fellow members, are striving prudently to harmonize the just demands of their members with the prosperity of their whole

---

14. Cf. Deut. 31:7.
15. Cf. 2 Tim. 2:3.
16. 1 Tim. 2:4.

PART I: CHURCH TEACHING

occupation and also to promote these demands, and who do not let themselves be deterred from so noble a service by any obstacle or suspicion. Also, as anyone may see, many young men, who by reason of their talent or wealth will soon occupy high places among the leaders of society, are studying social problems with deeper interest, and they arouse the joyful hope that they will dedicate themselves wholly to the restoration of society.

141. The present state of affairs, Venerable Brethren, clearly indicates the way in which We ought to proceed. For We are now confronted, as more than once before in the history of the Church, with a world that in large part has almost fallen back into paganism. That these whole classes of men may be brought back to Christ Whom they have denied, we must recruit and train from among them, themselves, auxiliary soldiers of the Church who know them well and their minds and wishes, and can reach their hearts with a tender brotherly love. The first and immediate apostles to the workers ought to be workers; the apostles to those who follow industry and trade ought to be from among them themselves.

142. It is chiefly your duty, Venerable Brethren, and of your clergy, to search diligently for these lay apostles both of workers and of employers, to select them with prudence, and to train and instruct them properly. A difficult task, certainly, is thus imposed on priests, and to meet it, all who are growing up as the hope of the Church, must be duly prepared by an intensive study of the social question. Especially is it necessary that those whom you intend to assign in particular to this work should demonstrate that they are men possessed of the keenest sense of justice, who will resist with true manly courage the dishonest demands or the unjust acts of anyone, who will excel in the prudence and judgment which avoids every extreme, and, above all, who will be deeply permeated by the charity of Christ, which alone has the power to subdue firmly but gently the hearts and wills of men to the laws of justice and

equity. Upon this road so often tried by happy experience, there is no reason why we should hesitate to go forward with all speed.

143. These Our Beloved Sons who are chosen for so great a work, We earnestly exhort in the Lord to give themselves wholly to the training of the men committed to their care, and in the discharge of this eminently priestly and apostolic duty to make proper use of the resources of Christian education by teaching youth, forming Christian organizations, and founding study groups guided by principles in harmony with the Faith. But above all, let them hold in high esteem and assiduously employ for the good of their disciples that most valuable means of both personal and social restoration which, as We taught in Our Encyclical, *Mens Nostra*,[17] is to be found in the Spiritual Exercises. In that Letter We expressly mentioned and warmly recommended not only the Spiritual Exercises for all the laity, but also the highly beneficial Workers' Retreats. For in that school of the spirit, not only are the best of Christians developed but true apostles also are trained for every condition of life and are enkindled with the fire of the heart of Christ. From this school they will go forth as did the Apostles from the Upper Room of Jerusalem, strong in faith, endowed with an invincible steadfastness in persecution, burning with zeal, interested solely in spreading everywhere the Kingdom of Christ.

144. Certainly there is the greatest need now of such valiant soldiers of Christ who will work with all their strength to keep the human family safe from the dire ruin into which it would be plunged were the teachings of the Gospel to be flouted, and that order of things permitted to prevail which tramples underfoot no less the laws of nature than those of God. The Church of Christ, built upon an unshakable rock, has nothing to fear for herself, as she knows for a certainty that the gates of hell shall never prevail against her.[18] Rather, she knows full well, through the experience of many centuries, that she is wont to come forth from

---

17. Encyclical, *Mens Nostra*, Dec. 20, 1929.
18. Cf. Matt. 16:18.

the most violent storms stronger than ever and adorned with new triumphs. Yet her maternal heart cannot but be moved by the countless evils with which so many thousands would be afflicted during storms of this kind, and above all by the consequent enormous injury to spiritual life which would work eternal ruin to so many souls redeemed by the Blood of Jesus Christ.

145. To ward off such great evils from human society nothing, therefore, is to be left untried; to this end may all our labors turn, to this all our energies, to this our fervent and unremitting prayers to God! For with the assistance of Divine Grace the fate of the human family rests in our hands.

146. Venerable Brethren and Beloved Sons, let us not permit the children of this world to appear wiser in their generation than we who by the Divine Goodness are the children of the light.[19] We find them, indeed, selecting and training with the greatest shrewdness alert and resolute devotees who spread their errors ever wider day by day through all classes of men and in every part of the world. And whenever they undertake to attack the Church of Christ more violently, We see them put aside their internal quarrels, assembling in full harmony in a single battle line with a completely united effort, and work to achieve their common purpose.

147. Surely there is not one that does not know how many and how great are the works that the tireless zeal of Catholics is striving everywhere to carry out, both for social and economic welfare as well as in the fields of education and religion. But this admirable and unremitting activity not infrequently shows less effectiveness because of the dispersion of its energies in too many different directions. Therefore, let all men of good will stand united, all who under the Shepherds of the Church wish to fight this good and peaceful battle of Christ; and under the leadership and teaching guidance of the Church let all strive according to

---

19. Cf. Luke 16:8.

the talent, powers, and position of each to contribute something to the Christian reconstruction of human society which Leo XIII inaugurated through his immortal Encyclical, *On the Condition of Workers*, seeking not themselves and their own interests, but those of Jesus Christ,[20] not trying to press at all costs their own counsels, but ready to sacrifice them, however excellent, if the greater common good should seem to require it, so that in all and above all Christ may reign, Christ may command to Whom be "honor and glory and dominion forever and ever."[21]

---

20. Cf. Phil. 2:21.
21. Rev. 5:13.

CHAPTER 4

Mater et Magistra:
On Christianity and Social Progress

(Excerpt)

Pope St. John XXIII
May 15, 1961

Issued on the seventieth anniversary of Rerum Novarum, *Pope St. John XXIII's encyclical notes that true social progress is only possible when fundamental moral and spiritual values, which are rooted in God, are recognized and protected.*

✳

III. NEW ASPECTS OF THE SOCIAL QUESTION

[. . .]

Population Increase and Economic Development

185. How can economic development and the supply of food keep pace with the continual rise in population? This is a question which constantly obtrudes itself today—a world problem, as well as one for the poverty-stricken nations.

186. As a world problem, the case is put thus: According to sufficiently reliable statistics the next few decades will see a very great increase in human population, whereas economic development will proceed at a slower rate. Hence, we are told, if nothing is done to check this rise in

population, the world will be faced in the not too distant future with an increasing shortage in the necessities of life.

187. As it affects the less developed countries, the problem is stated thus: The resources of modern hygiene and medicine will very shortly bring about a notable decrease in the mortality rate, especially among infants, while the birth rate—which in such countries is unusually high—will tend to remain more or less constant, at least for a considerable period. The excess of births over deaths will therefore show a steep rise, whereas there will be no corresponding increase in the productive efficiency of the economy. Accordingly, the standard of living in these poorer countries cannot possibly improve. It must surely worsen, even to the point of extreme hardship. Hence there are those who hold the opinion that, in order to prevent a serious crisis from developing, the conception and birth of children should be secretly avoided, or, in any event, curbed in some way.

The Problem Examined

188. Truth to tell, we do not seem to be faced with any immediate or imminent world problem arising from the disproportion between the increase of population and the supply of food. Arguments to this effect are based on such unreliable and controversial data that they can only be of very uncertain validity.

189. Besides, the resources which God in His goodness and wisdom has implanted in Nature are well-nigh inexhaustible, and He has at the same time given man the intelligence to discover ways and means of exploiting these resources for his own advantage and his own livelihood. Hence, the real solution of the problem is not to be found in expedients which offend against the divinely established moral order and which attack human life at its very source, but in a renewed scientific and technical effort on man's part to deepen and extend his dominion over

Nature. The progress of science and technology that has already been achieved opens up almost limitless horizons in this field.

190. As for the problems which face the poorer nations in various parts of the world, We realize, of course, that these are very real. They are caused, more often than not, by a deficient economic and social organization, which does not offer living conditions proportionate to the increase in population. They are caused, also, by the lack of effective solidarity among such peoples.

191. But granting this, We must nevertheless state most emphatically that no statement of the problem and no solution to it is acceptable which does violence to man's essential dignity; those who propose such solutions base them on an utterly materialistic conception of man himself and his life.

Only Possible Solution

192. The only possible solution to this question is one which envisages the social and economic progress both of individuals and of the whole of human society, and which respects and promotes true human values. First consideration must obviously be given to those values which concern man's dignity generally, and the immense worth of each individual human life. Attention must then be turned to the need for worldwide co-operation among men, with a view to a fruitful and well-regulated interchange of useful knowledge, capital and manpower.

Respect for the Laws of Life

193. We must solemnly proclaim that human life is transmitted by means of the family, and the family is based upon a marriage which is one and indissoluble and, with respect to Christians, raised to the dignity of a sacrament. The transmission of human life is the result of a personal and conscious act, and, as such, is subject to the all-holy, inviolable and

immutable laws of God, which no man may ignore or disobey. He is not therefore permitted to use certain ways and means which are allowable in the propagation of plant and animal life.

194. Human life is sacred—all men must recognize that fact. From its very inception it reveals the creating hand of God. Those who violate His laws not only offend the divine majesty and degrade themselves and humanity, they also sap the vitality of the political community of which they are members.

Education Toward Sense of Responsibility

195. It is of the utmost importance that parents exercise their right and obligation toward the younger generation by securing for their children a sound cultural and religious formation. They must also educate them to a deep sense of responsibility in life, especially in such matters as concern the foundation of a family and the procreation and education of children. They must instill in them an unshakable confidence in Divine Providence and a determination to accept the inescapable sacrifices and hardships involved in so noble and important a task as the co-operation with God in the transmitting of human life and the bringing up of children.

To the attainment of this end nothing can be more effective than those principles and that supernatural aid which the Church supplies. On this score alone the right of the Church to full liberty in the exercise of her mission must be recognized.

Science in the Service of Life

196. Genesis relates how God gave two commandments to our first parents: to transmit human life—"Increase and multiply"[1]—and to bring

---

1. Gen. 1:28.

nature into their service—"Fill the earth, and subdue it."[2] These two commandments are complementary.

197. Nothing is said in the second of these commandments about destroying nature. On the contrary, it must be brought into the service of human life.

198. We are sick at heart, therefore, when We observe the contradiction which has beguiled so much modern thinking. On the one hand we are shown the fearful specter of want and misery which threatens to extinguish human life, and on the other hand we find scientific discoveries, technical inventions and economic resources being used to provide terrible instruments of ruin and death.

199. A provident God grants sufficient means to the human race to find a dignified solution to the problems attendant upon the transmission of human life. But these problems can become difficult of solution, or even insoluble, if man, led astray in mind and perverted in will, turns to such means as are opposed to right reason, and seeks ends that are contrary to his social nature and the intentions of Providence.

Worldwide Co-operation

200. The progress of science and technology in every aspect of life has led, particularly today, to increased relationships between nations, and made the nations more and more dependent on one another.

201. As a rule no single commonwealth has sufficient resources at its command to solve the more important scientific, technical, economic, social, political and cultural problems which confront it at the present time. These problems are necessarily the concern of a whole group of nations, and possibly of the whole world.

---

2. *Ibid.*

202. Individual political communities may indeed enjoy a high degree of culture and civilization. They may have a large and industrious population, an advanced economic structure, great natural resources and extensive territories. Yet, even so, in isolation from the rest of the world they are quite incapable of finding an adequate solution to their major problems. The nations, therefore, must work with each other for their mutual development and perfection. They can help themselves only in so far as they succeed in helping one another. That is why international understanding and co-operation are so necessary.

The Effects of Mutual Distrust

203. Yet although individuals and nations are becoming more and more convinced of this twofold necessity, it would seem that men in general, and particularly those with high responsibility in public life, are showing themselves quite incapable of achieving it. The root of such inability is not to be sought in scientific, technical or economic reasons, but in the absence of mutual trust. Men, and consequently States, are in mortal fear of each other. Each fears that the other harbors plans of conquest and is only waiting for a favorable moment to put these plans into effect. Hence each organizes its own defense and builds up munitions of war as a deterrent against the would-be aggressor.

204. The result is a vast expenditure of human energy and natural resources on projects which are disruptive of human society rather than beneficial to it; while a growing uneasiness gnaws at men's hearts and makes them less responsive to the call of nobler enterprises.

Failure to Acknowledge the Moral Order

205. The root cause of so much mistrust is the presence of ideological differences between nations, and more especially between their rulers. There are some indeed who go so far as to deny the existence of a moral

order which is transcendent, absolute, universal and equally binding upon all. And where the same law of justice is not adhered to by all, men cannot hope to come to open and full agreement on vital issues.

206. Yes, both sides speak of justice and the demands of justice, but these words frequently take on different or opposite meanings according to which side uses them. Hence, when rulers of nations appeal to justice and the demands of justice, they not only disagree on terms, but often increase the tension that exists between their States. And so the belief is engendered that if a nation is to assert its rights and pursue its own interests, there is only one way open to it: to have recourse to violence; ignoring the fact that violence is the source of the very greatest evils.

God, the Foundation of the Moral Order

207. Mutual trust among rulers of States cannot begin nor increase except by recognition of, and respect for, the moral order.

208. But the moral order has no existence except in God; cut off from God it must necessarily disintegrate. Moreover, man is not just a material organism. He consists also of spirit; he is endowed with reason and freedom. He demands, therefore, a moral and religious order; and it is this order—and not considerations of a purely extraneous, material order—which has the greatest validity in the solution of problems relating to his life as an individual and as a member of society, and problems concerning individual states and their inter-relations.

209. It has been claimed that in an era of scientific and technical triumphs such as ours man can well afford to rely on his own powers, and construct a very good civilization without God. But the truth is that these very advances in science and technology frequently involve the whole human race in such difficulties as can only be solved in the light of a sincere faith in God, the Creator and Ruler of man and his world.

Spiritual and Moral Values

210. The almost limitless horizons opened up by scientific research only go to confirm this truth. More and more men are beginning to realize that science has so far done little more than scratch the surface of nature and reality. There are vast hidden depths still to be explored and adequately explained. Such men are appalled when they consider how these gigantic forces for good can be turned by science into engines of destruction. They realize then the supreme importance of spiritual and moral values, if scientific and technical progress is to be used in the service of civilization, and not involve the whole human race in irremediable disaster.

211. Furthermore, the increasing sense of dissatisfaction with worldly goods which is making itself felt among citizens of the wealthier nations, is rapidly destroying the treasured illusion of an earthly paradise. Men, too, are becoming more and more conscious of their rights as human beings, rights which are universal and inviolable; and they are aspiring to more just and more human relations with their fellows. The effect of all this is to make the modern man more deeply aware of his own limitations, and to create in him a striving for spiritual values. All of which encourages Us in the hope that individuals and nations will one day learn to unite in a spirit of sincere understanding and profitable cooperation.

IV. THE REBUILDING OF A SOCIAL ORDER

212. After all this scientific and technical progress, and even because of it, the problem remains: how to build up a new order of society based on a more balanced human relationship between political communities on a national and international level?

Incomplete and False Ideologies

213. The attempt to find a solution to this problem has given birth to a number of theories. Some of these were little more than ephemeral; others have undergone, and are still undergoing, substantial change; others again are proving themselves less and less attractive to modern man.

Why is this? It is because these ideologies do not take account of the whole man, nor even of his most important part. In particular, they take little account of certain inevitable human weaknesses such as sickness and suffering, weaknesses which even the most advanced economic and social systems cannot completely eliminate. Finally, they fail to take account of that deep-rooted sense of religion which exists in all men everywhere, and which nothing, neither violence nor cunning, can eradicate.

214. The most fundamental modern error is that of imagining that man's natural sense of religion is nothing more than the outcome of feeling or fantasy, to be eradicated from his soul as an anachronism and an obstacle to human progress. And yet this very need for religion reveals a man for what he is: a being created by God and tending always toward God. As we read in St. Augustine: "Lord, you have made us for yourself, and our hearts can find no rest until they rest in you."[3]

The Real Source of Justice, Truth and Love

215. Let men make all the technical and economic progress they can; there will be no peace nor justice in the world until they return to a sense of their dignity as creatures and sons of God, who is the first and final cause of all created being. Separated from God a man is but a monster, in himself and toward others; for the right ordering of human society presupposes the right ordering of man's conscience with God, who is Himself the source of all justice, truth and love.

---

3. Augustine, *Confessions*, I, 1.

216. Here is a spectacle for all the world to see: thousands of Our sons and brothers, whom We love so dearly, suffering years of bitter persecution in many lands, even those of an ancient Christian culture. And will not men who see clearly and compare the superior dignity of the persecuted with that refined barbarity of their oppressors, soon return to their senses, if indeed they have not already done so?

"Unless the Lord Build the House . . ."

217. The most perniciously typical aspect of the modern era consists in the absurd attempt to reconstruct a solid and fruitful temporal order divorced from God, who is, in fact, the only foundation on which it can endure. In seeking to enhance man's greatness, men fondly imagine that they can do so by drying up the source from which that greatness springs and from which it is nourished. They want, that is, to restrain and, if possible, to eliminate the soul's upward surge toward God. But today's experience of so much disillusionment and bloodshed only goes to confirm those words of Scripture: "Unless the Lord build the house, they labor in vain that build it."[4]

The Enduring Validity of the Church's Social Teaching

218. The permanent validity of the Catholic Church's social teaching admits of no doubt.

The Fundamental Principle

219. This teaching rests on one basic principle: individual human beings are the foundation, the cause and the end of every social institution. That is necessarily so, for men are by nature social beings. This fact must be recognized, as also the fact that they are raised in the plan of Providence to an order of reality which is above nature.

---

4. Ps. 126:1.

220. On this basic principle, which guarantees the sacred dignity of the individual, the Church constructs her social teaching. She has formulated, particularly over the past hundred years, and through the efforts of a very well informed body of priests and laymen, a social doctrine which points out with clarity the sure way to social reconstruction. The principles she gives are of universal application, for they take human nature into account, and the varying conditions in which man's life is lived. They also take into account the principal characteristics of contemporary society, and are thus acceptable to all.

CHAPTER 5

Pacem in Terris: On Establishing Universal Peace in Truth, Justice, Charity, and Liberty

(Excerpt)

Pope St. John XXIII

April 11, 1963

In this encyclical, Pope St. John XXIII outlines the rights and duties that flow from the natural law and states that a just society must be founded upon them, as they are rooted in human nature and come from God himself.

Peace on Earth—which man throughout the ages has so longed for and sought after—can never be established, never guaranteed, except by the diligent observance of the divinely established order.

Order in the Universe

2. That a marvelous order predominates in the world of living beings and in the forces of nature, is the plain lesson which the progress of modern research and the discoveries of technology teach us. And it is part of the greatness of man that he can appreciate that order, and devise the means for harnessing those forces for his own benefit.

3. But what emerges first and foremost from the progress of scientific knowledge and the inventions of technology is the infinite greatness of

God Himself, who created both man and the universe. Yes; out of nothing He made all things, and filled them with the fullness of His own wisdom and goodness. Hence, these are the words the holy psalmist used in praise of God: "O Lord, our Lord: how admirable is thy name in the whole earth!"[1] And elsewhere he says: "How great are thy works, O Lord! Thou hast made all things in wisdom."[2]

Moreover, God created man "in His own image and likeness,"[3] endowed him with intelligence and freedom, and made him lord of creation. All this the psalmist proclaims when he says: "Thou hast made him a little less than the angels: thou hast crowned him with glory and honor, and hast set him over the works of thy hands. Thou hast subjected all things under his feet."[4]

Order in Human Beings

4. And yet there is a disunity among individuals and among nations which is in striking contrast to this perfect order in the universe. One would think that the relationships that bind men together could only be governed by force.

5. But the world's Creator has stamped man's inmost being with an order revealed to man by his conscience; and his conscience insists on his preserving it. Men "show the work of the law written in their hearts. Their conscience bears witness to them."[5] And how could it be otherwise? All created being reflects the infinite wisdom of God. It reflects it all the more clearly, the higher it stands in the scale of perfection.[6]

6. But the mischief is often caused by erroneous opinions. Many people think that the laws which govern man's relations with the State are the

---

1. Ps. 8:1.
2. Ps. 103:24.
3. Cf. Gen. 1:26.
4. Ps. 8:5–6.
5. Rom. 2:15.
6. Cf. Ps. 18:8–11.

same as those which regulate the blind, elemental forces of the universe. But it is not so; the laws which govern men are quite different. The Father of the universe has inscribed them in man's nature, and that is where we must look for them; there and nowhere else.

7. These laws clearly indicate how a man must behave toward his fellows in society, and how the mutual relationships between the members of a State and its officials are to be conducted. They show too what principles must govern the relations between States; and finally, what should be the relations between individuals or States on the one hand, and the world-wide community of nations on the other. Men's common interests make it imperative that at long last a world-wide community of nations be established.

I. ORDER BETWEEN MEN

8. We must devote our attention first of all to that order which should prevail among men.

9. Any well-regulated and productive association of men in society demands the acceptance of one fundamental principle: that each individual man is truly a person. His is a nature, that is, endowed with intelligence and free will. As such he has rights and duties, which together flow as a direct consequence from his nature. These rights and duties are universal and inviolable, and therefore altogether inalienable.[7]

10. When, furthermore, we consider man's personal dignity from the standpoint of divine revelation, inevitably our estimate of it is incomparably increased. Men have been ransomed by the blood of Jesus Christ. Grace has made them sons and friends of God, and heirs to eternal glory.

---

7. Cf. Pius XII's broadcast message, Christmas 1942, AAS 35 (1943), 9–24; and John XXIII's sermon, Jan. 4, 1963, AAS 55 (1963), 89–91.

Rights

11. But first We must speak of man's rights. Man has the right to live. He has the right to bodily integrity and to the means necessary for the proper development of life, particularly food, clothing, shelter, medical care, rest, and, finally, the necessary social services. In consequence, he has the right to be looked after in the event of ill health; disability stemming from his work; widowhood; old age; enforced unemployment; or whenever through no fault of his own he is deprived of the means of livelihood.[8]

Rights Pertaining to Moral and Cultural Values

12. Moreover, man has a natural right to be respected. He has a right to his good name. He has a right to freedom in investigating the truth, and—within the limits of the moral order and the common good—to freedom of speech and publication, and to freedom to pursue whatever profession he may choose. He has the right, also, to be accurately informed about public events.

13. He has the natural right to share in the benefits of culture, and hence to receive a good general education, and a technical or professional training consistent with the degree of educational development in his own country. Furthermore, a system must be devised for affording gifted members of society the opportunity of engaging in more advanced studies, with a view to their occupying, as far as possible, positions of responsibility in society in keeping with their natural talent and acquired skill.[9]

---

8. Cf. Pius XI's encyclical letter *Divini Redemptoris*, AAS 29 (1931), 78; and Pius XII's broadcast message, Pentecost, June 1, 1941, AAS 33 (1941), 195–205.

9. Cf. Pius XII's broadcast message, Christmas 1942, AAS 35 (1943), 9–24.

The Right to Worship God According to One's Conscience

14. Also among man's rights is that of being able to worship God in accordance with the right dictates of his own conscience, and to profess his religion both in private and in public. According to the clear teaching of Lactantius, "this is the very condition of our birth, that we render to the God who made us that just homage which is His due; that we acknowledge Him alone as God, and follow Him. It is from this ligature of piety, which binds us and joins us to God, that religion derives its name."[10]

Hence, too, Pope Leo XIII declared that "true freedom, freedom worthy of the sons of God, is that freedom which most truly safeguards the dignity of the human person. It is stronger than any violence or injustice. Such is the freedom which has always been desired by the Church, and which she holds most dear. It is the sort of freedom which the Apostles resolutely claimed for themselves. The apologists defended it in their writings; thousands of martyrs consecrated it with their blood."[11]

The Right to Choose Freely One's State in Life

15. Human beings have also the right to choose for themselves the kind of life which appeals to them: whether it is to found a family—in the founding of which both the man and the woman enjoy equal rights and duties—or to embrace the priesthood or the religious life.[12]

16. The family, founded upon marriage freely contracted, one and indissoluble, must be regarded as the natural, primary cell of human society. The interests of the family, therefore, must be taken very specially into

---

10. *Divinae Institutiones*, lib. IV, c. 28.2; PL 6.535.
11. Encyclical letter *Libertas praestantissimum*, *Acta Leonis XIII*, VIII, 1888, pp. 237–238.
12. Cf. Pius XII's broadcast message, Christmas 1942, AAS 35 (1943), 9–24.

consideration in social and economic affairs, as well as in the spheres of faith and morals. For all of these have to do with strengthening the family and assisting it in the fulfillment of its mission.

17. Of course, the support and education of children is a right which belongs primarily to the parents.[13]

Economic Rights

18. In the economic sphere, it is evident that a man has the inherent right not only to be given the opportunity to work, but also to be allowed the exercise of personal initiative in the work he does.[14]

19. The conditions in which a man works form a necessary corollary to these rights. They must not be such as to weaken his physical or moral fibre, or militate against the proper development of adolescents to manhood. Women must be accorded such conditions of work as are consistent with their needs and responsibilities as wives and mothers.[15]

20. A further consequence of man's personal dignity is his right to engage in economic activities suited to his degree of responsibility.[16] The worker is likewise entitled to a wage that is determined in accordance with the precepts of justice. This needs stressing. The amount a worker receives must be sufficient, in proportion to available funds, to allow him and his family a standard of living consistent with human dignity. Pope Pius XII expressed it in these terms: "Nature imposes work upon man as a duty, and man has the corresponding natural right to demand that the work he does shall provide him with the means of livelihood for himself and his children. Such is nature's categorical imperative for the preservation of man."[17]

---

13. Cf. Pius XI's encyclical letter *Casti connubii*, AAS 22 (1930), 539–592, and Pius XII's broadcast message, Christmas 1942, AAS 35 (1943), 9–24.

14. Cf. Pius XII's broadcast message, Pentecost, June 1, 1941, AAS 33 (1941), 201.

15. Cf. Leo XIII's encyclical letter *Rerum novarum*, *Acta Leonis XIII*, XI, 1891, pp. 128–129.

16. Cf John XXIII's encyclical letter *Mater et Magistra*, AAS 53 (1961), 422.

17. Cf. Pius XII's broadcast message, Pentecost, June 1, 1941, AAS 33 (1941), 201.

21. As a further consequence of man's nature, he has the right to the private ownership of property, including that of productive goods. This, as We have said elsewhere, is "a right which constitutes so efficacious a means of asserting one's personality and exercising responsibility in every field, and an element of solidity and security for family life, and of greater peace and prosperity in the State."[18]

22. Finally, it is opportune to point out that the right to own private property entails a social obligation as well.[19]

The Right of Meeting and Association

23. Men are by nature social, and consequently they have the right to meet together and to form associations with their fellows. They have the right to confer on such associations the type of organization which they consider best calculated to achieve their objectives. They have also the right to exercise their own initiative and act on their own responsibility within these associations for the attainment of the desired results.[20]

24. As We insisted in Our encyclical *Mater et Magistra*, the founding of a great many such intermediate groups or societies for the pursuit of aims which it is not within the competence of the individual to achieve efficiently, is a matter of great urgency. Such groups and societies must be considered absolutely essential for the safeguarding of man's personal freedom and dignity, while leaving intact a sense of responsibility.[21]

The Right to Emigrate and Immigrate

25. Again, every human being has the right to freedom of movement and of residence within the confines of his own State. When there are

---

18. John XXIII's encyclical letter *Mater et Magistra*, AAS 53 (1961), 428.
19. Cf. *Ibid.*, p. 430; TPS v. 7, no. 4, p. 318.
20. Cf. Leo XIII's encyclical letter *Rerum novarum*, Acta Leonis XIII, XI, 1891, pp. 134–142; Pius XI's encyclical letter *Quadragesimo anno*, AAS 23 (1931), 199–200; and Pius XII's encyclical letter *Sertum laetitiae*, AAS 31 (1939), 635–644.
21. Cf. AAS 53 (1961), 430.

just reasons in favor of it, he must be permitted to emigrate to other countries and take up residence there.[22] The fact that he is a citizen of a particular State does not deprive him of membership in the human family, nor of citizenship in that universal society, the common, world-wide fellowship of men.

Political Rights

26. Finally, man's personal dignity involves his right to take an active part in public life, and to make his own contribution to the common welfare of his fellow citizens. As Pope Pius XII said, "man as such, far from being an object or, as it were, an inert element in society, is rather its subject, its basis and its purpose; and so must he be esteemed."[23]

27. As a human person he is entitled to the legal protection of his rights, and such protection must be effective, unbiased, and strictly just. To quote again Pope Pius XII: "In consequence of that juridical order willed by God, man has his own inalienable right to juridical security. To him is assigned a certain, well-defined sphere of law, immune from arbitrary attack."[24]

Duties

28. The natural rights of which We have so far been speaking are inextricably bound up with as many duties, all applying to one and the same person. These rights and duties derive their origin, their sustenance, and their indestructibility from the natural law, which in conferring the one imposes the other.

29. Thus, for example, the right to live involves the duty to preserve one's life; the right to a decent standard of living, the duty to live in a

---

22. Cf. Pius XII's broadcast message, Christmas 1952, AAS 45 (1953), 36–46.
23. Cf. Pius XII's broadcast message, Christmas 1944, AAS 37 (1945), 12.
24. Cf. Pius XII's broadcast message, Christmas 1942, AAS 35 (1943), 21.

becoming fashion; the right to be free to seek out the truth, the duty to devote oneself to an ever deeper and wider search for it.

Reciprocity of Rights and Duties Between Persons

30. Once this is admitted, it follows that in human society one man's natural right gives rise to a corresponding duty in other men; the duty, that is, of recognizing and respecting that right. Every basic human right draws its authoritative force from the natural law, which confers it and attaches to it its respective duty. Hence, to claim one's rights and ignore one's duties, or only half fulfill them, is like building a house with one hand and tearing it down with the other.

Mutual Collaboration

31. Since men are social by nature, they must live together and consult each other's interests. That men should recognize and perform their respective rights and duties is imperative to a well ordered society. But the result will be that each individual will make his whole-hearted contribution to the creation of a civic order in which rights and duties are ever more diligently and more effectively observed.

32. For example, it is useless to admit that a man has a right to the necessities of life, unless we also do all in our power to supply him with means sufficient for his livelihood.

33. Hence society must not only be well ordered, it must also provide men with abundant resources. This postulates not only the mutual recognition and fulfillment of rights and duties, but also the involvement and collaboration of all men in the many enterprises which our present civilization makes possible, encourages or indeed demands.

An Attitude of Responsibility

34. Man's personal dignity requires besides that he enjoy freedom and be able to make up his own mind when he acts. In his association with his fellows, therefore, there is every reason why his recognition of rights, observance of duties, and many-sided collaboration with other men, should be primarily a matter of his own personal decision. Each man should act on his own initiative, conviction, and sense of responsibility, not under the constant pressure of external coercion or enticement. There is nothing human about a society that is welded together by force. Far from encouraging, as it should, the attainment of man's progress and perfection, it is merely an obstacle to his freedom.

Social Life in Truth, Justice, Charity and Freedom

35. Hence, before a society can be considered well-ordered, creative, and consonant with human dignity, it must be based on truth. St. Paul expressed this as follows: "Putting away lying, speak ye the truth every man with his neighbor, for we are members one of another."[25] And so will it be, if each man acknowledges sincerely his own rights and his own duties toward others.

Human society, as We here picture it, demands that men be guided by justice, respect the rights of others and do their duty. It demands, too, that they be animated by such love as will make them feel the needs of others as their own, and induce them to share their goods with others, and to strive in the world to make all men alike heirs to the noblest of intellectual and spiritual values. Nor is this enough; for human society thrives on freedom, namely, on the use of means which are consistent with the dignity of its individual members, who, being endowed with reason, assume responsibility for their own actions.

---

25. Eph. 4:25.

36. And so, dearest sons and brothers, we must think of human society as being primarily a spiritual reality. By its means enlightened men can share their knowledge of the truth, can claim their rights and fulfill their duties, receive encouragement in their aspirations for the goods of the spirit, share their enjoyment of all the wholesome pleasures of the world, and strive continually to pass on to others all that is best in themselves and to make their own the spiritual riches of others. It is these spiritual values which exert a guiding influence on culture, economics, social institutions, political movements and forms, laws, and all the other components which go to make up the external community of men and its continual development.

God and the Moral Order

37. Now the order which prevails in human society is wholly incorporeal in nature. Its foundation is truth, and it must be brought into effect by justice. It needs to be animated and perfected by men's love for one another, and, while preserving freedom intact, it must make for an equilibrium in society which is increasingly more human in character.

38. But such an order—universal, absolute and immutable in its principles—finds its source in the true, personal and transcendent God. He is the first truth, the sovereign good, and as such the deepest source from which human society, if it is to be properly constituted, creative, and worthy of man's dignity, draws its genuine vitality.[26] This is what St. Thomas means when he says: "Human reason is the standard which measures the degree of goodness of the human will, and as such it derives from the eternal law, which is divine reason . . . Hence it is clear that the goodness of the human will depends much more on the eternal law than on human reason."[27]

---

26. Cf. Pius XII's broadcast message, Christmas 1942, AAS 35 (1943), 14.
27. *Summa Theol. Ia-IIae*, q. 19, a. 4; cf. a. 9.

Characteristics of the Present Day

39. There are three things which characterize our modern age.

40. In the first place we notice a progressive improvement in the economic and social condition of working men. They began by claiming their rights principally in the economic and social spheres, and then proceeded to lay claim to their political rights as well. Finally, they have turned their attention to acquiring the more cultural benefits of society.

Today, therefore, working men all over the world are loud in their demands that they shall in no circumstances be subjected to arbitrary treatment, as though devoid of intelligence and freedom. They insist on being treated as human beings, with a share in every sector of human society: in the socio-economic sphere, in government, and in the realm of learning and culture.

41. Secondly, the part that women are now playing in political life is everywhere evident. This is a development that is perhaps of swifter growth among Christian nations, but it is also happening extensively, if more slowly, among nations that are heirs to different traditions and imbued with a different culture. Women are gaining an increasing awareness of their natural dignity. Far from being content with a purely passive role or allowing themselves to be regarded as a kind of instrument, they are demanding both in domestic and in public life the rights and duties which belong to them as human persons.

42. Finally, we are confronted in this modern age with a form of society which is evolving on entirely new social and political lines. Since all peoples have either attained political independence or are on the way to attaining it, soon no nation will rule over another and none will be subject to an alien power.

43. Thus all over the world men are either the citizens of an independent State, or are shortly to become so; nor is any nation nowadays content to submit to foreign domination. The longstanding inferiority complex of certain classes because of their economic and social status, sex, or position in the State, and the corresponding superiority complex of other classes, is rapidly becoming a thing of the past.

Equality of Men

44. Today, on the contrary, the conviction is widespread that all men are equal in natural dignity; and so, on the doctrinal and theoretical level, at least, no form of approval is being given to racial discrimination. All this is of supreme significance for the formation of a human society animated by the principles We have mentioned above, for man's awareness of his rights must inevitably lead him to the recognition of his duties. The possession of rights involves the duty of implementing those rights, for they are the expression of a man's personal dignity. And the possession of rights also involves their recognition and respect by other people.

45. When society is formed on a basis of rights and duties, men have an immediate grasp of spiritual and intellectual values, and have no difficulty in understanding what is meant by truth, justice, charity and freedom. They become, moreover, conscious of being members of such a society. And that is not all. Inspired by such principles, they attain to a better knowledge of the true God—a personal God transcending human nature. They recognize that their relationship with God forms the very foundation of their life—the interior life of the spirit, and the life which they live in the society of their fellows.

CHAPTER 6

Dignitatis Humanae:
On the Right of the Person and of Communities to Social and Civil Freedom in Matters Religious

(Full Text)

Second Vatican Council
(promulgated by Pope St. Paul VI)
December 7, 1965

The Second Vatican Council's declaration on religious freedom affirms that all people have a right to religious freedom and are not to be coerced against their will in matters religious. But people cannot be indifferent to religious truth. Rather, they are obligated to seek the truth and to hold fast to the truth that they have found. The document opens with the affirmation that the Catholic faith is the "one true religion" and that the Church is commissioned by Christ to spread this truth throughout the world.

1. A sense of the dignity of the human person has been impressing itself more and more deeply on the consciousness of contemporary man,[1] and the demand is increasingly made that men should act on their own judgment, enjoying and making use of a responsible freedom, not driven by coercion but motivated by a sense of duty. The demand is likewise made that constitutional limits should be set to the powers of government, in order that there may be no encroachment on the rightful freedom of the person and of associations. This demand for freedom in human

---

1. Cf. John XXIII, encycl. *"Pacem in Terris,"* April 11, 1963: AAS 55 (1963) p. 279; *ibid.,* p. 265; Pius XII, radio message, Dec. 24, 1944: AAS 37 (1945), p. 14.

society chiefly regards the quest for the values proper to the human spirit. It regards, in the first place, the free exercise of religion in society. This Vatican Council takes careful note of these desires in the minds of men. It proposes to declare them to be greatly in accord with truth and justice. To this end, it searches into the sacred tradition and doctrine of the Church—the treasury out of which the Church continually brings forth new things that are in harmony with the things that are old.

First, the council professes its belief that God Himself has made known to mankind the way in which men are to serve Him, and thus be saved in Christ and come to blessedness. We believe that this one true religion subsists in the Catholic and Apostolic Church, to which the Lord Jesus committed the duty of spreading it abroad among all men. Thus He spoke to the Apostles: "Go, therefore, and make disciples of all nations, baptizing them in the name of the Father and of the Son and of the Holy Spirit, teaching them to observe all things whatsoever I have enjoined upon you" (Matt. 28:19–20). On their part, all men are bound to seek the truth, especially in what concerns God and His Church, and to embrace the truth they come to know, and to hold fast to it.

This Vatican Council likewise professes its belief that it is upon the human conscience that these obligations fall and exert their binding force. The truth cannot impose itself except by virtue of its own truth, as it makes its entrance into the mind at once quietly and with power.

Religious freedom, in turn, which men demand as necessary to fulfill their duty to worship God, has to do with immunity from coercion in civil society. Therefore it leaves untouched traditional Catholic doctrine on the moral duty of men and societies toward the true religion and toward the one Church of Christ.

Over and above all this, the council intends to develop the doctrine of recent popes on the inviolable rights of the human person and the constitutional order of society.

2. This Vatican Council declares that the human person has a right to religious freedom. This freedom means that all men are to be immune from coercion on the part of individuals or of social groups and of any human power, in such wise that no one is to be forced to act in a manner contrary to his own beliefs, whether privately or publicly, whether alone or in association with others, within due limits.

The council further declares that the right to religious freedom has its foundation in the very dignity of the human person as this dignity is known through the revealed word of God and by reason itself.[2] This right of the human person to religious freedom is to be recognized in the constitutional law whereby society is governed and thus it is to become a civil right.

It is in accordance with their dignity as persons—that is, beings endowed with reason and free will and therefore privileged to bear personal responsibility—that all men should be at once impelled by nature and also bound by a moral obligation to seek the truth, especially religious truth. They are also bound to adhere to the truth, once it is known, and to order their whole lives in accord with the demands of truth. However, men cannot discharge these obligations in a manner in keeping with their own nature unless they enjoy immunity from external coercion as well as psychological freedom. Therefore the right to religious freedom has its foundation not in the subjective disposition of the person, but in his very nature. In consequence, the right to this immunity continues to exist even in those who do not live up to their obligation of seeking the truth and adhering to it and the exercise of this right is not to be impeded, provided that just public order be observed.

3. Further light is shed on the subject if one considers that the highest norm of human life is the divine law—eternal, objective and

---

2. Cf. John XXIII, encycl. "*Pacem in Terris*," April 11, 1963: AAS 55 (1963), pp. 260–261; Pius XII, radio message, Dec. 24, 1942: AAS 35 (1943), p. 19; Pius XI, encycl. "*Mit Brennender Sorge*," March 14, 1937: AAS 29 (1937), p. 160; Leo XIII, encycl. "*Libertas Praestantissimum*," June 20, 1888: Acts of Leo XIII 8 (1888), p. 237–238.

universal—whereby God orders, directs and governs the entire universe and all the ways of the human community by a plan conceived in wisdom and love. Man has been made by God to participate in this law, with the result that, under the gentle disposition of divine Providence, he can come to perceive ever more fully the truth that is unchanging. Wherefore every man has the duty, and therefore the right, to seek the truth in matters religious in order that he may with prudence form for himself right and true judgments of conscience, under use of all suitable means.

Truth, however, is to be sought after in a manner proper to the dignity of the human person and his social nature. The inquiry is to be free, carried on with the aid of teaching or instruction, communication and dialogue, in the course of which men explain to one another the truth they have discovered, or think they have discovered, in order thus to assist one another in the quest for truth.

Moreover, as the truth is discovered, it is by a personal assent that men are to adhere to it.

On his part, man perceives and acknowledges the imperatives of the divine law through the mediation of conscience. In all his activity a man is bound to follow his conscience in order that he may come to God, the end and purpose of life. It follows that he is not to be forced to act in a manner contrary to his conscience. Nor, on the other hand, is he to be restrained from acting in accordance with his conscience, especially in matters religious. The reason is that the exercise of religion, of its very nature, consists before all else in those internal, voluntary and free acts whereby man sets the course of his life directly toward God. No merely human power can either command or prohibit acts of this kind.[3] The social nature of man, however, itself requires that he should give external expression to his internal acts of religion: that he should

---

3. Cf. John XXIII, encycl. *"Pacem in Terris,"* April 11, 1963: AAS 55 (1963), p. 270; Paul VI, radio message, Dec. 22, 1964: AAS 57 (1965), pp. 181–182.

PART I: CHURCH TEACHING

share with others in matters religious; that he should profess his religion in community. Injury therefore is done to the human person and to the very order established by God for human life, if the free exercise of religion is denied in society, provided just public order is observed.

There is a further consideration. The religious acts whereby men, in private and in public and out of a sense of personal conviction, direct their lives to God transcend by their very nature the order of terrestrial and temporal affairs. Government therefore ought indeed to take account of the religious life of the citizenry and show it favor, since the function of government is to make provision for the common welfare. However, it would clearly transgress the limits set to its power, were it to presume to command or inhibit acts that are religious.

4. The freedom or immunity from coercion in matters religious which is the endowment of persons as individuals is also to be recognized as their right when they act in community. Religious communities are a requirement of the social nature both of man and of religion itself.

Provided the just demands of public order are observed, religious communities rightfully claim freedom in order that they may govern themselves according to their own norms, honor the Supreme Being in public worship, assist their members in the practice of the religious life, strengthen them by instruction, and promote institutions in which they may join together for the purpose of ordering their own lives in accordance with their religious principles.

Religious communities also have the right not to be hindered, either by legal measures or by administrative action on the part of government, in the selection, training, appointment, and transferral of their own ministers, in communicating with religious authorities and communities abroad, in erecting buildings for religious purposes, and in the acquisition and use of suitable funds or properties.

Religious communities also have the right not to be hindered in their public teaching and witness to their faith, whether by the spoken or by the written word. However, in spreading religious faith and in introducing religious practices everyone ought at all times to refrain from any manner of action which might seem to carry a hint of coercion or of a kind of persuasion that would be dishonorable or unworthy, especially when dealing with poor or uneducated people. Such a manner of action would have to be considered an abuse of one's right and a violation of the right of others.

In addition, it comes within the meaning of religious freedom that religious communities should not be prohibited from freely undertaking to show the special value of their doctrine in what concerns the organization of society and the inspiration of the whole of human activity. Finally, the social nature of man and the very nature of religion afford the foundation of the right of men freely to hold meetings and to establish educational, cultural, charitable and social organizations, under the impulse of their own religious sense.

5. The family, since it is a society in its own original right, has the right freely to live its own domestic religious life under the guidance of parents. Parents, moreover, have the right to determine, in accordance with their own religious beliefs, the kind of religious education that their children are to receive. Government, in consequence, must acknowledge the right of parents to make a genuinely free choice of schools and of other means of education, and the use of this freedom of choice is not to be made a reason for imposing unjust burdens on parents, whether directly or indirectly. Besides, the right of parents are violated, if their children are forced to attend lessons or instructions which are not in agreement with their religious beliefs, or if a single system of education, from which all religious formation is excluded, is imposed upon all.

6. Since the common welfare of society consists in the entirety of those conditions of social life under which men enjoy the possibility of achieving their own perfection in a certain fullness of measure and also with some relative ease, it chiefly consists in the protection of the rights, and in the performance of the duties, of the human person.[4] Therefore the care of the right to religious freedom devolves upon the whole citizenry, upon social groups, upon government, and upon the Church and other religious communities, in virtue of the duty of all toward the common welfare, and in the manner proper to each.

The protection and promotion of the inviolable rights of man ranks among the essential duties of government.[5] Therefore government is to assume the safeguard of the religious freedom of all its citizens, in an effective manner, by just laws and by other appropriate means.

Government is also to help create conditions favorable to the fostering of religious life, in order that the people may be truly enabled to exercise their religious rights and to fulfill their religious duties, and also in order that society itself may profit by the moral qualities of justice and peace which have their origin in men's faithfulness to God and to His holy will.[6]

If, in view of peculiar circumstances obtaining among peoples, special civil recognition is given to one religious community in the constitutional order of society, it is at the same time imperative that the right of all citizens and religious communities to religious freedom should be recognized and made effective in practice.

Finally, government is to see to it that equality of citizens before the law, which is itself an element of the common good, is never violated,

---

4. Cf. John XXIII, encycl. "*Mater et Magistra*," May 15, 1961: AAS 53 (1961), p. 417; idem, encycl. "*Pacem in Terris*," April 11, 1963: AAS 55 (1963), p. 273.

5. Cf. John XXIII, encycl. "*Pacem in Terris*," April 11, 1963: AAS 55 (1963), pp. 273–274; Pius XII, radio message, June 1 1941: AAS 33 (1941), p. 200.

6. Cf. Leo XIII, encycl. "*Immortale Dei*," Nov. 1, 1885: AAS 18 (1885), p. 161.

whether openly or covertly, for religious reasons. Nor is there to be discrimination among citizens.

It follows that a wrong is done when government imposes upon its people, by force or fear or other means, the profession or repudiation of any religion, or when it hinders men from joining or leaving a religious community. All the more is it a violation of the will of God and of the sacred rights of the person and the family of nations when force is brought to bear in any way in order to destroy or repress religion, either in the whole of mankind or in a particular country or in a definite community.

7. The right to religious freedom is exercised in human society: hence its exercise is subject to certain regulatory norms. In the use of all freedoms the moral principle of personal and social responsibility is to be observed. In the exercise of their rights, individual men and social groups are bound by the moral law to have respect both for the rights of others and for their own duties toward others and for the common welfare of all. Men are to deal with their fellows in justice and civility.

Furthermore, society has the right to defend itself against possible abuses committed on the pretext of freedom of religion. It is the special duty of government to provide this protection.

However, government is not to act in an arbitrary fashion or in an unfair spirit of partisanship. Its action is to be controlled by juridical norms which are in conformity with the objective moral order. These norms arise out of the need for the effective safeguard of the rights of all citizens and for the peaceful settlement of conflicts of rights, also out of the need for an adequate care of genuine public peace, which comes about when men live together in good order and in true justice, and finally out of the need for a proper guardianship of public morality.

These matters constitute the basic component of the common welfare: they are what is meant by public order. For the rest, the usages of society are to be the usages of freedom in their full range: that is, the freedom of man is to be respected as far as possible and is not to be curtailed except when and insofar as necessary.

8. Many pressures are brought to bear upon the men of our day, to the point where the danger arises lest they lose the possibility of acting on their own judgment. On the other hand, not a few can be found who seem inclined to use the name of freedom as the pretext for refusing to submit to authority and for making light of the duty of obedience. Wherefore this Vatican Council urges everyone, especially those who are charged with the task of educating others, to do their utmost to form men who, on the one hand, will respect the moral order and be obedient to lawful authority, and on the other hand, will be lovers of true freedom—men, in other words, who will come to decisions on their own judgment and in the light of truth, govern their activities with a sense of responsibility, and strive after what is true and right, willing always to join with others in cooperative effort.

Religious freedom therefore ought to have this further purpose and aim, namely, that men may come to act with greater responsibility in fulfilling their duties in community life.

9. The declaration of this Vatican Council on the right of man to religious freedom has its foundation in the dignity of the person, whose exigencies have come to be more fully known to human reason through centuries of experience. What is more, this doctrine of freedom has roots in divine revelation, and for this reason Christians are bound to respect it all the more conscientiously. Revelation does not indeed affirm in so many words the right of man to immunity from external coercion in matters religious. It does, however, disclose the dignity of the human person in its full dimensions. It gives evidence of the respect which Christ showed toward the freedom with which man is to fulfill his duty of belief in the word of God and it gives us lessons in the spirit which disciples of such a Master ought to adopt and continually follow.

Thus further light is cast upon the general principles upon which the doctrine of this declaration on religious freedom is based. In particular, religious freedom in society is entirely consonant with the freedom of the act of Christian faith.

10. It is one of the major tenets of Catholic doctrine that man's response to God in faith must be free: no one therefore is to be forced to embrace the Christian faith against his own will.[7] This doctrine is contained in the word of God and it was constantly proclaimed by the Fathers of the Church.[8] The act of faith is of its very nature a free act. Man, redeemed by Christ the Savior and through Christ Jesus called to be God's adopted son,[9] cannot give his adherence to God revealing Himself unless, under the drawing of the Father,[10] he offers to God the reasonable and free submission of faith. It is therefore completely in accord with the nature of faith that in matters religious every manner of coercion on the part of men should be excluded. In consequence, the principle of religious freedom makes no small contribution to the creation of an environment in which men can without hindrance be invited to the Christian faith, embrace it of their own free will, and profess it effectively in their whole manner of life.

11. God calls men to serve Him in spirit and in truth, hence they are bound in conscience but they stand under no compulsion. God has

---

7. Cf. CIC, c. *1351*; Pius XII, *allocution to prelate auditors and other officials and administrators of the tribune of the Holy Roman Rota*, Oct. 6, 1946: AAS 38 (1946), p. 394; idem. Encycl. *"Mystici Corporis,"* June 29, 1943: AAS (1943), p. 243.

8. Cf. Lactantius *"Divinarum Institutionum,"* Book V, 19: CSEL 19, pp. 463–464, 465: PL 6, 614 and 616 (ch. 20); St. Ambrose, *"Epistola ad Valentianum Imp.,"* Letter 21: PL 16, 1005; St. Augustine, *"Contra Litteras Petiliani,"* Book II, ch. 83: CSEL 52, p. 112: PL 43, 315; cf. C. 23, q. 5, c. 33 (ed. Friedberg, col. 939); idem, Letter 23: PL 33, 98, idem, Letter 34: PL 33, 132; idem, Letter 35: PL 33, 135; St. Gregory the Great, *"Epistola ad Virgilium et Theodorum Episcopos Massiliae Galliarum,"* Register of Letters I, 45: MGH Ep. 1, p. 72: PL 77, 510–511 (Book I, ep. 47); idem, *"Epistola ad Johannem Episcopum Constantinopolitanum,"* Register of Letters, III, 52: MGH Letter 1, p. 210: PL 77, 649 (Book III, Letter 53); cf. D. 45, c. 1 (ed. Friedberg, col. 160); Council of Toledo IV, c. 57: Mansi 10, 633; cf. D. 45, c. 5 (ed. Friedberg, col. 161–162); Clement III: X., V, 6, 9: ed. Friedberg, col. 774; Innocent III, *"Epistola ad Arelatensem Archiepiscopum,"* X., III, 42, 3: Friedberg, col. 646.

9. Cf. Eph. 1:5.

10. Cf. John 6:44.

regard for the dignity of the human person whom He Himself created and man is to be guided by his own judgment and he is to enjoy freedom. This truth appears at its height in Christ Jesus, in whom God manifested Himself and His ways with men. Christ is at once our Master and our Lord[11] and also meek and humble of heart.[12] In attracting and inviting His disciples He used patience.[13] He wrought miracles to illuminate His teaching and to establish its truth, but His intention was to rouse faith in His hearers and to confirm them in faith, not to exert coercion upon them.[14] He did indeed denounce the unbelief of some who listened to Him, but He left vengeance to God in expectation of the day of judgment.[15] When He sent His Apostles into the world, He said to them: "He who believes and is baptized will be saved. He who does not believe will be condemned" (Mark 16:16). But He Himself, noting that the cockle had been sown amid the wheat, gave orders that both should be allowed to grow until the harvest time, which will come at the end of the world.[16] He refused to be a political messiah, ruling by force:[17] He preferred to call Himself the Son of Man, who came "to serve and to give his life as a ransom for the many" (Mark 10:45). He showed Himself the perfect servant of God,[18] who "does not break the bruised reed nor extinguish the smoking flax" (Matt. 12:20).

He acknowledged the power of government and its rights, when He commanded that tribute be given to Caesar: but He gave clear warning that the higher rights of God are to be kept inviolate: "Render to Caesar the things that are Caesar's and to God the things that are God's" (Matt. 22:21). In the end, when He completed on the cross the work of redemption whereby He achieved salvation and true freedom for men, He brought His revelation to completion. For He bore witness to the

---

11. Cf. John 13:13.
12. Cf. Matt. 11:29.
13. Cf. Matt. 11:28–30; John 6:67–68.
14. Cf. Matt. 9:28–29; Mark 9:23–24; 6:5–6; Paul VI, encycl. *"Ecclesiam Suam,"* Aug. 6, 1964: AAS 56 (1964), pp. 642–643.
15. Cf. Matt. 11:20–24; Rom. 12:19–20; 2 Thess. 1:8.
16. Cf. Matt. 13:30 and 40–42.
17. Cf. Matt. 4:8–10; John 6:15.
18. Cf. Is. 42:1–4.

truth,[19] but He refused to impose the truth by force on those who spoke against it. Not by force of blows does His rule assert its claims.[20] It is established by witnessing to the truth and by hearing the truth, and it extends its dominion by the love whereby Christ, lifted up on the cross, draws all men to Himself.[21]

Taught by the word and example of Christ, the Apostles followed the same way. From the very origins of the Church the disciples of Christ strove to convert men to faith in Christ as the Lord; not, however, by the use of coercion or of devices unworthy of the Gospel, but by the power, above all, of the word of God.[22] Steadfastly they proclaimed to all the plan of God our Savior, "who wills that all men should be saved and come to the acknowledgment of the truth" (1 Tim. 2:4). At the same time, however, they showed respect for those of weaker stuff, even though they were in error, and thus they made it plain that "each one of us is to render to God an account of himself" (Romans 14:12),[23] and for that reason is bound to obey his conscience. Like Christ Himself, the Apostles were unceasingly bent upon bearing witness to the truth of God, and they showed the fullest measure of boldness in "speaking the word with confidence" (Acts 4:31)[24] before the people and their rulers. With a firm faith they held that the Gospel is indeed the power of God unto salvation for all who believe.[25] Therefore they rejected all "carnal weapons":[26] they followed the example of the gentleness and respectfulness of Christ and they preached the word of God in the full confidence that there was resident in this word itself a divine power able to destroy all the forces arrayed against God[27] and bring men to faith in Christ and to His service.[28] As the Master, so too the Apostles recognized

---

19. Cf. John 18:37.
20. Cf. Matt. 26:51–53; John 18:36.
21. Cf. John 12:32.
22. Cf. 1 Cor. 2:3–5; 1 Thess. 2:3–5.
23. Cf. Rom. 14:1–23; 1 Cor. 8:9–13; 10:23–33.
24. Cf. Eph. 6:19–20.
25. Cf. Rom. 1:16.
26. Cf. 2 Cor. 10:4; 1 Thess. 5:8–9.
27. Cf. Eph. 6:11–17.
28. Cf. 2 Cor. 10:3–5.

legitimate civil authority. "For there is no power except from God," the Apostle teaches, and thereafter commands: "Let everyone be subject to higher authorities. . . . He who resists authority resists God's ordinance" (Romans 13:1–5).[29] At the same time, however, they did not hesitate to speak out against governing powers which set themselves in opposition to the holy will of God: "It is necessary to obey God rather than men" (Acts 5:29).[30] This is the way along which the martyrs and other faithful have walked through all ages and over all the earth.

12. In faithfulness therefore to the truth of the Gospel, the Church is following the way of Christ and the apostles when she recognizes and gives support to the principle of religious freedom as befitting the dignity of man and as being in accord with divine revelation. Throughout the ages the Church has kept safe and handed on the doctrine received from the Master and from the apostles. In the life of the People of God, as it has made its pilgrim way through the vicissitudes of human history, there has at times appeared a way of acting that was hardly in accord with the spirit of the Gospel or even opposed to it. Nevertheless, the doctrine of the Church that no one is to be coerced into faith has always stood firm.

Thus the leaven of the Gospel has long been about its quiet work in the minds of men, and to it is due in great measure the fact that in the course of time men have come more widely to recognize their dignity as persons, and the conviction has grown stronger that the person in society is to be kept free from all manner of coercion in matters religious.

13. Among the things that concern the good of the Church and indeed the welfare of society here on earth—things therefore that are always and everywhere to be kept secure and defended against all injury—this certainly is preeminent, namely, that the Church should enjoy that full measure of freedom which her care for the salvation of men requires.[31]

---

29. Cf. 1 Pet. 2:13–17.
30. Cf. Acts 4:19–20.
31. Cf. Leo XIII, letter "*Officio Sanctissimo*," Dec. 22 1887: AAS 20 (1887), p. 269; idem, letter "*Ex Litteris*," April 7 1887: AAS 19 (1886), p. 465.

This is a sacred freedom, because the only-begotten Son endowed with it the Church which He purchased with His blood. Indeed it is so much the property of the Church that to act against it is to act against the will of God. The freedom of the Church is the fundamental principle in what concerns the relations between the Church and governments and the whole civil order.

In human society and in the face of government the Church claims freedom for herself in her character as a spiritual authority, established by Christ the Lord, upon which there rests, by divine mandate, the duty of going out into the whole world and preaching the Gospel to every creature.[32] The Church also claims freedom for herself in her character as a society of men who have the right to live in society in accordance with the precepts of the Christian faith.[33]

In turn, where the principle of religious freedom is not only proclaimed in words or simply incorporated in law but also given sincere and practical application, there the Church succeeds in achieving a stable situation of right as well as of fact and the independence which is necessary for the fulfillment of her divine mission.

This independence is precisely what the authorities of the Church claim in society.[34] At the same time, the Christian faithful, in common with all other men, possess the civil right not to be hindered in leading their lives in accordance with their consciences. Therefore, a harmony exists between the freedom of the Church and the religious freedom which is to be recognized as the right of all men and communities and sanctioned by constitutional law.

14. In order to be faithful to the divine command, "teach all nations" (Matt. 28:19–20), the Catholic Church must work with all urgency and

---

32. Cf. Mark 16:15; Matt. 28:18–20, Pius XII, encycl. "*Summi Pontificatus*," Oct. 20, 1939: AAS 31 (1939). pp. 445–446.

33. Cf. Pius XI, letter "*Firmissiman Constantiam*," March 28, 1937: AAS 29 (1937), p. 196.

34. Cf. Pius XII, allocution, "*Ci Riesce*," Dec. 6, 1953: AAS 45 (1953), p. 802.

PART I: CHURCH TEACHING

concern "that the word of God be spread abroad and glorified" (2 Thess. 3:1). Hence the Church earnestly begs of its children that, "first of all, supplications, prayers, petitions, acts of thanksgiving be made for all men. . . . For this is good and agreeable in the sight of God our Savior, who wills that all men be saved and come to the knowledge of the truth" (1 Tim. 2:1–4). In the formation of their consciences, the Christian faithful ought carefully to attend to the sacred and certain doctrine of the Church.[35] For the Church is, by the will of Christ, the teacher of the truth. It is her duty to give utterance to, and authoritatively to teach, that truth which is Christ Himself, and also to declare and confirm by her authority those principles of the moral order which have their origins in human nature itself. Furthermore, let Christians walk in wisdom in the face of those outside, "in the Holy Spirit, in unaffected love, in the word of truth" (2 Cor. 6:6–7), and let them be about their task of spreading the light of life with all confidence[36] and apostolic courage, even to the shedding of their blood.

The disciple is bound by a grave obligation toward Christ, his Master, ever more fully to understand the truth received from Him, faithfully to proclaim it, and vigorously to defend it, never—be it understood— having recourse to means that are incompatible with the spirit of the Gospel. At the same time, the charity of Christ urges him to love and have prudence and patience in his dealings with those who are in error or in ignorance with regard to the faith.[37] All is to be taken into account—the Christian duty to Christ, the life-giving word which must be proclaimed, the rights of the human person, and the measure of grace granted by God through Christ to men who are invited freely to accept and profess the faith.

15. The fact is that men of the present day want to be able freely to profess their religion in private and in public. Indeed, religious freedom

---

35. Cf. Pius XII, radio message, March 23, 1952: AAS 44 (1952), pp. 270–278.
36. Cf. Acts 4:29.
37. Cf. John XXIII, encycl. "Pacem in Terris," April 11, 1963: AAS 55 (1963), pp. 299–300.

has already been declared to be a civil right in most constitutions, and it is solemnly recognized in international documents.[38] The further fact is that forms of government still exist under which, even though freedom of religious worship receives constitutional recognition, the powers of government are engaged in the effort to deter citizens from the profession of religion and to make life very difficult and dangerous for religious communities.

This council greets with joy the first of these two facts as among the signs of the times. With sorrow, however, it denounces the other fact, as only to be deplored. The council exhorts Catholics, and it directs a plea to all men, most carefully to consider how greatly necessary religious freedom is, especially in the present condition of the human family. All nations are coming into even closer unity. Men of different cultures and religions are being brought together in closer relationships. There is a growing consciousness of the personal responsibility that every man has. All this is evident. Consequently, in order that relationships of peace and harmony be established and maintained within the whole of mankind, it is necessary that religious freedom be everywhere provided with an effective constitutional guarantee and that respect be shown for the high duty and right of man freely to lead his religious life in society.

May the God and Father of all grant that the human family, through careful observance of the principle of religious freedom in society, may be brought by the grace of Christ and the power of the Holy Spirit to the sublime and unending and "glorious freedom of the sons of God" (Rom. 8:21).

---

38. Cf. John XXIII, encycl. *"Pacem in Terris,"* April 11, 1963: AAS 55 (1963) pp. 295–296.

CHAPTER 7

Gaudium et Spes:
On the Church in the Modern World

(Excerpt)

Second Vatican Council
(promulgated by Pope St. Paul VI)
December 7, 1965

*The Second Vatican Council's pastoral constitution on
the Church in the modern world outlines the place of individuals and
societies in God's divine plan of salvation, and the Church's role
and mission in this period of history.*

PART I: THE CHURCH AND MAN'S CALLING

11. The People of God believes that it is led by the Lord's Spirit, Who fills the earth. Motivated by this faith, it labors to decipher authentic signs of God's presence and purpose in the happenings, needs and desires in which this People has a part along with other men of our age. For faith throws a new light on everything, manifests God's design for man's total vocation, and thus directs the mind to solutions which are fully human.

This council, first of all, wishes to assess in this light those values which are most highly prized today and to relate them to their divine source. Insofar as they stem from endowments conferred by God on man, these values are exceedingly good. Yet they are often wrenched from their rightful function by the taint in man's heart, and hence stand in need of purification.

What does the Church think of man? What needs to be recommended for the upbuilding of contemporary society? What is the ultimate significance of human activity throughout the world? People are waiting for an answer to these questions. From the answers it will be increasingly clear that the People of God and the human race in whose midst it lives render service to each other. Thus the mission of the Church will show its religious, and by that very fact, its supremely human character.

Chapter 1: The Dignity of the Human Person

12. According to the almost unanimous opinion of believers and unbelievers alike, all things on earth should be related to man as their center and crown.

But what is man? About himself he has expressed, and continues to express, many divergent and even contradictory opinions. In these he often exalts himself as the absolute measure of all things or debases himself to the point of despair. The result is doubt and anxiety. The Church certainly understands these problems. Endowed with light from God, she can offer solutions to them, so that man's true situation can be portrayed and his defects explained, while at the same time his dignity and destiny are justly acknowledged.

For Sacred Scripture teaches that man was created "to the image of God," is capable of knowing and loving his Creator, and was appointed by Him as master of all earthly creatures[1] that he might subdue them and use them to God's glory.[2] "What is man that you should care for him? You have made him little less than the angels, and crowned him with glory and honor. You have given him rule over the works of your hands, putting all things under his feet" (Ps. 8:5–7).

---

1. Cf. Gen. 1:26; Wis. 2:23.
2. Cf. Sir. 17:3–10.

But God did not create man as a solitary, for from the beginning "male and female he created them" (Gen. 1:27). Their companionship produces the primary form of interpersonal communion. For by his innermost nature man is a social being, and unless he relates himself to others he can neither live nor develop his potential.

Therefore, as we read elsewhere in Holy Scripture God saw "all that he had made, and it was very good" (Gen. 1:31).

13. Although he was made by God in a state of holiness, from the very onset of his history man abused his liberty, at the urging of the Evil One. Man set himself against God and sought to attain his goal apart from God. Although they knew God, they did not glorify Him as God, but their senseless minds were darkened and they served the creature rather than the Creator.[3] What divine revelation makes known to us agrees with experience. Examining his heart, man finds that he has inclinations toward evil too, and is engulfed by manifold ills which cannot come from his good Creator. Often refusing to acknowledge God as his beginning, man has disrupted also his proper relationship to his own ultimate goal as well as his whole relationship toward himself and others and all created things.

Therefore man is split within himself. As a result, all of human life, whether individual or collective, shows itself to be a dramatic struggle between good and evil, between light and darkness. Indeed, man finds that by himself he is incapable of battling the assaults of evil successfully, so that everyone feels as though he is bound by chains. But the Lord Himself came to free and strengthen man, renewing him inwardly and casting out that "prince of this world" (John 12:31) who held him in the bondage of sin.[4] For sin has diminished man, blocking his path to fulfillment.

---

3. Cf. Rom. 1:21–25.
4. Cf. John 8:34.

The call to grandeur and the depths of misery, both of which are a part of human experience, find their ultimate and simultaneous explanation in the light of this revelation.

14. Though made of body and soul, man is one. Through his bodily composition he gathers to himself the elements of the material world; thus they reach their crown through him, and through him raise their voice in free praise of the Creator.[5] For this reason man is not allowed to despise his bodily life, rather he is obliged to regard his body as good and honorable since God has created it and will raise it up on the last day. Nevertheless, wounded by sin, man experiences rebellious stirrings in his body. But the very dignity of man postulates that man glorify God in his body and forbid it to serve the evil inclinations of his heart.[6]

Now, man is not wrong when he regards himself as superior to bodily concerns, and as more than a speck of nature or a nameless constituent of the city of man. For by his interior qualities he outstrips the whole sum of mere things. He plunges into the depths of reality whenever he enters into his own heart; God, Who probes the heart,[7] awaits him there; there he discerns his proper destiny beneath the eyes of God. Thus, when he recognizes in himself a spiritual and immortal soul, he is not being mocked by a fantasy born only of physical or social influences, but is rather laying hold of the proper truth of the matter.

15. Man judges rightly that by his intellect he surpasses the material universe, for he shares in the light of the divine mind. By relentlessly employing his talents through the ages he has indeed made progress in the practical sciences and in technology and the liberal arts. In our times he has won superlative victories, especially in his probing of the material world and in subjecting it to himself. Still he has always searched for more penetrating truths, and finds them. For his intelligence is not confined to observable data alone, but can with genuine

---

5. Cf. Dan. 3:57–90.
6. Cf. 1 Cor. 6:13–20.
7. Cf. 1 Kings 16:7; Jer. 17:10.

certitude attain to reality itself as knowable, though in consequence of sin that certitude is partly obscured and weakened.

The intellectual nature of the human person is perfected by wisdom and needs to be, for wisdom gently attracts the mind of man to a quest and a love for what is true and good. Steeped in wisdom, man passes through visible realities to those which are unseen.

Our era needs such wisdom more than bygone ages if the discoveries made by man are to be further humanized. For the future of the world stands in peril unless wiser men are forthcoming. It should also be pointed out that many nations, poorer in economic goods, are quite rich in wisdom and can offer noteworthy advantages to others.

It is, finally, through the gift of the Holy Spirit that man comes by faith to the contemplation and appreciation of the divine plan.[8]

16. In the depths of his conscience, man detects a law which he does not impose upon himself, but which holds him to obedience. Always summoning him to love good and avoid evil, the voice of conscience when necessary speaks to his heart: do this, shun that. For man has in his heart a law written by God; to obey it is the very dignity of man; according to it he will be judged.[9] Conscience is the most secret core and sanctuary of a man. There he is alone with God, Whose voice echoes in his depths.[10] In a wonderful manner conscience reveals that law which is fulfilled by love of God and neighbor.[11] In fidelity to conscience, Christians are joined with the rest of men in the search for truth, and for the genuine solution to the numerous problems which arise in the life of individuals from social relationships. Hence the more right conscience holds sway, the more persons and groups turn aside from blind choice and strive to be guided by the objective norms of

---

8. Cf. Sir. 17:7–8.
9. Cf. Rom. 2:15–16.
10. Cf. Pius XII, *Radio address on the correct formation of a Christian conscience in the young,* March 23, 1952: AAS (1952), p. 271.
11. Cf. Matt. 22:37–40; Gal. 5:14.

morality. Conscience frequently errs from invincible ignorance without losing its dignity. The same cannot be said for a man who cares but little for truth and goodness, or for a conscience which by degrees grows practically sightless as a result of habitual sin.

17. Only in freedom can man direct himself toward goodness. Our contemporaries make much of this freedom and pursue it eagerly; and rightly to be sure. Often however they foster it perversely as a license for doing whatever pleases them, even if it is evil. For its part, authentic freedom is an exceptional sign of the divine image within man. For God has willed that man remain "under the control of his own decisions,"[12] so that he can seek his Creator spontaneously, and come freely to utter and blissful perfection through loyalty to Him. Hence man's dignity demands that he act according to a knowing and free choice that is personally motivated and prompted from within, not under blind internal impulse nor by mere external pressure. Man achieves such dignity when, emancipating himself from all captivity to passion, he pursues his goal in a spontaneous choice of what is good, and procures for himself through effective and skilful action, apt helps to that end. Since man's freedom has been damaged by sin, only by the aid of God's grace can he bring such a relationship with God into full flower. Before the judgement seat of God each man must render an account of his own life, whether he has done good or evil.[13]

18. It is in the face of death that the riddle of human existence grows most acute. Not only is man tormented by pain and by the advancing deterioration of his body, but even more so by a dread of perpetual extinction. He rightly follows the intuition of his heart when he abhors and repudiates the utter ruin and total disappearance of his own person. He rebels against death because he bears in himself an eternal seed which cannot be reduced to sheer matter. All the endeavors of technology, though useful in the extreme, cannot calm his anxiety; for

---

12. Cf. Sir. 15:14.
13. Cf. 2 Cor. 5:10.

PART I: CHURCH TEACHING

prolongation of biological life is unable to satisfy that desire for higher life which is inescapably lodged in his breast.

Although the mystery of death utterly beggars the imagination, the Church has been taught by divine revelation and firmly teaches that man has been created by God for a blissful purpose beyond the reach of earthly misery. In addition, that bodily death from which man would have been immune had he not sinned[14] will be vanquished, according to the Christian faith, when man who was ruined by his own doing is restored to wholeness by an almighty and merciful Saviour. For God has called man and still calls him so that with his entire being he might be joined to Him in an endless sharing of a divine life beyond all corruption. Christ won this victory when He rose to life, for by His death He freed man from death.[15] Hence to every thoughtful man a solidly established faith provides the answer to his anxiety about what the future holds for him. At the same time faith gives him the power to be united in Christ with his loved ones who have already been snatched away by death; faith arouses the hope that they have found true life with God.

19. The root reason for human dignity lies in man's call to communion with God. From the very circumstance of his origin man is already invited to converse with God. For man would not exist were he not created by God's love and constantly preserved by it; and he cannot live fully according to truth unless he freely acknowledges that love and devotes himself to His Creator. Still, many of our contemporaries have never recognized this intimate and vital link with God, or have explicitly rejected it. Thus atheism must be accounted among the most serious problems of this age, and is deserving of closer examination.

The word atheism is applied to phenomena which are quite distinct from one another. For while God is expressly denied by some, others believe that man can assert absolutely nothing about Him. Still others use such

---

14. Cf. Wis. 1:13; 2:23–24; Rom. 5:21; 6:23; Jas. 1:15.
15. Cf. 1 Cor. 15:56–57.

a method to scrutinize the question of God as to make it seem devoid of meaning. Many, unduly transgressing the limits of the positive sciences, contend that everything can be explained by this kind of scientific reasoning alone, or by contrast, they altogether disallow that there is any absolute truth. Some laud man so extravagantly that their faith in God lapses into a kind of anemia, though they seem more inclined to affirm man than to deny God. Again some form for themselves such a fallacious idea of God that when they repudiate this figment they are by no means rejecting the God of the Gospel. Some never get to the point of raising questions about God, since they seem to experience no religious stirrings nor do they see why they should trouble themselves about religion. Moreover, atheism results not rarely from a violent protest against the evil in this world, or from the absolute character with which certain human values are unduly invested, and which thereby already accords them the stature of God. Modern civilization itself often complicates the approach to God not for any essential reason but because it is so heavily engrossed in earthly affairs.

Undeniably, those who willfully shut out God from their hearts and try to dodge religious questions are not following the dictates of their consciences, and hence are not free of blame; yet believers themselves frequently bear some responsibility for this situation. For, taken as a whole, atheism is not a spontaneous development but stems from a variety of causes, including a critical reaction against religious beliefs, and in some places against the Christian religion in particular. Hence believers can have more than a little to do with the birth of atheism. To the extent that they neglect their own training in the faith, or teach erroneous doctrine, or are deficient in their religious, moral or social life, they must be said to conceal rather than reveal the authentic face of God and religion.

20. Modern atheism often takes on a systematic expression which, in addition to other causes, stretches the desires for human independence

to such a point that it poses difficulties against any kind of dependence on God. Those who profess atheism of this sort maintain that it gives man freedom to be an end unto himself, the sole artisan and creator of his own history. They claim that this freedom cannot be reconciled with the affirmation of a Lord Who is author and purpose of all things, or at least that this freedom makes such an affirmation altogether superfluous. Favoring this doctrine can be the sense of power which modern technical progress generates in man.

Not to be overlooked among the forms of modern atheism is that which anticipates the liberation of man especially through his economic and social emancipation. This form argues that by its nature religion thwarts this liberation by arousing man's hope for a deceptive future life, thereby diverting him from the constructing of the earthly city. Consequently when the proponents of this doctrine gain governmental power they vigorously fight against religion, and promote atheism by using, especially in the education of youth, those means of pressure which public power has at its disposal.

21. In her loyal devotion to God and men, the Church has already repudiated[16] and cannot cease repudiating, sorrowfully but as firmly as possible, those poisonous doctrines and actions which contradict reason and the common experience of humanity, and dethrone man from his native excellence.

Still, she strives to detect in the atheistic mind the hidden causes for the denial of God; conscious of how weighty are the questions which atheism raises, and motivated by love for all men, she believes these questions ought to be examined seriously and more profoundly.

The Church holds that the recognition of God is in no way hostile to man's dignity, since this dignity is rooted and perfected in God. For man

---

16. Cf. Pius XI, encyclical letter *Divini Redemptoris*, March 19, 1937: AAS 29 (1937), pp. 65–106; Pius XII, encyclical letter *Ad Apostolorum Principis*, June 29, 1958: AAS 50 (1958), pp. 601–614; John XXIII, encyclical letter *Mater et Magistra*, May 15, 1961: AAS 53 (1961), pp. 451–453; Paul VI, *Ecclesiam Suam*, Aug. 6, 1964: AAS 56 (1964), pp. 651–653.

was made an intelligent and free member of society by God Who created him, but even more important, he is called as a son to commune with God and share in His happiness. She further teaches that a hope related to the end of time does not diminish the importance of intervening duties but rather undergirds the acquittal of them with fresh incentives. By contrast, when a divine instruction and the hope of life eternal are wanting, man's dignity is most grievously lacerated, as current events often attest; riddles of life and death, of guilt and of grief go unsolved with the frequent result that men succumb to despair.

Meanwhile every man remains to himself an unsolved puzzle, however obscurely he may perceive it. For on certain occasions no one can entirely escape the kind of self-questioning mentioned earlier, especially when life's major events take place. To this questioning only God fully and most certainly provides an answer as He summons man to higher knowledge and humbler probing.

The remedy which must be applied to atheism, however, is to be sought in a proper presentation of the Church's teaching as well as in the integral life of the Church and her members. For it is the function of the Church, led by the Holy Spirit Who renews and purifies her ceaselessly,[17] to make God the Father and His Incarnate Son present and in a sense visible. This result is achieved chiefly by the witness of a living and mature faith, namely, one trained to see difficulties clearly and to master them. Many martyrs have given luminous witness to this faith and continue to do so. This faith needs to prove its fruitfulness by penetrating the believer's entire life, including its worldly dimensions, and by activating him toward justice and love, especially regarding the needy. What does the most to reveal God's presence, however, is the brotherly charity of the faithful who are united in spirit as they work together for the faith of the Gospel[18] and who prove themselves a sign of unity.

---

17. Cf. Second Vatican Council, *Dogmatic Constitution on the Church*, Chapter I, n. 8: AAS 57 (1965), p. 12.

18. Cf. Phil. 1:27.

While rejecting atheism, root and branch, the Church sincerely professes that all men, believers and unbelievers alike, ought to work for the rightful betterment of this world in which all alike live; such an ideal cannot be realized, however, apart from sincere and prudent dialogue. Hence the Church protests against the distinction which some state authorities make between believers and unbelievers, with prejudice to the fundamental rights of the human person. The Church calls for the active liberty of believers to build up in this world God's temple too. She courteously invites atheists to examine the Gospel of Christ with an open mind.

Above all the Church knows that her message is in harmony with the most secret desires of the human heart when she champions the dignity of the human vocation, restoring hope to those who have already despaired of anything higher than their present lot. Far from diminishing man, her message brings to his development light, life and freedom. Apart from this message nothing will avail to fill up the heart of man: "Thou hast made us for Thyself," O Lord, "and our hearts are restless till they rest in Thee."[19]

22. The truth is that only in the mystery of the incarnate Word does the mystery of man take on light. For Adam, the first man, was a figure of Him Who was to come,[20] namely Christ the Lord. Christ, the final Adam, by the revelation of the mystery of the Father and His love, fully reveals man to man himself and makes his supreme calling clear. It is not surprising, then, that in Him all the aforementioned truths find their root and attain their crown.

He Who is "the image of the invisible God" (Col. 1:15),[21] is Himself the perfect man. To the sons of Adam He restores the divine likeness which

---

19. St. Augustine, *Confessions*, I, 1: PL 32, 661.
20. Cf. Rom. 5:14. Cf. Tertullian, *De carnis resurrectione* 6: "The shape that the slime of the earth was given was intended with a view to Christ, the future man": p. 2, 282; CSEL 47, p. 33, 1. 12–13.
21. Cf. 2 Cor. 4:4.

had been disfigured from the first sin onward. Since human nature as He assumed it was not annulled,[22] by that very fact it has been raised up to a divine dignity in our respect too. For by His incarnation the Son of God has united Himself in some fashion with every man. He worked with human hands, He thought with a human mind, acted by human choice[23] and loved with a human heart. Born of the Virgin Mary, He has truly been made one of us, like us in all things except sin.[24]

As an innocent lamb He merited for us life by the free shedding of His own blood. In Him God reconciled us[25] to Himself and among ourselves; from bondage to the devil and sin He delivered us, so that each one of us can say with the Apostle: The Son of God "loved me and gave Himself up for me" (Gal. 2:20). By suffering for us He not only provided us with an example for our imitation,[26] He blazed a trail, and if we follow it, life and death are made holy and take on a new meaning.

The Christian man, conformed to the likeness of that Son Who is the firstborn of many brothers,[27] received "the first-fruits of the Spirit" (Rom. 8:23) by which he becomes capable of discharging the new law of love.[28] Through this Spirit, who is "the pledge of our inheritance" (Eph. 1:14), the whole man is renewed from within, even to the achievement of "the redemption of the body" (Rom. 8:23): "If the Spirit of him who raised Jesus from the death dwells in you, then he who raised Jesus Christ from the dead will also bring to life your mortal bodies because of his Spirit

---

22. Cf. Second Council of Constantinople, canon 7: "The divine Word was not changed into a human nature, nor was a human nature absorbed by the Word." Denzinger 219 (428); Cf. also Third Council of Constantinople: "For just as His most holy and immaculate human nature, though deified, was not destroyed (theotheisa ouk anerethe), but rather remained in its proper state and mode of being": Denzinger 291 (556); Cf. Council of Chalcedon: "to be acknowledged in two natures, without confusion, change, division, or separation." Denzinger 148 (302).

23. Cf. Third Council of Constantinople: "and so His human will, though deified, is not destroyed": Denzinger 291 (556).

24. Cf. Heb. 4:15.

25. Cf. 2 Cor. 5:18–19; Col. 1:20–22.

26. Cf. 1 Pet. 2:21; Matt. 16:24; Luke 14:27.

27. Cf. Rom. 8:29; Col. 3:10–14.

28. Cf. Rom. 8:1–11.

who dwells in you" (Rom. 8:11).[29] Pressing upon the Christian to be sure, are the need and the duty to battle against evil through manifold tribulations and even to suffer death. But, linked with the paschal mystery and patterned on the dying Christ, he will hasten forward to resurrection in the strength which comes from hope.[30]

All this holds true not only for Christians, but for all men of good will in whose hearts grace works in an unseen way.[31] For, since Christ died for all men,[32] and since the ultimate vocation of man is in fact one, and divine, we ought to believe that the Holy Spirit in a manner known only to God offers to every man the possibility of being associated with this paschal mystery.

Such is the mystery of man, and it is a great one, as seen by believers in the light of Christian revelation. Through Christ and in Christ, the riddles of sorrow and death grow meaningful. Apart from His Gospel, they overwhelm us. Christ has risen, destroying death by His death; He has lavished life upon us[33] so that, as sons in the Son, we can cry out in the Spirit: Abba, Father.[34]

Chapter 2: The Community of Mankind

23. One of the salient features of the modern world is the growing interdependence of men one on the other, a development promoted chiefly by modern technical advances. Nevertheless brotherly dialogue among men does not reach its perfection on the level of technical progress, but on the deeper level of interpersonal relationships. These demand a mutual respect for the full spiritual dignity of the person. Christian revelation contributes greatly to the promotion of this communion

---

29. Cf. 2 Cor. 4:14.
30. Cf. Phil. 3:19; Rom. 8:17.
31. Cf. Second Vatican Council, *Dogmatic Constitution on the Church*, Chapter 2, n. 16: *AAS* 57 (1965), p. 20.
32. Cf. Rom. 8:32.
33. Cf. The *Byzantine Easter Liturgy*.
34. Cf. Rom. 8:15 and Gal. 4:6; cf. also John 1:22 and John 3:1–2.

between persons, and at the same time leads us to a deeper understanding of the laws of social life which the Creator has written into man's moral and spiritual nature.

Since rather recent documents of the Church's teaching authority have dealt at considerable length with Christian doctrine about human society,[35] this council is merely going to call to mind some of the more basic truths, treating their foundations under the light of revelation. Then it will dwell more at length on certain of their implications having special significance for our day.

24. God, Who has fatherly concern for everyone, has willed that all men should constitute one family and treat one another in a spirit of brotherhood. For having been created in the image of God, Who "from one man has created the whole human race and made them live all over the face of the earth" (Acts 17:26), all men are called to one and the same goal, namely God Himself.

For this reason, love for God and neighbor is the first and greatest commandment. Sacred Scripture, however, teaches us that the love of God cannot be separated from love of neighbor: "If there is any other commandment, it is summed up in this saying: Thou shalt love thy neighbor as thyself. . . . Love therefore is the fulfillment of the Law" (Rom. 13:9–10; cf. 1 John 4:20). To men growing daily more dependent on one another, and to a world becoming more unified every day, this truth proves to be of paramount importance.

Indeed, the Lord Jesus, when He prayed to the Father, "that all may be one . . . as we are one" (John 17:21–22) opened up vistas closed to human reason, for He implied a certain likeness between the union of the divine Persons, and the unity of God's sons in truth and charity. This likeness reveals that man, who is the only creature on earth which

---

35. Cf. John XXIII, encyclical letter, *Mater et Magistra*, May 15, 1961: AAS 53 (1961), pp. 401–464, and encyclical letter *Pacem in Terris*, April 11, 1963: AAS 55 (1963), pp. 257–304; Paul VI encyclical letter *Ecclesiam Suam*, Aug. 6, 1964: AAS 54 (1864), pp. 609–659.

God willed for itself, cannot fully find himself except through a sincere gift of himself.[36]

25. Man's social nature makes it evident that the progress of the human person and the advance of society itself hinge on one another. For the beginning, the subject and the goal of all social institutions is and must be the human person which for its part and by its very nature stands completely in need of social life.[37] Since this social life is not something added on to man, through his dealings with others, through reciprocal duties, and through fraternal dialogue he develops all his gifts and is able to rise to his destiny.

Among those social ties which man needs for his development some, like the family and political community, relate with greater immediacy to his innermost nature; others originate rather from his free decision. In our era, for various reasons, reciprocal ties and mutual dependencies increase day by day and give rise to a variety of associations and organizations, both public and private. This development, which is called socialization, while certainly not without its dangers, brings with it many advantages with respect to consolidating and increasing the qualities of the human person, and safeguarding his rights.[38]

But if by this social life the human person is greatly aided in responding to his destiny, even in its religious dimensions, it cannot be denied that men are often diverted from doing good and spurred toward and by the social circumstances in which they live and are immersed from their birth. To be sure the disturbances which so frequently occur in the social order result in part from the natural tensions of economic, political and social forms. But at a deeper level they flow from man's pride and selfishness, which contaminate even the social sphere. When the structure of affairs is flawed by the consequences of sin, man, already born with a bent toward evil, finds there new inducements to sin, which

---

36. Cf. Luke 17:33.
37. Cf. St. Thomas, 1 *Ethica Lect.* 1.
38. Cf. John XXIII, encyclical letter *Mater et Magistra: AAS* 53 (1961), p. 418. Cf. also Pius XI, encyclical letter *Quadragesimo Anno: AAS* 23 (1931), p. 222 ff.

cannot be overcome without strenuous efforts and the assistance of grace.

26. Every day human interdependence grows more tightly drawn and spreads by degrees over the whole world. As a result the common good, that is, the sum of those conditions of social life which allow social groups and their individual members relatively thorough and ready access to their own fulfillment, today takes on an increasingly universal complexion and consequently involves rights and duties with respect to the whole human race. Every social group must take account of the needs and legitimate aspirations of other groups, and even of the general welfare of the entire human family.[39]

At the same time, however, there is a growing awareness of the exalted dignity proper to the human person, since he stands above all things, and his rights and duties are universal and inviolable. Therefore, there must be made available to all men everything necessary for leading a life truly human, such as food, clothing, and shelter; the right to choose a state of life freely and to found a family, the right to education, to employment, to a good reputation, to respect, to appropriate information, to activity in accord with the upright norm of one's own conscience, to protection of privacy and rightful freedom even in matters religious.

Hence, the social order and its development must invariably work to the benefit of the human person if the disposition of affairs is to be subordinate to the personal realm and not contrariwise, as the Lord indicated when He said that the Sabbath was made for man, and not man for the Sabbath.[40]

This social order requires constant improvement. It must be founded on truth, built on justice and animated by love; in freedom it should grow every day toward a more humane balance.[41] An improvement in

---

39. Cf. John XXIII, encyclical letter *Mater et Magistra*: AAS 53 (1961).
40. Cf. Mark 2:27.
41. Cf. John XXIII, encyclical letter *Pacem in Terris*: AAS 55 (1963), p. 266.

attitudes and abundant changes in society will have to take place if these objectives are to be gained.

God's Spirit, Who with a marvelous providence directs the unfolding of time and renews the face of the earth, is not absent from this development. The ferment of the Gospel too has aroused and continues to arouse in man's heart the irresistible requirements of his dignity.

27. Coming down to practical and particularly urgent consequences, this council lays stress on reverence for man; everyone must consider his every neighbor without exception as another self, taking into account first of all His life and the means necessary to living it with dignity,[42] so as not to imitate the rich man who had no concern for the poor man Lazarus.[43]

In our times a special obligation binds us to make ourselves the neighbor of every person without exception and of actively helping him when he comes across our path, whether he be an old person abandoned by all, a foreign laborer unjustly looked down upon, a refugee, a child born of an unlawful union and wrongly suffering for a sin he did not commit, or a hungry person who disturbs our conscience by recalling the voice of the Lord, "As long as you did it for one of these the least of my brethren, you did it for me" (Matt. 25:40).

Furthermore, whatever is opposed to life itself, such as any type of murder, genocide, abortion, euthanasia or wilful self-destruction, whatever violates the integrity of the human person, such as mutilation, torments inflicted on body or mind, attempts to coerce the will itself; whatever insults human dignity, such as subhuman living conditions, arbitrary imprisonment, deportation, slavery, prostitution, the selling of women and children; as well as disgraceful working conditions, where men are treated as mere tools for profit, rather than as free and responsible persons; all these things and others of their like are infamies indeed.

---

42. Cf. Jas. 2:15–16.
43. Cf. Luke 16:18–31.

They poison human society, but they do more harm to those who practice them than those who suffer from the injury. Moreover, they are a supreme dishonor to the Creator.

28. Respect and love ought to be extended also to those who think or act differently than we do in social, political and even religious matters. In fact, the more deeply we come to understand their ways of thinking through such courtesy and love, the more easily will we be able to enter into dialogue with them.

This love and good will, to be sure, must in no way render us indifferent to truth and goodness. Indeed love itself impels the disciples of Christ to speak the saving truth to all men. But it is necessary to distinguish between error, which always merits repudiation, and the person in error, who never loses the dignity of being a person even when he is flawed by false or inadequate religious notions.[44] God alone is the judge and searcher of hearts, for that reason He forbids us to make judgments about the internal guilt of anyone.[45]

The teaching of Christ even requires that we forgive injuries,[46] and extends the law of love to include every enemy, according to the command of the New Law: "You have heard that it was said: Thou shalt love thy neighbor and hate thy enemy. But I say to you: love your enemies, do good to those who hate you, and pray for those who persecute and calumniate you" (Matt. 5:43–44).

29. Since all men possess a rational soul and are created in God's likeness, since they have the same nature and origin, have been redeemed by Christ and enjoy the same divine calling and destiny, the basic equality of all must receive increasingly greater recognition.

True, all men are not alike from the point of view of varying physical power and the diversity of intellectual and moral resources. Nevertheless,

---

44. Cf. John XXIII, encyclical letter *Pacem in Terris: AAS* 55 (1963), p. 299 and 300.
45. Cf. Luke 6:37–38; Matt. 7:1–2; Rom. 2:1–11; 14:10, 14:10–12.
46. Cf. Matt. 5:43–47.

with respect to the fundamental rights of the person, every type of discrimination, whether social or cultural, whether based on sex, race, color, social condition, language or religion, is to be overcome and eradicated as contrary to God's intent. For in truth it must still be regretted that fundamental personal rights are still not being universally honored. Such is the case of a woman who is denied the right to choose a husband freely, to embrace a state of life or to acquire an education or cultural benefits equal to those recognized for men.

Therefore, although rightful differences exist between men, the equal dignity of persons demands that a more humane and just condition of life be brought about. For excessive economic and social differences between the members of the one human family or population groups cause scandal, and militate against social justice, equity, the dignity of the human person, as well as social and international peace.

Human institutions, both private and public, must labor to minister to the dignity and purpose of man. At the same time let them put up a stubborn fight against any kind of slavery, whether social or political, and safeguard the basic rights of man under every political system. Indeed human institutions themselves must be accommodated by degrees to the highest of all realities, spiritual ones, even though meanwhile, a long enough time will be required before they arrive at the desired goal.

30. Profound and rapid changes make it more necessary that no one ignoring the trend of events or drugged by laziness, content himself with a merely individualistic morality. It grows increasingly true that the obligations of justice and love are fulfilled only if each person, contributing to the common good, according to his own abilities and the needs of others, also promotes and assists the public and private institutions dedicated to bettering the conditions of human life. Yet there are those who, while possessing grand and rather noble sentiments, nevertheless in reality live always as if they cared nothing for the needs of society. Many in various places even make light of social laws and

precepts, and do not hesitate to resort to various frauds and deceptions in avoiding just taxes or other debts due to society. Others think little of certain norms of social life, for example those designed for the protection of health, or laws establishing speed limits; they do not even avert to the fact that by such indifference they imperil their own life and that of others.

Let everyone consider it his sacred obligation to esteem and observe social necessities as belonging to the primary duties of modern man. For the more unified the world becomes, the more plainly do the offices of men extend beyond particular groups and spread by degrees to the whole world. But this development cannot occur unless individual men and their associations cultivate in themselves the moral and social virtues, and promote them in society; thus, with the needed help of divine grace men who are truly new and artisans of a new humanity can be forthcoming.

31. In order for individual men to discharge with greater exactness the obligations of their conscience toward themselves and the various group to which they belong, they must be carefully educated to a higher degree of culture through the use of the immense resources available today to the human race. Above all the education of youth from every social background has to be undertaken, so that there can be produced not only men and women of refined talents, but those great-souled persons who are so desperately required by our times.

Now a man can scarcely arrive at the needed sense of responsibility, unless his living conditions allow him to become conscious of his dignity, and to rise to his destiny by spending himself for God and for others. But human freedom is often crippled when a man encounters extreme poverty just as it withers when he indulges in too many of life's comforts and imprisons himself in a kind of splendid isolation. Freedom acquires new strength, by contrast, when a man consents to the unavoidable requirements of social life, takes on the manifold demands of human partnership, and commits himself to the service of the human community.

Hence, the will to play one's role in common endeavors should be everywhere encouraged. Praise is due to those national procedures which allow the largest possible number of citizens to participate in public affairs with genuine freedom. Account must be taken, to be sure, of the actual conditions of each people and the decisiveness required by public authority. If every citizen is to feel inclined to take part in the activities of the various groups which make up the social body, these must offer advantages which will attract members and dispose them to serve others. We can justly consider that the future of humanity lies in the hands of those who are strong enough to provide coming generations with reasons for living and hoping.

32. As God did not create man for life in isolation, but for the formation of social unity, so also "it has pleased God to make men holy and save them not merely as individuals, without bond or link between them, but by making them into a single people, a people which acknowledges Him in truth and serves Him in holiness."[47] So from the beginning of salvation history He has chosen men not just as individuals but as members of a certain community. Revealing His mind to them, God called these chosen ones "His people" (Ex. 3:7–12), and even made a covenant with them on Sinai.[48]

This communitarian character is developed and consummated in the work of Jesus Christ. For the very Word made flesh willed to share in the human fellowship. He was present at the wedding of Cana, visited the house of Zacchaeus, ate with publicans and sinners. He revealed the love of the Father and the sublime vocation of man in terms of the most common of social realities and by making use of the speech and the imagery of plain everyday life. Willingly obeying the laws of his country

---

47. Cf. *Dogmatic Constitution on the Church*, Chapter II, n. 9: AAS 57 (1965), pp. 12–13
48. Cf. Exod. 24:1–8.

He sanctified those human ties, especially family ones, which are the source of social structures. He chose to lead the life proper to an artisan of His time and place.

In His preaching He clearly taught the sons of God to treat one another as brothers. In His prayers He pleaded that all His disciples might be "one." Indeed as the redeemer of all, He offered Himself for all even to point of death. "Greater love than this no one has, that one lay down his life for his friends" (John 15:13). He commanded His Apostles to preach to all peoples the Gospel's message that the human race was to become the Family of God, in which the fullness of the Law would be love.

As the firstborn of many brethren and by the giving of His Spirit, He founded after His death and resurrection a new brotherly community composed of all those who receive Him in faith and in love. This He did through His Body, which is the Church. There everyone, as members one of the other, would render mutual service according to the different gifts bestowed on each.

This solidarity must be constantly increased until that day on which it will be brought to perfection. Then, saved by grace, men will offer flawless glory to God as a family beloved of God and of Christ their Brother.

Chapter 3: Man's Activity Throughout the World

33. Through his labors and his native endowments man has ceaselessly striven to better his life. Today, however, especially with the help of science and technology, he has extended his mastery over nearly the whole of nature and continues to do so. Thanks to increased opportunities for many kinds of social contact among nations, the human family is gradually recognizing that it comprises a single world community and is making itself so. Hence many benefits once looked for, especially from heavenly powers, man has now enterprisingly procured for himself.

In the face of these immense efforts which already preoccupy the whole human race, men agitate numerous questions among themselves. What is the meaning and value of this feverish activity? How should all these things be used? To the achievement of what goal are the strivings of individuals and societies heading? The Church guards the heritage of God's word and draws from it moral and religious principles without always having at hand the solution to particular problems. As such she desires to add the light of revealed truth to mankind's store of experience, so that the path which humanity has taken in recent times will not be a dark one.

34. Throughout the course of the centuries, men have labored to better the circumstances of their lives through a monumental amount of individual and collective effort. To believers, this point is settled: considered in itself, this human activity accords with God's will. For man, created to God's image, received a mandate to subject to himself the earth and all it contains, and to govern the world with justice and holiness;[49] a mandate to relate himself and the totality of things to Him Who was to be acknowledged as the Lord and Creator of all. Thus, by the subjection of all things to man, the name of God would be wonderful in all the earth.[50]

This mandate concerns the whole of everyday activity as well. For while providing the substance of life for themselves and their families, men and women are performing their activities in a way which appropriately benefits society. They can justly consider that by their labor they are unfolding the Creator's work, consulting the advantages of their brother men, and are contributing by their personal industry to the realization in history of the divine plan.[51]

Thus, far from thinking that works produced by man's own talent and energy are in opposition to God's power, and that the rational creature

---

49. Cf. Gen. 1:26–27; 9:3; Wis. 9:3.
50. Cf. Ps. 8:7 and 10.
51. Cf. John XXIII, encyclical letter *Pacem in Terris*: AAS 55 (1963), p. 297.

exists as a kind of rival to the Creator, Christians are convinced that the triumphs of the human race are a sign of God's grace and the flowering of His own mysterious design. For the greater man's power becomes, the farther his individual and community responsibility extends. Hence it is clear that men are not deterred by the Christian message from building up the world, or impelled to neglect the welfare of their fellows, but that they are rather more stringently bound to do these very things.[52]

35. Human activity, to be sure, takes its significance from its relationship to man. Just as it proceeds from man, so it is ordered toward man. For when a man works he not only alters things and society, he develops himself as well. He learns much, he cultivates his resources, he goes outside of himself and beyond himself. Rightly understood this kind of growth is of greater value than any external riches which can be garnered. A man is more precious for what he is than for what he has.[53] Similarly, all that men do to obtain greater justice, wider brotherhood, a more humane disposition of social relationships has greater worth than technical advances. For these advances can supply the material for human progress, but of themselves alone they can never actually bring it about.

Hence, the norm of human activity is this: that in accord with the divine plan and will, it harmonize with the genuine good of the human race, and that it allow men as individuals and as members of society to pursue their total vocation and fulfill it.

36. Now many of our contemporaries seem to fear that a closer bond between human activity and religion will work against the independence of men, of societies, or of the sciences.

If by the autonomy of earthly affairs we mean that created things and societies themselves enjoy their own laws and values which must be gradually deciphered, put to use, and regulated by men, then it is entirely

---

52. Cf. Message to all mankind sent by the Fathers at the beginning of the Second Vatican Council, Oct. 20, 1962: AAS 54 (1962), p. 823.
53. Cf. Paul VI, Address to the diplomatic corps Jan. 7, 1965: AAS 57 (1965), p. 232.

right to demand that autonomy. Such is not merely required by modern man, but harmonizes also with the will of the Creator. For by the very circumstance of their having been created, all things are endowed with their own stability, truth, goodness, proper laws and order. Man must respect these as he isolates them by the appropriate methods of the individual sciences or arts. Therefore if methodical investigation within every branch of learning is carried out in a genuinely scientific manner and in accord with moral norms, it never truly conflicts with faith, for earthly matters and the concerns of faith derive from the same God.[54] Indeed whoever labors to penetrate the secrets of reality with a humble and steady mind, even though he is unaware of the fact, is nevertheless being led by the hand of God, who holds all things in existence, and gives them their identity. Consequently, we cannot but deplore certain habits of mind, which are sometimes found too among Christians, which do not sufficiently attend to the rightful independence of science and which, from the arguments and controversies they spark, lead many minds to conclude that faith and science are mutually opposed.[55]

But if the expression, the independence of temporal affairs, is taken to mean that created things do not depend on God, and that man can use them without any reference to their Creator, anyone who acknowledges God will see how false such a meaning is. For without the Creator the creature would disappear. For their part, however, all believers of whatever religion always hear His revealing voice in the discourse of creatures. When God is forgotten, however, the creature itself grows unintelligible.

37. Sacred Scripture teaches the human family what the experience of the ages confirms: that while human progress is a great advantage to man, it brings with it a strong temptation. For when the order of values is jumbled and bad is mixed with the good, individuals and groups pay heed solely to their own interests, and not to those of others. Thus it happens that

---

54. Cf. First Vatican Council, *Dogmatic Constitution on the Catholic Faith*, Chapter III: Denz. 1785–1786 (3004–3005).

55. Cf. Msgr. Pio Paschini, *Vita e opere di Galileo Galilei*, 2 volumes, Vatican Press (1964).

the world ceases to be a place of true brotherhood. In our own day, the magnified power of humanity threatens to destroy the race itself.

For a monumental struggle against the powers of darkness pervades the whole history of man. The battle was joined from the very origins of the world and will continue until the last day, as the Lord has attested.[56] Caught in this conflict, man is obliged to wrestle constantly if he is to cling to what is good, nor can he achieve his own integrity without great efforts and the help of God's grace.

That is why Christ's Church, trusting in the design of the Creator, acknowledges that human progress can serve man's true happiness, yet she cannot help echoing the Apostle's warning: "Be not conformed to this world" (Rom. 12:2). Here by the world is meant that spirit of vanity and malice which transforms into an instrument of sin those human energies intended for the service of God and man.

Hence if anyone wants to know how this unhappy situation can be overcome, Christians will tell him that all human activity, constantly imperiled by man's pride and deranged self-love, must be purified and perfected by the power of Christ's cross and resurrection. For redeemed by Christ and made a new creature in the Holy Spirit, man is able to love the things themselves created by God, and ought to do so. He can receive them from God and respect and reverence them as flowing constantly from the hand of God. Grateful to his Benefactor for these creatures, using and enjoying them in detachment and liberty of spirit, man is led forward into a true possession of them, as having nothing, yet possessing all things.[57] "All are yours, and you are Christ's, and Christ is God's" (1 Cor. 3:22–23).

38. For God's Word, through Whom all things were made, was Himself made flesh and dwelt on the earth of men.[58] Thus He entered the world's

---

56. Cf. Matt. 24:13; 13:24–30 and 36–43.
57. Cf. 2 Cor. 6:10.
58. Cf. John 1:3 and 14.

history as a perfect man, taking that history up into Himself and summarizing it.[59] He Himself revealed to us that "God is love" (1 John 4:8) and at the same time taught us that the new command of love was the basic law of human perfection and hence of the world's transformation.

To those, therefore, who believe in divine love, He gives assurance that the way of love lies open to men and that the effort to establish a universal brotherhood is not a hopeless one. He cautions them at the same time that this charity is not something to be reserved for important matters, but must be pursued chiefly in the ordinary circumstances of life. Undergoing death itself for all of us sinners,[60] He taught us by example that we too must shoulder that cross which the world and the flesh inflict upon those who search after peace and justice. Appointed Lord by His resurrection and given plenary power in heaven and on earth,[61] Christ is now at work in the hearts of men through the energy of His Holy Spirit, arousing not only a desire for the age to come, but by that very fact animating, purifying and strengthening those noble longings too by which the human family makes its life more human and strives to render the whole earth submissive to this goal.

Now, the gifts of the Spirit are diverse: while He calls some to give clear witness to the desire for a heavenly home and to keep that desire green among the human family, He summons others to dedicate themselves to the earthly service of men and to make ready the material of the celestial realm by this ministry of theirs. Yet He frees all of them so that by putting aside love of self and bringing all earthly resources into the service of human life they can devote themselves to that future when humanity itself will become an offering accepted by God.[62]

The Lord left behind a pledge of this hope and strength for life's journey in that sacrament of faith where natural elements refined by man are

---

59. Cf. Eph. 1:10.
60. Cf. John 3:16; Rom. 5:8.
61. Cf. Acts 2:36; Matt. 28:18.
62. Cf. Rom. 15:16.

gloriously changed into His Body and Blood, providing a meal of brotherly solidarity and a foretaste of the heavenly banquet.

39. We do not know the time for the consummation of the earth and of humanity,[63] nor do we know how all things will be transformed. As deformed by sin, the shape of this world will pass away;[64] but we are taught that God is preparing a new dwelling place and a new earth where justice will abide,[65] and whose blessedness will answer and surpass all the longings for peace which spring up in the human heart.[66] Then, with death overcome, the sons of God will be raised up in Christ, and what was sown in weakness and corruption will be invested with incorruptibility.[67] Enduring with charity and its fruits,[68] all that creation[69] which God made on man's account will be unchained from the bondage of vanity.

Therefore, while we are warned that it profits a man nothing if he gain the whole world and lose himself,[70] the expectation of a new earth must not weaken but rather stimulate our concern for cultivating this one. For here grows the body of a new human family, a body which even now is able to give some kind of foreshadowing of the new age.

Hence, while earthly progress must be carefully distinguished from the growth of Christ's kingdom, to the extent that the former can contribute to the better ordering of human society, it is of vital concern to the Kingdom of God.[71]

For after we have obeyed the Lord, and in His Spirit nurtured on earth the values of human dignity, brotherhood and freedom, and indeed all the good fruits of our nature and enterprise, we will find them again,

---

63. Cf. Acts 1:7.
64. Cf. 1 Cor. 7:31; St. Irenaeus, *Adversus haereses*, V, 36: PG, VIII, 1221.
65. Cf. 2 Cor. 5:2; 2 Pet. 3:13.
66. Cf. 1 Cor. 2:9; Rev. 21:4–5.
67. Cf. 1 Cor. 15:42 and 53.
68. Cf. 1 Cor. 13:8; 3:14.
69. Cf. Rom. 8:19–21.
70. Cf. Luke 9:25.
71. Cf. Pius XI, encyclical letter *Quadragesimo Anno*: AAS 23 (1931), p. 207.

but freed of stain, burnished and transfigured, when Christ hands over to the Father: "a kingdom eternal and universal, a kingdom of truth and life, of holiness and grace, of justice, love and peace."[72] On this earth that Kingdom is already present in mystery. When the Lord returns it will be brought into full flower.

Chapter 4: The Role of the Church in the Modern World

40. Everything we have said about the dignity of the human person, and about the human community and the profound meaning of human activity, lays the foundation for the relationship between the Church and the world, and provides the basis for dialogue between them.[73] In this chapter, presupposing everything which has already been said by this council concerning the mystery of the Church, we must now consider this same Church inasmuch as she exists in the world, living and acting with it.

Coming forth from the eternal Father's love,[74] founded in time by Christ the Redeemer and made one in the Holy Spirit,[75] the Church has a saving and an eschatological purpose which can be fully attained only in the future world. But she is already present in this world, and is composed of men, that is, of members of the earthly city who have a call to form the family of God's children during the present history of the human race, and to keep increasing it until the Lord returns. United on behalf of heavenly values and enriched by them, this family has been "constituted and structured as a society in this world"[76] by Christ, and is equipped "by appropriate means for visible and social union."[77] Thus the Church, at once "a visible association and a spiritual community,"[78]

---

72. Preface of the Feast of Christ the King.

73. Cf. Paul VI, encyclical letter *Ecclesiam Suam*, III: AAS 56 (1964), pp. 637–659.

74. Cf. Titus 3:4: "love of mankind."

75. Cf. Eph. 1:3; 5:6, 13–14, 23.

76. Second Vatican Council, *Dogmatic Constitution on the Church*, Chapter I, n. 8: AAS 57 (1965), p. 12.

77. *Ibid.*, Chapter II, no. 9: AAS 57 (1965), p. 14; Cf. n. 8: AAS *loc. cit.*, p. 11.

78. *Ibid.*, Chapter I, n. 8: AAS 57 (1965), p. 11.

goes forward together with humanity and experiences the same earthly lot which the world does. She serves as a leaven and as a kind of soul for human society[79] as it is to be renewed in Christ and transformed into God's family.

That the earthly and the heavenly city penetrate each other is a fact accessible to faith alone; it remains a mystery of human history, which sin will keep in great disarray until the splendor of God's sons, is fully revealed. Pursuing the saving purpose which is proper to her, the Church does not only communicate divine life to men but in some way casts the reflected light of that life over the entire earth, most of all by its healing and elevating impact on the dignity of the person, by the way in which it strengthens the seams of human society and imbues the everyday activity of men with a deeper meaning and importance. Thus through her individual matters and her whole community, the Church believes she can contribute greatly toward making the family of man and its history more human.

In addition, the Catholic Church gladly holds in high esteem the things which other Christian Churches and ecclesial communities have done or are doing cooperatively by way of achieving the same goal. At the same time, she is convinced that she can be abundantly and variously helped by the world in the matter of preparing the ground for the Gospel. This help she gains from the talents and industry of individuals and from human society as a whole. The council now sets forth certain general principles for the proper fostering of this mutual exchange and assistance in concerns which are in some way common to the world and the Church.

41. Modern man is on the road to a more thorough development of his own personality, and to a growing discovery and vindication of his own rights. Since it has been entrusted to the Church to reveal the mystery of God, Who is the ultimate goal of man, she opens up to man at the

---

79. Cf. *ibid.*, Chapter IV, n. 38: AAS 57 (1965), p. 43, with note 120.

same time the meaning of his own existence, that is, the innermost truth about himself. The Church truly knows that only God, Whom she serves, meets the deepest longings of the human heart, which is never fully satisfied by what this world has to offer.

She also knows that man is constantly worked upon by God's spirit, and hence can never be altogether indifferent to the problems of religion. The experience of past ages proves this, as do numerous indications in our own times. For man will always yearn to know, at least in an obscure way, what is the meaning of his life, of his activity, of his death. The very presence of the Church recalls these problems to his mind. But only God, Who created man to His own image and ransomed him from sin, provides the most adequate answer to the questions, and this He does through what He has revealed in Christ His Son, Who became man. Whoever follows after Christ, the perfect man, becomes himself more of a man. For by His incarnation the Father's Word assumed, and sanctified through His cross and resurrection, the whole of man, body and soul, and through that totality the whole of nature created by God for man's use.

Thanks to this belief, the Church can anchor the dignity of human nature against all tides of opinion, for example those which undervalue the human body or idolize it. By no human law can the personal dignity and liberty of man be so aptly safeguarded as by the Gospel of Christ which has been entrusted to the Church. For this Gospel announces and proclaims the freedom of the sons of God, and repudiates all the bondage which ultimately results from sin;[80] it has a sacred reverence for the dignity of conscience and its freedom of choice, constantly advises that all human talents be employed in God's service and men's, and, finally, commends all to the charity of all.[81]

This agrees with the basic law of the Christian dispensation. For though the same God is Savior and Creator, Lord of human history as well as

---

80. Cf. Rom. 8:14–17.
81. Cf. Matt. 22:39.

of salvation history, in the divine arrangement itself, the rightful autonomy of the creature, and particularly of man is not withdrawn, but is rather re-established in its own dignity and strengthened in it.

The Church, therefore, by virtue of the Gospel committed to her, proclaims the rights of man; she acknowledges and greatly esteems the dynamic movements of today by which these rights are everywhere fostered. Yet these movements must be penetrated by the spirit of the Gospel and protected against any kind of false autonomy. For we are tempted to think that our personal rights are fully ensured only when we are exempt from every requirement of divine law. But this way lies not the maintenance of the dignity of the human person, but its annihilation.

42. The union of the human family is greatly fortified and fulfilled by the unity, founded on Christ,[82] of the family of God's sons.

Christ, to be sure, gave His Church no proper mission in the political, economic or social order. The purpose which He set before her is a religious one.[83] But out of this religious mission itself comes a function, a light and an energy which can serve to structure and consolidate the human community according to the divine law. As a matter of fact, when circumstances of time and place produce the need, she can and indeed should initiate activities on behalf of all men, especially those designed for the needy, such as the works of mercy and similar undertakings.

The Church recognizes that worthy elements are found in today's social movements, especially an evolution toward unity, a process

---

82. *Dogmatic Constitution on the Church*, Chapter II, n. 9: AAS 57 (1965), pp. 12–14.

83. Cf. Pius XII, Address to the International Union of Institutes of Archeology, History and History of Art, March 9, 1956: AAS 48 (1965), p. 212: "Its divine Founder, Jesus Christ, has not given it any mandate or fixed any end of the cultural order. The goal which Christ assigns to it is strictly religious. . . . The Church must lead men to God, in order that they may be given over to him without reserve. . . . The Church can never lose sight of the strictly religious, supernatural goal. The meaning of all its activities, down to the last canon of its Code, can only cooperate directly or indirectly in this goal."

of wholesome socialization and of association in civic and economic realms. The promotion of unity belongs to the innermost nature of the Church, for she is, "thanks to her relationship with Christ, a sacramental sign and an instrument of intimate union with God, and of the unity of the whole human race."[84] Thus she shows the world that an authentic union, social and external, results from a union of minds and hearts, namely from that faith and charity by which her own unity is unbreakably rooted in the Holy Spirit. For the force which the Church can inject into the modern society of man consists in that faith and charity put into vital practice, not in any external dominion exercised by merely human means.

Moreover, since in virtue of her mission and nature she is bound to no particular form of human culture, nor to any political, economic or social system, the Church by her very universality can be a very close bond between diverse human communities and nations, provided these trust her and truly acknowledge her right to true freedom in fulfilling her mission. For this reason, the Church admonishes her own sons, but also humanity as a whole, to overcome all strife between nations and race in this family spirit of God's children, and in the same way, to give internal strength to human associations which are just.

With great respect, therefore, this council regards all the true, good and just elements inherent in the very wide variety of institutions which the human race has established for itself and constantly continues to establish. The council affirms, moreover, that the Church is willing to assist and promote all these institutions to the extent that such a service depends on her and can be associated with her mission. She has no fiercer desire than that in pursuit of the welfare of all she may be able to develop herself freely under any kind of government which grants recognition to the basic rights of person and family, to the demands of the common good and to the free exercise of her own mission.

---

84. *Dogmatic Constitution on the Church*, Chapter I, n. 1: AAS 57 (1965), p. 5.

43. This council exhorts Christians, as citizens of two cities, to strive to discharge their earthly duties conscientiously and in response to the Gospel spirit. They are mistaken who, knowing that we have here no abiding city but seek one which is to come,[85] think that they may therefore shirk their earthly responsibilities. For they are forgetting that by the faith itself they are more obliged than ever to measure up to these duties, each according to his proper vocation.[86] Nor, on the contrary, are they any less wide of the mark who think that religion consists in acts of worship alone and in the discharge of certain moral obligations, and who imagine they can plunge themselves into earthly affairs in such a way as to imply that these are altogether divorced from the religious life. This split between the faith which many profess and their daily lives deserves to be counted among the more serious errors of our age. Long since, the Prophets of the Old Testament fought vehemently against this scandal[87] and even more so did Jesus Christ Himself in the New Testament threaten it with grave punishments.[88] Therefore, let there be no false opposition between professional and social activities on the one part, and religious life on the other. The Christian who neglects his temporal duties, neglects his duties toward his neighbor and even God, and jeopardizes his eternal salvation. Christians should rather rejoice that, following the example of Christ Who worked as an artisan, they are free to give proper exercise to all their earthly activities and to their humane, domestic, professional, social and technical enterprises by gathering them into one vital synthesis with religious values, under whose supreme direction all things are harmonized unto God's glory.

Secular duties and activities belong properly although not exclusively to laymen. Therefore acting as citizens in the world, whether individually or socially, they will keep the laws proper to each discipline, and labor to equip themselves with a genuine expertise in their various fields. They will gladly work with men seeking the same goals. Acknowledging the

---

85. Cf. Heb. 13:14.
86. Cf. 2 Thess. 3:6–13; Eph. 4:28.
87. Cf. Is. 58:1–12.
88. Cf. Matt. 23:3–23; Mark 7:10–13.

demands of faith and endowed with its force, they will unhesitatingly devise new enterprises, where they are appropriate, and put them into action. Laymen should also know that it is generally the function of their well-formed Christian conscience to see that the divine law is inscribed in the life of the earthly city; from priests they may look for spiritual light and nourishment. Let the layman not imagine that his pastors are always such experts, that to every problem which arises, however complicated, they can readily give him a concrete solution, or even that such is their mission. Rather, enlightened by Christian wisdom and giving close attention to the teaching authority of the Church,[89] let the layman take on his own distinctive role.

Often enough the Christian view of things will itself suggest some specific solution in certain circumstances. Yet it happens rather frequently, and legitimately so, that with equal sincerity some of the faithful will disagree with others on a given matter. Even against the intentions of their proponents, however, solutions proposed on one side or another may be easily confused by many people with the Gospel message. Hence it is necessary for people to remember that no one is allowed in the aforementioned situations to appropriate the Church's authority for his opinion. They should always try to enlighten one another through honest discussion, preserving mutual charity and caring above all for the common good.

Since they have an active role to play in the whole life of the Church, laymen are not only bound to penetrate the world with a Christian spirit, but are also called to be witnesses to Christ in all things in the midst of human society.

Bishops, to whom is assigned the task of ruling the Church of God, should, together with their priests, so preach the news of Christ that all the earthly activities of the faithful will be bathed in the light of the Gospel. All pastors should remember too that by their daily conduct and

---

89. Cf. John XXIII, encyclical letter *Mater et Magistra*, IV: AAS 53 (1961), pp. 456–457; cf. I: AAS *loc. cit.*, pp. 407, 410–41.

concern[90] they are revealing the face of the Church to the world, and men will judge the power and truth of the Christian message thereby. By their lives and speech, in union with Religious and their faithful, may they demonstrate that even now the Church by her presence alone and by all the gifts which she contains, is an unspent fountain of those virtues which the modern world needs the most.

By unremitting study they should fit themselves to do their part in establishing dialogue with the world and with men of all shades of opinion. Above all let them take to heart the words which this council has spoken: "Since humanity today increasingly moves toward civil, economic and social unity, it is more than ever necessary that priests, with joint concern and energy, and under the guidance of the bishops and the supreme pontiff, erase every cause of division, so that the whole human race may be led to the unity of God's family."[91]

Although by the power of the Holy Spirit the Church will remain the faithful spouse of her Lord and will never cease to be the sign of salvation on earth, still she is very well aware that among her members,[92] both clerical and lay, some have been unfaithful to the Spirit of God during the course of many centuries; in the present age, too, it does not escape the Church how great a distance lies between the message she offers and the human failings of those to whom the Gospel is entrusted. Whatever be the judgement of history on these defects, we ought to be conscious of them, and struggle against them energetically, lest they inflict harm on spread of the Gospel. The Church also realizes that in working out her relationship with the world she always has great need of the ripening which comes with the experience of the centuries. Led by the Holy Spirit, Mother Church unceasingly exhorts her sons "to purify and renew themselves so that the sign of Christ can shine more brightly on the face of the Church."[93]

---

90. Cf. *Dogmatic Constitution on the Church*, Chapter III, n. 28: AAS 57 (1965), p. 35.
91. *Ibid.*, n. 28: AAS *loc. cit.*, pp. 35–36.
92. Cf. St. Ambrose, *De virginitate*, Chapter VIII, n. 48: ML 16, 278.
93. Cf. *Dogmatic Constitution on the Church*, Chapter II, n. 15: AAS 57 (1965), p. 20.

44. Just as it is in the world's interest to acknowledge the Church as an historical reality, and to recognize her good influence, so the Church herself knows how richly she has profited by the history and development of humanity.

The experience of past ages, the progress of the sciences, and the treasures hidden in the various forms of human culture, by all of which the nature of man himself is more clearly revealed and new roads to truth are opened, these profit the Church, too. For, from the beginning of her history she has learned to express the message of Christ with the help of the ideas and terminology of various philosophers, and has tried to clarify it with their wisdom, too. Her purpose has been to adapt the Gospel to the grasp of all as well as to the needs of the learned, insofar as such was appropriate. Indeed this accommodated preaching of the revealed word ought to remain the law of all evangelization. For thus the ability to express Christ's message in its own way is developed in each nation, and at the same time there is fostered a living exchange between the Church and the diverse cultures of people.[94] To promote such exchange, especially in our days, the Church requires the special help of those who live in the world, are versed in different institutions and specialties, and grasp their innermost significance in the eyes of both believers and unbelievers. With the help of the Holy Spirit, it is the task of the entire People of God, especially pastors and theologians, to hear, distinguish and interpret the many voices of our age, and to judge them in the light of the divine word, so that revealed truth can always be more deeply penetrated, better understood and set forth to greater advantage.

Since the Church has a visible and social structure as a sign of her unity in Christ, she can and ought to be enriched by the development of human social life, not that there is any lack in the constitution given her by Christ, but that she can understand it more penetratingly, express it better, and adjust it more successfully to our times. Moreover,

---

94. Cf. *Dogmatic Constitution on the Church*, Chapter II, n. 13: AAS 57 (1965), p. 17.

she gratefully understands that in her community life no less than in her individual sons, she receives a variety of helps from men of every rank and condition, for whoever promotes the human community at the family level, culturally, in its economic, social and political dimensions, both nationally and internationally, such a one, according to God's design, is contributing greatly to the Church as well, to the extent that she depends on things outside herself. Indeed, the Church admits that she has greatly profited and still profits from the antagonism of those who oppose or who persecute her.[95]

45. While helping the world and receiving many benefits from it, the Church has a single intention: that God's kingdom may come, and that the salvation of the whole human race may come to pass. For every benefit which the People of God during its earthly pilgrimage can offer to the human family stems from the fact that the Church is "the universal sacrament of salvation,"[96] simultaneously manifesting and exercising the mystery of God's love.

For God's Word, by whom all things were made, was Himself made flesh so that as perfect man He might save all men and sum up all things in Himself. The Lord is the goal of human history, the focal point of the longings of history and of civilization, the center of the human race, the joy of every heart and the answer to all its yearnings.[97] He it is Whom the Father raised from the dead, lifted on high and stationed at His right hand, making Him judge of the living and the dead. Enlivened and united in His Spirit, we journey toward the consummation of human history, one which fully accords with the counsel of God's love: "To reestablish all things in Christ, both those in the heavens and those on the earth" (Eph. 1:10).

---

95. Cf. Justin, *Dialogus cum Tryphene*, Chapter 110: PG 6, 729 (ed. Otto), 1897, pp. 391–393: ". . . but the greater the number of persecutions which are inflicted upon us, so much the greater the number of other men who become devout believers through the name of Jesus." Cf. Tertullian, *Apologeticus*, Chapter L, 13: "Every time you mow us down like grass, we increase in number: the blood of Christians is a seed!" Cf. *Dogmatic Constitution on the Church*, Chapter II, no. 9: AAS 57 (1965), p. 14.

96. Cf. *Dogmatic Constitution on the Church*, Chapter II n. 15: AAS 57 (1965), p. 20.

97. Cf. Paul VI, address given on Feb. 3, 1965.

The Lord Himself speaks: "Behold I come quickly! And my reward is with me, to render to each one according to his works. I am the Alpha and the Omega, the first and the last, the beginning and the end (Rev. 22:12–13).

CHAPTER 8

Populorum Progressio:
On the Development of Peoples

(Excerpt)

Pope St. Paul VI
March 26, 1967

Pope St. Paul VI's encyclical on the development of peoples emphasizes the nature of true development, which can only be measured and understood in light of the supernatural destiny of human beings.

✳

The Present Need

13. In the present day . . . the world situation requires the concerted effort of everyone, a thorough examination of every facet of the problem—social, economic, cultural and spiritual.

The Church, which has long experience in human affairs and has no desire to be involved in the political activities of any nation, "seeks but one goal: to carry forward the work of Christ under the lead of the befriending Spirit. And Christ entered this world to give witness to the truth; to save, not to judge; to serve, not to be served."[1]

Founded to build the kingdom of heaven on earth rather than to acquire temporal power, the Church openly avows that the two powers—Church and State—are distinct from one another; that each is

---

1. Cf. *Church in the World of Today* no. 3: AAS 58 (1966), 1026 [cf. TPS XI, 261].

supreme in its own sphere of competency.[2] But since the Church does dwell among men, she has the duty "of scrutinizing the signs of the times and of interpreting them in the light of the Gospel."[3] Sharing the noblest aspirations of men and suffering when she sees these aspirations not satisfied, she wishes to help them attain their full realization. So she offers man her distinctive contribution: a global perspective on man and human realities.

Authentic Development

14. The development We speak of here cannot be restricted to economic growth alone. To be authentic, it must be well rounded; it must foster the development of each man and of the whole man. As an eminent specialist on this question has rightly said: "We cannot allow economics to be separated from human realities, nor development from the civilization in which it takes place. What counts for us is man—each individual man, each human group, and humanity as a whole."[4]

Personal Responsibility

15. In God's plan, every man is born to seek self-fulfillment, for every human life is called to some task by God. At birth a human being possesses certain aptitudes and abilities in germinal form, and these qualities are to be cultivated so that they may bear fruit. By developing these traits through formal education of personal effort, the individual works his way toward the goal set for him by the Creator.

Endowed with intellect and free will, each man is responsible for his self-fulfillment even as he is for his salvation. He is helped, and sometimes hindered, by his teachers and those around him; yet whatever be the outside influences exerted on him, he is the chief architect of his

---

2. Cf. Leo XIII, Encyc. letter *Immortale Dei: Acta Leonis XIII 5* (1885), 127.

3. *Church in the World of Today*, no. 4: AAS 58 (1966), 1027 [cf. TPS XI, 261].

4. Cf. L. J. Lebret, O.P., *Dynamique concrète du développement*, Paris: Economie et Humanisme, Les editions ouvrières (1961), 28.

own success or failure. Utilizing only his talent and willpower, each man can grow in humanity, enhance his personal worth, and perfect himself.

Man's Supernatural Destiny

16. Self-development, however, is not left up to man's option. Just as the whole of creation is ordered toward its Creator, so too the rational creature should of his own accord direct his life to God, the first truth and the highest good. Thus human self-fulfillment may be said to sum up our obligations.

Moreover, this harmonious integration of our human nature, carried through by personal effort and responsible activity, is destined for a higher state of perfection. United with the life-giving Christ, man's life is newly enhanced; it acquires a transcendent humanism which surpasses its nature and bestows new fullness of life. This is the highest goal of human self-fulfillment.

Ties With All Men

17. Each man is also a member of society; hence he belongs to the community of man. It is not just certain individuals but all men who are called to further the development of human society as a whole. Civilizations spring up, flourish and die. As the waves of the sea gradually creep farther and farther in along the shoreline, so the human race inches its way forward through history.

We are the heirs of earlier generations, and we reap benefits from the efforts of our contemporaries; we are under obligation to all men. Therefore we cannot disregard the welfare of those who will come after us to increase the human family. The reality of human solidarity brings us not only benefits but also obligations.

Development in Proper Perspective

18. Man's personal and collective fulfillment could be jeopardized if the proper scale of values were not maintained. The pursuit of life's necessities is quite legitimate; hence we are duty-bound to do the work which enables us to obtain them: "If anyone is unwilling to work, do not let him eat."[5] But the acquisition of worldly goods can lead men to greed, to the unrelenting desire for more, to the pursuit of greater personal power. Rich and poor alike—be they individuals, families or nations—can fall prey to avarice and soulstifling materialism.

Latent Dangers

19. Neither individuals nor nations should regard the possession of more and more goods as the ultimate objective. Every kind of progress is a two-edged sword. It is necessary if man is to grow as a human being; yet it can also enslave him, if he comes to regard it as the supreme good and cannot look beyond it. When this happens, men harden their hearts, shut out others from their minds and gather together solely for reasons of self-interest rather than out of friendship; dissension and disunity follow soon after.

Thus the exclusive pursuit of material possessions prevents man's growth as a human being and stands in opposition to his true grandeur. Avarice, in individuals and in nations, is the most obvious form of stultified moral development.

A New Humanism Needed

20. If development calls for an ever-growing number of technical experts, even more necessary still is the deep thought and reflection of wise men in search of a new humanism, one which will enable our contemporaries to enjoy the higher values of love and friendship, of

---

5. 2 Thess. 3:10.

prayer and contemplation,[6] and thus find themselves. This is what will guarantee man's authentic development—his transition from less than human conditions to truly human ones.

The Scale of Values

21. What are less than human conditions? The material poverty of those who lack the bare necessities of life, and the moral poverty of those who are crushed under the weight of their own self-love; oppressive political structures resulting from the abuse of ownership or the improper exercise of power, from the exploitation of the worker or unjust transactions.

What are truly human conditions? The rise from poverty to the acquisition of life's necessities; the elimination of social ills; broadening the horizons of knowledge; acquiring refinement and culture. From there one can go on to acquire a growing awareness of other people's dignity, a taste for the spirit of poverty,[7] an active interest in the common good, and a desire for peace. Then man can acknowledge the highest values and God Himself, their author and end. Finally and above all, there is faith—God's gift to men of good will—and our loving unity in Christ, who calls all men to share God's life as sons of the living God, the Father of all men.

Issues and Principles

22. In the very first pages of Scripture we read these words: "Fill the earth and subdue it."[8] This teaches us that the whole of creation is for man, that he has been charged to give it meaning by his intelligent activity, to complete and perfect it by his own efforts and to his own advantage.

---

6. Cf., for example, J. Maritain, *Les conditions spintuelles du progrès et de la paix*, in an anthology entitled *Rencontre des cultures à l'UNESCO sous le signe du Concile Oecuménique Vatican II*, Paris: Mame (1966), 66.

7. Cf. Matt. 5:3.

8. Gen. 1:28.

Now if the earth truly was created to provide man with the necessities of life and the tools for his own progress, it follows that every man has the right to glean what he needs from the earth. The recent Council reiterated this truth: "God intended the earth and everything in it for the use of all human beings and peoples. Thus, under the leadership of justice and in the company of charity, created goods should flow fairly to all."[9]

All other rights, whatever they may be, including the rights of property and free trade, are to be subordinated to this principle. They should in no way hinder it; in fact, they should actively facilitate its implementation. Redirecting these rights back to their original purpose must be regarded as an important and urgent social duty.

The Use of Private Property

23. "He who has the goods of this world and sees his brother in need and closes his heart to him, how does the love of God abide in him?"[10] Everyone knows that the Fathers of the Church laid down the duty of the rich toward the poor in no uncertain terms. As St. Ambrose put it: "You are not making a gift of what is yours to the poor man, but you are giving him back what is his. You have been appropriating things that are meant to be for the common use of everyone. The earth belongs to everyone, not to the rich."[11] These words indicate that the right to private property is not absolute and unconditional.

No one may appropriate surplus goods solely for his own private use when others lack the bare necessities of life. In short, "as the Fathers of the Church and other eminent theologians tell us, the right of private property may never be exercised to the detriment of the common

---

9. *Church in the World of Today*, no. 69: AAS 58 (1966), 1090 [cf. TPS XI, 306].
10. 1 John 3:17.
11. *De Nabute*, c. 12, n. 53: PL 14, 747; cf. J. R. Palanque, *Saint Ambroise et l'empire romain*, Paris: de Boccard (1933), 336 ff.

good." When "private gain and basic community needs conflict with one another," it is for the public authorities "to seek a solution to these questions, with the active involvement of individual citizens and social groups."[12]

The Common Good

24. If certain landed estates impede the general prosperity because they are extensive, unused or poorly used, or because they bring hardship to peoples or are detrimental to the interests of the country, the common good sometimes demands their expropriation.

Vatican II affirms this emphatically.[13] At the same time it clearly teaches that income thus derived is not for man's capricious use, and that the exclusive pursuit of personal gain is prohibited. Consequently, it is not permissible for citizens who have garnered sizeable income from the resources and activities of their own nation to deposit a large portion of their income in foreign countries for the sake of their own private gain alone, taking no account of their country's interests; in doing this, they clearly wrong their country.[14]

The Value of Industrialization

25. The introduction of industrialization, which is necessary for economic growth and human progress, is both a sign of development and a spur to it. By dint of intelligent thought and hard work, man gradually uncovers the hidden laws of nature and learns to make better use of natural resources. As he takes control over his way of life, he is stimulated to undertake new investigations and fresh discoveries, to take prudent risks and launch new ventures, to act responsibly and give of himself unselfishly.

---

12. Letter to the 52nd Social Week at Brest, in *L'homme et la révolution urbaine*, Lyon: Chronique sociale (1965), 8–9.

13. *Church in the World of Today*, no. 71: AAS 58 (1966), 1093 [cf. TPS XI, 308].

14. *Ibid.*, no. 65: AAS 58 (1966), 1086 [cf. TPS XI, 303].

Unbridled Liberalism

26. However, certain concepts have somehow arisen out of these new conditions and insinuated themselves into the fabric of human society. These concepts present profit as the chief spur to economic progress, free competition as the guiding norm of economics, and private ownership of the means of production as an absolute right, having no limits nor concomitant social obligations.

This unbridled liberalism paves the way for a particular type of tyranny, rightly condemned by Our predecessor Pius XI, for it results in the "international imperialism of money."[15]

Such improper manipulations of economic forces can never be condemned enough; let it be said once again that economics is supposed to be in the service of man.[16]

But if it is true that a type of capitalism, as it is commonly called, has given rise to hardships, unjust practices, and fratricidal conflicts that persist to this day, it would be a mistake to attribute these evils to the rise of industrialization itself, for they really derive from the pernicious economic concepts that grew up along with it. We must in all fairness acknowledge the vital role played by labor systemization and industrial organization in the task of development.

Nobility of Work

27. The concept of work can turn into an exaggerated mystique. Yet, for all that, it is something willed and approved by God. Fashioned in the image of his Creator, "man must cooperate with Him in completing the work of creation and engraving on the earth the spiritual imprint

---

15. Encyc. letter *Quadragesimo anno: AAS* 23 (1931), 212.
16. Cf., for example, Colin Clark, *The Conditions of Economic Progress*, 3rd ed., New York: St. Martin's Press (1960), 3–6.

which he himself has received."[17] God gave man intelligence, sensitivity and the power of thought—tools with which to finish and perfect the work He began. Every worker is, to some extent, a creator—be he artist, craftsman, executive, laborer or farmer.

Bent over a material that resists his efforts, the worker leaves his imprint on it, at the same time developing his own powers of persistence, inventiveness and concentration. Further, when work is done in common—when hope, hardship, ambition and joy are shared—it brings together and firmly unites the wills, minds and hearts of men. In its accomplishment, men find themselves to be brothers.[18]

Dangers and Ideals

28. Work, too, has a double edge. Since it promises money, pleasure and power, it stirs up selfishness in some and incites others to revolt. On the other hand, it also fosters a professional outlook, a sense of duty, and love of neighbor. Even though it is now being organized more scientifically and efficiently, it still can threaten man's dignity and enslave him; for work is human only if it results from man's use of intellect and free will.

Our predecessor John XXIII stressed the urgent need of restoring dignity to the worker and making him a real partner in the common task: "Every effort must be made to ensure that the enterprise is indeed a true human community, concerned about the needs, the activities and the standing of each of its members."[19]

Considered from a Christian point of view, work has an even loftier connotation. It is directed to the establishment of a supernatural order

---

17. Letter to the 51st Social Week at Lyon, in *Le travail et les travailleurs dans la societé contemporaine*, Lyon: Chronique sociale (1965), 6.

18. Cf., for example, M. D. Chenu, O.P., *Pour une théologie du travail*, Paris: Editions du Seuil (1955) [Eng. tr. *The Theology of Work*, Dublin: Gill, 1963].

19. Encyc. letter *Mater et Magistra*: AAS 53 (1961), 423 [cf. TPS VII, 312].

here on earth,[20] a task that will not be completed until we all unite to form that perfect manhood of which St. Paul speaks, "the mature measure of the fullness of Christ."[21]

Balanced Progress Required

29. We must make haste. Too many people are suffering. While some make progress, others stand still or move backwards; and the gap between them is widening. However, the work must proceed in measured steps if the proper equilibrium is to be maintained. Makeshift agrarian reforms may fall short of their goal. Hasty industrialization can undermine vital institutions and produce social evils, causing a setback to true human values.

Reform, Not Revolution

30. The injustice of certain situations cries out for God's attention. Lacking the bare necessities of life, whole nations are under the thumb of others; they cannot act on their own initiative; they cannot exercise personal responsibility; they cannot work toward a higher degree of cultural refinement or a greater participation in social and public life. They are sorely tempted to redress these insults to their human nature by violent means.

31. Everyone knows, however, that revolutionary uprisings—except where there is manifest, longstanding tyranny which would do great damage to fundamental personal rights and dangerous harm to the common good of the country—engender new injustices, introduce new inequities and bring new disasters. The evil situation that exists, and it surely is evil, may not be dealt with in such a way that an even worse situation results.

---

20. Cf., for example, O. von Nell-Breuning, S.J., *Wirtschaft und Gesellschaft*, vol. 1: Grundfragen, Freiburg: Herder (1956), 183–184.

21. Eph. 4:13.

A Task for Everyone

32. We want to be clearly understood on this point: The present state of affairs must be confronted boldly, and its concomitant injustices must be challenged and overcome. Continuing development calls for bold innovations that will work profound changes. The critical state of affairs must be corrected for the better without delay.

Everyone must lend a ready hand to this task, particularly those who can do most by reason of their education, their office, or their authority. They should set a good example by contributing part of their own goods, as several of Our brother bishops have done.[22] In this way they will be responsive to men's longings and faithful to the Holy Spirit, because "the ferment of the Gospel, too, has aroused and continues to arouse in man's heart the irresistible requirements of his dignity.[23]

Programs and Planning

33. Individual initiative alone and the interplay of competition will not ensure satisfactory development. We cannot proceed to increase the wealth and power of the rich while we entrench the needy in their poverty and add to the woes of the oppressed. Organized programs are necessary for "directing, stimulating, coordinating, supplying and integrating"[24] the work of individuals and intermediary organizations.

It is for the public authorities to establish and lay down the desired goals, the plans to be followed, and the methods to be used in fulfilling them; and it is also their task to stimulate the efforts of those involved in this common activity. But they must also see to it that private initiative and intermediary organizations are involved in this work. In this way they will avoid total collectivization and the dangers of a planned

---

22. Cf., for example, Emmanuel Larrain Errázuriz, Bishop of Talca, Chile, President of CELAM, *Lettre pastorale sur le développement et la paix*, Paris: Pax Christi (1965).

23. *Church in the World of Today*, no. 26: AAS 58 (1966), 1046 [TPS XI, 275].

24. John XXIII, Encyc. letter *Mater et Magistra*: AAS 53 (1961), 414.

economy which might threaten human liberty and obstruct the exercise of man's basic human rights.

The Ultimate Purpose

34. Organized programs designed to increase productivity should have but one aim: to serve human nature. They should reduce inequities, eliminate discrimination, free men from the bonds of servitude, and thus give them the capacity, in the sphere of temporal realities, to improve their lot, to further their moral growth and to develop their spiritual endowments. When we speak of development, we should mean social progress as well as economic growth.

It is not enough to increase the general fund of wealth and then distribute it more fairly. It is not enough to develop technology so that the earth may become a more suitable living place for human beings. The mistakes of those who led the way should help those now on the road to development to avoid certain dangers. The reign of technology—technocracy, as it is called—can cause as much harm to the world of tomorrow as liberalism did to the world of yesteryear. Economics and technology are meaningless if they do not benefit man, for it is he they are to serve. Man is truly human only if he is the master of his own actions and the judge of their worth, only if he is the architect of his own progress. He must act according to his God-given nature, freely accepting its potentials and its claims upon him.

Basic Education

35. We can even say that economic growth is dependent on social progress, the goal to which it aspires; and that basic education is the first objective for any nation seeking to develop itself. Lack of education is as serious as lack of food; the illiterate is a starved spirit. When someone learns how to read and write, he is equipped to do a job and to shoulder a profession, to develop self-confidence and realize that he can progress

along with others. As We said in Our message to the UNESCO meeting at Teheran, literacy is the "first and most basic tool for personal enrichment and social integration; and it is society's most valuable tool for furthering development and economic progress."[25]

We also rejoice at the good work accomplished in this field by private initiative, by the public authorities, and by international organizations. These are the primary agents of development, because they enable man to act for himself.

Role of the Family

36. Man is not really himself, however, except within the framework of society and there the family plays the basic and most important role. The family's influence may have been excessive at some periods of history and in some places, to the extent that it was exercised to the detriment of the fundamental rights of the individual. Yet time honored social frameworks, proper to the developing nations, are still necessary for awhile, even as their excessive strictures are gradually relaxed. The natural family, stable and monogamous—as fashioned by God[26] and sanctified by Christianity—"in which different generations live together, helping each other to acquire greater wisdom and to harmonize personal rights with other social needs, is the basis of society."[27]

Population Growth

37. There is no denying that the accelerated rate of population growth brings many added difficulties to the problems of development where the size of the population grows more rapidly than the quantity of available resources to such a degree that things seem to have reached an impasse. In such circumstances people are inclined to apply drastic remedies to reduce the birth rate.

25. L'Osservatore Romano, Sept. 11, 1965; La Documentation Catholique, 62 (1965), 1674–1675.
26. Cf. Matt. 19:6.
27. Church in the World of Today, no. 52: AAS 58 (1966), 1073 [cf. TPS XI, 294].

There is no doubt that public authorities can intervene in this matter, within the bounds of their competence. They can instruct citizens on this subject and adopt appropriate measures, so long as these are in conformity with the dictates of the moral law and the rightful freedom of married couples is preserved completely intact. When the inalienable right of marriage and of procreation is taken away, so is human dignity.

Finally, it is for parents to take a thorough look at the matter and decide upon the number of their children. This is an obligation they take upon themselves, before their children already born, and before the community to which they belong—following the dictates of their own consciences informed by God's law authentically interpreted, and bolstered by their trust in Him.[28]

Professional Organizations

38. In the task of development man finds the family to be the first and most basic social structure; but he is often helped by professional organizations. While such organizations are founded to aid and assist their members, they bear a heavy responsibility for the task of education which they can and must carry out. In training and developing individual men, they do much to cultivate in them an awareness of the common good and of its demands upon all.

39. Every form of social action involves some doctrine; and the Christian rejects that which is based on a materialistic and atheistic philosophy, namely one which shows no respect for a religious outlook on life, for freedom or human dignity. So long as these higher values are preserved intact, however, the existence of a variety of professional organizations and trade unions is permissible. Variety may even help to preserve freedom and create friendly rivalry. We gladly commend those people who unselfishly serve their brothers by working in such organizations.

---

28. *Ibid.*, nos. 50–51, with note 14: AAS 58 (1966), 1070–1073 [cf. TPS XI, 292–293]; also no. 87, p. 1110 [cf. TPS XI, 319–320].

Cultural Institutions

40. Cultural institutions also do a great deal to further the work of development. Their important role was stressed by the Council: ". . . the future of the world stands in peril unless wiser men are forthcoming. It should also be pointed out that many nations, poorer in economic goods, are quite rich in wisdom and can offer noteworthy advantages to others."[29]

Every country, rich or poor, has a cultural tradition handed down from past generations. This tradition includes institutions required by life in the world, and higher manifestations—artistic, intellectual and religious—of the life of the spirit. When the latter embody truly human values, it would be a great mistake to sacrifice them for the sake of the former. Any group of people who would consent to let this happen, would be giving up the better portion of their heritage; in order to live, they would be giving up their reason for living. Christ's question is directed to nations also: "What does it profit a man, if he gain the whole world but suffer the loss of his own soul?"[30]

Avoiding Past Temptations

41. The poorer nations can never be too much on guard against the temptation posed by the wealthier nations. For these nations, with their favorable results from a highly technical and culturally developed civilization, provide an example of work and diligence with temporal prosperity the main pursuit. Not that temporal prosperity of itself precludes the activity of the human spirit. Indeed, with it, "the human spirit, being less subjected to material things, can be more easily drawn to the worship and contemplation of the Creator."[31] On the other hand, "modern civilization itself often complicates the approach to God, not

---

29. Cf. *ibid.*, no. 15: AAS 58 (1966), 1036 [cf. TPS XI, 268].
30. Matt. 16:26.
31. *Church in the World of Today*, no. 57: AAS 58 (1966), 1078 [cf. TPS XI, 297].

for any essential reason, but because it is so much engrossed in worldly affairs."[32]

The developing nations must choose wisely from among the things that are offered to them. They must test and reject false values that would tarnish a truly human way of life, while accepting noble and useful values in order to develop them in their own distinctive way, along with their own indigenous heritage.

A Full-Bodied Humanism

42. The ultimate goal is a full-bodied humanism.[33] And does this not mean the fulfillment of the whole man and of every man? A narrow humanism, closed in on itself and not open to the values of the spirit and to God who is their source, could achieve apparent success, for man can set about organizing terrestrial realities without God. But "closed off from God, they will end up being directed against man. A humanism closed off from other realities becomes inhuman."[34]

True humanism points the way toward God and acknowledges the task to which we are called, the task which offers us the real meaning of human life. Man is not the ultimate measure of man. Man becomes truly man only by passing beyond himself. In the words of Pascal: "Man infinitely surpasses man."[35]

---

32. *Ibid.*, no. 19: AAS 58 (1966), 1039 [cf. TPS XI, 270].

33. Cf., for example, J. Maritain, *L'humanisme intégral*, Paris: Aubier (1936) [Eng. tr. *True Humanism*, New York: Charles Scribner's Sons (1938)].

34. Cf. H. de Lubac, S.J., *Le drame de l'humanisme athée*, 3rd ed., Paris: Spes (1945), 10 [Eng. tr. *The Drama of Atheistic Humanism*, London: Sheed and Ward (1949), 7].

35. Pensées, ed. Brunschvicg, n. 434; cf. Maurice Zundel, *L'homme passe l'homme*, Le Caire: Editions du lien (1944).

CHAPTER 9

Octogesima Adveniens:
On the Eightieth Anniversary of
Rerum Novarum

(Excerpt)

Pope St. Paul VI
May 14, 1971

Released on the eightieth anniversary of Rerum Novarum, *this apostolic letter of Pope St. Paul VI warns of the dangers of both Marxism and philosophical liberalism, and emphasizes the role of Christians in the "positive transformation of society."*

FUNDAMENTAL ASPIRATIONS AND CURRENTS OF IDEAS

22. While scientific and technological progress continues to overturn man's surroundings, his patterns of knowledge, work, consumption and relationships, two aspirations persistently make themselves felt in these new contexts, and they grow stronger to the extent that he becomes better informed and better educated: the aspiration to equality and the aspiration to participation, two forms of man's dignity and freedom.

Advantages and limitations of juridical recognition

23. Through the statement of the rights of man and the seeking for international agreements for the application of these rights, progress

has been made towards inscribing these two aspirations in deeds and structures.[1] Nevertheless various forms of discrimination continually reappear—ethnic, cultural, religious, political and so on. In fact, human rights are still too often disregarded, if not scoffed at, or else they receive only formal recognition. In many cases legislation does not keep up with real situations. Legislation is necessary, but it is not sufficient for setting up true relationships of justice and equity. In teaching us charity, the Gospel instructs us in the preferential respect due to the poor and the special situation they have in society: the more fortunate should renounce some of their rights so as to place their goods more generously at the service of others. If, beyond legal rules, there is really no deeper feeling of respect for and service to others, then even equality before the law can serve as an alibi for flagrant discrimination, continued exploitation and actual contempt. Without a renewed education in solidarity, an overemphasis of equality can give rise to an individualism in which each one claims his own rights without wishing to be answerable for the common good.

In this field, everyone sees the highly important contribution of the Christian spirit, which moreover answers man's yearning to be loved. "Love for man, the prime value of the earthly order" ensures the conditions for peace, both social peace and international peace, by affirming our universal brotherhood.[2]

The political society

24. The two aspirations, to equality and to participation, seek to promote a democratic type of society. Various models are proposed, some are tried out, none of them gives complete satisfaction, and the search goes on between ideological and pragmatic tendencies. The Christian has the duty to take part in this search and in the organization and life of political society. As a social being, man builds his destiny within a series of particular groupings which demand, as their completion and as

---

1. Cf. Pope John XXIII, *Pacem in Terris*: AAS 55 (1963), p. 261ff.
2. Cf. Message for the World Day of Peace, 1971: AAS 63 (1971), pp. 5–9.

a necessary condition for their development, a vaster society, one of a universal character, the political society. All particular activity must be placed within that wider society, and thereby it takes on the dimension of the common good.[3]

This indicates the importance of education for life in society, in which there are called to mind, not only information on each one's rights, but also their necessary correlative: the recognition of the duties of each one in regard to others. The sense, and practice of duty are themselves conditioned by self-mastery and by the acceptance of responsibility and of the limits placed upon the freedom of the individual or of the group.

25. Political activity—need one remark that we are dealing primarily with an activity, not an ideology?—should be the projection of a plan of society which is consistent in its concrete means and in its inspiration, and which springs from a complete conception of man's vocation and of its differing social expressions. It is not for the State or even for political parties, which would be closed unto themselves, to try to impose an ideology by means that would lead to a dictatorship over minds, the worst kind of all. It is for cultural and religious groupings, in the freedom of acceptance which they presume, to develop in the social body, disinterestedly and in their own ways, those ultimate convictions on the nature, origin and end of man and society.

In this field, it is well to keep in mind the principle proclaimed at the Second Vatican Council: "The truth cannot impose itself except by virtue of its own truth, and it makes its entrance into the mind at once quietly and with power."[4]

Ideologies and human liberty

26. Therefore the Christian who wishes to live his faith in a political activity which he thinks of as service cannot without contradicting

---

3. Cf. *Gaudium et Spes*, 74: AAS 58 (1966), pp. 1095–1096.
4. *Dignitatis Humanae*, 1: AAS 58 (1966), p. 930.

himself adhere to ideological systems which radically or substantially go against his faith and his concept of man. He cannot adhere to the Marxist ideology, to its atheistic materialism, to its dialectic of violence and to the way it absorbs individual freedom in the collectivity, at the same time denying all transcendence to man and his personal and collective history; nor can he adhere to the liberal ideology which believes it exalts individual freedom by withdrawing it from every limitation, by stimulating it through exclusive seeking of interest and power, and by considering social solidarities as more or less automatic consequences of individual initiatives, not as an aim and a major criterion of the value of the social organization.

27. Is there need to stress the possible ambiguity of every social ideology? Sometimes it leads political or social activity to be simply the application of an abstract, purely theoretical idea; at other times it is thought which becomes a mere instrument at the service of activity as a simple means of a strategy.

In both cases is it not man that risks finding himself alienated? The Christian faith is above and is sometimes opposed to the ideologies, in that it recognizes God, who is transcendent and the Creator, and who, through all the levels of creation, calls on man as endowed with responsibility and freedom.

28. There would also be the danger of giving adherence to an ideology which does not rest on a true and organic doctrine, to take refuge in it as a final and sufficient explanation of everything, and thus to build a new idol, accepting, at times without being aware of doing so, its totalitarian and coercive character. And people imagine they find in it a justification for their activity, even violent activity, and an adequate response to a generous desire to serve. The desire remains but it allows itself to be consumed by an ideology which, even if it suggests certain paths to man's liberation, ends up by making him a slave.

29. It has been possible today to speak of a retreat of ideologies. In this respect the present time may be favorable for an openness to the concrete transcendence of Christianity. It may also be a more accentuated sliding towards a new positivism: universalized technology as the dominant form of activity, as the overwhelming pattern of existence, even as a language, without the question of its meaning being really asked.

Historical movements

30. But outside of this positivism which reduces man to a single dimension even if it be an important one today and by so doing mutilates him, the Christian encounters in his activity concrete historical movements sprung from ideologies and in part distinct from them. Our venerated predecessor Pope John XXIII in *Pacem in Terris* already showed that it is possible to make a distinction: "Neither can false philosophical teachings regarding the nature, origin and destiny of the universe and of man be identified with historical movements that have economic, social, cultural or political ends, not even when these movements have originated from those teachings and have drawn and still draw inspiration therefrom. Because the teachings, once they are drawn up and defined, remain always the same, while the movements, being concerned with historical situations in constant evolution, cannot but be influenced by these latter and cannot avoid, therefore, being subject to changes, even of a profound nature. Besides, who can deny that those movements, in so far as they conform to the dictates of right reason and are interpreters of the lawful aspirations of the human person, contain elements that are positive and deserving of approval?"[5]

Attraction of socialist currents

31. Some Christians are today attracted by socialist currents and their various developments. They try to recognize therein a certain number of aspirations which they carry within themselves in the name of their

---

5. AAS 55 (1963), p. 300.

faith. They feel that they are part of that historical current and wish to play a part within it. Now this historical current takes on, under the same name, different forms according to different continents and cultures, even if it drew its inspiration, and still does in many cases, from ideologies incompatible with faith. Careful judgment is called for. Too often Christians attracted by socialism tend to idealize it in terms which, apart from anything else, are very general: a will for justice, solidarity and equality. They refuse to recognize the limitations of the historical socialist movements, which remain conditioned by the ideologies from which they originated. Distinctions must be made to guide concrete choices between the various levels of expression of socialism: a generous aspiration and a seeking for a more just society, historical movements with a political organization and aim, and an ideology which claims to give a complete and self-sufficient picture of man. Nevertheless, these distinctions must not lead one to consider such levels as completely separate and independent. The concrete link which, according to circumstances, exists between them must be clearly marked out. This insight will enable Christians to see the degree of commitment possible along these lines, while safeguarding the values, especially those of liberty, responsibility and openness to the spiritual, which guarantee the integral development of man.

Historical evolution of Marxism

32. Other Christians even ask whether an historical development of Marxism might not authorize certain concrete rapprochements. They note in fact a certain splintering of Marxism, which until now showed itself to be a unitary ideology which explained in atheistic terms the whole of man and the world since it did not go outside their development process. Apart from the ideological confrontation officially separating the various champions of Marxism-Leninism in their individual interpretations of the thought of its founders, and apart from the open opposition between the political systems which make use of

its name today, some people lay down distinctions between Marxism's various levels of expression.

33. For some, Marxism remains essentially the active practice of class struggle. Experiencing the ever present and continually renewed force of the relationships of domination and exploitation among men, they reduce Marxism to no more than a struggle—at times with no other purpose—to be pursued and even stirred up in permanent fashion. For others, it is first and foremost the collective exercise of political and economic power under the direction of a single party, which would be the sole expression and guarantee of the welfare of all, and would deprive individuals and other groups of any possibility of initiative and choice. At a third level, Marxism, whether in power or not, is viewed as a socialist ideology based on historical materialism and the denial of everything transcendent. At other times, finally, it presents itself in a more attenuated form, one also more attractive to the modern mind: as a scientific activity, as a rigorous method of examining social and political reality, and as the rational link, tested by history, between theoretical knowledge and the practice of revolutionary transformation. Although this type of analysis gives a privileged position to certain aspects of reality to the detriment of the rest, and interprets them in the light of its ideology, it nevertheless furnishes some people not only with a working tool but also a certitude preliminary to action: the claim to decipher in a scientific manner the mainsprings of the evolution of society.

34. While, through the concrete existing form of Marxism, one can distinguish these various aspects and the questions they pose for the reflection and activity of Christians, it would be illusory and dangerous to reach a point of forgetting the intimate link which radically binds them together, to accept the elements of Marxist analysis without recognizing their relationships with ideology, and to enter into the practice of class struggle and its Marxist interpretations, while failing to note the kind of totalitarian and violent society to which this process leads.

The liberal ideology

35. On another side, we are witnessing a renewal of the liberal ideology. This current asserts itself both in the name of economic efficiency, and for the defense of the individual against the increasingly overwhelming hold of organizations, and as a reaction against the totalitarian tendencies of political powers. Certainly, personal initiative must be maintained and developed. But do not Christians who take this path tend to idealize liberalism in their turn, making it a proclamation in favor of freedom? They would like a new model, more adapted to present-day conditions, while easily forgetting that at the very root of philosophical liberalism is an erroneous affirmation of the autonomy of the individual in his activity, his motivation and the exercise of his liberty. Hence, the liberal ideology likewise calls for careful discernment on their part.

Christian discernment

36. In this renewed encounter of the various ideologies, the Christian will draw from the sources of his faith and the Church's teaching the necessary principles and suitable criteria to avoid permitting himself to be first attracted by and then imprisoned within a system whose limitations and totalitarianism may well become evident to him too late, if he does not perceive them in their roots. Going beyond every system, without however failing to commit himself concretely to serving his brothers, he will assert, in the very midst of his options, the specific character of the Christian contribution for a positive transformation of society.[6]

Rebirth of utopias

37. Today moreover the weaknesses of the ideologies are better perceived through the concrete systems in which they are trying to affirm themselves. Bureaucratic socialism, technocratic capitalism and authoritarian

---

6. Cf. *Gaudium et Spes*, 11: AAS 58 (1966), p. 1033.

democracy are showing how difficult it is to solve the great human problem of living together in justice and equality. How in fact could they escape the materialism, egoism or constraint which inevitably go with them? This is the source of a protest which is springing up more or less everywhere, as a sign of a deep-seated sickness, while at the same time we are witnessing the rebirth of what it is agreed to call "utopias." These claim to resolve the political problem of modern societies better than the ideologies. It would be dangerous to disregard this. The appeal to a utopia is often a convenient excuse for those who wish to escape from concrete tasks in order to take refuge in an imaginary world. To live in a hypothetical future is a facile alibi for rejecting immediate responsibilities. But it must clearly be recognized that this kind of criticism of existing society often provokes the forward-looking imagination both to perceive in the present the disregarded possibility hidden within it, and to direct itself towards a fresh future; it thus sustains social dynamism by the confidence that it gives to the inventive powers of the human mind and heart; and, if it refuses no overture, it can also meet the Christian appeal. The Spirit of the Lord, who animates man renewed in Christ, continually breaks down the horizons within which his understanding likes to find security and the limits to which his activity would willingly restrict itself; here dwells within him a power which urges him to go beyond every system and every ideology. At the heart of the world there dwells the mystery of man discovering himself to be God's son in the course of a historical and psychological process in which constraint and freedom as well as the weight of sin and the breath of the Spirit alternate and struggle for the upper hand.

The dynamism of Christian faith here triumphs over the narrow calculations of egoism. Animated by the power of the Spirit of Jesus Christ, the Savior of mankind, and upheld by hope, the Christian involves himself in the building up of the human city, one that is to be peaceful, just and fraternal and acceptable as an offering to God.[7] In fact,

---

7. Cf. Rom. 15:16.

"the expectation of a new earth must not weaken but rather stimulate our concern for cultivating this one. For here grows the body of a new human family, a body which even now is able to give some kind of fore-shadowing of the new age."[8]

The questioning of the human sciences

38. In this world dominated by scientific and technological change, which threatens to drag it towards a new positivism, another more fundamental doubt is raised. Having subdued nature by using his reason, man now finds that he himself is as it were imprisoned within his own rationality; he in turn becomes the object of science. The "human sciences" are today enjoying a significant flowering. On the one hand they are subjecting to critical and radical examination the hitherto accepted knowledge about man, on the grounds that this knowledge seems either too empirical or too theoretical. On the other hand, methodological necessity and ideological presuppositions too often lead the human sciences to isolate, in the various situations, certain aspects of man, and yet to give these an explanation which claims to be complete or at least an interpretation which is meant to be all-embracing from a purely quantitative or phenomenological point of view. This scientific reduction betrays a dangerous presupposition. To give a privileged position in this way to such an aspect of analysis is to mutilate man and, under the pretext of a scientific procedure, to make it impossible to understand man in his totality.

39. One must be no less attentive to the action which the human sciences can instigate, giving rise to the elaboration of models of society to be subsequently imposed on men as scientifically tested types of behavior. Man can then become the object of manipulations directing his desires and needs and modifying his behavior and even his system of values. There is no doubt that there exists here a grave danger for the societies of tomorrow and for man himself. For even if all agree to build

---

8. *Gaudium et Spes*, 39: AAS 58 (1966), p. 1057.

a new society at the service of men, it is still essential to know what sort of man is in question.

Widening the horizons

40. Suspicion of the human sciences affects the Christian more than others, but it does not find him disarmed. For, as we ourself wrote in *Populorum Progressio*, it is here that there is found the specific contribution of the Church to civilizations: "Sharing the noblest aspirations of men and suffering when she sees them not satisfied, she wishes to help them attain their full flowering, and that is why she offers men what she possesses as her characteristic attribute: a global vision of man and of the human race."[9] Should the Church in its turn contest the proceedings of the human sciences, and condemn their pretentions? As in the case of the natural sciences, the Church has confidence in this research also and urges Christians to play an active part in it.[10] Prompted by the same scientific demands and the desire to know man better, but at the same time enlightened by their faith, Christians who devote themselves to the human sciences will begin a dialogue between the Church and this new field of discovery, a dialogue which promises to be fruitful. Of course, each individual scientific discipline will be able, in its own particular sphere, to grasp only a partial—yet true—aspect of man; the complete picture and the full meaning will escape it. But within these limits the human sciences give promise of a positive function that the Church willingly recognizes. They can even widen the horizons of human liberty to a greater extent than the conditioning circumstances perceived enable one to foresee. They could thus assist Christian social morality, which no doubt will see its field restricted when it comes to suggesting certain models of society, while its function of making a critical judgment and taking an overall view will be strengthened by its showing the relative character of the behavior and values presented by such and such a society as definitive and inherent

9. *Populorum Progressio*, 13: AAS 59 (1967), p. 264.
10. Cf. *Gaudium et Spes*, 36: AAS 58 (1966), p. 1054.

in the very nature of man. These sciences are a condition at once indispensable and inadequate for a better discovery of what is human. They are a language which becomes more and more complex, yet one that deepens rather than solves the mystery of the heart of man; nor does it provide the complete and definitive answer to the desire which springs from his innermost being.

Ambiguous nature of progress

41. This better knowledge of man makes it possible to pass a better critical judgment upon and to elucidate a fundamental notion that remains at the basis of modern societies as their motive, their measure and their goal: namely, progress. Since the nineteenth century, western societies and, as a result, many others have put their hopes in ceaselessly renewed and indefinite progress. They saw this progress as man's effort to free himself in face of the demands of nature and of social constraints; progress was the condition for and the yardstick of human freedom. Progress, spread by the modern media of information and by the demand for wider knowledge and greater consumption, has become an omnipresent ideology. Yet a doubt arises today regarding both its value and its result. What is the meaning of this never-ending, breathless pursuit of a progress that always eludes one just when one believes one has conquered it sufficiently in order to enjoy it in peace? If it is not attained, it leaves one dissatisfied. Without doubt, there has been just condemnation of the limits and even the misdeeds of a merely quantitative economic growth; there is a desire to attain objectives of a qualitative order also. The quality and the truth of human relations, the degree of participation and of responsibility, are no less significant and important for the future of society than the quantity and variety of the goods produced and consumed.

Overcoming the temptation to wish to measure everything in terms of efficiency and of trade, and in terms of the interplay of forces and interests, man today wishes to replace these quantitative criteria with the intensity of communication, the spread of knowledge and culture, mutual service and a combining of efforts for a common task. Is not genuine progress to be found in the development of moral consciousness, which will lead man to exercise a wider solidarity and to open himself freely to others and to God? For a Christian, progress necessarily comes up against the eschatological mystery of death. The death of Christ and his resurrection and the outpouring of the Spirit of the Lord help man to place his freedom, in creativity and gratitude, within the context of the truth of all progress and the only hope which does not deceive.[11]

---

11. Cf. Rom. 5:5.

CHAPTER 10

Sollicitudo Rei Socialis: The Concern of the Church for the Social Order

(Excerpt)

Pope St. John Paul II

December 30, 1987

Issued on the twentieth anniversary of Populorum Progessio, *Pope St. John Paul II's encyclical emphasizes that mere economic growth is not equivalent to true development, which is founded on justice and the full flourishing of human nature. He emphasizes the responsibility of all in supporting the true development of the poorer nations of the world, while always respecting their rights and dignity.*

IV. AUTHENTIC HUMAN DEVELOPMENT

27. The examination which the Encyclical invites us to make of the contemporary world leads us to note in the first place that development is not a straightforward process, as it were automatic and in itself limitless, as though, given certain conditions, the human race were able to progress rapidly towards an undefined perfection of some kind.[1]

Such an idea—linked to a notion of "progress" with philosophical connotations deriving from the Enlightenment, rather than to the notion

1. Cf. Apostolic Exhortation *Familiaris Consortio* (November 22, 1981), n. 6: *AAS* 74 (1982), p. 88: ". . . history is not simply a fixed progression toward what is better, but rather an event of freedom, and even a struggle between freedoms. . . ."

of "development"[2] which is used in a specifically economic and social sense—now seems to be seriously called into doubt, particularly since the tragic experience of the two world wars, the planned and partly achieved destruction of whole peoples, and the looming atomic peril. A naive mechanistic optimism has been replaced by a well founded anxiety for the fate of humanity.

28. At the same time, however, the "economic" concept itself, linked to the word development, has entered into crisis. In fact there is a better understanding today that the mere accumulation of goods and services, even for the benefit of the majority, is not enough for the realization of human happiness. Nor, in consequence, does the availability of the many real benefits provided in recent times by science and technology, including the computer sciences, bring freedom from every form of slavery. On the contrary, the experience of recent years shows that unless all the considerable body of resources and potential at man's disposal is guided by a moral understanding and by an orientation towards the true good of the human race, it easily turns against man to oppress him.

A disconcerting conclusion about the most recent period should serve to enlighten us: side-by-side with the miseries of underdevelopment, themselves unacceptable, we find ourselves up against a form of super-development, equally inadmissible, because like the former it is contrary to what is good and to true happiness. This super-development, which consists in an excessive availability of every kind of material good for the benefit of certain social groups, easily makes people slaves of "possession" and of immediate gratification, with no other horizon than the multiplication or continual replacement of the things already owned with others still better. This is the so-called civilization of "consumption" or "consumerism," which involves so much "throwing-away" and "waste." An object already owned but now superseded by something better is discarded, with no thought of its possible lasting value in itself, nor of some other human being who is poorer.

---

2. For this reason the word "development" was used in the Encyclical rather than the word "progress," but with an attempt to give the word "development" its fullest meaning.

All of us experience firsthand the sad effects of this blind submission to pure consumerism: in the first place a crass materialism, and at the same time a radical dissatisfaction, because one quickly learns—unless one is shielded from the flood of publicity and the ceaseless and tempting offers of products—that the more one possesses the more one wants, while deeper aspirations remain unsatisfied and perhaps even stifled.

The Encyclical of Pope Paul VI pointed out the difference, so often emphasized today, between "having" and "being,"[3] which had been expressed earlier in precise words by the Second Vatican Council.[4] To "have" objects and goods does not in itself perfect the human subject, unless it contributes to the maturing and enrichment of that subject's "being," that is to say unless it contributes to the realization of the human vocation as such.

Of course, the difference between "being" and "having," the danger inherent in a mere multiplication or replacement of things possessed compared to the value of "being," need not turn into a contradiction. One of the greatest injustices in the contemporary world consists precisely in this: that the ones who possess much are relatively few and those who possess almost nothing are many. It is the injustice of the poor distribution of the goods and services originally intended for all.

This then is the picture: there are some people—the few who possess much—who do not really succeed in "being" because, through a reversal of the hierarchy of values, they are hindered by the cult of "having"; and there are others—the many who have little or nothing—who do not succeed in realizing their basic human vocation because they are deprived of essential goods.

---

3. Encyclical Letter *Populorum Progressio*, n. 19: AAS 59 (1967), pp. 266f.: "Increased possession is not the ultimate goal of nations or of individuals. All growth is ambivalent. . . . The exclusive pursuit of possessions thus becomes an obstacle to individual fulfillment and to man's true greatness . . . both for nations and for individual men, avarice is the most evident form of moral underdevelopment"; cf. also Paul VI, Apostolic Letter *Octogesima Adveniens* (May 14, 1971), n. 9: AAS 63 (1971), pp. 407f.

4. Cf. Pastoral Constitution on the Church in the Modern World, *Gaudium et Spes*, n. 35: Paul VI, *Address to the Diplomatic Corps* (January 7, 1965): AAS 57 (1965), p. 232.

The evil does not consist in "having" as such, but in possessing without regard for the quality and the ordered hierarchy of the goods one has. Quality and hierarchy arise from the subordination of goods and their availability to man's "being" and his true vocation.

This shows that although development has a necessary economic dimension, since it must supply the greatest possible number of the world's inhabitants with an availability of goods essential for them "to be," it is not limited to that dimension. If it is limited to this, then it turns against those whom it is meant to benefit.

The characteristics of full development, one which is "more human" and able to sustain itself at the level of the true vocation of men and women without denying economic requirements, were described by Paul VI.[5]

29. Development which is not only economic must be measured and oriented according to the reality and vocation of man seen in his totality, namely, according to his interior dimension. There is no doubt that he needs created goods and the products of industry, which is constantly being enriched by scientific and technological progress. And the ever greater availability of material goods not only meets needs but also opens new horizons. The danger of the misuse of material goods and the appearance of artificial needs should in no way hinder the regard we have for the new goods and resources placed at our disposal and the use we make of them. On the contrary, we must see them as a gift from God and as a response to the human vocation, which is fully realized in Christ.

However, in trying to achieve true development we must never lose sight of that dimension which is in the specific nature of man, who has been created by God in his image and likeness (cf. Gen 1:26). It is a bodily and a spiritual nature, symbolized in the second creation account

---

5. Cf. Encyclical Letter *Populorum Progressio*, nn. 20–21: *loc. cit.*, pp. 267f.

by the two elements: the earth, from which God forms man's body, and the breath of life which he breathes into man's nostrils (cf. Gen 2:7).

Thus man comes to have a certain affinity with other creatures: he is called to use them, and to be involved with them. As the Genesis account says (cf. Gen 2:15), he is placed in the garden with the duty of cultivating and watching over it, being superior to the other creatures placed by God under his dominion (cf. Gen 1:25–26). But at the same time man must remain subject to the will of God, who imposes limits upon his use and dominion over things (cf. Gen 2:16–17), just as he promises him immortality (cf. Gen 2:9; Wis 2:23). Thus man, being the image of God, has a true affinity with him too. On the basis of this teaching, development cannot consist only in the use, dominion over and indiscriminate possession of created things and the products of human industry, but rather in subordinating the possession, dominion and use to man's divine likeness and to his vocation to immortality. This is the transcendent reality of the human being, a reality which is seen to be shared from the beginning by a couple, a man and a woman (cf. Gen 1:27), and is therefore fundamentally social.

30. According to Sacred Scripture therefore, the notion of development is not only "lay" or "profane," but it is also seen to be, while having a socio-economic dimension of its own, the modern expression of an essential dimension of man's vocation.

The fact is that man was not created, so to speak, immobile and static. The first portrayal of him, as given in the Bible, certainly presents him as a creature and image, defined in his deepest reality by the origin and affinity that constitute him. But all this plants within the human being—man and woman—the seed and the requirement of a special task to be accomplished by each individually and by them as a couple. The task is "to have dominion" over the other created beings, "to cultivate the garden." This is to be accomplished within the framework of obedience to the divine law and therefore with respect for the image received, the image which is the clear foundation of the power of dominion recognized as belonging to man as the means to his perfection (cf. Gen 1:26–30; 2:15–16; Wis 9:2–3).

When man disobeys God and refuses to submit to his rule, nature rebels against him and no longer recognizes him as its "master," for he has tarnished the divine image in himself. The claim to ownership and use of created things remains still valid, but after sin its exercise becomes difficult and full of suffering (cf. Gen 3:17–19).

In fact, the following chapter of Genesis shows us that the descendants of Cain build "a city," engage in sheep farming, practice the arts (music) and technical skills (metallurgy); while at the same time people began to "call upon the name of the Lord" (cf. Gen 4:17–26).

The story of the human race described by Sacred Scripture is, even after the fall into sin, a story of constant achievements, which, although always called into question and threatened by sin, are nonetheless repeated, increased and extended in response to the divine vocation given from the beginning to man and to woman (cf. Gen 1:26–28) and inscribed in the image which they received.

It is logical to conclude, at least on the part of those who believe in the word of God, that today's "development" is to be seen as a moment in the story which began at creation, a story which is constantly endangered by reason of infidelity to the Creator's will, and especially by the temptation to idolatry. But this "development" fundamentally corresponds to the first premises. Anyone wishing to renounce the difficult yet noble task of improving the lot of man in his totality, and of all people, with the excuse that the struggle is difficult and that constant effort is required, or simply because of the experience of defeat and the need to begin again, that person would be betraying the will of God the Creator. In this regard, in the Encyclical *Laborem Exercens* I referred to man's vocation to work, in order to emphasize the idea that it is always man who is the protagonist of development.[6]

Indeed, the Lord Jesus himself, in the parable of the talents, emphasizes the severe treatment given to the man who dared to hide the gift received: "You wicked slothful servant! You knew that I reap where I have not sowed and gather where I have not winnowed? . . . So take the talent from him, and give it to him who has the ten talents" (Mt 25:26–28). It falls to us, who receive the gifts of God in order to make them fruitful, to "sow" and "reap." If we do not, even what we have will be taken away from us.

A deeper study of these harsh words will make us commit ourselves more resolutely to the duty, which is urgent for everyone today, to work together for the full development of others: "development of the whole human being and of all people."[7]

31. Faith in Christ the Redeemer, while it illuminates from within the nature of development, also guides us in the task of collaboration. In the Letter of St. Paul to the Colossians, we read that Christ is "the first-born of all creation," and that "all things were created through him" and for him (1:15–16). In fact, "all things hold together in him," since "in him all the fullness of God was pleased to dwell, and through him to reconcile to himself all things" (v. 20).

A part of this divine plan, which begins from eternity in Christ, the perfect "image" of the Father, and which culminates in him, "the first-born from the dead" (v. 18), is our own history, marked by our personal and collective effort to raise up the human condition and to overcome the obstacles which are continually arising along our way. It thus prepares us to share in the fullness which "dwells in the Lord" and which he communicates "to his body, which is the Church" (v. 18; cf.

---

6. Cf. Encyclical Letter *Laborem Exercens* (September 14, 1981), n. 4: *AAS* 73 (1981), pp. 584f., Paul VI Encyclical Letter *Populorum Progressio*, n. 15: *loc. cit.*, p. 265.
7. Encyclical Letter *Populorum Progressio*, n. 42: *loc. cit.*, p. 278.

Eph 1:22–23). At the same time sin, which is always attempting to trap us and which jeopardizes our human achievements, is conquered and redeemed by the "reconciliation" accomplished by Christ (cf. Col 1:20).

Here the perspectives widen. The dream of "unlimited progress" reappears, radically transformed by the new outlook created by Christian faith, assuring us that progress is possible only because God the Father has decided from the beginning to make man a sharer of his glory in Jesus Christ risen from the dead, in whom "we have redemption through his blood . . . the forgiveness of our trespasses" (Eph 1:7). In him God wished to conquer sin and make it serve our greater good,[8] which infinitely surpasses what progress could achieve.

We can say therefore—as we struggle amidst the obscurities and deficiencies of underdevelopment and superdevelopment—that one day this corruptible body will put on incorruptibility, this mortal body immortality (cf. 1 Cor 15:54), when the Lord "delivers the Kingdom to God the Father" (v. 24) and all the works and actions that are worthy of man will be redeemed.

Furthermore, the concept of faith makes quite clear the reasons which impel the Church to concern herself with the problems of development, to consider them a duty of her pastoral ministry, and to urge all to think about the nature and characteristics of authentic human development. Through her commitment she desires, on the one hand, to place herself at the service of the divine plan which is meant to order all things to the fullness which dwells in Christ (cf. Col 1:19) and which he communicated to his body; and on the other hand she desires to respond to her fundamental vocation of being a "sacrament," that is to say "a sign and instrument of intimate union with God and of the unity of the whole human race."[9]

---

8. Cf. Praeconium Paschale, *Missale Romanum*, ed. typ. altera, 1975, p. 272: "O certe necessarium Adae peccatum, quod Christi morte deletum est! O felix culpa, quae talem ac tantum meruit habere Redemptorem!"

9. Second Vatican Ecumenical Council, Dogmatic Constitution on the Church, *Lumen Gentium*, n. 1.

Some Fathers of the Church were inspired by this idea to develop in original ways a concept of the meaning of history and of human work, directed towards a goal which surpasses this meaning and which is always defined by its relationship to the work of Christ. In other words, one can find in the teaching of the Fathers an optimistic vision of history and work, that is to say of the perennial value of authentic human achievements, inasmuch as they are redeemed by Christ and destined for the promised Kingdom.[10]

Thus, part of the teaching and most ancient practice of the Church is her conviction that she is obliged by her vocation—she herself, her ministers and each of her members—to relieve the misery of the suffering, both far and near, not only out of her "abundance" but also out of her "necessities." Faced by cases of need, one cannot ignore them in favor of superfluous church ornaments and costly furnishings for divine worship; on the contrary it could be obligatory to sell these goods in order to provide food, drink, clothing and shelter for those who lack these things.[11] As has been already noted, here we are shown a "hierarchy of values"—in the framework of the right to property—between "having" and "being," especially when the "having" of a few can be to the detriment of the "being" of many others.

In his Encyclical Pope Paul VI stands in the line of this teaching, taking his inspiration from the Pastoral Constitution *Gaudium et Spes*.[12] For my own part, I wish to insist once more on the seriousness and urgency of

---

10. Cf. for example, St. Basil the Great, *Regulae Fusius Tractatae, Interrogatio* XXXVII, nn. 1–2: PG 31, 1009–1012 Theodoret of Cyr, *De Providentia*, Oratio VII: PG 83, 665–686; St. Augustine, *De Civitate Dei*, XIX, n. 17: CCL 48 683–685.

11. Cf. for example, St. John Chrysostom, In Evang. S. Matthaei, *Hom.* 50, 3–4: PG 58, 508–510, St. Ambrose *De Officiis Ministrorum*, lib. II, XXVIII, 136–140: PL 16, 139–141; St. Possidius, *Vita S. Augustini Episcopi*, XXIV: PL 32, 53f.

12. Encyclical Letter *Populorum Progressio*, n. 23: *loc. cit.*, p. 268: "If someone who has the riches of this world sees his brother in need and closes his heart to him, how does the love of God abide in him?" (1 Jn 3:17). It is well known how strong were the words used by the Fathers of the Church to describe the proper attitude of persons who possess any thing toward persons in need." In the previous number, the Pope had cited n. 69 of the Pastoral Constitution, *Gaudium et Spes*, of the Second Vatican Ecumenical Council.

that teaching, and I ask the Lord to give all Christians the strength to put it faithfully into practice.

32. The obligation to commit oneself to the development of peoples is not just an individual duty, and still less an individualistic one, as if it were possible to achieve this development through the isolated efforts of each individual. It is an imperative which obliges each and every man and woman, as well as societies and nations. In particular, it obliges the Catholic Church and the other Churches and Ecclesial Communities, with which we are completely willing to collaborate in this field. In this sense, just as we Catholics invite our Christian brethren to share in our initiatives, so too we declare that we are ready to collaborate in theirs, and we welcome the invitations presented to us. In this pursuit of integral human development we can also do much with the members of other religions, as in fact is being done in various places.

Collaboration in the development of the whole person and of every human being is in fact a duty of all towards all, and must be shared by the four parts of the world: East and West, North and South; or, as we say today, by the different "worlds." If, on the contrary, people try to achieve it in only one part, or in only one world, they do so at the expense of the others; and, precisely because the others are ignored, their own development becomes exaggerated and misdirected.

Peoples or nations too have a right to their own full development, which while including—as already said—the economic and social aspects, should also include individual cultural identity and openness to the transcendent. Not even the need for development can be used as an excuse for imposing on others one's own way of life or own religious belief.

33. Nor would a type of development which did not respect and promote human rights—personal and social, economic and political, including the rights of nations and of peoples—be really worthy of man.

Today, perhaps more than in the past, the intrinsic contradiction of a development limited only to its economic element is seen more clearly. Such development easily subjects the human person and his deepest needs to the demands of economic planning and selfish profit.

The intrinsic connection between authentic development and respect for human rights once again reveals the moral character of development: the true elevation of man, in conformity with the natural and historical vocation of each individual, is not attained only by exploiting the abundance of goods and services, or by having available perfect infrastructures.

When individuals and communities do not see a rigorous respect for the moral, cultural and spiritual requirements, based on the dignity of the person and on the proper identity of each community, beginning with the family and religious societies, then all the rest—availability of goods, abundance of technical resources applied to daily life, a certain level of material well-being—will prove unsatisfying and in the end contemptible. The Lord clearly says this in the Gospel, when he calls the attention of all to the true hierarchy of values: "For what will it profit a man, if he gains the whole world and forfeits his life?" (Mt 16:26).

True development, in keeping with the specific needs of the human being—man or woman, child, adult or old person—implies, especially for those who actively share in this process and are responsible for it, a lively awareness of the value of the rights of all and of each person. It likewise implies a lively awareness of the need to respect the right of every individual to the full use of the benefits offered by science and technology.

On the internal level of every nation, respect for all rights takes on great importance, especially: the right to life at every stage of its existence; the rights of the family, as the basic social community, or "cell of society"; justice in employment relationships; the rights inherent in the life of the political community as such; the rights based on the transcendent vocation of the human being, beginning with the right of freedom to profess and practice one's own religious belief.

On the international level, that is, the level of relations between States or, in present-day usage, between the different "worlds," there must be complete respect for the identity of each people, with its own historical and cultural characteristics. It is likewise essential, as the Encyclical *Populorum Progressio* already asked, to recognize each people's equal right "to be seated at the table of the common banquet,"[13] instead of lying outside the door like Lazarus, while "the dogs come and lick his sores" (cf. Lk 16:21). Both peoples and individuals must enjoy the fundamental equality[14] which is the basis, for example, of the Charter of the United Nations Organization: the equality which is the basis of the right of all to share in the process of full development.

In order to be genuine, development must be achieved within the framework of solidarity and freedom, without ever sacrificing either of them under whatever pretext. The moral character of development and its necessary promotion are emphasized when the most rigorous respect is given to all the demands deriving from the order of truth and good proper to the human person. Furthermore the Christian who is taught to see that man is the image of God, called to share in the truth and the good which is God himself, does not understand a commitment to development and its application which excludes regard and respect for the unique dignity of this "image." In other words, true development

---

13. Cf. Encyclical Letter *Populorum Progressio*, n. 47: ". . . a world where freedom is not an empty word and where the poor man Lazarus can sit down at the same table with the rich man."

14. Cf. Encyclical Letter *Populorum Progressio*, n. 47: "It is a question, rather, of building a world where every man, no matter what his race, religion or nationality, can live a fully human life, freed from servitude imposed on him by other men . . ."; cf. also Second Vatican Ecumenical Council, Pastoral Constitution on the Church in the Modern World, *Gaudium et Spes*, n. 29. Such fundamental equality is one of the basic reasons why the Church has always been opposed to every form of racism.

must be based on the love of God and neighbor, and must help to promote the relationships between individuals and society. This is the "civilization of love" of which Paul VI often spoke.

CHAPTER II

Centesimus Annus:
On the Hundredth Anniversary
of *Rerum Novarum*

(Full Text)

Pope St. John Paul II

May 1, 1991

Released on the one hundredth anniversary of Rerum Novarum,
*Pope St. John Paul II's encyclical emphasizes the "permanent value"
of Pope Leo XIII's teaching, showing how the principles laid down
in his encyclical can be applied to the new challenges facing the world
on the eve of the new millennium.*

INTRODUCTION

1. The Centenary of the promulgation of the Encyclical which begins with the words *"Rerum novarum,"*[1] by my predecessor of venerable memory Pope Leo XIII, is an occasion of great importance for the present history of the Church and for my own Pontificate. It is an Encyclical that has the distinction of having been commemorated by solemn Papal documents from its fortieth anniversary to its ninetieth. It may be said that its path through history has been marked by other documents which paid tribute to it and applied it to the circumstances of the day.[2]

---

1. Leo XIII, Encyclical Letter *Rerum Novarum* (May 15, 1891): *Leonis XIII P.M. Acta*, XI, Romae 1892, 97–144.

2. Pius XI, Encyclical Letter *Quadragesimo Anno* (May 15, 1931): AAS 23 (1931), 177–228; Pius XII, Radio Message of June 1, 1941: AAS 33 (1941), 195–205; John XXIII, Encyclical Letter *Mater et Magistra* (May 15, 1961): AAS 53 (1961), 401–464; Paul VI, Apostolic Epistle *Octogesima Adveniens* (May 14, 1971): AAS 63 (1971), 401–441.

In doing likewise for the hundredth anniversary, in response to requests from many Bishops, Church institutions, and study centers, as well as business leaders and workers, both individually and as members of associations, I wish first and foremost to satisfy the debt of gratitude which the whole Church owes to this great Pope and his "immortal document."[3] I also mean to show that the *vital energies* rising from that root have not been spent with the passing of the years, but rather *have increased even more.* This is evident from the various initiatives which have preceded, and which are to accompany and follow the celebration, initiatives promoted by Episcopal Conferences, by international agencies, universities and academic institutes, by professional associations and by other institutions and individuals in many parts of the world.

2. The present Encyclical is part of these celebrations, which are meant to thank God—the origin of "every good endowment and every perfect gift" (Jas 1:17)—for having used a document published a century ago by the See of Peter to achieve so much good and to radiate so much light in the Church and in the world. Although the commemoration at hand is meant to honor *Rerum novarum*, it also honors those Encyclicals and other documents of my Predecessors which have helped to make Pope Leo's Encyclical present and alive in history, thus constituting what would come to be called the Church's "social doctrine," "social teaching" or even "social magisterium."

The validity of this teaching has already been pointed out in two Encyclicals published during my Pontificate: *Laborem exercens* on human work, and *Sollicitudo rei socialis* on current problems regarding the development of individuals and peoples.[4]

3. I now wish to propose a "re-reading" of Pope Leo's Encyclical by issuing an invitation to "look back" at the text itself in order to discover anew the richness of the fundamental principles which it formulated

---

3. Cf. Pius XI, Encyclical Letter *Quadragesimo Anno*, III, *loc. cit.*, 228.

4. Encyclical Letter *Laborem Exercens* (September 14, 1981): AAS 73 (1981), 577–647; Encyclical Letter *Sollicitudo Rei Socialis* (December 30, 1987): AAS 80 (1988), 513–586.

for dealing with the question of the condition of workers. But this is also an invitation to "look around" at the "new things" which surround us and in which we find ourselves caught up, very different from the "new things" which characterized the final decade of the last century. Finally, it is an invitation to "look to the future" at a time when we can already glimpse the third Millennium of the Christian era, so filled with uncertainties but also with promises—uncertainties and promises which appeal to our imagination and creativity, and which reawaken our responsibility, as disciples of the "one teacher" (cf. Mt 23:8), to show the way, to proclaim the truth and to communicate the life which is Christ (cf. Jn 14:6).

A re-reading of this kind will not only confirm *the permanent value of such teaching,* but will also manifest *the true meaning of the Church's Tradition* which, being ever living and vital, builds upon the foundation laid by our fathers in the faith, and particularly upon what "the Apostles passed down to the Church"[5] in the name of Jesus Christ, who is her irreplaceable foundation (cf. 1 Cor 3:11).

It was out of an awareness of his mission as the Successor of Peter that Pope Leo XIII proposed to speak out, and Peter's Successor today is moved by that same awareness. Like Pope Leo and the Popes before and after him, I take my inspiration from the Gospel image of "the scribe who has been trained for the kingdom of heaven," whom the Lord compares to "a householder who brings out of his treasure what is new and what is old" (Mt 13:52). The treasure is the great outpouring of the Church's Tradition, which contains "what is old"—received and passed on from the very beginning—and which enables us to interpret the "new things" in the midst of which the life of the Church and the world unfolds.

Among the things which become "old" as a result of being incorporated into Tradition, and which offer opportunities and material for enriching

---

5. Cf. St. Irenaeus, *Adversus Haereses,* I, 10, 1; III, 4, 1: PG 7, 549f.; 855f.; S. Ch. 264, 154f.; 211, 44–46.

both Tradition and the life of faith, there is the fruitful activity of many millions of people, who, spurred on by the social Magisterium, have sought to make that teaching the inspiration for their involvement in the world. Acting either as individuals or joined together in various groups, associations and organizations, these people represent *a great movement for the defense of the human person* and the safeguarding of human dignity. Amid changing historical circumstances, this movement has contributed to the building up of a more just society or at least to the curbing of injustice.

The present Encyclical seeks to show the fruitfulness of the principles enunciated by Leo XIII, which belong to the Church's doctrinal patrimony and, as such, involve the exercise of her teaching authority. But pastoral solicitude also prompts me to propose *an analysis of some events of recent history.* It goes without saying that part of the responsibility of Pastors is to give careful consideration to current events in order to discern the new requirements of evangelization. However, such an analysis is not meant to pass definitive judgments since this does not fall *per se* within the Magisterium's specific domain.

I. CHARACTERISTICS OF "RERUM NOVARUM"

4. Towards the end of the last century the Church found herself facing an historical process which had already been taking place for some time, but which was by then reaching a critical point. The determining factor in this process was a combination of radical changes which had taken place in the political, economic and social fields, and in the areas of science and technology, to say nothing of the wide influence of the prevailing ideologies. In the sphere of politics, the result of these changes was a *new conception of society and of the State,* and consequently *of authority* itself. A traditional society was passing away and another was beginning to be formed—one which brought the hope of new freedoms but also the threat of new forms of injustice and servitude.

In the sphere of economics, in which scientific discoveries and their practical application come together, new structures for the production of consumer goods had progressively taken shape. A new form of *property* had appeared—capital; and a *new form of labor*—labor for wages, characterized by high rates of production which lacked due regard for sex, age or family situation, and were determined solely by efficiency, with a view to increasing profits.

In this way labor became a commodity to be freely bought and sold on the market, its price determined by the law of supply and demand, without taking into account the bare minimum required for the support of the individual and his family. Moreover, the worker was not even sure of being able to sell "his own commodity," continually threatened as he was by unemployment, which, in the absence of any kind of social security, meant the specter of death by starvation.

The result of this transformation was a society "divided into two classes, separated by a deep chasm."[6] This situation was linked to the marked change taking place in the political order already mentioned. Thus the prevailing political theory of the time sought to promote total economic freedom by appropriate laws, or, conversely, by a deliberate lack of any intervention. At the same time, another conception of property and economic life was beginning to appear in an organized and often violent form, one which implied a new political and social structure.

At the height of this clash, when people finally began to realize fully the very grave injustice of social realities in many places and the danger of a revolution fanned by ideals which were then called "socialist," Pope Leo XIII intervened with a document which dealt in a systematic way with the "condition of the workers." The Encyclical had been preceded by others devoted to teachings of a political character; still

---

6. Leo XIII, Encyclical Letter *Rerum Novarum: loc. cit.,* 132.

others would appear later.[7] Here, particular mention must be made of the Encyclical *Libertas praestantissimum*, which called attention to the essential bond between human freedom and truth, so that freedom which refused to be bound to the truth would fall into arbitrariness and end up submitting itself to the vilest of passions, to the point of self-destruction. Indeed, what is the origin of all the evils to which *Rerum Novarum* wished to respond, if not a kind of freedom which, in the area of economic and social activity, cuts itself off from the truth about man?

The Pope also drew inspiration from the teaching of his Predecessors, as well as from the many documents issued by Bishops, from scientific studies promoted by members of the laity, from the work of Catholic movements and associations, and from the Church's practical achievements in the social field during the second half of the nineteenth century.

5. The "new things" to which the Pope devoted his attention were anything but positive. The first paragraph of the Encyclical describes in strong terms the "new things" (*rerum novarum*) which gave it its name: "That *the spirit of revolutionary change* which has long been disturbing the nations of the world should have passed beyond the sphere of politics and made its influence felt in the related sphere of practical economics is not surprising. Progress in industry, the development of new trades, the changing relationship between employers and workers, the enormous wealth of a few as opposed to the poverty of the many, the increasing self-reliance of the workers and their closer association with each other, as well as a notable decline in morality: all these elements have led to the conflict now taking place."[8]

The Pope and the Church with him were confronted, as was the civil community, by a society which was torn by a conflict all the more harsh

7. Cf., e.g., Leo XIII, Encyclical Epistle *Arcanum Divinae Sapientiae* (February 10, 1880): *Leonis XIII P.M. Acta*, II, Romae 1882, 10–40; Encyclical Epistle *Diuturnum Illud* (June 29, 1881): *Leonis XIII P.M. Acta*, II, Romae 1882, 269–287; Encyclical Letter *Libertas Praestantissimum* (June 20, 1888): *Leonis XIII P.M. Acta*, VIII, Romae 1889, 212–246; Encyclical Epistle *Graves de communi* (January 18, 1901): *Leonis XIII P.M. Acta*, XXI, Romae 1902, 320.
8. Encyclical Letter *Rerum Novarum*: loc. cit., 97.

and inhumane because it knew no rule or regulation. It was *the conflict between capital and labor,* or—as the Encyclical puts it—the worker question. It is precisely about this conflict, in the very pointed terms in which it then appeared, that the Pope did not hesitate to speak.

Here we find the first reflection for our times as suggested by the Encyclical. In the face of a conflict which set man against man, almost as if they were "wolves," a conflict between the extremes of mere physical survival on the one side and opulence on the other, the Pope did not hesitate to intervene by virtue of his "apostolic office,"[9] that is, on the basis of the mission received from Jesus Christ himself to "feed his lambs and tend his sheep" (cf. Jn 21:15–17), and to "bind and loose" on earth for the Kingdom of Heaven (cf. Mt 16:19). The Pope's intention was certainly to restore peace, and the present-day reader cannot fail to note his severe condemnation, in no uncertain terms, of the class struggle.[10] However, the Pope was very much aware that *peace is built on the foundation of justice:* what was essential to the Encyclical was precisely its proclamation of the fundamental conditions for justice in the economic and social situation of the time.[11]

In this way, Pope Leo XIII, in the footsteps of his Predecessors, created a lasting paradigm for the Church. The Church, in fact, has something to say about specific human situations, both individual and communal, national and international. She formulates a genuine doctrine for these situations, a *corpus* which enables her to analyze social realities, to make judgments about them and to indicate directions to be taken for the just resolution of the problems involved.

In Pope Leo XIII's time such a concept of the Church's right and duty was far from being commonly admitted. Indeed, a two-fold approach prevailed: one directed to this world and this life, to which faith ought to remain extraneous; the other directed towards a purely other-worldly

---

9. *Ibid.: loc. cit.,* 98.

10. Cf. *ibid.: loc. cit.,* 109f.

11. Cf. *ibid.:* description of working conditions; 44: anti-Christian workers' associations: *loc. cit.,* 110f.; 136f.

salvation, which neither enlightens nor directs existence on earth. The Pope's approach in publishing *Rerum novarum* gave the Church "citizenship status" as it were, amid the changing realities of public life, and this standing would be more fully confirmed later on. In effect, to teach and to spread her social doctrine pertains to the Church's evangelizing mission and is an essential part of the Christian message, since this doctrine points out the direct consequences of that message in the life of society and situates daily work and struggles for justice in the context of bearing witness to Christ the Savior. This doctrine is likewise a source of unity and peace in dealing with the conflicts which inevitably arise in social and economic life. Thus it is possible to meet these new situations without degrading the human person's transcendent dignity, either in oneself or in one's adversaries, and to direct those situations towards just solutions.

Today, at a distance of a hundred years, the validity of this approach affords me the opportunity to contribute to the development of Christian social doctrine. The "new evangelization," which the modern world urgently needs and which I have emphasized many times, must include among its essential elements a proclamation of the Church's social doctrine. As in the days of Pope Leo XIII, this doctrine is still suitable for indicating the right way to respond to the great challenges of today, when ideologies are being increasingly discredited. Now, as then, we need to repeat that there can be *no genuine solution of the "social question" apart from the Gospel*, and that the "new things" can find in the Gospel the context for their correct understanding and the proper moral perspective for judgment on them.

6. With the intention of shedding light on the *conflict* which had arisen between capital and labor, Pope Leo XIII affirmed the fundamental rights of workers. Indeed, the key to reading the Encyclical is the *dignity of the worker* as such, and, for the same reason, the *dignity of work*, which is defined as follows: "to exert oneself for the sake of procuring what is necessary for the various purposes of life, and first of

all for self-preservation."[12] The Pope describes work as "personal, inasmuch as the energy expended is bound up with the personality and is the exclusive property of him who acts, and, furthermore, was given to him for his advantage."[13] Work thus belongs to the vocation of every person; indeed, man expresses and fulfils himself by working. At the same time, work has a "social" dimension through its intimate relationship not only to the family, but also to the common good, since "it may truly be said that it is only by the labor of working-men that States grow rich."[14] These are themes that I have taken up and developed in my Encyclical *Laborem exercens.*[15]

Another important principle is undoubtedly that of the *right to "private property.*"[16] The amount of space devoted to this subject in the Encyclical shows the importance attached to it. The Pope is well aware that private property is not an absolute value, nor does he fail to proclaim the necessary complementary principles, such as the *universal destination of the earth's goods.*[17]

On the other hand, it is certainly true that the type of private property which Leo XIII mainly considers is land ownership.[18] But this does not mean that the reasons adduced to safeguard private property or to affirm the right to possess the things necessary for one's personal development and the development of one's family, whatever the concrete form which that right may assume, are not still valid today. This is something which must be affirmed once more in the face of the changes we are witnessing in systems formerly dominated by collective ownership of the means of production, as well as in the face of the increasing instances of poverty or, more precisely, of hindrances to private ownership in many parts of the world, including those where systems predominate which are

---

12. *Ibid.: loc. cit.,* 130; cf. also 114f.
13. *Ibid.: loc. cit.,* 130.
14. *Ibid.: loc. cit.,* 123.
15. Cf. Encyclical Letter *Laborem Exercens*, 1, 2, 6: *loc. cit.,* 578–583; 589–592.
16. Cf. Encyclical Letter *Rerum Novarum: loc. cit.,* 99–107.
17. Cf. *ibid.: loc. cit.,* 102f.
18. Cf. *ibid.: loc. cit.,* 101–104.

based on an affirmation of the right to private property. As a result of these changes and of the persistence of poverty, a deeper analysis of the problem is called for, an analysis which will be developed later in this document.

7. In close connection with the right to private property, Pope Leo XIII's Encyclical also affirms *other rights* as inalienable and proper to the human person. Prominent among these, because of the space which the Pope devotes to it and the importance which he attaches to it, is the "natural human right" to form private associations. This means above all *the right to establish professional associations* of employers and workers, or of workers alone.[19] Here we find the reason for the Church's defense and approval of the establishment of what are commonly called trade unions: certainly not because of ideological prejudices or in order to surrender to a class mentality, but because the right of association is a natural right of the human being, which therefore precedes his or her incorporation into political society. Indeed, the formation of unions "cannot . . . be prohibited by the State," because "the State is bound to protect natural rights, not to destroy them; and if it forbids its citizens to form associations, it contradicts the very principle of its own existence."[20]

Together with this right, which—it must be stressed—the Pope explicitly acknowledges as belonging to workers, or, using his own language, to "the working class," the Encyclical affirms just as clearly the right to the "limitation of working hours," the right to legitimate rest and the right of children and women[21] to be treated differently with regard to the type and duration of work.

If we keep in mind what history tells us about the practices permitted or at least not excluded by law regarding the way in which workers were employed, without any guarantees as to working hours or the hygienic

---

19. Cf. *ibid.*: *loc. cit.*, 134f.; 137f.
20. *Ibid.*: *loc. cit.*, 135.
21. Cf. *Ibid.*: *loc. cit.*, 128–129.

conditions of the work-place, or even regarding the age and sex of apprentices, we can appreciate the Pope's severe statement: "It is neither just nor human so to grind men down with excessive labor as to stupefy their minds and wear out their bodies." And referring to the "contract" aimed at putting into effect "labor relations" of this sort, he affirms with greater precision, that "in all agreements between employers and workers there is always the condition expressed or understood" that proper rest be allowed, proportionate to "the wear and tear of one's strength." He then concludes: "To agree in any other sense would be against what is right and just."[22]

8. The Pope immediately adds *another right* which the worker has as a person. This is the right to a "just wage," which cannot be left to the "free consent of the parties, so that the employer, having paid what was agreed upon, has done his part and seemingly is not called upon to do anything beyond."[23] It was said at the time that the State does not have the power to intervene in the terms of these contracts, except to ensure the fulfilment of what had been explicitly agreed upon. This concept of relations between employers and employees, purely pragmatic and inspired by a thorough-going individualism, is severely censured in the Encyclical as contrary to the twofold nature of work as a personal and necessary reality. For if work *as something personal* belongs to the sphere of the individual's free use of his own abilities and energy, *as something necessary* it is governed by the grave obligation of every individual to ensure "the preservation of life." "It necessarily follows," the Pope concludes, "that every individual has a natural right to procure what is required to live; and the poor can procure that in no other way than by what they can earn through their work."[24]

A workman's wages should be sufficient to enable him to support himself, his wife and his children. "If through necessity or fear of a worse evil the

---

22. *Ibid.: loc. cit.,* 129.
23. *Ibid.: loc. cit.,* 129.
24. *Ibid.: loc. cit.,* 130f.

workman accepts harder conditions because an employer or contractor will afford no better, he is made the victim of force and injustice."[25]

Would that these words, written at a time when what has been called "unbridled capitalism" was pressing forward, should not have to be repeated today with the same severity. Unfortunately, even today one finds instances of contracts between employers and employees which lack reference to the most elementary justice regarding the employment of children or women, working hours, the hygienic condition of the work-place and fair pay; and this is the case despite the *International Declarations* and *Conventions* on the subject[26] and the *internal laws* of States. The Pope attributed to the "public authority" the "strict duty" of providing properly for the welfare of the workers, because a failure to do so violates justice; indeed, he did not hesitate to speak of "distributive justice."[27]

9. To these rights Pope Leo XIII adds another right regarding the condition of the working class, one which I wish to mention because of its importance: namely, the right to discharge freely one's religious duties. The Pope wished to proclaim this right within the context of the other rights and duties of workers, notwithstanding the general opinion, even in his day, that such questions pertained exclusively to an individual's private life. He affirms the need for Sunday rest so that people may turn their thoughts to heavenly things and to the worship which they owe to Almighty God.[28] No one can take away this human right, which is based on a commandment; in the words of the Pope: "no man may with impunity violate that human dignity which God himself treats with great reverence," and consequently, the State must guarantee to the worker the exercise of this freedom.[29]

---

25. *Ibid.: loc. cit.*, 131.
26. Cf. Universal Declaration of Human Rights.
27. Cf. Encyclical Letter *Rerum Novarum: loc. cit.*, 121–123.
28. Cf. *ibid.: loc. cit.*, 127.
29. *Ibid.: loc. cit.*, 126f.

It would not be mistaken to see in this clear statement a springboard for the principle of the right to religious freedom, which was to become the subject of many solemn *International Declarations* and *Conventions*,[30] as well as of the Second Vatican Council's well-known *Declaration* and of my own repeated teaching.[31] In this regard, one may ask whether existing laws and the practice of industrialized societies effectively ensure in our own day the exercise of this basic right to Sunday rest.

10. Another important aspect, which has many applications to our own day, is the concept of the relationship between the State and its citizens. *Rerum novarum* criticizes two social and economic systems: socialism and liberalism. The opening section, in which the right to private property is reaffirmed, is devoted to socialism. Liberalism is not the subject of a special section, but it is worth noting that criticisms of it are raised in the treatment of the duties of the State.[32] The State cannot limit itself to "favoring one portion of the citizens," namely the rich and prosperous, nor can it "neglect the other," which clearly represents the majority of society. Otherwise, there would be a violation of that law of justice which ordains that every person should receive his due. "When there is question of defending the rights of individuals, the defenseless and the poor have a claim to special consideration. The richer class has many ways of shielding itself, and stands less in need of help from the State; whereas the mass of the poor have no resources of their own to fall back on, and must chiefly depend on the assistance of the State. It is for this reason that wage-earners, since they mostly belong to the latter class, should be specially cared for and protected by the Government."[33]

These passages are relevant today, especially in the face of the new forms of poverty in the world, and also because they are affirmations

---

30. Cf. Universal Declaration of Human Rights; Declaration on the elimination of every form of intolerance and discrimination based on religion or convictions.

31. Second Vatican Ecumenical Council, Declaration on Religious Freedom *Dignitatis Humanae*; John Paul II, Letter to Heads of State (September 1, 1980): AAS 72 (1980), 1252–1260; Message for the 1988 World Day of Peace (January 1, 1988): AAS 80 (1988), 278–286.

32. Cf. Encyclical Letter *Rerum Novarum*: 42: *loc. cit.*, 99–105; 130f.; 135.

33. *Ibid.*: *loc. cit.*, 125.

which do not depend on a specific notion of the State or on a particular political theory. Leo XIII is repeating an elementary principle of sound political organization, namely, the more that individuals are defenseless within a given society, the more they require the care and concern of others, and in particular the intervention of governmental authority.

In this way what we nowadays call the principle of solidarity, the validity of which both in the internal order of each nation and in the international order I have discussed in the Encyclical *Sollicitudo rei socialis*,[34] is clearly seen to be one of the fundamental principles of the Christian view of social and political organization. This principle is frequently stated by Pope Leo XIII, who uses the term "friendship," a concept already found in Greek philosophy. Pope Pius XI refers to it with the equally meaningful term "social charity." Pope Paul VI, expanding the concept to cover the many modern aspects of the social question, speaks of a "civilization of love."[35]

11. Re-reading the Encyclical in the light of contemporary realities enables us to appreciate *the Church's constant concern for and dedication to* categories of people who are especially beloved to the Lord Jesus. The content of the text is an excellent testimony to the continuity within the Church of the so-called "preferential option for the poor," an option which I defined as a "special form of primacy in the exercise of Christian charity."[36] Pope Leo's Encyclical on the "condition of the workers" is thus an Encyclical on the poor and on the terrible conditions to which the new and often violent process of industrialization had reduced great multitudes of people. Today, in many parts of the world, similar processes of economic, social and political transformation are creating the same evils.

---

34. Cf. Encyclical Letter *Sollicitudo Rei Socialis*, 38–40: *loc. cit.*, 564–569; cf. also John XXIII, Encyclical Letter *Mater et Magistra, loc. cit.*, 407.

35. Cf. Leo XIII, Encyclical Letter *Rerum Novarum*: *loc. cit.*, 114–116; Pius XI, Encyclical Letter *Quadragesimo Anno*, III, *loc. cit.*, 208; Paul VI, Homily for the Closing of the Holy Year (December 25,1975): *AAS* 68 (1976), 145; Message for the 1977 World Day of Peace (January 1, 1977): *AAS* 68 (1976), 709.

36. Encyclical Letter *Sollicitudo Rei Socialis*, 42: *loc. cit.*, 572.

PART I: CHURCH TEACHING

If Pope Leo XIII calls upon the State to remedy the condition of the poor in accordance with justice, he does so because of his timely awareness that the State has the duty of watching over the common good and of ensuring that every sector of social life, not excluding the economic one, contributes to achieving that good, while respecting the rightful autonomy of each sector. This should not however lead us to think that Pope Leo expected the State to solve every social problem. On the contrary, he frequently insists on necessary limits to the State's intervention and on its instrumental character, inasmuch as the individual, the family and society are prior to the State, and inasmuch as the State exists in order to protect their rights and not stifle them.[37]

The relevance of these reflections for our own day is inescapable. It will be useful to return later to this important subject of the limits inherent in the nature of the state. For now, the points which have been emphasized (certainly not the only ones in the Encyclical) are situated in continuity with the Church's social teaching, and in the light of a sound view of private property, work, the economic process, the reality of the State and, above all, of man himself. Other themes will be mentioned later when we examine certain aspects of the contemporary situation. From this point forward it will be necessary to keep in mind that the main thread and, in a certain sense, the guiding principle of Pope Leo's Encyclical, and of all of the Church's social doctrine, is a *correct view of the human person* and of his unique value, inasmuch as "man . . . is the only creature on earth which God willed for itself."[38] God has imprinted his own image and likeness on man (cf. Gen 1:26), conferring upon him an incomparable dignity, as the Encyclical frequently insists. In effect, beyond the rights which man acquires by his own work, there exist rights which do not correspond to any work he performs, but which flow from his essential dignity as a person.

---

37. Cf. Encyclical Letter *Rerum Novarum*: loc. cit., 101f.; 104f.; 130f.; 136.
38. Second Vatican Ecumenical Council, Pastoral Constitution on the Church in the World of Today *Gaudium et Spes*, 24.

II. TOWARDS THE "NEW THINGS" OF TODAY

12. The commemoration of *Rerum novarum* would be incomplete unless reference were also made to the situation of the world today. The document lends itself to such a reference, because the historical picture and the prognosis which it suggests have proved to be surprisingly accurate in the light of what has happened since then.

This is especially confirmed by the events which took place near the end of 1989 and at the beginning of 1990. These events, and the radical transformations which followed, can only be explained by the preceding situations which, to a certain extent, crystallized or institutionalized Leo XIII's predictions and the increasingly disturbing signs noted by his Successors. Pope Leo foresaw the negative consequences—political, social and economic—of the social order proposed by "socialism," which at that time was still only a social philosophy and not yet a fully structured movement. It may seem surprising that "socialism" appeared at the beginning of the Pope's critique of solutions to the "question of the working class" at a time when "socialism" was not yet in the form of a strong and powerful State, with all the resources which that implies, as was later to happen. However, he correctly judged the danger posed to the masses by the attractive presentation of this simple and radical solution to the "question of the working class" of the time—all the more so when one considers the terrible situation of injustice in which the working classes of the recently industrialized nations found themselves.

Two things must be emphasized here: first, the great clarity in perceiving, in all its harshness, the actual condition of the working class—men, women and children; secondly, equal clarity in recognizing the evil of a solution which, by appearing to reverse the positions of the poor and the rich, was in reality detrimental to the very people whom it was meant to help. The remedy would prove worse than the sickness. By defining the nature of the socialism of his day as the suppression of private property, Leo XIII arrived at the crux of the problem.

His words deserve to be re-read attentively: "To remedy these wrongs (the unjust distribution of wealth and the poverty of the workers), the Socialists encourage the poor man's envy of the rich and strive to do away with private property, contending that individual possessions should become the common property of all . . . ; but their contentions are so clearly powerless to end the controversy that, were they carried into effect, the working man himself would be among the first to suffer. They are moreover emphatically unjust, for they would rob the lawful possessor, distort the functions of the State, and create utter confusion in the community."[39] The evils caused by the setting up of this type of socialism as a State system—what would later be called "Real Socialism"—could not be better expressed.

13. Continuing our reflections, and referring also to what has been said in the Encyclicals *Laborem exercens* and *Sollicitudo rei socialis*, we have to add that the fundamental error of socialism is anthropological in nature. Socialism considers the individual person simply as an element, a molecule within the social organism, so that the good of the individual is completely subordinated to the functioning of the socioeconomic mechanism. Socialism likewise maintains that the good of the individual can be realized without reference to his free choice, to the unique and exclusive responsibility which he exercises in the face of good or evil. Man is thus reduced to a series of social relationships, and the concept of the person as the autonomous subject of moral decision disappears, the very subject whose decisions build the social order. From this mistaken conception of the person there arise both a distortion of law, which defines the sphere of the exercise of freedom, and an opposition to private property. A person who is deprived of something he can call "his own," and of the possibility of earning a living through his own initiative, comes to depend on the social machine and on those who control it. This makes it much more difficult for him to recognize his dignity as a person, and hinders progress towards the building up of an authentic human community.

---

39. Encyclical Letter *Rerum Novarum: loc. cit.*, 99.

In contrast, from the Christian vision of the human person there necessarily follows a correct picture of society. According to *Rerum novarum* and the whole social doctrine of the Church, the social nature of man is not completely fulfilled in the State, but is realized in various intermediary groups, beginning with the family and including economic, social, political and cultural groups which stem from human nature itself and have their own autonomy, always with a view to the common good. This is what I have called the "subjectivity" of society which, together with the subjectivity of the individual, was cancelled out by "Real Socialism."[40]

If we then inquire as to the source of this mistaken concept of the nature of the person and the "subjectivity" of society, we must reply that its first cause is atheism. It is by responding to the call of God contained in the being of things that man becomes aware of his transcendent dignity. Every individual must give this response, which constitutes the apex of his humanity, and no social mechanism or collective subject can substitute for it. The denial of God deprives the person of his foundation, and consequently leads to a reorganization of the social order without reference to the person's dignity and responsibility.

The atheism of which we are speaking is also closely connected with the rationalism of the Enlightenment, which views human and social reality in a mechanistic way. Thus there is a denial of the supreme insight concerning man's true greatness, his transcendence in respect to earthly realities, the contradiction in his heart between the desire for the fullness of what is good and his own inability to attain it and, above all, the need for salvation which results from this situation.

14. From the same atheistic source, socialism also derives its choice of the means of action condemned in *Rerum novarum*, namely, class struggle. The Pope does not, of course, intend to condemn every possible form of social conflict. The Church is well aware that in the course of history conflicts of interest between different social groups inevitably arise, and

40. Cf. Encyclical Letter *Sollicitudo Rei Socialis*, 15, 28: *loc. cit.*, 530; 548ff.

that in the face of such conflicts Christians must often take a position, honestly and decisively. The Encyclical *Laborem exercens* moreover clearly recognized the positive role of conflict when it takes the form of a "struggle for social justice";[41] *Quadragesimo anno* had already stated that "if the class struggle abstains from enmities and mutual hatred, it gradually changes into an honest discussion of differences founded on a desire for justice."[42]

However, what is condemned in class struggle is the idea that conflict is not restrained by ethical or juridical considerations, or by respect for the dignity of others (and consequently of oneself); a reasonable compromise is thus excluded, and what is pursued is not the general good of society, but a partisan interest which replaces the common good and sets out to destroy whatever stands in its way. In a word, it is a question of transferring to the sphere of internal conflict between social groups the doctrine of "total war," which the militarism and imperialism of that time brought to bear on international relations. As a result of this doctrine, the search for a proper balance between the interests of the various nations was replaced by attempts to impose the absolute domination of one's own side through the destruction of the other side's capacity to resist, using every possible means, not excluding the use of lies, terror tactics against citizens, and weapons of utter destruction (which precisely in those years were beginning to be designed). Therefore class struggle in the Marxist sense and militarism have the same root, namely, atheism and contempt for the human person, which place the principle of force above that of reason and law.

15. *Rerum novarum* is opposed to State control of the means of production, which would reduce every citizen to being a "cog" in the State machine. It is no less forceful in criticizing a concept of the State which completely excludes the economic sector from the State's range of interest and action. There is certainly a legitimate sphere of autonomy in economic life which the State should not enter. The State, however, has

---

41. Cf. Encyclical Letter *Laborem Exercens*, 11–15: *loc. cit.*, 602–618.
42. Pius XI, Encyclical Letter *Quadragesimo Anno*, III, 113: *loc. cit.*, 213.

the task of determining the juridical framework within which economic affairs are to be conducted, and thus of safeguarding the prerequisites of a free economy, which presumes a certain equality between the parties, such that one party would not be so powerful as practically to reduce the other to subservience.[43]

In this regard, *Rerum novarum* points the way to just reforms which can restore dignity to work as the free activity of man. These reforms imply that society and the State will both assume responsibility, especially for protecting the worker from the nightmare of unemployment. Historically, this has happened in two converging ways: either through economic policies aimed at ensuring balanced growth and full employment, or through unemployment insurance and retraining programs capable of ensuring a smooth transfer of workers from crisis sectors to those in expansion.

Furthermore, society and the State must ensure wage levels adequate for the maintenance of the worker and his family, including a certain amount for savings. This requires a continuous effort to improve workers' training and capability so that their work will be more skilled and productive, as well as careful controls and adequate legislative measures to block shameful forms of exploitation, especially to the disadvantage of the most vulnerable workers, of immigrants and of those on the margins of society. The role of trade unions in negotiating minimum salaries and working conditions is decisive in this area.

Finally, "humane" working hours and adequate free-time need to be guaranteed, as well as the right to express one's own personality at the work-place without suffering any affront to one's conscience or personal dignity. This is the place to mention once more the role of trade unions, not only in negotiating contracts, but also as "places" where workers can express themselves. They serve the development of an authentic culture

---

43. Cf. Encyclical Letter *Rerum Novarum: loc. cit.*, 121–125.

of work and help workers to share in a fully human way in the life of their place of employment.[44]

The State must contribute to the achievement of these goals both directly and indirectly. Indirectly and according to the *principle of subsidiarity*, by creating favorable conditions for the free exercise of economic activity, which will lead to abundant opportunities for employment and sources of wealth. Directly and according to the *principle of solidarity*, by defending the weakest, by placing certain limits on the autonomy of the parties who determine working conditions, and by ensuring in every case the necessary minimum support for the unemployed worker.[45]

The Encyclical and the related social teaching of the Church had far-reaching influence in the years bridging the nineteenth and twentieth centuries. This influence is evident in the numerous reforms which were introduced in the areas of social security, pensions, health insurance and compensation in the case of accidents, within the framework of greater respect for the rights of workers.[46]

16. These reforms were carried out in part by States, but in the struggle to achieve them *the role of the workers' movement* was an important one. This movement, which began as a response of moral conscience to unjust and harmful situations, conducted a widespread campaign for reform, far removed from vague ideology and closer to the daily needs of workers. In this context its efforts were often joined to those of Christians in order to improve workers' living conditions. Later on, this movement was dominated to a certain extent by the Marxist ideology against which *Rerum novarum* had spoken.

These same reforms were also partly the result of *an open process by which society organized itself* through the establishment of effective instruments

---

44. Cf. Encyclical Letter *Laborem Exercens*, 20: *loc. cit.*, 629–632; Discourse to the International Labor Organization (I.L.O.) in Geneva (June 15, 1982): *Insegnamenti* V/2 (1982), 2250–2266; Paul VI, Discourse to the same Organization (June 10, 1969): *AAS* 61 (1969), 491–502.

45. Cf. Encyclical Letter *Laborem Exercens*, 8: *loc. cit.*, 594–598.

46. Cf. Pius XI, Encyclical Letter *Quadragesimo Anno*, 14: *loc. cit.*, 178–181.

of solidarity, which were capable of sustaining an economic growth more respectful of the values of the person. Here we should remember the numerous efforts to which Christians made a notable contribution in establishing producers', consumers' and credit cooperatives, in promoting general education and professional training, in experimenting with various forms of participation in the life of the work-place and in the life of society in general.

Thus, as we look at the past, there is good reason to thank God that the great Encyclical was not without an echo in human hearts and indeed led to a generous response on the practical level. Still, we must acknowledge that its prophetic message was not fully accepted by people at the time. Precisely for this reason there ensued some very serious tragedies.

17. Reading the Encyclical within the context of Pope Leo's whole magisterium,[47] we see how it points essentially to the socio-economic consequences of an error which has even greater implications. As has been mentioned, this error consists in an understanding of human freedom which detaches it from obedience to the truth, and consequently from the duty to respect the rights of others. The essence of freedom then becomes self-love carried to the point of contempt for God and neighbor, a self-love which leads to an unbridled affirmation of self-interest and which refuses to be limited by any demand of justice.[48]

This very error had extreme consequences in the tragic series of wars which ravaged Europe and the world between 1914 and 1945. Some of these resulted from militarism and exaggerated nationalism, and from related forms of totalitarianism; some derived from the class struggle;

---

47. Cf. Encyclical Epistle *Arcanum Divinae Sapientiae* (February 10, 1880): *Leonis XIII P.M. Acta,* II, Romae 1882, 10–40; Encyclical Epistle *Diuturnum Illud* (June 29, 1881): *Leonis XIII P.M. Acta,* II, Romae 1882, 269287; Encyclical Epistle *Immortale Dei* (November 1, 1885): *Leonis XIII P.M. Acta,* V, Romae 1886, 118–150; Encyclical Letter *Sapientiae Christianae* (January 10, 1890): *Leonis XIII P.M. Acta,* X, Romae 1891, 10–41; Encyclical Epistle *Quod Apostolici Muneris* (December 28,1878): *Leonis XIII P.M. Acta,* I, Romae 1881, 170–183; Encyclical Letter *Libertas Praestantissimum* (June 20, 1888): *Leonis XIII P.M. Acta,* VIII, Romae 1889, 212–246.

48. Cf. Leo XIII, Encyclical Letter *Libertas Praestantissimum,* 10: *loc. cit.,* 224–226.

still others were civil wars or wars of an ideological nature. Without the terrible burden of hatred and resentment which had built up as a result of so many injustices both on the international level and within individual States, such cruel wars would not have been possible, in which great nations invested their energies and in which there was no hesitation to violate the most sacred human rights, with the extermination of entire peoples and social groups being planned and carried out. Here we recall the Jewish people in particular, whose terrible fate has become a symbol of the aberration of which man is capable when he turns against God.

However, it is only when hatred and injustice are sanctioned and organized by the ideologies based on them, rather than on the truth about man, that they take possession of entire nations and drive them to act.[49] *Rerum novarum* opposed ideologies of hatred and showed how violence and resentment could be overcome by justice. May the memory of those terrible events guide the actions of everyone, particularly the leaders of nations in our own time, when other forms of injustice are fueling new hatreds and when new ideologies which exalt violence are appearing on the horizon.

18. While it is true that since 1945 weapons have been silent on the European continent, it must be remembered that true peace is never simply the result of military victory, but rather implies both the removal of the causes of war and genuine reconciliation between peoples. For many years there has been in Europe and the world a situation of non-war rather than genuine peace. Half of the continent fell under the domination of a Communist dictatorship, while the other half organized itself in defense against this threat. Many peoples lost the ability to control their own destiny and were enclosed within the suffocating boundaries of an empire in which efforts were made to destroy their

---

49. Cf. Message for the 1980 World Day of Peace: AAS 71 (1979), 1572–1580.

historical memory and the centuries-old roots of their culture. As a result of this violent division of Europe, enormous masses of people were compelled to leave their homeland or were forcibly deported.

An insane arms race swallowed up the resources needed for the development of national economies and for assistance to the less developed nations. Scientific and technological progress, which should have contributed to man's well-being, was transformed into an instrument of war: science and technology were directed to the production of ever more efficient and destructive weapons. Meanwhile, an ideology, a perversion of authentic philosophy, was called upon to provide doctrinal justification for the new war. And this war was not simply expected and prepared for, but was actually fought with enormous bloodshed in various parts of the world. The logic of power blocs or empires, denounced in various Church documents and recently in the Encyclical *Sollicitudo rei socialis*,[50] led to a situation in which controversies and disagreements among Third World countries were systematically aggravated and exploited in order to create difficulties for the adversary.

Extremist groups, seeking to resolve such controversies through the use of arms, found ready political and military support and were equipped and trained for war; those who tried to find peaceful and humane solutions, with respect for the legitimate interests of all parties, remained isolated and often fell victim to their opponents. In addition, the precariousness of the peace which followed the Second World War was one of the principal causes of the militarization of many Third World countries and the fratricidal conflicts which afflicted them, as well as of the spread of terrorism and of increasingly barbaric means of political and military conflict. Moreover, the whole world was oppressed by the threat of an atomic war capable of leading to the extinction of humanity. Science used for military purposes had placed this decisive instrument at the disposal of hatred, strengthened by ideology. But if

---

50. Cf. Encyclical Letter *Sollicitudo Rei Socialis*, 20: *loc. cit.*, 536f.

PART I: CHURCH TEACHING

war can end without winners or losers in a suicide of humanity, then we must repudiate the logic which leads to it: the idea that the effort to destroy the enemy, confrontation and war itself are factors of progress and historical advancement.[51] When the need for this repudiation is understood, the concepts of "total war" and "class struggle" must necessarily be called into question.

19. At the end of the Second World War, however, such a development was still being formed in people's consciences. What received attention was the spread of Communist totalitarianism over more than half of Europe and over other parts of the world. The war, which should have re-established freedom and restored the right of nations, ended without having attained these goals. Indeed, in a way, for many peoples, especially those which had suffered most during the war, it openly contradicted these goals. It may be said that the situation which arose has evoked different responses.

Following the destruction caused by the war, we see in some countries and under certain aspects a positive effort to rebuild a democratic society inspired by social justice, so as to deprive Communism of the revolutionary potential represented by masses of people subjected to exploitation and oppression. In general, such attempts endeavor to preserve free-market mechanisms, ensuring, by means of a stable currency and the harmony of social relations, the conditions for steady and healthy economic growth in which people through their own work can build a better future for themselves and their families. At the same time, these attempts try to avoid making market mechanisms the only point of reference for social life, and they tend to subject them to public control which upholds the principle of the common destination of material goods. In this context, an abundance of work opportunities, a solid system of social security and professional training, the freedom to join trade unions and the effective action of unions, the assistance

---

51. Cf. John XXIII, Encyclical Letter *Pacem in Terris* (April 11, 1963), III: *AAS* 55 (1963), 286–289.

provided in cases of unemployment, the opportunities for democratic participation in the life of society—all these are meant to deliver work from the mere condition of "a commodity," and to guarantee its dignity.

Then there are the other social forces and ideological movements which oppose Marxism by setting up systems of "national security," aimed at controlling the whole of society in a systematic way, in order to make Marxist infiltration impossible. By emphasizing and increasing the power of the State, they wish to protect their people from Communism, but in doing so they run the grave risk of destroying the freedom and values of the person, the very things for whose sake it is necessary to oppose Communism.

Another kind of response, practical in nature, is represented by the affluent society or the consumer society. It seeks to defeat Marxism on the level of pure materialism by showing how a free-market society can achieve a greater satisfaction of material human needs than Communism, while equally excluding spiritual values. In reality, while on the one hand it is true that this social model shows the failure of Marxism to contribute to a humane and better society, on the other hand, insofar as it denies an autonomous existence and value to morality, law, culture and religion, it agrees with Marxism, in the sense that it totally reduces man to the sphere of economics and the satisfaction of material needs.

20. During the same period a widespread process of "decolonization" occurred, by which many countries gained or regained their independence and the right freely to determine their own destiny. With the formal re-acquisition of State sovereignty, however, these countries often find themselves merely at the beginning of the journey towards the construction of genuine independence. Decisive sectors of the economy still remain *de facto* in the hands of large foreign companies which are unwilling to commit themselves to the long-term development of the host country. Political life itself is controlled by foreign powers, while within the national boundaries there are tribal groups

not yet amalgamated into a genuine national community. Also lacking is a class of competent professional people capable of running the State apparatus in an honest and just way, nor are there qualified personnel for managing the economy in an efficient and responsible manner.

Given this situation, many think that Marxism can offer a sort of short-cut for building up the nation and the State; thus many variants of socialism emerge with specific national characteristics. Legitimate demands for national recovery, forms of nationalism and also of militarism, principles drawn from ancient popular traditions (which are sometimes in harmony with Christian social doctrine) and Marxist-Leninist concepts and ideas—all these mingle in the many ideologies which take shape in ways that differ from case to case.

21. Lastly, it should be remembered that after the Second World War, and in reaction to its horrors, there arose a more lively sense of human rights, which found recognition in a number of *International Documents*[52] and, one might say, in the drawing up of a new "right of nations," to which the Holy See has constantly contributed. The focal point of this evolution has been the United Nations Organization. Not only has there been a development in awareness of the rights of individuals, but also in awareness of the rights of nations, as well as a clearer realization of the need to act in order to remedy the grave imbalances that exist between the various geographical areas of the world. In a certain sense, these imbalances have shifted the center of the social question from the national to the international level.[53]

While noting this process with satisfaction, nevertheless one cannot ignore the fact that the overall balance of the various policies of aid for development has not always been positive. The United Nations,

---

52. Cf. Universal Declaration of Human Rights, issued in 1948; John XXIII, Encyclical Letter *Pacem in Terris*, IV: loc. cit., 291–296; "Final Act" of the Conference on Cooperation and Security in Europe, Helsinki, 1975.

53. Cf. Paul VI, Encyclical Letter *Populorum Progressio* (March 26, 1967), 61–65: AAS 59 (1967), 287–289.

moreover, has not yet succeeded in establishing, as alternatives to war, effective means for the resolution of international conflicts. This seems to be the most urgent problem which the international community has yet to resolve.

III. THE YEAR 1989

22. It is on the basis of the world situation just described, and already elaborated in the Encyclical *Sollicitudo rei socialis,* that the unexpected and promising significance of the events of recent years can be understood. Although they certainly reached their climax in 1989 in the countries of Central and Eastern Europe, they embrace a longer period of time and a wider geographical area. In the course of the 80s, certain dictatorial and oppressive regimes fell one by one in some countries of Latin America and also of Africa and Asia. In other cases there began a difficult but productive transition towards more participatory and more just political structures. An important, even decisive, contribution was made by *the Church's commitment to defend and promote human rights.* In situations strongly influenced by ideology, in which polarization obscured the awareness of a human dignity common to all, the Church affirmed clearly and forcefully that every individual—whatever his or her personal convictions—bears the image of God and therefore deserves respect. Often, the vast majority of people identified themselves with this kind of affirmation, and this led to a search for forms of protest and for political solutions more respectful of the dignity of the person.

From this historical process new forms of democracy have emerged which offer a hope for change in fragile political and social structures weighed down by a painful series of injustices and resentments, as well as by a heavily damaged economy and serious social conflicts. Together with the whole Church, I thank God for the often heroic witness borne in such difficult circumstances by many Pastors, entire Christian communities, individual members of the faithful, and other people of good will; at the same time I pray that he will sustain the efforts being made by everyone to build a better future. This is, in fact, a responsibility which falls not only to the citizens of the countries in question, but to all Christians and people of good will. It is a question of showing that the complex problems faced by those peoples can be resolved through dialogue and solidarity, rather than by a struggle to destroy the enemy through war.

23. Among the many factors involved in the fall of oppressive regimes, some deserve special mention. Certainly, the decisive factor which gave rise to the changes was the violation of the rights of workers. It cannot be forgotten that the fundamental crisis of systems claiming to express the rule and indeed the dictatorship of the working class began with the great upheavals which took place in Poland in the name of solidarity. It was the throngs of working people which foreswore the ideology which presumed to speak in their name. On the basis of a hard, lived experience of work and of oppression, it was they who recovered and, in a sense, rediscovered the content and principles of the Church's social doctrine.

Also worthy of emphasis is the fact that the fall of this kind of "bloc" or empire was accomplished almost everywhere by means of peaceful protest, using only the weapons of truth and justice. While Marxism held that only by exacerbating social conflicts was it possible to resolve them through violent confrontation, the protests which led to the collapse of Marxism tenaciously insisted on trying every avenue of negotiation, dialogue, and witness to the truth, appealing to the conscience of the adversary and seeking to reawaken in him a sense of shared human dignity.

It seemed that the European order resulting from the Second World War and sanctioned by the *Yalta Agreements* could only be overturned by another war. Instead, it has been overcome by the non-violent commitment of people who, while always refusing to yield to the force of power, succeeded time after time in finding effective ways of bearing witness to the truth. This disarmed the adversary, since violence always needs to justify itself through deceit, and to appear, however falsely, to be defending a right or responding to a threat posed by others.[54] Once again I thank God for having sustained people's hearts amid difficult trials, and I pray that this example will prevail in other places and other circumstances. May people learn to fight for justice without violence, renouncing class struggle in their internal disputes, and war in international ones.

24. The second factor in the crisis was certainly the inefficiency of the economic system, which is not to be considered simply as a technical problem, but rather a consequence of the violation of the human rights to private initiative, to ownership of property and to freedom in the economic sector. To this must be added the cultural and national dimension: it is not possible to understand man on the basis of economics alone, nor to define him simply on the basis of class membership. Man is understood in a more complete way when he is situated within the sphere of culture through his language, history, and the position he takes towards the fundamental events of life, such as birth, love, work and death. At the heart of every culture lies the attitude man takes to the greatest mystery: the mystery of God. Different cultures are basically different ways of facing the question of the meaning of personal existence. When this question is eliminated, the culture and moral life of nations are corrupted. For this reason the struggle to defend work was spontaneously linked to the struggle for culture and for national rights.

But the true cause of the new developments was the spiritual void brought about by atheism, which deprived the younger generations of a sense of direction and in many cases led them, in the irrepressible search for personal identity and for the meaning of life, to rediscover the religious roots of their national cultures, and to rediscover the person of Christ himself as the existentially adequate response to the desire in

---

54. Cf. Message for the 1980 World Day of Peace: *loc. cit.*, 1572–1580.

PART I: CHURCH TEACHING

every human heart for goodness, truth and life. This search was supported by the witness of those who, in difficult circumstances and under persecution, remained faithful to God. Marxism had promised to uproot the need for God from the human heart, but the results have shown that it is not possible to succeed in this without throwing the heart into turmoil.

25. The events of 1989 are an example of the success of willingness to negotiate and of the Gospel spirit in the face of an adversary determined not to be bound by moral principles. These events are a warning to those who, in the name of political realism, wish to banish law and morality from the political arena. Undoubtedly, the struggle which led to the changes of 1989 called for clarity, moderation, suffering and sacrifice. In a certain sense, it was a struggle born of prayer, and it would have been unthinkable without immense trust in God, the Lord of history, who carries the human heart in his hands. It is by uniting his own sufferings for the sake of truth and freedom to the sufferings of Christ on the Cross that man is able to accomplish the miracle of peace and is in a position to discern the often narrow path between the cowardice which gives in to evil and the violence which, under the illusion of fighting evil, only makes it worse.

Nevertheless, it cannot be forgotten that the manner in which the individual exercises his freedom is conditioned in innumerable ways. While these certainly have an influence on freedom, they do not determine it; they make the exercise of freedom more difficult or less difficult, but they cannot destroy it. Not only is it wrong from the ethical point of view to disregard human nature, which is made for freedom, but in practice it is impossible to do so. Where society is so organized as to reduce arbitrarily or even suppress the sphere in which freedom is legitimately exercised, the result is that the life of society becomes progressively disorganized and goes into decline.

Moreover, man, who was created for freedom, bears within himself the wound of original sin, which constantly draws him towards evil and puts him in need of redemption. Not only is *this doctrine an integral part of Christian revelation*; it also has great hermeneutical value insofar as it helps one to understand human reality. Man tends towards good, but he is also capable of evil. He can transcend his immediate interest and still remain bound to it. The social order will be all the more stable, the more it takes this fact into account and does not place in opposition personal interest and the interests of society as a whole, but rather seeks ways to bring them into fruitful harmony. In fact, where self-interest is violently suppressed, it is replaced by a burdensome system of bureaucratic control which dries up the wellsprings of initiative and creativity. When people think they possess the secret of a perfect social organization which makes evil impossible, they also think that they can use any means, including violence and deceit, in order to bring that organization into being. Politics then becomes a "secular religion" which operates under the illusion of creating paradise in this world. But no political society—which possesses its own autonomy and laws[55]—can ever be confused with the Kingdom of God. The Gospel parable of the weeds among the wheat (cf. Mt 13:24–30; 36–43) teaches that it is for God alone to separate the subjects of the Kingdom from the subjects of the Evil One, and that this judgment will take place at the end of time. By presuming to anticipate judgment here and now, man puts himself in the place of God and sets himself against the patience of God.

Through Christ's sacrifice on the Cross, the victory of the Kingdom of God has been achieved once and for all. Nevertheless, the Christian life involves a struggle against temptation and the forces of evil. Only at the end of history will the Lord return in glory for the final judgment (cf. Mt 25:31) with the establishment of a new heaven and a new earth (cf. 2 Pt 3:13; Rev 21:1); but as long as time lasts the struggle between good and evil continues even in the human heart itself.

---

55. Cf. Second Vatican Ecumenical Council, Pastoral Constitution on the Church in the World of Today *Gaudium et Spes*, 36; 39.

What Sacred Scripture teaches us about the prospects of the Kingdom of God is not without consequences for the life of temporal societies, which, as the adjective indicates, belong to the realm of time, with all that this implies of imperfection and impermanence. The Kingdom of God, being *in* the world without being *of* the world, throws light on the order of human society, while the power of grace penetrates that order and gives it life. In this way the requirements of a society worthy of man are better perceived, deviations are corrected, the courage to work for what is good is reinforced. In union with all people of good will, Christians, especially the laity, are called to this task of imbuing human realities with the Gospel.[56]

26. The events of 1989 took place principally in the countries of Eastern and Central Europe. However, they have worldwide importance because they have positive and negative consequences which concern the whole human family. These consequences are not mechanistic or fatalistic in character, but rather are opportunities for human freedom to cooperate with the merciful plan of God who acts within history.

The first consequence was *an encounter* in some countries *between the Church and the workers' movement*, which came about as a result of an ethical and explicitly Christian reaction against a widespread situation of injustice. For about a century the workers' movement had fallen in part under the dominance of Marxism, in the conviction that the working class, in order to struggle effectively against oppression, had to appropriate its economic and materialistic theories.

In the crisis of Marxism, the natural dictates of the consciences of workers have re-emerged in a demand for justice and a recognition of the dignity of work, in conformity with the social doctrine of the Church.[57] The worker movement is part of a more general movement among workers and other people of good will for the liberation of the

---

56. Cf. Apostolic Exhortation *Christifideles Laici* (December 30, 1988), 32–44: *AAS* 81 (1989), 431–481.

57. Cf. Encyclical Letter *Laborem Exercens*, 20: *loc. cit.*, 629–632.

human person and for the affirmation of human rights. It is a movement which today has spread to many countries, and which, far from opposing the Catholic Church, looks to her with interest.

The crisis of Marxism does not rid the world of the situations of injustice and oppression which Marxism itself exploited and on which it fed. To those who are searching today for a new and authentic theory and praxis of liberation, the Church offers not only her social doctrine and, in general, her teaching about the human person redeemed in Christ, but also her concrete commitment and material assistance in the struggle against marginalization and suffering.

In the recent past, the sincere desire to be on the side of the oppressed and not to be cut off from the course of history has led many believers to seek in various ways an impossible compromise between Marxism and Christianity. Moving beyond all that was short-lived in these attempts, present circumstances are leading to a reaffirmation of the positive value of an authentic theology of integral human liberation.[58] Considered from this point of view, the events of 1989 are proving to be important also for the countries of the Third World, which are searching for their own path to development, just as they were important for the countries of Central and Eastern Europe.

27. The second consequence concerns the peoples of Europe themselves. Many individual, social, regional and national injustices were committed during and prior to the years in which Communism dominated; much hatred and ill-will have accumulated. There is a real danger that these will re-explode after the collapse of dictatorship, provoking serious conflicts and casualties, should there be a lessening of the moral commitment and conscious striving to bear witness to the truth which were the inspiration for past efforts. It is to be hoped that hatred and violence will not triumph in people's hearts, especially among those

---

58. Cf. Congregation for the Doctrine of the Faith, Instruction on Christian Freedom and Liberation *Libertatis Conscientia* (March 22, 1986): AAS 79 (1987), 554–599.

PART I: CHURCH TEACHING

who are struggling for justice, and that all people will grow in the spirit of peace and forgiveness.

What is needed are concrete steps to create or consolidate international structures capable of intervening through appropriate arbitration in the conflicts which arise between nations, so that each nation can uphold its own rights and reach a just agreement and peaceful settlement vis-à-vis the rights of others. This is especially needed for the nations of Europe, which are closely united in a bond of common culture and an age old history. A great effort is needed to rebuild morally and economically the countries which have abandoned Communism. For a long time the most elementary economic relationships were distorted, and basic virtues of economic life, such as truthfulness, trustworthiness and hard work were denigrated. A patient material and moral reconstruction is needed, even as people, exhausted by longstanding privation, are asking their governments for tangible and immediate results in the form of material benefits and an adequate fulfilment of their legitimate aspirations.

The fall of Marxism has naturally had a great impact on the division of the planet into worlds which are closed to one another and in jealous competition. It has further highlighted the reality of interdependence among peoples, as well as the fact that human work, by its nature, is meant to unite peoples, not divide them. Peace and prosperity, in fact, are goods which belong to the whole human race: it is not possible to enjoy them in a proper and lasting way if they are achieved and maintained at the cost of other peoples and nations, by violating their rights or excluding them from the sources of well-being.

28. In a sense, for some countries of Europe the real post-war period is just beginning. The radical reordering of economic systems, hitherto collectivized, entails problems and sacrifices comparable to those which the countries of Western Europe had to face in order to rebuild after the Second World War. It is right that in the present difficulties the

formerly Communist countries should be aided by the united effort of other nations. Obviously they themselves must be the primary agents of their own development, but they must also be given a reasonable opportunity to accomplish this goal, something that cannot happen without the help of other countries. Moreover, their present condition, marked by difficulties and shortages, is the result of an historical process in which the formerly Communist countries were often objects and not subjects. Thus they find themselves in the present situation not as a result of free choice or mistakes which were made, but as a consequence of tragic historical events which were violently imposed on them, and which prevented them from following the path of economic and social development.

Assistance from other countries, especially the countries of Europe which were part of that history and which bear responsibility for it, represents a debt in justice. But it also corresponds to the interest and welfare of Europe as a whole, since Europe cannot live in peace if the various conflicts which have arisen as a result of the past are to become more acute because of a situation of economic disorder, spiritual dissatisfaction and desperation.

This need, however, must not lead to a slackening of efforts to sustain and assist the countries of the Third World, which often suffer even more serious conditions of poverty and want.[59] What is called for is a special effort to mobilize resources, which are not lacking in the world as a whole, for the purpose of economic growth and common development, redefining the priorities and hierarchies of values on the basis of which economic and political choices are made. Enormous resources can be made available by disarming the huge military machines which were constructed for the conflict between East and West. These resources could become even more abundant if, in place of war, reliable procedures for the resolution of conflicts could be set up, with the resulting spread

---

59. Cf. Discourse at the Headquarters of the E.C.W.A. on the occasion of the Tenth Anniversary of the "Appeal for the Sahel" (Ouagadougou, Burkina Faso, January 29, 1990): AAS 82 (1990), 816–821.

of the principle of arms control and arms reduction, also in the countries of the Third World, through the adoption of appropriate measures against the arms trade.[60] But it will be necessary above all to abandon a mentality in which the poor—as individuals and as peoples—are considered a burden, as irksome intruders trying to consume what others have produced. The poor ask for the right to share in enjoying material goods and to make good use of their capacity for work, thus creating a world that is more just and prosperous for all. The advancement of the poor constitutes a great opportunity for the moral, cultural and even economic growth of all humanity.

29. Finally, development must not be understood solely in economic terms, but in a way that is fully human.[61] It is not only a question of raising all peoples to the level currently enjoyed by the richest countries, but rather of building up a more decent life through united labor, of concretely enhancing every individual's dignity and creativity, as well as his capacity to respond to his personal vocation, and thus to God's call. The apex of development is the exercise of the right and duty to seek God, to know him and to live in accordance with that knowledge.[62] In the totalitarian and authoritarian regimes, the principle that force predominates over reason was carried to the extreme. Man was compelled to submit to a conception of reality imposed on him by coercion, and not reached by virtue of his own reason and the exercise of his own freedom. This principle must be overturned and total recognition must be given to *the rights of the human conscience*, which is bound only to the truth, both natural and revealed. The recognition of these rights represents the primary foundation of every authentically free political order.[63] It is important to reaffirm this latter principle for several reasons:

---

60. Cf. John XXIII, Encyclical Letter *Pacem in Terris*, III: *loc. cit.*, 286–288.

61. Cf. Encyclical Letter *Sollicitudo Rei Socialis*, 27-28: *loc. cit.*, 547–550; Paul VI, Encyclical Letter *Populorum Progressio*, 43–44: *loc. cit.*, 278f.

62. Cf. Encyclical Letter *Sollicitudo Rei Socialis*, 29–31: *loc. cit.*, 550–556.

63. Cf. Helsinki Final Act and Vienna Accord; Leo XIII, Encyclical Letter *Libertas Praestantissimum*, 5: *loc. cit.*, 215–217.

a) because the old forms of totalitarianism and authoritarianism are not yet completely vanquished; indeed there is a risk that they will regain their strength. This demands renewed efforts of cooperation and solidarity between all countries;

b) because in the developed countries there is sometimes an excessive promotion of purely utilitarian values, with an appeal to the appetites and inclinations towards immediate gratification, making it difficult to recognize and respect the hierarchy of the true values of human existence;

c) because in some countries new forms of religious fundamentalism are emerging which covertly, or even openly, deny to citizens of faiths other than that of the majority the full exercise of their civil and religious rights, preventing them from taking part in the cultural process, and restricting both the Church's right to preach the Gospel and the rights of those who hear this preaching to accept it and to be converted to Christ. No authentic progress is possible without respect for the natural and fundamental right to know the truth and live according to that truth. The exercise and development of this right includes the right to discover and freely to accept Jesus Christ, who is man's true good.[64]

IV. PRIVATE PROPERTY AND THE UNIVERSAL DESTINATION OF MATERIAL GOODS

30. In *Rerum novarum*, Leo XIII strongly affirmed the natural character of the right to private property, using various arguments against the socialism of his time.[65] This right, which is fundamental for the autonomy and development of the person, has always been defended by the Church up to our own day. At the same time, the Church teaches that the possession of material goods is not an absolute right, and that its limits are inscribed in its very nature as a human right.

---

64. Cf. Encyclical Letter *Redemptoris Missio* (December 7, 1990), 7: *L'Osservatore Romano*, January 23, 1991.
65. Cf. Encyclical Letter *Rerum Novarum: loc. cit.*, 99–107; 131–133.

While the Pope proclaimed the right to private ownership, he affirmed with equal clarity that the "use" of goods, while marked by freedom, is subordinated to their original common destination as created goods, as well as to the will of Jesus Christ as expressed in the Gospel. Pope Leo wrote: "those whom fortune favors are admonished . . . that they should tremble at the warnings of Jesus Christ . . . and that a most strict account must be given to the Supreme Judge for the use of all they possess"; and quoting Saint Thomas Aquinas, he added: "But if the question be asked, how must one's possessions be used? the Church replies without hesitation that man should not consider his material possessions as his own, but as common to all . . . ," because "above the laws and judgments of men stands the law, the judgment of Christ."[66]

The Successors of Leo XIII have repeated this twofold affirmation: the necessity and therefore the legitimacy of private ownership, as well as the limits which are imposed on it.[67] The Second Vatican Council likewise clearly restated the traditional doctrine in words which bear repeating: "In making use of the exterior things we lawfully possess, we ought to regard them not just as our own but also as common, in the sense that they can profit not only the owners but others too"; and a little later we read: "Private property or some ownership of external goods affords each person the scope needed for personal and family autonomy, and should be regarded as an extension of human freedom . . . Of its nature private property also has a social function which is based on the law of the *common purpose of goods*."[68] I have returned to this same doctrine, first in my address to the Third Conference of the Latin American Bishops at Puebla, and later in the Encyclicals *Laborem exercens* and *Sollicitudo rei socialis*.[69]

---

66. *Ibid.*, 111–113f.

67. Cf. Pius XI, Encyclical Letter *Quadragesimo Anno*, II; *loc. cit.*, 191; Pius XII, Radio Message on June 1, 1941: *loc. cit.*, 199; John XXIII, Encyclical Letter *Mater et Magistra*: *loc. cit.*, 428–429; Paul VI, Encyclical Letter *Populorum Progressio*, 22–24: *loc. cit.*, 268f.

68. Second Vatican Ecumenical Council, Pastoral Constitution on the Church in the World of Today *Gaudium et Spes*, 69; 71.

69. Cf. Discourse to Latin American Bishops at Puebla (January 28, 1979), III, 4: *AAS* 71 (1979), 199–201; Encyclical Letter *Laborem Exercens*, 14: *loc. cit.*, 612–616; Encyclical Letter *Sollicitudo Rei Socialis*, 42: *loc. cit.*, 572–574.

31. Re-reading this teaching on the right to property and the common destination of material wealth as it applies to the present time, the question can be raised concerning the origin of the material goods which sustain human life, satisfy people's needs and are an object of their rights.

The original source of all that is good is the very act of God, who created both the earth and man, and who gave the earth to man so that he might have dominion over it by his work and enjoy its fruits (Gen 1:28). God gave the earth to the whole human race for the sustenance of all its members, without excluding or favoring anyone. This is *the foundation of the universal destination of the earth's goods.* The earth, by reason of its fruitfulness and its capacity to satisfy human needs, is God's first gift for the sustenance of human life. But the earth does not yield its fruits without a particular human response to God's gift, that is to say, without work. It is through work that man, using his intelligence and exercising his freedom, succeeds in dominating the earth and making it a fitting home. In this way, he makes part of the earth his own, precisely the part which he has acquired through work; this is *the origin of individual property.* Obviously, he also has the responsibility not to hinder others from having their own part of God's gift; indeed, he must cooperate with others so that together all can dominate the earth.

In history, these two factors—*work* and *the land*—are to be found at the beginning of every human society. However, they do not always stand in the same relationship to each other. At one time *the natural fruitfulness of the earth* appeared to be, and was in fact, the primary factor of wealth, while work was, as it were, the help and support for this fruitfulness. In our time, *the role of human work* is becoming increasingly important as the productive factor both of non-material and of material wealth. Moreover, it is becoming clearer how a person's work is naturally interrelated with the work of others. More than ever, work is *work with others* and *work for others:* it is a matter of doing something for someone else. Work becomes ever more fruitful and productive to the extent that people become more knowledgeable of the productive potentialities of the earth and more profoundly cognizant of the needs of those for whom their work is done.

32. In our time, in particular, there exists another form of ownership which is becoming no less important than land: *the possession of know-how, technology and skill.* The wealth of the industrialized nations is based much more on this kind of ownership than on natural resources.

Mention has just been made of the fact that *people work with each other,* sharing in a "community of work" which embraces ever widening circles. A person who produces something other than for his own use generally does so in order that others may use it after they have paid a just price, mutually agreed upon through free bargaining. It is precisely the ability to foresee both the needs of others and the combinations of productive factors most adapted to satisfying those needs that constitutes another important source of wealth in modern society. Besides, many goods cannot be adequately produced through the work of an isolated individual; they require the cooperation of many people in working towards a common goal. Organizing such a productive effort, planning its duration in time, making sure that it corresponds in a positive way to the demands which it must satisfy, and taking the necessary risks—all this too is a source of wealth in today's society. In this way, the *role* of disciplined and creative *human work* and, as an essential part of that work, *initiative and entrepreneurial ability* becomes increasingly evident and decisive.[70]

This process, which throws practical light on a truth about the person which Christianity has constantly affirmed, should be viewed carefully and favorably. Indeed, besides the earth, man's principal resource is *man himself.* His intelligence enables him to discover the earth's productive potential and the many different ways in which human needs can be satisfied. It is his disciplined work in close collaboration with others that

---

70. Cf. Encyclical Letter *Sollicitudo Rei Socialis,* 15: *loc. cit.,* 528–531.

makes possible the creation of ever more extensive *working communities* which can be relied upon to transform man's natural and human environments. Important virtues are involved in this process, such as diligence, industriousness, prudence in undertaking reasonable risks, reliability and fidelity in interpersonal relationships, as well as courage in carrying out decisions which are difficult and painful but necessary, both for the overall working of a business and in meeting possible setbacks.

The modern *business economy* has positive aspects. Its basis is human freedom exercised in the economic field, just as it is exercised in many other fields. Economic activity is indeed but one sector in a great variety of human activities, and like every other sector, it includes the right to freedom, as well as the duty of making responsible use of freedom. But it is important to note that there are specific differences between the trends of modern society and those of the past, even the recent past. Whereas at one time the decisive factor of production was *the land,* and later capital—understood as a total complex of the instruments of production—today the decisive factor is increasingly *man himself,* that is, his knowledge, especially his scientific knowledge, his capacity for interrelated and compact organization, as well as his ability to perceive the needs of others and to satisfy them.

33. However, the risks and problems connected with this kind of process should be pointed out. The fact is that many people, perhaps the majority today, do not have the means which would enable them to take their place in an effective and humanly dignified way within a productive system in which work is truly central. They have no possibility of acquiring the basic knowledge which would enable them to express their creativity and develop their potential. They have no way of entering the network of knowledge and intercommunication which would enable them to see their qualities appreciated and utilized. Thus, if not actually exploited, they are to a great extent marginalized; economic development takes place over their heads, so to speak, when it does

not actually reduce the already narrow scope of their old subsistence economies. They are unable to compete against the goods which are produced in ways which are new and which properly respond to needs, needs which they had previously been accustomed to meeting through traditional forms of organization. Allured by the dazzle of an opulence which is beyond their reach, and at the same time driven by necessity, these people crowd the cities of the Third World where they are often without cultural roots, and where they are exposed to situations of violent uncertainty, without the possibility of becoming integrated. Their dignity is not acknowledged in any real way, and sometimes there are even attempts to eliminate them from history through coercive forms of demographic control which are contrary to human dignity.

Many other people, while not completely marginalized, live in situations in which the struggle for a bare minimum is uppermost. These are situations in which the rules of the earliest period of capitalism still flourish in conditions of "ruthlessness" in no way inferior to the darkest moments of the first phase of industrialization. In other cases the land is still the central element in the economic process, but those who cultivate it are excluded from ownership and are reduced to a state of quasi-servitude.[71] In these cases, it is still possible today, as in the days of *Rerum novarum*, to speak of inhuman exploitation. In spite of the great changes which have taken place in the more advanced societies, the human inadequacies of capitalism and the resulting domination of things over people are far from disappearing. In fact, for the poor, to the lack of material goods has been added a lack of knowledge and training which prevents them from escaping their state of humiliating subjection.

Unfortunately, the great majority of people in the Third World still live in such conditions. It would be a mistake, however, to understand this *"world"* in purely geographic terms. In some regions and in some social sectors of that world, development programs have been set up

---

71. Cf. Encyclical Letter *Laborem Exercens*, 21: *loc. cit.*, 632–634.

which are centered on the use not so much of the material resources available but of the "human resources."

Even in recent years it was thought that the poorest countries would develop by isolating themselves from the world market and by depending only on their own resources. Recent experience has shown that countries which did this have suffered stagnation and recession, while the countries which experienced development were those which succeeded in taking part in the general interrelated economic activities at the international level. It seems therefore that the chief problem is that of gaining fair access to the international market, based not on the unilateral principle of the exploitation of the natural resources of these countries but on the proper use of human resources.[72]

However, aspects typical of the Third World also appear in developed countries, where the constant transformation of the methods of production and consumption devalues certain acquired skills and professional expertise, and thus requires a continual effort of re-training and updating. Those who fail to keep up with the times can easily be marginalized, as can the elderly, the young people who are incapable of finding their place in the life of society and, in general, those who are weakest or part of the so-called Fourth World. The situation of women too is far from easy in these conditions.

34. It would appear that, on the level of individual nations and of international relations, the *free market* is the most efficient instrument for utilizing resources and effectively responding to needs. But this is true only for those needs which are "solvent," insofar as they are endowed with purchasing power, and for those resources which are "marketable," insofar as they are capable of obtaining a satisfactory price. But there are many human needs which find no place on the market. It is a strict duty of justice and truth not to allow fundamental human needs to remain unsatisfied, and not to allow those burdened by such needs to

---

72. Cf. Paul VI, Encyclical Letter *Populorum Progressio*, 33–42: *loc. cit.*, 273–278.

perish. It is also necessary to help these needy people to acquire expertise, to enter the circle of exchange, and to develop their skills in order to make the best use of their capacities and resources. Even prior to the logic of a fair exchange of goods and the forms of justice appropriate to it, there exists *something which is due to man because he is man*, by reason of his lofty dignity. Inseparable from that required "something" is the possibility to survive and, at the same time, to make an active contribution to the common good of humanity.

In Third World contexts, certain objectives stated by *Rerum novarum* remain valid, and, in some cases, still constitute a goal yet to be reached, if man's work and his very being are not to be reduced to the level of a mere commodity. These objectives include a sufficient wage for the support of the family, social insurance for old age and unemployment, and adequate protection for the conditions of employment.

35. Here we find a wide range of *opportunities for commitment and effort* in the name of justice on the part of trade unions and other workers' organizations. These defend workers' rights and protect their interests as persons, while fulfilling a vital cultural role, so as to enable workers to participate more fully and honorably in the life of their nation and to assist them along the path of development.

In this sense, it is right to speak of a struggle against an economic system, if the latter is understood as a method of upholding the absolute predominance of capital, the possession of the means of production and of the land, in contrast to the free and personal nature of human work.[73] In the struggle against such a system, what is being proposed as an alternative is not the socialist system, which in fact turns out to be State capitalism, but rather *a society of free work, of enterprise and of participation*. Such a society is not directed against the market, but demands that the market be appropriately controlled by the forces of society and by the State, so as to guarantee that the basic needs of the whole of society are satisfied.

---

73. Cf. Encyclical Letter *Laborem Exercens*, 7: loc. cit., 592–594.

The Church acknowledges the legitimate *role of profit* as an indication that a business is functioning well. When a firm makes a profit, this means that productive factors have been properly employed and corresponding human needs have been duly satisfied. But profitability is not the only indicator of a firm's condition. It is possible for the financial accounts to be in order, and yet for the people—who make up the firm's most valuable asset—to be humiliated and their dignity offended. Besides being morally inadmissible, this will eventually have negative repercussions on the firm's economic efficiency. In fact, the purpose of a business firm is not simply to make a profit, but is to be found in its very existence as a *community of persons* who in various ways are endeavoring to satisfy their basic needs, and who form a particular group at the service of the whole of society. Profit is a regulator of the life of a business, but it is not the only one; *other human and moral factors* must also be considered which, in the long term, are at least equally important for the life of a business.

We have seen that it is unacceptable to say that the defeat of so-called "Real Socialism" leaves capitalism as the only model of economic organization. It is necessary to break down the barriers and monopolies which leave so many countries on the margins of development, and to provide all individuals and nations with the basic conditions which will enable them to share in development. This goal calls for programmed and responsible efforts on the part of the entire international community. Stronger nations must offer weaker ones opportunities for taking their place in international life, and the latter must learn how to use these opportunities by making the necessary efforts and sacrifices and by ensuring political and economic stability, the certainty of better prospects for the future, the improvement of workers' skills, and the training of competent business leaders who are conscious of their responsibilities.[74]

---

74. Cf. *ibid.*, 8: *loc. cit.*, 594–598.

At present, the positive efforts which have been made along these lines are being affected by the still largely unsolved problem of the foreign debt of the poorer countries. The principle that debts must be paid is certainly just. However, it is not right to demand or expect payment when the effect would be the imposition of political choices leading to hunger and despair for entire peoples. It cannot be expected that the debts which have been contracted should be paid at the price of unbearable sacrifices. In such cases it is necessary to find—as in fact is partly happening—ways to lighten, defer or even cancel the debt, compatible with the fundamental right of peoples to subsistence and progress.

36. It would now be helpful to direct our attention to the specific problems and threats emerging within the more advanced economies and which are related to their particular characteristics. In earlier stages of development, man always lived under the weight of necessity. His needs were few and were determined, to a degree, by the objective structures of his physical make-up. Economic activity was directed towards satisfying these needs. It is clear that today the problem is not only one of supplying people with a sufficient quantity of goods, but also of responding to a *demand for quality:* the quality of the goods to be produced and consumed, the quality of the services to be enjoyed, the quality of the environment and of life in general.

To call for an existence which is qualitatively more satisfying is of itself legitimate, but one cannot fail to draw attention to the new responsibilities and dangers connected with this phase of history. The manner in which new needs arise and are defined is always marked by a more or less appropriate concept of man and of his true good. A given culture reveals its overall understanding of life through the choices it makes in production and consumption. It is here that *the phenomenon of consumerism* arises. In singling out new needs and new means to meet them, one must be guided by a comprehensive picture of man which respects all the dimensions of his being and which subordinates his material and instinctive dimensions to his interior and spiritual ones. If, on the contrary, a direct appeal is made to his instincts—while ignoring in various ways the reality of the person as intelligent and free—then *consumer attitudes* and *life-styles* can be created which are objectively improper and often damaging to his physical and spiritual health. Of itself, an economic system does not possess criteria for correctly distinguishing new and higher forms of satisfying human needs from artificial new needs which hinder the formation of a mature personality. *Thus a great deal of educational and cultural work* is urgently needed, including the education of consumers in the responsible use of their power of choice, the formation of a strong sense of responsibility among producers and among people in the mass media in particular, as well as the necessary intervention by public authorities.

A striking example of artificial consumption contrary to the health and dignity of the human person, and certainly not easy to control, is the use of drugs. Widespread drug use is a sign of a serious malfunction in the social system; it also implies a materialistic and, in a certain sense, destructive "reading" of human needs. In this way the innovative capacity of a free economy is brought to a one-sided and inadequate conclusion. Drugs, as well as pornography and other forms of consumerism which exploit the frailty of the weak, tend to fill the resulting spiritual void.

It is not wrong to want to live better; what is wrong is a style of life which is presumed to be better when it is directed towards "having" rather than "being," and which wants to have more, not in order to be more but in order to spend life in enjoyment as an end in itself.[75] It is therefore necessary to create life-styles in which the quest for truth, beauty, goodness and communion with others for the sake of common growth are the factors which determine consumer choices, savings and investments. In this regard, it is not a matter of the duty of charity alone, that is, the duty to give from one's "abundance," and sometimes

---

75. Cf. Second Vatican Ecumenical Council, Pastoral Constitution on the Church in the World of Today *Gaudium et Spes*, 35; Paul VI, Encyclical Letter *Populorum Progressio*, 19: *loc. cit.*, 266f.

even out of one's needs, in order to provide what is essential for the life of a poor person. I am referring to the fact that even the decision to invest in one place rather than another, in one productive sector rather than another, is always *a moral and cultural choice*. Given the utter necessity of certain economic conditions and of political stability, the decision to invest, that is, to offer people an opportunity to make good use of their own labor, is also determined by an attitude of human sympathy and trust in Providence, which reveal the human quality of the person making such decisions.

37. Equally worrying is *the ecological question* which accompanies the problem of consumerism and which is closely connected to it. In his desire to have and to enjoy rather than to be and to grow, man consumes the resources of the earth and his own life in an excessive and disordered way. At the root of the senseless destruction of the natural environment lies an anthropological error, which unfortunately is widespread in our day. Man, who discovers his capacity to transform and in a certain sense create the world through his own work, forgets that this is always based on God's prior and original gift of the things that are. Man thinks that he can make arbitrary use of the earth, subjecting it without restraint to his will, as though it did not have its own requisites and a prior God-given purpose, which man can indeed develop but must not betray. Instead of carrying out his role as a co-operator with God in the work of creation, man sets himself up in place of God and thus ends up provoking a rebellion on the part of nature, which is more tyrannized than governed by him.[76]

In all this, one notes first the poverty or narrowness of man's outlook, motivated as he is by a desire to possess things rather than to relate them to the truth, and lacking that disinterested, unselfish and aesthetic attitude that is born of wonder in the presence of being and of the beauty which enables one to see in visible things the message of the

---

76. Cf. Encyclical Letter *Sollicitudo Rei Socialis*, 34: *loc. cit.*, 559f.; Message for the 1990 World Day of Peace: AAS 82 (1990), 147–156.

invisible God who created them. In this regard, humanity today must be conscious of its duties and obligations towards future generations.

38. In addition to the irrational destruction of the natural environment, we must also mention the more serious destruction of the *human environment*, something which is by no means receiving the attention it deserves. Although people are rightly worried—though much less than they should be—about preserving the natural habitats of the various animal species threatened with extinction, because they realize that each of these species makes its particular contribution to the balance of nature in general, too little effort is made to *safeguard the moral conditions for an authentic "human ecology."* Not only has God given the earth to man, who must use it with respect for the original good purpose for which it was given to him, but man too is God's gift to man. He must therefore respect the natural and moral structure with which he has been endowed. In this context, mention should be made of the serious problems of modern urbanization, of the need for urban planning which is concerned with how people are to live, and of the attention which should be given to a "social ecology" of work.

Man receives from God his essential dignity and with it the capacity to transcend every social order so as to move towards truth and goodness. But he is also conditioned by the social structure in which he lives, by the education he has received and by his environment. These elements can either help or hinder his living in accordance with the truth. The decisions which create a human environment can give rise to specific structures of sin which impede the full realization of those who are in any way oppressed by them. To destroy such structures and replace them with more authentic forms of living in community is a task which demands courage and patience.[77]

39. The first and fundamental structure for "human ecology" is the family, in which man receives his first formative ideas about truth and

---

77. Cf. Apostolic Exhortation *Reconciliatio et Paenitentia* (December 2, 1984), 16: AAS 77 (1985), 213–217; Pius XI, Encyclical Letter *Quadragesimo Anno*, III: *loc. cit.*, 219.

goodness, and learns what it means to love and to be loved, and thus what it actually means to be a person. Here we mean the *family founded on marriage,* in which the mutual gift of self by husband and wife creates an environment in which children can be born and develop their potentialities, become aware of their dignity and prepare to face their unique and individual destiny. But it often happens that people are discouraged from creating the proper conditions for human reproduction and are led to consider themselves and their lives as a series of sensations to be experienced rather than as a work to be accomplished. The result is a lack of freedom, which causes a person to reject a commitment to enter into a stable relationship with another person and to bring children into the world, or which leads people to consider children as one of the many "things" which an individual can have or not have, according to taste, and which compete with other possibilities.

It is necessary to go back to seeing the family as the *sanctuary of life.* The family is indeed sacred: it is the place in which life—the gift of God—can be properly welcomed and protected against the many attacks to which it is exposed, and can develop in accordance with what constitutes authentic human growth. In the face of the so-called culture of death, the family is the heart of the culture of life.

Human ingenuity seems to be directed more towards limiting, suppressing or destroying the sources of life—including recourse to abortion, which unfortunately is so widespread in the world—than towards defending and opening up the possibilities of life. The Encyclical *Sollicitudo rei socialis* denounced systematic anti-childbearing campaigns which, on the basis of a distorted view of the demographic problem and in a climate of "absolute lack of respect for the freedom of choice of the parties involved," often subject them "to intolerable pressures . . . in order to force them to submit to this new form of oppression."[78] These policies are extending their field of action by the use of new techniques,

---

78. Encyclical Letter *Sollicitudo Rei Socialis,* 25: *loc. cit.,* 544.

to the point of poisoning the lives of millions of defenseless human beings, as if in a form of "chemical warfare."

These criticisms are directed not so much against an economic system as against an ethical and cultural system. The economy in fact is only one aspect and one dimension of the whole of human activity. If economic life is absolutized, if the production and consumption of goods become the center of social life and society's only value, not subject to any other value, the reason is to be found not so much in the economic system itself as in the fact that the entire socio-cultural system, by ignoring the ethical and religious dimension, has been weakened, and ends by limiting itself to the production of goods and services alone.[79]

All of this can be summed up by repeating once more that economic freedom is only one element of human freedom. When it becomes autonomous, when man is seen more as a producer or consumer of goods than as a subject who produces and consumes in order to live, then economic freedom loses its necessary relationship to the human person and ends up by alienating and oppressing him.[80]

40. It is the task of the State to provide for the defense and preservation of common goods such as the natural and human environments, which cannot be safeguarded simply by market forces. Just as in the time of primitive capitalism the State had the duty of defending the basic rights of workers, so now, with the new capitalism, the State and all of society have the duty of *defending those collective goods* which, among others, constitute the essential framework for the legitimate pursuit of personal goals on the part of each individual.

Here we find a new limit on the market: there are collective and qualitative needs which cannot be satisfied by market mechanisms. There are important human needs which escape its logic. There are goods which by their very nature cannot and must not be bought or sold. Certainly

---

79. Cf. *ibid.*, 34: *loc. cit.*, 559f.
80. Cf. Encyclical Letter *Redemptor Hominis* (March 4, 1979), 15: AAS 71 (1979), 286–289.

the mechanisms of the market offer secure advantages: they help to utilize resources better; they promote the exchange of products; above all they give central place to the person's desires and preferences, which, in a contract, meet the desires and preferences of another person. Nevertheless, these mechanisms carry the risk of an "idolatry" of the market, an idolatry which ignores the existence of goods which by their nature are not and cannot be mere commodities.

41. Marxism criticized capitalist bourgeois societies, blaming them for the commercialization and alienation of human existence. This rebuke is of course based on a mistaken and inadequate idea of alienation, derived solely from the sphere of relationships of production and ownership, that is, giving them a materialistic foundation and moreover denying the legitimacy and positive value of market relationships even in their own sphere. Marxism thus ends up by affirming that only in a collective society can alienation be eliminated. However, the historical experience of socialist countries has sadly demonstrated that collectivism does not do away with alienation but rather increases it, adding to it a lack of basic necessities and economic inefficiency.

The historical experience of the West, for its part, shows that even if the Marxist analysis and its foundation of alienation are false, nevertheless alienation—and the loss of the authentic meaning of life—is a reality in Western societies too. This happens in consumerism, when people are ensnared in a web of false and superficial gratifications rather than being helped to experience their personhood in an authentic and concrete way. Alienation is found also in work, when it is organized so as to ensure maximum returns and profits with no concern whether the worker, through his own labor, grows or diminishes as a person, either through increased sharing in a genuinely supportive community or through increased isolation in a maze of relationships marked by destructive competitiveness and estrangement, in which he is considered only a means and not an end.

The concept of alienation needs to be led back to the Christian vision of reality, by recognizing in alienation a reversal of means and ends. When man does not recognize in himself and in others the value and grandeur of the human person, he effectively deprives himself of the possibility of benefitting from his humanity and of entering into that relationship of solidarity and communion with others for which God created him. Indeed, it is through the free gift of self that man truly finds himself.[81] This gift is made possible by the human person's essential "capacity for transcendence." Man cannot give himself to a purely human plan for reality, to an abstract ideal or to a false utopia. As a person, he can give himself to another person or to other persons, and ultimately to God, who is the author of his being and who alone can fully accept his gift.[82] A man is alienated if he refuses to transcend himself and to live the experience of self-giving and of the formation of an authentic human community oriented towards his final destiny, which is God. A society is alienated if its forms of social organization, production and consumption make it more difficult to offer this gift of self and to establish this solidarity between people.

Exploitation, at least in the forms analyzed and described by Karl Marx, has been overcome in Western society. Alienation, however, has not been overcome as it exists in various forms of exploitation, when people use one another, and when they seek an ever more refined satisfaction of their individual and secondary needs, while ignoring the principal and authentic needs which ought to regulate the manner of satisfying the other ones too.[83] A person who is concerned solely or primarily with possessing and enjoying, who is no longer able to control his instincts and passions, or to subordinate them by obedience to the truth, cannot be free: *obedience to the truth* about God and man is the first condition of freedom, making it possible for a person to order his needs and desires and to choose the means of satisfying them according to a correct scale

---

81. Cf. Second Vatican Ecumenical Council, Pastoral Constitution on the Church in the World of Today *Gaudium et Spes*, 24.
82. Cf. *ibid.*, 41.
83. Cf. *ibid.*, 26.

PART I: CHURCH TEACHING

of values, so that the ownership of things may become an occasion of growth for him. This growth can be hindered as a result of manipulation by the means of mass communication, which impose fashions and trends of opinion through carefully orchestrated repetition, without it being possible to subject to critical scrutiny the premises on which these fashions and trends are based.

42. Returning now to the initial question: can it perhaps be said that, after the failure of Communism, capitalism is the victorious social system, and that capitalism should be the goal of the countries now making efforts to rebuild their economy and society? Is this the model which ought to be proposed to the countries of the Third World which are searching for the path to true economic and civil progress?

The answer is obviously complex. If by "capitalism" is meant an economic system which recognizes the fundamental and positive role of business, the market, private property and the resulting responsibility for the means of production, as well as free human creativity in the economic sector, then the answer is certainly in the affirmative, even though it would perhaps be more appropriate to speak of a "business economy," "market economy" or simply "free economy." But if by "capitalism" is meant a system in which freedom in the economic sector is not circumscribed within a strong juridical framework which places it at the service of human freedom in its totality, and which sees it as a particular aspect of that freedom, the core of which is ethical and religious, then the reply is certainly negative.

The Marxist solution has failed, but the realities of marginalization and exploitation remain in the world, especially the Third World, as does the reality of human alienation, especially in the more advanced countries. Against these phenomena the Church strongly raises her voice. Vast multitudes are still living in conditions of great material and moral poverty. The collapse of the Communist system in so many countries certainly removes an obstacle to facing these problems in an appropriate and realistic way, but it is not enough to bring about their solution. Indeed, there is a risk that a radical capitalistic ideology could spread which refuses even to consider these problems, in the *a priori* belief that any attempt to solve them is doomed to failure, and which blindly entrusts their solution to the free development of market forces.

43. The Church has no models to present; models that are real and truly effective can only arise within the framework of different historical situations, through the efforts of all those who responsibly confront concrete problems in all their social, economic, political and cultural aspects, as these interact with one another.[84] For such a task the Church offers her social teaching as an *indispensable and ideal orientation*, a teaching which, as already mentioned, recognizes the positive value of the market and of enterprise, but which at the same time points out that these need to be oriented towards the common good. This teaching also recognizes the legitimacy of workers' efforts to obtain full respect for their dignity and to gain broader areas of participation in the life of industrial enterprises so that, while cooperating with others and under the direction of others, they can in a certain sense "work for themselves"[85] through the exercise of their intelligence and freedom.

The integral development of the human person through work does not impede but rather promotes the greater productivity and efficiency of work itself, even though it may weaken consolidated power structures. A business cannot be considered only as a "society of capital goods"; it is also a "society of persons" in which people participate in different ways and with specific responsibilities, whether they supply the necessary capital for the company's activities or take part in such activities through their labor. To achieve these goals there is still need for a broad associated workers' movement, directed towards the liberation and promotion of the whole person.

---

84. Cf. Second Vatican Ecumenical Council, Pastoral Constitution on the Church in the World of Today *Gaudium et Spes*, 36; Paul VI, Apostolic Epistle *Octogesima Adveniens*, 2–5: *loc. cit.*, 402–405.

85. Cf. Encyclical Letter *Laborem Exercens*, 15: *loc. cit.*, 616–618.

In the light of today's "new things," we have re-read *the relationship between individual or private property and the universal destination of material wealth.* Man fulfils himself by using his intelligence and freedom. In so doing he utilizes the things of this world as objects and instruments and makes them his own. The foundation of the right to private initiative and ownership is to be found in this activity. By means of his work man commits himself, not only for his own sake but also *for others* and *with others.* Each person collaborates in the work of others and for their good. Man works in order to provide for the needs of his family, his community, his nation, and ultimately all humanity.[86] Moreover, he collaborates in the work of his fellow employees, as well as in the work of suppliers and in the customers' use of goods, in a progressively expanding chain of solidarity. Ownership of the means of production, whether in industry or agriculture, is just and legitimate if it serves useful work. It becomes illegitimate, however, when it is not utilized or when it serves to impede the work of others, in an effort to gain a profit which is not the result of the overall expansion of work and the wealth of society, but rather is the result of curbing them or of illicit exploitation, speculation or the breaking of solidarity among working people.[87] Ownership of this kind has no justification, and represents an abuse in the sight of God and man.

The obligation to earn one's bread by the sweat of one's brow also presumes the right to do so. A society in which this right is systematically denied, in which economic policies do not allow workers to reach satisfactory levels of employment, cannot be justified from an ethical point of view, nor can that society attain social peace.[88] Just as the person fully realizes himself in the free gift of self, so too ownership morally justifies itself in the creation, at the proper time and in the proper way, of opportunities for work and human growth for all.

---

86. Cf. *ibid.,* 10: *loc. cit.,* 600–602.
87. *Ibid.,* 14: *loc. cit.,* 612–616.
88. Cf. *ibid.,* 18: *loc. cit.,* 622–625.

V. STATE AND CULTURE

44. Pope Leo XIII was aware of the need for a sound *theory of the State* in order to ensure the normal development of man's spiritual and temporal activities, both of which are indispensable.[89] For this reason, in one passage of *Rerum novarum* he presents the organization of society according to the three powers—legislative, executive and judicial—something which at the time represented a novelty in Church teaching.[90] Such an ordering reflects a realistic vision of man's social nature, which calls for legislation capable of protecting the freedom of all. To that end, it is preferable that each power be balanced by other powers and by other spheres of responsibility which keep it within proper bounds. This is the principle of the "rule of law," in which the law is sovereign, and not the arbitrary will of individuals.

In modern times, this concept has been opposed by totalitarianism, which, in its Marxist-Leninist form, maintains that some people, by virtue of a deeper knowledge of the laws of the development of society, or through membership of a particular class or through contact with the deeper sources of the collective consciousness, are exempt from error and can therefore arrogate to themselves the exercise of absolute power. It must be added that totalitarianism arises out of a denial of truth in the objective sense. If there is no transcendent truth, in obedience to which man achieves his full identity, then there is no sure principle for guaranteeing just relations between people. Their self-interest as a class, group or nation would inevitably set them in opposition to one another. If one does not acknowledge transcendent truth, then the force of power takes over, and each person tends to make full use of the means at his disposal in order to impose his own interests or his own opinion, with no regard for the rights of others. People are then respected only to the extent that they can be exploited for selfish ends. Thus, the root of modern totalitarianism is to be found in the denial of the transcendent

---

89. Cf. Encyclical Letter *Rerum Novarum: loc. cit.,* 126–128.
90. *Ibid.,* 121f.

dignity of the human person who, as the visible image of the invisible God, is therefore by his very nature the subject of rights which no one may violate—no individual, group, class, nation or State. Not even the majority of a social body may violate these rights, by going against the minority, by isolating, oppressing, or exploiting it, or by attempting to annihilate it.[91]

45. The culture and praxis of totalitarianism also involve a rejection of the Church. The State or the party which claims to be able to lead history towards perfect goodness, and which sets itself above all values, cannot tolerate the affirmation of an *objective criterion of good and evil* beyond the will of those in power, since such a criterion, in given circumstances, could be used to judge their actions. This explains why totalitarianism attempts to destroy the Church, or at least to reduce her to submission, making her an instrument of its own ideological apparatus.[92]

Furthermore, the totalitarian State tends to absorb within itself the nation, society, the family, religious groups and individuals themselves. In defending her own freedom, the Church is also defending the human person, who must obey God rather than men (cf. Acts 5:29), as well as defending the family, the various social organizations and nations—all of which enjoy their own spheres of autonomy and sovereignty.

46. The Church values the democratic system inasmuch as it ensures the participation of citizens in making political choices, guarantees to the governed the possibility both of electing and holding accountable those who govern them, and of replacing them through peaceful means when appropriate.[93] Thus she cannot encourage the formation of narrow ruling groups which usurp the power of the State for individual interests or for ideological ends.

---

91. Cf. Leo XIII, Encyclical Letter *Libertas Praestantissimum: loc. cit.*, 224–226.
92. Cf. Second Vatican Ecumenical Council, Pastoral Constitution on the Church in the World of Today *Gaudium et Spes*, 76.
93. Cf. *ibid.*, 29; Pius XII, Christmas Radio Message on December 24, 1944: *AAS* 37 (1945), 10–20.

Authentic democracy is possible only in a State ruled by law, and on the basis of a correct conception of the human person. It requires that the necessary conditions be present for the advancement both of the individual through education and formation in true ideals, and of the "subjectivity" of society through the creation of structures of participation and shared responsibility. Nowadays there is a tendency to claim that agnosticism and skeptical relativism are the philosophy and the basic attitude which correspond to democratic forms of political life. Those who are convinced that they know the truth and firmly adhere to it are considered unreliable from a democratic point of view, since they do not accept that truth is determined by the majority, or that it is subject to variation according to different political trends. It must be observed in this regard that if there is no ultimate truth to guide and direct political activity, then ideas and convictions can easily be manipulated for reasons of power. As history demonstrates, a democracy without values easily turns into open or thinly disguised totalitarianism.

Nor does the Church close her eyes to the danger of fanaticism or fundamentalism among those who, in the name of an ideology which purports to be scientific or religious, claim the right to impose on others their own concept of what is true and good. *Christian truth* is not of this kind. Since it is not an ideology, the Christian faith does not presume to imprison changing socio-political realities in a rigid schema, and it recognizes that human life is realized in history in conditions that are diverse and imperfect. Furthermore, in constantly reaffirming the transcendent dignity of the person, the Church's method is always that of respect for freedom.[94]

But freedom attains its full development only by accepting the truth. In a world without truth, freedom loses its foundation and man is exposed to the violence of passion and to manipulation, both open and hidden. The Christian upholds freedom and serves it, constantly offering to

---

94. Cf. Second Vatican Ecumenical Council, Declaration on Religious Freedom *Dignitatis Humanae.*

others the truth which he has known (cf. Jn 8:31–32), in accordance with the missionary nature of his vocation. While paying heed to every fragment of truth which he encounters in the life experience and in the culture of individuals and of nations, he will not fail to affirm in dialogue with others all that his faith and the correct use of reason have enabled him to understand.[95]

47. Following the collapse of Communist totalitarianism and of many other totalitarian and "national security" regimes, today we are witnessing a predominance, not without signs of opposition, of the democratic ideal, together with lively attention to and concern for human rights. But for this very reason it is necessary for peoples in the process of reforming their systems to give democracy an authentic and solid foundation through the explicit recognition of those rights.[96] Among the most important of these rights, mention must be made of the right to life, an integral part of which is the right of the child to develop in the mother's womb from the moment of conception; the right to live in a united family and in a moral environment conducive to the growth of the child's personality; the right to develop one's intelligence and freedom in seeking and knowing the truth; the right to share in the work which makes wise use of the earth's material resources, and to derive from that work the means to support oneself and one's dependents; and the right freely to establish a family, to have and to rear children through the responsible exercise of one's sexuality. In a certain sense, the source and synthesis of these rights is religious freedom, understood as the right to live in the truth of one's faith and in conformity with one's transcendent dignity as a person.[97]

Even in countries with democratic forms of government, these rights are not always fully respected. Here we are referring not only to the scandal

---

95. Cf. Encyclical Letter *Redemptoris Missio*, 11: *L'Osservatore Romano*, January 23, 1991.

96. Cf. Encyclical Letter *Redemptor Hominis*, 17: loc. cit., 270–272.

97. Cf. Message for the 1988 World Day of Peace: loc. cit., 1572–1580; Message for the 1991 World Day of Peace: *L'Osservatore Romano*, December 19, 1990; Second Vatican Ecumenical Council, Declaration on Religious Freedom *Dignitatis Humanae*, 1–2.

of abortion, but also to different aspects of a crisis within democracies themselves, which seem at times to have lost the ability to make decisions aimed at the common good. Certain demands which arise within society are sometimes not examined in accordance with criteria of justice and morality, but rather on the basis of the electoral or financial power of the groups promoting them. With time, such distortions of political conduct create distrust and apathy, with a subsequent decline in the political participation and civic spirit of the general population, which feels abused and disillusioned. As a result, there is a growing inability to situate particular interests within the framework of a coherent vision of the common good. The latter is not simply the sum total of particular interests; rather it involves an assessment and integration of those interests on the basis of a balanced hierarchy of values; ultimately, it demands a correct understanding of the dignity and the rights of the person.[98]

The Church respects *the legitimate autonomy of the democratic order* and is not entitled to express preferences for this or that institutional or constitutional solution. Her contribution to the political order is precisely her vision of the dignity of the person revealed in all its fullness in the mystery of the Incarnate Word.[99]

48. These general observations also apply to the *role of the State in the economic sector*. Economic activity, especially the activity of a market economy, cannot be conducted in an institutional, juridical or political vacuum. On the contrary, it presupposes sure guarantees of individual freedom and private property, as well as a stable currency and efficient public services. Hence the principal task of the State is to guarantee this security, so that those who work and produce can enjoy the fruits of their labors and thus feel encouraged to work efficiently and honestly. The absence of stability, together with the corruption of public officials

---

98. Second Vatican Ecumenical Council, Pastoral Constitution on the Church in the World of Today *Gaudium et Spes*, 26.

99. Cf. *ibid.*, 22.

PART I: CHURCH TEACHING

and the spread of improper sources of growing rich and of easy profits deriving from illegal or purely speculative activities, constitutes one of the chief obstacles to development and to the economic order.

Another task of the State is that of overseeing and directing the exercise of human rights in the economic sector. However, primary responsibility in this area belongs not to the State but to individuals and to the various groups and associations which make up society. The State could not directly ensure the right to work for all its citizens unless it controlled every aspect of economic life and restricted the free initiative of individuals. This does not mean, however, that the State has no competence in this domain, as was claimed by those who argued against any rules in the economic sphere. Rather, the State has a duty to sustain business activities by creating conditions which will ensure job opportunities, by stimulating those activities where they are lacking or by supporting them in moments of crisis.

The State has the further right to intervene when particular monopolies create delays or obstacles to development. In addition to the tasks of harmonizing and guiding development, in exceptional circumstances the State can also exercise *a substitute function,* when social sectors or business systems are too weak or are just getting under way, and are not equal to the task at hand. Such supplementary interventions, which are justified by urgent reasons touching the common good, must be as brief as possible, so as to avoid removing permanently from society and business systems the functions which are properly theirs, and so as to avoid enlarging excessively the sphere of State intervention to the detriment of both economic and civil freedom.

In recent years the range of such intervention has vastly expanded, to the point of creating a new type of State, the so-called "Welfare State." This has happened in some countries in order to respond better to many needs and demands, by remedying forms of poverty and deprivation unworthy of the human person. However, excesses and abuses, especially in recent years, have provoked very harsh criticisms of the Welfare State, dubbed the "Social Assistance State."

Malfunctions and defects in the Social Assistance State are the result of an inadequate understanding of the tasks proper to the State. Here again *the principle of subsidiarity* must be respected: a community of a higher order should not interfere in the internal life of a community of a lower order, depriving the latter of its functions, but rather should support it in case of need and help to coordinate its activity with the activities of the rest of society, always with a view to the common good.[100]

By intervening directly and depriving society of its responsibility, the Social Assistance State leads to a loss of human energies and an inordinate increase of public agencies, which are dominated more by bureaucratic ways of thinking than by concern for serving their clients, and which are accompanied by an enormous increase in spending. In fact, it would appear that needs are best understood and satisfied by people who are closest to them and who act as neighbors to those in need. It should be added that certain kinds of demands often call for a response which is not simply material but which is capable of perceiving the deeper human need. One thinks of the condition of refugees, immigrants, the elderly, the sick, and all those in circumstances which call for assistance, such as drug abusers: all these people can be helped effectively only by those who offer them genuine fraternal support, in addition to the necessary care.

49. Faithful to the mission received from Christ her Founder, the Church has always been present and active among the needy, offering them material assistance in ways that neither humiliate nor reduce them to mere objects of assistance, but which help them to escape their precarious situation by promoting their dignity as persons. With heartfelt gratitude to God it must be pointed out that active charity has never

---

100. Pius XI, Encyclical Letter *Quadragesimo Anno* (May 15, 1931), 1: *loc. cit.*, 184–186.

ceased to be practiced in the Church; indeed, today it is showing a manifold and gratifying increase. In this regard, special mention must be made of *volunteer work*, which the Church favors and promotes by urging everyone to cooperate in supporting and encouraging its undertakings.

In order to overcome today's widespread individualistic mentality, what is required is *a concrete commitment to solidarity and charity*, beginning in the family with the mutual support of husband and wife and the care which the different generations give to one another. In this sense the family too can be called a community of work and solidarity. It can happen, however, that when a family does decide to live up fully to its vocation, it finds itself without the necessary support from the State and without sufficient resources. It is urgent therefore to promote not only family policies, but also those social policies which have the family as their principal object, policies which assist the family by providing adequate resources and efficient means of support, both for bringing up children and for looking after the elderly, so as to avoid distancing the latter from the family unit and in order to strengthen relations between generations.[101]

Apart from the family, other intermediate communities exercise primary functions and give life to specific networks of solidarity. These develop as real communities of persons and strengthen the social fabric, preventing society from becoming an anonymous and impersonal mass, as unfortunately often happens today. It is in interrelationships on many levels that a person lives, and that society becomes more "personalized." The individual today is often suffocated between two poles represented by the State and the marketplace. At times it seems as though he exists only as a producer and consumer of goods, or as an object of State administration. People lose sight of the fact that life in society has neither the market nor the State as its final purpose, since life itself has a

---

101. Cf. Apostolic Exhortation *Familiaris Consortio* (November 22, 1981), 45: *AAS* 74 (1982), 136f.

unique value which the State and the market must serve. Man remains above all a being who seeks the truth and strives to live in that truth, deepening his understanding of it through a dialogue which involves past and future generations.[102]

50. From this open search for truth, which is renewed in every generation, *the culture of a nation* derives its character. Indeed, the heritage of values which has been received and handed down is always challenged by the young. To challenge does not necessarily mean to destroy or reject *a priori*, but above all to put these values to the test in one's own life, and through this existential verification to make them more real, relevant and personal, distinguishing the valid elements in the tradition from false and erroneous ones, or from obsolete forms which can be usefully replaced by others more suited to the times.

In this context, it is appropriate *to recall that evangelization too plays a role in the culture of the various nations*, sustaining culture in its progress towards the truth, and assisting in the work of its purification and enrichment.[103] However, when a culture becomes inward looking, and tries to perpetuate obsolete ways of living by rejecting any exchange or debate with regard to the truth about man, then it becomes sterile and is heading for decadence.

51. All human activity takes place within a culture and interacts with culture. For an adequate formation of a culture, the involvement of the whole man is required, whereby he exercises his creativity, intelligence, and knowledge of the world and of people. Furthermore, he displays his capacity for self-control, personal sacrifice, solidarity and readiness to promote the common good. Thus the first and most important task is accomplished within man's heart. The way in which he is involved in building his own future depends on the understanding he has of himself and of his own destiny. It is on this level that *the Church's specific and*

---

102. Cf. Discourse to UNESCO (June 2, 1980): AAS 72 (1980), 735–752.
103. Cf. Encyclical Letter *Redemptoris Missio*, 39; 52 *L'Osservatore Romano*, January 23, 1991.

decisive contribution to true culture is to be found. The Church promotes those aspects of human behavior which favor a true culture of peace, as opposed to models in which the individual is lost in the crowd, in which the role of his initiative and freedom is neglected, and in which his greatness is posited in the arts of conflict and war. The Church renders this service to human society *by preaching the truth about the creation of the world,* which God has placed in human hands so that people may make it fruitful and more perfect through their work; and *by preaching the truth about the Redemption,* whereby the Son of God has saved mankind and at the same time has united all people, making them responsible for one another. Sacred Scripture continually speaks to us of an active commitment to our neighbor and demands of us a shared responsibility for all of humanity.

This duty is not limited to one's own family, nation or State, but extends progressively to all mankind, since no one can consider himself extraneous or indifferent to the lot of another member of the human family. No one can say that he is not responsible for the well-being of his brother or sister (cf. Gen 4:9; Lk 10:29–37; Mt 25:31–46). Attentive and pressing concern for one's neighbor in a moment of need—made easier today because of the new means of communication which have brought people closer together—is especially important with regard to the search for ways to resolve international conflicts other than by war. It is not hard to see that the terrifying power of the means of destruction—to which even medium and small-sized countries have access—and the ever closer links between the peoples of the whole world make it very difficult or practically impossible to limit the consequences of a conflict.

52. Pope Benedict XV and his Successors clearly understood this danger.[104] I myself, on the occasion of the recent tragic war in the Persian Gulf, repeated the cry: "Never again war!" No, never again war, which

---

104. Cf. Benedict XV, Exhortation *Ubi Primum* (September 8, 1914): AAS 6 (1914), 501f.; Pius XI, Radio Message to the Catholic Faithful and to the entire world (September 29, 1938): AAS 30 (1938), 309f.; Pius XII, Radio Message to the entire world (August 24, 1939): AAS 31 (1939), 333–335; John XXIII, Encyclical Letter *Pacem in Terris,* III: *loc. cit.,* 285–289; Paul VI, Discourse at the United Nations (October 4, 1965): AAS 57 (1965), 877–885.

destroys the lives of innocent people, teaches how to kill, throws into upheaval even the lives of those who do the killing and leaves behind a trail of resentment and hatred, thus making it all the more difficult to find a just solution of the very problems which provoked the war. Just as the time has finally come when in individual States a system of private vendetta and reprisal has given way to the rule of law, so too a similar step forward is now urgently needed in the international community. Furthermore, it must not be forgotten that at the root of war there are usually real and serious grievances: injustices suffered, legitimate aspirations frustrated, poverty, and the exploitation of multitudes of desperate people who see no real possibility of improving their lot by peaceful means.

For this reason, another name for peace is *development*.[105] Just as there is a collective responsibility for avoiding war, so too there is a collective responsibility for promoting development. Just as within individual societies it is possible and right to organize a solid economy which will direct the functioning of the market to the common good, so too there is a similar need for adequate interventions on the international level. For this to happen, *a great effort must be made to enhance mutual understanding and knowledge, and to increase the sensitivity of consciences.* This is the culture which is hoped for, one which fosters trust in the human potential of the poor, and consequently in their ability to improve their condition through work or to make a positive contribution to economic prosperity. But to accomplish this, the poor—be they individuals or nations—need to be provided with realistic opportunities. Creating such conditions calls for a *concerted worldwide effort to promote development,* an effort which also involves sacrificing the positions of income and of power enjoyed by the more developed economies.[106]

This may mean making important changes in established life-styles, in order to limit the waste of environmental and human resources, thus enabling every individual and all the peoples of the earth to have a

---

105. Cf. Paul VI, Encyclical Letter *Populorum Progressio*, 76–77: *loc. cit.*, 294f.
106. Cf. Apostolic Exhortation *Familiaris Consortio*, 48: *loc. cit.*, 139f.

sufficient share of those resources. In addition, the new material and spiritual resources must be utilized which are the result of the work and culture of peoples who today are on the margins of the international community, so as to obtain an overall human enrichment of the family of nations.

VI. MAN IS THE WAY OF THE CHURCH

53. Faced with the poverty of the working class, Pope Leo XIII wrote: "We approach this subject with confidence, and in the exercise of the rights which manifestly pertain to us . . . By keeping silence we would seem to neglect the duty incumbent on us."[107] During the last hundred years the Church has repeatedly expressed her thinking, while closely following the continuing development of the social question. She has certainly not done this in order to recover former privileges or to impose her own vision. Her sole purpose has been *care and responsibility* for man, who has been entrusted to her by Christ himself: for *this man,* whom, as the Second Vatican Council recalls, is the only creature on earth which God willed for its own sake, and for which God has his plan, that is, a share in eternal salvation. We are not dealing here with man in the "abstract," but with the real, "concrete," "historical" man. We are dealing with *each individual,* since each one is included in the mystery of Redemption, and through this mystery Christ has united himself with each one for ever.[108] It follows that the Church cannot abandon man, and that "*this man* is the primary route that the Church must travel in fulfilling her mission . . . the way traced out by Christ himself, the way that leads invariably through the mystery of the Incarnation and the Redemption."[109]

This, and this alone, is the principle which inspires the Church's social doctrine. The Church has gradually developed that doctrine in

---

107. Encyclical Letter *Rerum Novarum: loc. cit.,* 107.
108. Cf. Encyclical Letter *Redemptor Hominis,* 13: *loc. cit.,* 283.
109. *Ibid.,* 14: *loc. cit.,* 284f.

a systematic way, above all in the century that has followed the date we are commemorating, precisely because the horizon of the Church's whole wealth of doctrine is man in his concrete reality as sinful and righteous.

54. Today, the Church's social doctrine focuses especially *on man* as he is involved in a complex network of relationships within modern societies. The human sciences and philosophy are helpful for interpreting *man's central place within society* and for enabling him to understand himself better as a "social being." However, man's true identity is only fully revealed to him through faith, and it is precisely from faith that the Church's social teaching begins. While drawing upon all the contributions made by the sciences and philosophy, her social teaching is aimed at helping man on the path of salvation.

The Encyclical *Rerum novarum* can be read as a valid contribution to socio-economic analysis at the end of the nineteenth century, but its specific value derives from the fact that it is a document of the Magisterium and is fully a part of the Church's evangelizing mission, together with many other documents of this nature. Thus the Church's *social teaching* is itself a valid *instrument of evangelization.* As such, it proclaims God and his mystery of salvation in Christ to every human being, and for that very reason reveals man to himself. In this light, and only in this light, does it concern itself with everything else: the human rights of the individual, and in particular of the "working class," the family and education, the duties of the State, the ordering of national and international society, economic life, culture, war and peace, and respect for life from the moment of conception until death.

55. The Church receives "the meaning of man" from Divine Revelation. "In order to know man, authentic man, man in his fullness, one must know God," said Pope Paul VI, and he went on to quote Saint Catherine

of Siena, who, in prayer, expressed the same idea: "In your nature, O eternal Godhead, I shall know my own nature."[110]

Christian anthropology therefore is really a chapter of theology, and for this reason, the Church's social doctrine, by its concern for man and by its interest in him and in the way he conducts himself in the world, "belongs to the field . . . of theology and particularly of moral theology."[111] The theological dimension is needed both for interpreting and solving present-day problems in human society. It is worth noting that this is true in contrast both to the "atheistic" solution, which deprives man of one of his basic dimensions, namely the spiritual one, and to permissive and consumerist solutions, which under various pretexts seek to convince man that he is free from every law and from God himself, thus imprisoning him within a selfishness which ultimately harms both him and others.

When the Church proclaims God's salvation *to man*, when she offers and communicates the life of God through the sacraments, when she gives direction to human life through the commandments of love of God and neighbor, she contributes to the enrichment of human dignity. But just as the Church can never abandon her religious and transcendent mission on behalf of man, so too she is aware that today her activity meets with particular difficulties and obstacles. That is why she devotes herself with ever new energies and methods to an evangelization which promotes the whole human being. Even on the eve of the third Millennium she continues to be "a sign and safeguard of the transcendence of the human person,"[112] as indeed she has always sought to be from the beginning of her existence, walking together with man through history. The Encyclical *Rerum novarum* itself is a significant sign of this.

---

110. Paul VI, Homily at the Final Public Session of the Second Vatican Ecumenical Council (December 7, 1965): AAS 58 (1966), 58.

111. Encyclical Letter *Sollicitudo Rei Socialis*, 41: *loc. cit.*, 571.

112. Second Vatican Ecumenical Council, Pastoral Constitution on the Church in the World of Today *Gaudium et Spes*, 76; cf. John Paul II, Encyclical Letter *Redemptor Hominis*, 13: *loc. cit.*, 283.

56. On the hundredth anniversary of that Encyclical I wish to thank all those who have devoted themselves to studying, expounding and making better known Christian social teaching. To this end, the cooperation of the local Churches is indispensable, and I would hope that the present anniversary will be a source of fresh enthusiasm for studying, spreading and applying that teaching in various contexts.

In particular, I wish this teaching to be made known and applied in the countries which, following the collapse of "Real Socialism," are experiencing a serious lack of direction in the work of rebuilding. The Western countries, in turn, run the risk of seeing this collapse as a one-sided victory of their own economic system, and thereby failing to make necessary corrections in that system. Meanwhile, the countries of the Third World are experiencing more than ever the tragedy of underdevelopment, which is becoming more serious with each passing day.

After formulating principles and guidelines for the solution of the worker question, Pope Leo XIII made this incisive statement: "Everyone should put his hand to the work which falls to his share, and that at once and straightway, lest the evil which is already so great become through delay absolutely beyond remedy," and he added, "in regard to the Church, her cooperation will never be found lacking."[113]

57. As far as the Church is concerned, the social message of the Gospel must not be considered a theory, but above all else a basis and a motivation for action. Inspired by this message, some of the first Christians distributed their goods to the poor, bearing witness to the fact that, despite different social origins, it was possible for people to live together in peace and harmony. Through the power of the Gospel, down the centuries monks tilled the land, men and women Religious founded hospitals and shelters for the poor, Confraternities as well as individual men and women of all states of life devoted themselves to the needy and to those on the margins of society, convinced as they were that Christ's

---

113. Encyclical Letter *Rerum Novarum*: *loc. cit.*, 143.

words "as you did it to one of the least of these my brethren, you did it to me" (Mt 25:40) were not intended to remain a pious wish, but were meant to become a concrete life commitment.

Today more than ever, the Church is aware that her social message will gain credibility more immediately from the *witness of actions* than as a result of its internal logic and consistency. This awareness is also a source of her preferential option for the poor, which is never exclusive or discriminatory towards other groups. This option is not limited to material poverty, since it is well known that there are many other forms of poverty, especially in modern society—not only economic but cultural and spiritual poverty as well. The Church's love for the poor, which is essential for her and a part of her constant tradition, impels her to give attention to a world in which poverty is threatening to assume massive proportions in spite of technological and economic progress. In the countries of the West, different forms of poverty are being experienced by groups which live on the margins of society, by the elderly and the sick, by the victims of consumerism, and even more immediately by so many refugees and migrants. In the developing countries, tragic crises loom on the horizon unless internationally coordinated measures are taken before it is too late.

58. Love for others, and in the first place love for the poor, in whom the Church sees Christ himself, is made concrete in the *promotion of justice*. Justice will never be fully attained unless people see in the poor person, who is asking for help in order to survive, not an annoyance or a burden, but an opportunity for showing kindness and a chance for greater enrichment. Only such an awareness can give the courage needed to face the risk and the change involved in every authentic attempt to come to the aid of another. It is not merely a matter of "giving from one's surplus," but of helping entire peoples which are presently excluded or marginalized to enter into the sphere of economic and human development. For this to happen, it is not enough to draw

on the surplus goods which in fact our world abundantly produces; it requires above all a change of life-styles, of models of production and consumption, and of the established structures of power which today govern societies. Nor is it a matter of eliminating instruments of social organization which have proved useful, but rather of orienting them according to an adequate notion of the common good in relation to the whole human family. Today we are facing the so-called "globalization" of the economy, a phenomenon which is not to be dismissed, since it can create unusual opportunities for greater prosperity. There is a growing feeling, however, that this increasing internationalization of the economy ought to be accompanied by effective international agencies which will oversee and direct the economy to the common good, something that an individual State, even if it were the most powerful on earth, would not be in a position to do. In order to achieve this result, it is necessary that there be increased coordination among the more powerful countries, and that in international agencies the interests of the whole human family be equally represented. It is also necessary that in evaluating the consequences of their decisions, these agencies always give sufficient consideration to peoples and countries which have little weight in the international market, but which are burdened by the most acute and desperate needs, and are thus more dependent on support for their development. Much remains to be done in this area.

59. Therefore, in order that the demands of justice may be met, and attempts to achieve this goal may succeed, what is needed is *the gift of grace, a gift* which comes from God. Grace, in cooperation with human freedom, constitutes that mysterious presence of God in history which is Providence.

The newness which is experienced in following Christ demands to be communicated to other people in their concrete difficulties, struggles, problems and challenges, so that these can then be illuminated and made more human in the light of faith. Faith not only helps people to find solutions; it makes even situations of suffering humanly bearable, so that in these situations people will not become lost or forget their dignity and vocation.

In addition, the Church's social teaching has an important interdisciplinary dimension. In order better to incarnate the one truth about man in different and constantly changing social, economic and political contexts, this teaching enters into dialogue with the various disciplines concerned with man. It assimilates what these disciplines have to contribute, and helps them to open themselves to a broader horizon, aimed at serving the individual person who is acknowledged and loved in the fullness of his or her vocation.

Parallel with the interdisciplinary aspect, mention should also be made of the practical and as it were experiential dimension of this teaching, which is to be found at the crossroads where Christian life and conscience come into contact with the real world. This teaching is seen in the efforts of individuals, families, people involved in cultural and social life, as well as politicians and statesmen to give it a concrete form and application in history.

60. In proclaiming the principles for a solution of the worker question, Pope Leo XIII wrote: "This most serious question demands the attention and the efforts of others."[114] He was convinced that the grave problems caused by industrial society could be solved only by cooperation between all forces. This affirmation has become a permanent element of the Church's social teaching, and also explains why Pope John XXIII addressed his Encyclical on peace to "all people of good will."

Pope Leo, however, acknowledged with sorrow that the ideologies of his time, especially Liberalism and Marxism, rejected such cooperation. Since then, many things have changed, especially in recent years. The world today is ever more aware that solving serious national and

---

114. *Ibid.*, 107.

international problems is not just a matter of economic production or of juridical or social organization, but also calls for specific ethical and religious values, as well as changes of mentality, behavior and structures. The Church feels a particular responsibility to offer this contribution and, as I have written in the Encyclical *Sollicitudo rei socialis*, there is a reasonable hope that the many people who profess no religion will also contribute to providing the social question with the necessary ethical foundation.[115]

In that same Encyclical I also addressed an appeal to the Christian Churches and to all the great world religions, inviting them to offer the unanimous witness of our common convictions regarding the dignity of man, created by God.[116] In fact I am convinced that the various religions, now and in the future, will have a preeminent role in preserving peace and in building a society worthy of man.

Indeed, openness to dialogue and to cooperation is required of all people of good will, and in particular of individuals and groups with specific responsibilities in the areas of politics, economics and social life, at both the national and international levels.

61. At the beginning of industrialized society, it was "a yoke little better than that of slavery itself" which led my Predecessor to speak out *in defense of man*. Over the past hundred years the Church has remained faithful to this duty. Indeed, she intervened in the turbulent period of class struggle after the First World War in order to defend man from economic exploitation and from the tyranny of the totalitarian systems. After the Second World War, she put the dignity of the person at the center of her social messages, insisting that material goods were meant for all, and that the social order ought to be free of oppression and based on a spirit of cooperation and solidarity. The Church has constantly repeated that the person and society need not only material goods but

---

115. Cf. Encyclical Letter *Sollicitudo Rei Socialis*, 38: *loc. cit.*, 564–566.
116. *Ibid.*, 47: *loc. cit.*, 582.

spiritual and religious values as well. Furthermore, as she has become more aware of the fact that too many people live, not in the prosperity of the Western world, but in the poverty of the developing countries amid conditions which are still "a yoke little better than that of slavery itself," she has felt and continues to feel obliged to denounce this fact with absolute clarity and frankness, although she knows that her call will not always win favor with everyone.

One hundred years after the publication of *Rerum novarum*, the Church finds herself still facing "new things" and new challenges. The centenary celebration should therefore confirm the commitment of all people of good will and of believers in particular.

62. The present Encyclical has looked at the past, but above all it is directed to the future. Like *Rerum novarum*, it comes almost at the threshold of a new century, and its intention, with God's help, is to prepare for that moment.

In every age the true and perennial "newness of things" comes from the infinite power of God, who says: "Behold, I make all things new" (Rev 21:5). These words refer to the fulfilment of history, when Christ "delivers the Kingdom to God the Father . . . that God may be everything to everyone" (1 Cor 15:24, 28). But the Christian well knows that the newness which we await in its fullness at the Lord's second coming has been present since the creation of the world, and in a special way since the time when God became man in Jesus Christ and brought about a "new creation" with him and through him (2 Cor 5:17; Gal 6:15).

In concluding this Encyclical I again give thanks to Almighty God, who has granted his Church the light and strength to accompany humanity on its earthly journey towards its eternal destiny. In the Third Millennium too, the Church will be faithful *in making man's way her own*, knowing that she does not walk alone, but with Christ her Lord. It is Christ who made man's way his own, and who guides him, even when he is unaware of it.

Mary, the Mother of the Redeemer, constantly remained beside Christ in his journey towards the human family and in its midst, and she goes before the Church on the pilgrimage of faith. May her maternal intercession accompany humanity towards the next Millennium, in fidelity to him who "is the same yesterday and today and for ever" (cf. Heb 13:8), Jesus Christ our Lord, in whose name I cordially impart my blessing to all.

Given in Rome, at Saint Peter's, on 1 May, the Memorial of Saint Joseph the Worker, in the year 1991, the thirteenth of my Pontificate.

JOHN PAUL II

CHAPTER 12

Evangelium Vitae: On the Value and Inviolability of Human Life

(Excerpt)

Pope St. John Paul II

March 25, 1995

Latin for "the Gospel of life," Pope St. John Paul II's encyclical speaks of the need to build a "culture of life and love"—founded on the "value and inviolability" of each human life—to combat the "culture of death."

CHAPTER IV: YOU DID IT TO ME

For a New Culture of Human Life

"You are God's own people, that you may declare the wonderful deeds of him who called you out of darkness into his marvelous light" (1 Pet 2:9): a people of life and for life

78. The Church has received the Gospel as a proclamation and a source of joy and salvation. She has received it as a gift from Jesus, sent by the Father "to preach good news to the poor" (Lk 4:18). She has received it through the Apostles, sent by Christ to the whole world (cf. Mk 16:15; Mt 28:19–20). Born from this evangelizing activity, the Church hears every day the echo of Saint Paul's words of warning: "Woe to me if I do not preach the Gospel!" (1 Cor 9:16). As Paul VI wrote, "evangelization

is the grace and vocation proper to the Church, her deepest identity. She exists in order to evangelize."[1]

Evangelization is an all-embracing, progressive activity through which the Church participates in the prophetic, priestly and royal mission of the Lord Jesus. It is therefore inextricably linked to preaching, celebration and the service of charity. Evangelization is a profoundly ecclesial act, which calls all the various workers of the Gospel to action, according to their individual charisms and ministry.

This is also the case with regard to the proclamation of the Gospel of life, an integral part of that Gospel which is Jesus Christ himself. We are at the service of this Gospel, sustained by the awareness that we have received it as a gift and are sent to preach it to all humanity, "to the ends of the earth" (Acts 1:8). With humility and gratitude we know that we are the people of life and for life, and this is how we present ourselves to everyone.

79. We are the people of life because God, in his unconditional love, has given us the Gospel of life and by this same Gospel we have been transformed and saved. We have been ransomed by the "Author of life" (Acts 3:15) at the price of his precious blood (cf. 1 Cor 6:20; 7:23; 1 Pet 1:19). Through the waters of Baptism we have been made a part of him (cf. Rom 6:4–5; Col 2:12), as branches which draw nourishment and fruitfulness from the one tree (cf. Jn 15:5). Interiorly renewed by the grace of the Spirit, "who is the Lord and giver of life," we have become a people for life and we are called to act accordingly.

We have been sent. For us, being at the service of life is not a boast but rather a duty, born of our awareness of being "God's own people, that we may declare the wonderful deeds of him who called us out of darkness into his marvelous light" (cf. 1 Pet 2:9). On our journey we are guided and sustained by the law of love: a love which has as its source

---

1. Apostolic Exhortation *Evangelii Nuntiandi* (8 December 1975), 14: AAS 68 (1976), 13.

and model the Son of God made man, who "by dying gave life to the world."[2]

We have been sent as a people. Everyone has an obligation to be at the service of life. This is a properly "ecclesial" responsibility, which requires concerted and generous action by all the members and by all sectors of the Christian community. This community commitment does not however eliminate or lessen the responsibility of each individual, called by the Lord to "become the neighbour" of everyone: "Go and do likewise" (Lk 10:37).

Together we all sense our duty to preach the Gospel of life, to celebrate it in the Liturgy and in our whole existence, and to serve it with the various programmes and structures which support and promote life.

"That which we have seen and heard we proclaim also to you" (1 Jn 1:3): proclaiming the Gospel of life

80. "That which was from the beginning, which we have heard, which we have seen with our eyes, which we have looked upon and touched with our hands, concerning the word of life . . . we proclaim also to you, so that you may have fellowship with us" (1 Jn 1:1, 3). Jesus is the only Gospel: we have nothing further to say or any other witness to bear.

To proclaim Jesus is itself to proclaim life. For Jesus is "the word of life" (1 Jn 1:1). In him "life was made manifest" (1 Jn 1:2); he himself is "the eternal life which was with the Father and was made manifest to us" (1 Jn 1:2). By the gift of the Spirit, this same life has been bestowed on us. It is in being destined to life in its fullness, to "eternal life," that every person's earthly life acquires its full meaning.

Enlightened by this Gospel of life, we feel a need to proclaim it and to bear witness to it in all its marvelous newness. Since it is one with Jesus

---

2. Cf. *Roman Missal*, prayer of the celebrant before communion.

himself, who makes all things new[3] and conquers the "oldness" which comes from sin and leads to death,[4] this Gospel exceeds every human expectation and reveals the sublime heights to which the dignity of the human person is raised through grace. This is how Saint Gregory of Nyssa understands it: "Man, as a being, is of no account; he is dust, grass, vanity. But once he is adopted by the God of the universe as a son, he becomes part of the family of that Being, whose excellence and greatness no one can see, hear or understand. What words, thoughts or flight of the spirit can praise the superabundance of this grace? Man surpasses his nature: mortal, he becomes immortal; perishable, he becomes imperishable; fleeting, he becomes eternal; human, he becomes divine."[5]

Gratitude and joy at the incomparable dignity of man impel us to share this message with everyone: "that which we have seen and heard we proclaim also to you, so that you may have fellowship with us" (1 Jn 1:3). We need to bring the Gospel of life to the heart of every man and woman and to make it penetrate every part of society.

81. This involves above all proclaiming the core of this Gospel. It is the proclamation of a living God who is close to us, who calls us to profound communion with himself and awakens in us the certain hope of eternal life. It is the affirmation of the inseparable connection between the person, his life and his bodiliness. It is the presentation of human life as a life of relationship, a gift of God, the fruit and sign of his love. It is the proclamation that Jesus has a unique relationship with every person, which enables us to see in every human face the face of Christ. It is the call for a "sincere gift of self" as the fullest way to realize our personal freedom.

---

3. Cf. Saint Irenaeus: "Omnem novitatem attulit, semetipsum afferens, qui fuerat annuntiatus," *Adversus Haereses*: IV, 34, 1: SCh 100/2, 846–847.
4. Cf. Saint Thomas Aquinas, "Peccator inveterascit, recedens a novitate Christi," *In Psalmos Davidis Lectura*: 6, 5.
5. *De Beatitudinibus*, Oratio VII: PG 44, 1280.

It also involves making clear all the consequences of this Gospel. These can be summed up as follows: human life, as a gift of God, is sacred and inviolable. For this reason procured abortion and euthanasia are absolutely unacceptable. Not only must human life not be taken, but it must be protected with loving concern. The meaning of life is found in giving and receiving love, and in this light human sexuality and procreation reach their true and full significance. Love also gives meaning to suffering and death; despite the mystery which surrounds them, they can become saving events. Respect for life requires that science and technology should always be at the service of man and his integral development. Society as a whole must respect, defend and promote the dignity of every human person, at every moment and in every condition of that person's life.

82. To be truly a people at the service of life we must propose these truths constantly and courageously from the very first proclamation of the Gospel, and thereafter in catechesis, in the various forms of preaching, in personal dialogue and in all educational activity. Teachers, catechists and theologians have the task of emphasizing the anthropological reasons upon which respect for every human life is based. In this way, by making the newness of the Gospel of life shine forth, we can also help everyone discover in the light of reason and of personal experience how the Christian message fully reveals what man is and the meaning of his being and existence. We shall find important points of contact and dialogue also with non-believers, in our common commitment to the establishment of a new culture of life.

Faced with so many opposing points of view, and a widespread rejection of sound doctrine concerning human life, we can feel that Paul's entreaty to Timothy is also addressed to us: "Preach the word, be urgent in season and out of season, convince, rebuke, and exhort, be unfailing in patience and in teaching" (2 Tim 4:2). This exhortation should resound with special force in the hearts of those members of the Church who directly share, in different ways, in her mission as "teacher" of the truth. May it resound above all for us who are Bishops: we are the first ones called to be untiring preachers of the Gospel of life. We are also entrusted with the task of ensuring that the doctrine which is once again being set forth in this Encyclical is faithfully handed on in its integrity. We must use appropriate means to defend the faithful from all teaching which is contrary to it. We need to make sure that in theological faculties, seminaries and Catholic institutions sound doctrine is taught, explained and more fully investigated.[6] May Paul's exhortation strike a chord in all theologians, pastors, teachers and in all those responsible for catechesis and the formation of consciences. Aware of their specific role, may they never be so grievously irresponsible as to betray the truth and their own mission by proposing personal ideas contrary to the Gospel of life as faithfully presented and interpreted by the Magisterium.

In the proclamation of this Gospel, we must not fear hostility or unpopularity, and we must refuse any compromise or ambiguity which might conform us to the world's way of thinking (cf. Rom 12:2). We must be in the world but not of the world (cf. Jn 15:19; 17:16), drawing our strength from Christ, who by his Death and Resurrection has overcome the world (cf. Jn 16:33).

"I give you thanks that I am fearfully, wonderfully made" (Ps 139:14): celebrating the Gospel of life

83. Because we have been sent into the world as a "people for life," our proclamation must also become a genuine celebration of the Gospel of life. This celebration, with the evocative power of its gestures, symbols and rites, should become a precious and significant setting in which the beauty and grandeur of this Gospel is handed on.

---

6. Cf. John Paul II, Encyclical Letter *Veritatis Splendor* (6 August 1993), 116: AAS 85 (1993), 1224.

For this to happen, we need first of all to foster, in ourselves and in others, a contemplative outlook.[7] Such an outlook arises from faith in the God of life, who has created every individual as a "wonder" (cf. Ps 139:14). It is the outlook of those who see life in its deeper meaning, who grasp its utter gratuitousness, its beauty and its invitation to freedom and responsibility. It is the outlook of those who do not presume to take possession of reality but instead accept it as a gift, discovering in all things the reflection of the Creator and seeing in every person his living image (cf. Gen 1:27; Ps 8:5). This outlook does not give in to discouragement when confronted by those who are sick, suffering, outcast or at death's door. Instead, in all these situations it feels challenged to find meaning, and precisely in these circumstances it is open to perceiving in the face of every person a call to encounter, dialogue and solidarity.

It is time for all of us to adopt this outlook, and with deep religious awe to rediscover the ability to revere and honor every person, as Paul VI invited us to do in one of his first Christmas messages.[8] Inspired by this contemplative outlook, the new people of the redeemed cannot but respond with songs of joy, praise and thanksgiving for the priceless gift of life, for the mystery of every individual's call to share through Christ in the life of grace and in an existence of unending communion with God our Creator and Father.

84. To celebrate the Gospel of life means to celebrate the God of life, the God who gives life: "We must celebrate Eternal Life, from which every other life proceeds. From this, in proportion to its capacities, every being which in any way participates in life, receives life. This Divine Life, which is above every other life, gives and preserves life. Every life and every living movement proceed from this Life which transcends all life and every principle of life. It is to this that souls owe their incorruptibility; and because of this all animals and plants live, which receive only the faintest glimmer of life. To men, beings made of spirit and matter,

---

7. Cf. John Paul II, Encyclical Letter *Centesimus Annus* (1 May 1991), 37: AAS 83 (1991), 840.
8. Cf. Message for Christmas 1967: AAS 60 (1968), 40.

Life grants life. Even if we should abandon Life, because of its overflowing love for man, it converts us and calls us back to itself. Not only this: it promises to bring us, soul and body, to perfect life, to immortality. It is too little to say that this Life is alive: it is the Principle of life, the Cause and sole Wellspring of life. Every living thing must contemplate it and give it praise: it is Life which overflows with life."[9]

Like the Psalmist, we too, in our daily prayer as individuals and as a community, praise and bless God our Father, who knitted us together in our mother's womb, and saw and loved us while we were still without form (cf. Ps 139:13, 15–16). We exclaim with overwhelming joy: "I give you thanks that I am fearfully, wonderfully made; wonderful are your works. You know me through and through" (Ps 139:14). Indeed, "despite its hardships, its hidden mysteries, its suffering and its inevitable frailty, this mortal life is a most beautiful thing, a marvel ever new and moving, an event worthy of being exalted in joy and glory."[10] Moreover, man and his life appear to us not only as one of the greatest marvels of creation: for God has granted to man a dignity which is near to divine (Ps 8:5–6). In every child which is born and in every person who lives or dies we see the image of God's glory. We celebrate this glory in every human being, a sign of the living God, an icon of Jesus Christ.

We are called to express wonder and gratitude for the gift of life and to welcome, savour and share the Gospel of life not only in our personal and community prayer, but above all in the celebrations of the liturgical year. Particularly important in this regard are the Sacraments, the efficacious signs of the presence and saving action of the Lord Jesus in Christian life. The Sacraments make us sharers in divine life, and provide the spiritual strength necessary to experience life, suffering and death in their fullest meaning. Thanks to a genuine rediscovery and a better appreciation of the significance of these rites, our liturgical celebrations, especially celebrations of the Sacraments, will be ever more

---

9. Pseudo-Dionysius the Areopagite, *On the Divine Names*, 6, 1–3: PG 3, 856–857.
10. Paul VI, *Pensiero alla Morte*, Istituto Paolo VI, Brescia 1988, 24.

capable of expressing the full truth about birth, life, suffering and death, and will help us to live these moments as a participation in the Paschal Mystery of the Crucified and Risen Christ.

85. In celebrating the Gospel of life we also need to appreciate and make good use of the wealth of gestures and symbols present in the traditions and customs of different cultures and peoples. There are special times and ways in which the peoples of different nations and cultures express joy for a newborn life, respect for and protection of individual human lives, care for the suffering or needy, closeness to the elderly and the dying, participation in the sorrow of those who mourn, and hope and desire for immortality.

In view of this and following the suggestion made by the Cardinals in the Consistory of 1991, I propose that a Day for Life be celebrated each year in every country, as already established by some Episcopal Conferences. The celebration of this Day should be planned and carried out with the active participation of all sectors of the local Church. Its primary purpose should be to foster in individual consciences, in families, in the Church and in civil society a recognition of the meaning and value of human life at every stage and in every condition. Particular attention should be drawn to the seriousness of abortion and euthanasia, without neglecting other aspects of life which from time to time deserve to be given careful consideration, as occasion and circumstances demand.

86. As part of the spiritual worship acceptable to God (cf. Rom 12:1), the Gospel of life is to be celebrated above all in daily living, which should be filled with self-giving love for others. In this way, our lives will become a genuine and responsible acceptance of the gift of life and a heartfelt song of praise and gratitude to God who has given us this gift. This is already happening in the many different acts of selfless generosity, often humble and hidden, carried out by men and women, children and adults, the young and the old, the healthy and the sick.

It is in this context, so humanly rich and filled with love, that heroic actions too are born. These are the most solemn celebration of the Gospel of life, for they proclaim it by the total gift of self. They are the radiant manifestation of the highest degree of love, which is to give one's life for the person loved (cf. Jn 15:13). They are a sharing in the mystery of the Cross, in which Jesus reveals the value of every person, and how life attains its fullness in the sincere gift of self. Over and above such outstanding moments, there is an everyday heroism, made up of gestures of sharing, big or small, which build up an authentic culture of life. A particularly praiseworthy example of such gestures is the donation of organs, performed in an ethically acceptable manner, with a view to offering a chance of health and even of life itself to the sick who sometimes have no other hope.

Part of this daily heroism is also the silent but effective and eloquent witness of all those "brave mothers who devote themselves to their own family without reserve, who suffer in giving birth to their children and who are ready to make any effort, to face any sacrifice, in order to pass on to them the best of themselves."[11] In living out their mission "these heroic women do not always find support in the world around them. On the contrary, the cultural models frequently promoted and broadcast by the media do not encourage motherhood. In the name of progress and modernity the values of fidelity, chastity, sacrifice, to which a host of Christian wives and mothers have borne and continue to bear outstanding witness, are presented as obsolete. . . . We thank you, heroic mothers, for your invincible love! We thank you for your intrepid trust in God and in his love. We thank you for the sacrifice of your life. . . . In the Paschal Mystery, Christ restores to you the gift you gave him. Indeed, he has the power to give you back the life you gave him as an offering."[12]

---

11. John Paul II, Homily for the Beatification of Isidore Bakanja, Elisabetta Canori Mora and Gianna Beretta Molla (24 April 1994): *L'Osservatore Romano*, 25–26 April 1994, 5.
12. *Ibid.*

"What does it profit, my brethren, if a man says he has faith but has not works?" (Jas 2:14): serving the Gospel of life

87. By virtue of our sharing in Christ's royal mission, our support and promotion of human life must be accomplished through the service of charity, which finds expression in personal witness, various forms of volunteer work, social activity and political commitment. This is a particularly pressing need at the present time, when the "culture of death" so forcefully opposes the "culture of life" and often seems to have the upper hand. But even before that it is a need which springs from "faith working through love" (Gal 5:6). As the Letter of James admonishes us: "What does it profit, my brethren, if a man says he has faith but has not works? Can his faith save him? If a brother or sister is ill-clad and in lack of daily food, and one of you says to them, 'Go in peace, be warmed and filled,' without giving them the things needed for the body, what does it profit? So faith by itself, if it has no works, is dead" (2:14–17).

In our service of charity, we must be inspired and distinguished by a specific attitude: we must care for the other as a person for whom God has made us responsible. As disciples of Jesus, we are called to become neighbours to everyone (cf. Lk 10:29–37), and to show special favour to those who are poorest, most alone and most in need. In helping the hungry, the thirsty, the foreigner, the naked, the sick, the imprisoned—as well as the child in the womb and the old person who is suffering or near death—we have the opportunity to serve Jesus. He himself said: "As you did it to one of the least of these my brethren, you did it to me" (Mt 25:40). Hence we cannot but feel called to account and judged by the ever relevant words of Saint John Chrysostom: "Do you wish to honor the body of Christ? Do not neglect it when you find it naked. Do not do it homage here in the church with silk fabrics only to neglect it outside where it suffers cold and nakedness."[13]

---

13. *In Matthaeum*, Hom. L, 3: PG 58, 508.

Where life is involved, the service of charity must be profoundly consistent. It cannot tolerate bias and discrimination, for human life is sacred and inviolable at every stage and in every situation; it is an indivisible good. We need then to "show care" for all life and for the life of everyone. Indeed, at an even deeper level, we need to go to the very roots of life and love.

It is this deep love for every man and woman which has given rise down the centuries to an outstanding history of charity, a history which has brought into being in the Church and society many forms of service to life which evoke admiration from all unbiased observers. Every Christian community, with a renewed sense of responsibility, must continue to write this history through various kinds of pastoral and social activity. To this end, appropriate and effective programmes of support for new life must be implemented, with special closeness to mothers who, even without the help of the father, are not afraid to bring their child into the world and to raise it. Similar care must be shown for the life of the marginalized or suffering, especially in its final phases.

88. All of this involves a patient and fearless work of education aimed at encouraging one and all to bear each other's burdens (cf. Gal 6:2). It requires a continuous promotion of vocations to service, particularly among the young. It involves the implementation of long-term practical projects and initiatives inspired by the Gospel.

Many are the means towards this end which need to be developed with skill and serious commitment. At the first stage of life, centres for natural methods of regulating fertility should be promoted as a valuable help to responsible parenthood, in which all individuals, and in the first place the child, are recognized and respected in their own right, and where every decision is guided by the ideal of the sincere gift of self. Marriage and family counselling agencies by their specific work of guidance and prevention, carried out in accordance with an anthropology consistent with the Christian vision of the person, of the couple and of sexuality, also offer valuable help in rediscovering the meaning of love and life, and in supporting and accompanying every family in its mission as the "sanctuary of life." Newborn life is also served by centres of assistance and homes or centres where new life receives a welcome. Thanks to the work of such centres, many unmarried mothers and couples in difficulty discover new hope and find assistance and support in overcoming hardship and the fear of accepting a newly conceived life or life which has just come into the world.

When life is challenged by conditions of hardship, maladjustment, sickness or rejection, other programmes—such as communities for treating drug addiction, residential communities for minors or the mentally ill, care and relief centres for AIDS patients, associations for solidarity especially towards the disabled—are eloquent expressions of what charity is able to devise in order to give everyone new reasons for hope and practical possibilities for life.

And when earthly existence draws to a close, it is again charity which finds the most appropriate means for enabling the elderly, especially those who can no longer look after themselves, and the terminally ill to enjoy genuinely humane assistance and to receive an adequate response to their needs, in particular their anxiety and their loneliness. In these cases the role of families is indispensable; yet families can receive much help from social welfare agencies and, if necessary, from recourse to palliative care, taking advantage of suitable medical and social services available in public institutions or in the home.

In particular, the role of hospitals, clinics and convalescent homes needs to be reconsidered. These should not merely be institutions where care is provided for the sick or the dying. Above all they should be places where suffering, pain and death are acknowledged and understood in their human and specifically Christian meaning. This must be especially evident and effective in institutes staffed by Religious or in any way connected with the Church.

89. Agencies and centres of service to life, and all other initiatives of support and solidarity which circumstances may from time to time suggest, need to be directed by people who are generous in their involvement and fully aware of the importance of the Gospel of life for the good of individuals and society.

A unique responsibility belongs to health-care personnel: doctors, pharmacists, nurses, chaplains, men and women religious, administrators and volunteers. Their profession calls for them to be guardians and servants of human life. In today's cultural and social context, in which science and the practice of medicine risk losing sight of their inherent ethical dimension, health-care professionals can be strongly tempted at times to become manipulators of life, or even agents of death. In the face of this temptation their responsibility today is greatly increased. Its deepest inspiration and strongest support lie in the intrinsic and undeniable ethical dimension of the health-care profession, something already recognized by the ancient and still relevant Hippocratic Oath, which requires every doctor to commit himself to absolute respect for human life and its sacredness.

Absolute respect for every innocent human life also requires the exercise of conscientious objection in relation to procured abortion and euthanasia. "Causing death" can never be considered a form of medical treatment, even when the intention is solely to comply with the patient's request. Rather, it runs completely counter to the health-care profession, which is meant to be an impassioned and unflinching affirmation of life. Bio-medical research too, a field which promises great benefits for humanity, must always reject experimentation, research or applications which disregard the inviolable dignity of the human being, and thus cease to be at the service of people and become instead means which, under the guise of helping people, actually harm them.

90. Volunteer workers have a specific role to play: they make a valuable contribution to the service of life when they combine professional

ability and generous, selfless love. The Gospel of life inspires them to lift their feelings of good will towards others to the heights of Christ's charity; to renew every day, amid hard work and weariness, their awareness of the dignity of every person; to search out people's needs and, when necessary, to set out on new paths where needs are greater but care and support weaker.

If charity is to be realistic and effective, it demands that the Gospel of life be implemented also by means of certain forms of social activity and commitment in the political field, as a way of defending and promoting the value of life in our ever more complex and pluralistic societies. Individuals, families, groups and associations, albeit for different reasons and in different ways, all have a responsibility for shaping society and developing cultural, economic, political and legislative projects which, with respect for all and in keeping with democratic principles, will contribute to the building of a society in which the dignity of each person is recognized and protected and the lives of all are defended and enhanced.

This task is the particular responsibility of civil leaders. Called to serve the people and the common good, they have a duty to make courageous choices in support of life, especially through legislative measures. In a democratic system, where laws and decisions are made on the basis of the consensus of many, the sense of personal responsibility in the consciences of individuals invested with authority may be weakened. But no one can ever renounce this responsibility, especially when he or she has a legislative or decision-making mandate, which calls that person to answer to God, to his or her own conscience and to the whole of society for choices which may be contrary to the common good. Although laws are not the only means of protecting human life, nevertheless they do play a very important and sometimes decisive role in influencing patterns of thought and behaviour. I repeat once more that a law which violates an innocent person's natural right to life is unjust and, as such, is not valid as a law. For this reason I urgently appeal once more to all political leaders not to pass laws which, by disregarding the dignity of the person, undermine the very fabric of society.

The Church well knows that it is difficult to mount an effective legal defence of life in pluralistic democracies, because of the presence of strong cultural currents with differing outlooks. At the same time, certain that moral truth cannot fail to make its presence deeply felt in every conscience, the Church encourages political leaders, starting with those who are Christians, not to give in, but to make those choices which, taking into account what is realistically attainable, will lead to the re-establishment of a just order in the defence and promotion of the value of life. Here it must be noted that it is not enough to remove unjust laws. The underlying causes of attacks on life have to be eliminated, especially by ensuring proper support for families and motherhood. A family policy must be the basis and driving force of all social policies. For this reason there need to be set in place social and political initiatives capable of guaranteeing conditions of true freedom of choice in matters of parenthood. It is also necessary to rethink labour, urban, residential and social service policies so as to harmonize working schedules with time available for the family, so that it becomes effectively possible to take care of children and the elderly.

91. Today an important part of policies which favour life is the issue of population growth. Certainly public authorities have a responsibility to "intervene to orient the demography of the population."[14] But such interventions must always take into account and respect the primary and inalienable responsibility of married couples and families, and cannot employ methods which fail to respect the person and fundamental human rights, beginning with the right to life of every innocent human being. It is therefore morally unacceptable to encourage, let alone impose, the use of methods such as contraception, sterilization and abortion in order to regulate births. The ways of solving the population problem are quite different. Governments and the various international

---

14. *Catechism of the Catholic Church*, no. 2372.

agencies must above all strive to create economic, social, public health and cultural conditions which will enable married couples to make their choices about procreation in full freedom and with genuine responsibility. They must then make efforts to ensure "greater opportunities and a fairer distribution of wealth so that everyone can share equitably in the goods of creation. Solutions must be sought on the global level by establishing a true economy of communion and sharing of goods, in both the national and international order."[15] This is the only way to respect the dignity of persons and families, as well as the authentic cultural patrimony of peoples.

Service of the Gospel of life is thus an immense and complex task. This service increasingly appears as a valuable and fruitful area for positive cooperation with our brothers and sisters of other Churches and ecclesial communities, in accordance with the practical ecumenism which the Second Vatican Council authoritatively encouraged.[16] It also appears as a providential area for dialogue and joint efforts with the followers of other religions and with all people of good will. No single person or group has a monopoly on the defence and promotion of life. These are everyone's task and responsibility. On the eve of the Third Millennium, the challenge facing us is an arduous one: only the concerted efforts of all those who believe in the value of life can prevent a setback of unforeseeable consequences for civilization.

"Your children will be like olive shoots around your table" (Ps 128:3): the family as the "sanctuary of life"

92. Within the "people of life and the people for life," the family has a decisive responsibility. This responsibility flows from its very nature as a community of life and love, founded upon marriage, and from its

---

15. John Paul II, Address to the Fourth General Conference of Latin American Bishops in Santo Domingo (12 October 1992), No. 15: AAS 85 (1993), 819.

16. Cf. Decree on Ecumenism Unitatis Redintegratio, 12; Pastoral Constitution on the Church in the Modern World Gaudium et Spes, 90.

mission to "guard, reveal and communicate love."[17] Here it is a matter of God's own love, of which parents are co-workers and as it were interpreters when they transmit life and raise it according to his fatherly plan.[18] This is the love that becomes selflessness, receptiveness and gift. Within the family each member is accepted, respected and honoured precisely because he or she is a person; and if any family member is in greater need, the care which he or she receives is all the more intense and attentive.

The family has a special role to play throughout the life of its members, from birth to death. It is truly "the sanctuary of life: the place in which life—the gift of God—can be properly welcomed and protected against the many attacks to which it is exposed, and can develop in accordance with what constitutes authentic human growth."[19] Consequently the role of the family in building a culture of life is decisive and irreplaceable.

As the domestic church, the family is summoned to proclaim, celebrate and serve the Gospel of life. This is a responsibility which first concerns married couples, called to be givers of life, on the basis of an ever greater awareness of the meaning of procreation as a unique event which clearly reveals that human life is a gift received in order then to be given as a gift. In giving origin to a new life, parents recognize that the child, "as the fruit of their mutual gift of love, is, in turn, a gift for both of them, a gift which flows from them."[20]

---

17. John Paul II, Post-Synodal Apostolic Exhortation *Familiaris Consortio* (22 November 1981), 17: AAS 74 (1982), 100.

18. Cf. Second Vatican Ecumenical Council, Pastoral Constitution on the Church in the Modern World *Gaudium et Spes*, 50.

19. John Paul II, Encyclical Letter *Centesimus Annus* (1 May 1991), 39: AAS 83 (1991), 842.

20. John Paul II, Address to Participants in the Seventh Symposium of European Bishops, on the theme of "Contemporary Attitudes towards Life and Death: A Challenge for Evangelization" (17 October 1989), No. 5: *Insegnamenti* XII, 2 (1989), 945. Children are presented in the biblical tradition precisely as God's gift (cf. Ps 127:3) and as a sign of his blessing on those who walk in his ways (cf. Ps 128:3–4).

It is above all in raising children that the family fulfils its mission to proclaim the Gospel of life. By word and example, in the daily round of relations and choices, and through concrete actions and signs, parents lead their children to authentic freedom, actualized in the sincere gift of self, and they cultivate in them respect for others, a sense of justice, cordial openness, dialogue, generous service, solidarity and all the other values which help people to live life as a gift. In raising children Christian parents must be concerned about their children's faith and help them to fulfil the vocation God has given them. The parents' mission as educators also includes teaching and giving their children an example of the true meaning of suffering and death. They will be able to do this if they are sensitive to all kinds of suffering around them and, even more, if they succeed in fostering attitudes of closeness, assistance and sharing towards sick or elderly members of the family.

93. The family celebrates the Gospel of life through daily prayer, both individual prayer and family prayer. The family prays in order to glorify and give thanks to God for the gift of life, and implores his light and strength in order to face times of difficulty and suffering without losing hope. But the celebration which gives meaning to every other form of prayer and worship is found in the family's actual daily life together, if it is a life of love and self-giving.

This celebration thus becomes a service to the Gospel of life, expressed through solidarity as experienced within and around the family in the form of concerned, attentive and loving care shown in the humble, ordinary events of each day. A particularly significant expression of solidarity between families is a willingness to adopt or take in children abandoned by their parents or in situations of serious hardship. True parental love is ready to go beyond the bonds of flesh and blood in order to accept children from other families, offering them whatever is necessary for their well-being and full development. Among the various forms of adoption, consideration should be given to adoption-at-a-distance, preferable in cases where the only reason for giving up the child is the extreme poverty of the child's family. Through this type of adoption, parents are given the help needed to support and raise their children, without their being uprooted from their natural environment.

As "a firm and persevering determination to commit oneself to the common good,"[21] solidarity also needs to be practised through participation in social and political life. Serving the Gospel of life thus means that the family, particularly through its membership of family associations, works to ensure that the laws and institutions of the State in no way violate the right to life, from conception to natural death, but rather protect and promote it.

94. Special attention must be given to the elderly. While in some cultures older people remain a part of the family with an important and active role, in others the elderly are regarded as a useless burden and are left to themselves. Here the temptation to resort to euthanasia can more easily arise.

Neglect of the elderly or their outright rejection are intolerable. Their presence in the family, or at least their closeness to the family in cases where limited living space or other reasons make this impossible, is of fundamental importance in creating a climate of mutual interaction and enriching communication between the different age-groups. It is therefore important to preserve, or to re-establish where it has been lost, a sort of "covenant" between generations. In this way parents, in their later years, can receive from their children the acceptance and solidarity which they themselves gave to their children when they brought them into the world. This is required by obedience to the divine commandment to honor one's father and mother (cf. Ex 20:12; Lev 19:3). But there is more. The elderly are not only to be considered the object of our concern, closeness and service. They themselves have a valuable contribution to make to the Gospel of life. Thanks to the rich treasury

---

21. John Paul II, Encyclical Letter *Sollicitudo Rei Socialis* (30 December 1987), 38: *AAS* 80 (1988), 565–566.

of experiences they have acquired through the years, the elderly can and must be sources of wisdom and witnesses of hope and love.

Although it is true that "the future of humanity passes by way of the family,"[22] it must be admitted that modern social, economic and cultural conditions make the family's task of serving life more difficult and demanding. In order to fulfil its vocation as the "sanctuary of life," as the cell of a society which loves and welcomes life, the family urgently needs to be helped and supported. Communities and States must guarantee all the support, including economic support, which families need in order to meet their problems in a truly human way. For her part, the Church must untiringly promote a plan of pastoral care for families, capable of making every family rediscover and live with joy and courage its mission to further the Gospel of life.

"Walk as children of light" (Eph 5:8): bringing about a transformation of culture

95. "Walk as children of light . . . and try to learn what is pleasing to the Lord. Take no part in the unfruitful works of darkness" (Eph 5:8, 10–11). In our present social context, marked by a dramatic struggle between the "culture of life" and the "culture of death," there is need to develop a deep critical sense, capable of discerning true values and authentic needs.

What is urgently called for is a general mobilization of consciences and a united ethical effort to activate a great campaign in support of life. All together, we must build a new culture of life: new, because it will be able to confront and solve today's unprecedented problems affecting human life; new, because it will be adopted with deeper and more dynamic conviction by all Christians; new, because it will be capable of bringing about a serious and courageous cultural dialogue among all parties.

---

22. John Paul II, Post-Synodal Apostolic Exhortation *Familiaris Consortio* (22 November 1981), 86: AAS 74 (1982), 188.

While the urgent need for such a cultural transformation is linked to the present historical situation, it is also rooted in the Church's mission of evangelization. The purpose of the Gospel, in fact, is "to transform humanity from within and to make it new."[23] Like the yeast which leavens the whole measure of dough (cf. Mt 13:33), the Gospel is meant to permeate all cultures and give them life from within,[24] so that they may express the full truth about the human person and about human life.

We need to begin with the renewal of a culture of life within Christian communities themselves. Too often it happens that believers, even those who take an active part in the life of the Church, end up by separating their Christian faith from its ethical requirements concerning life, and thus fall into moral subjectivism and certain objectionable ways of acting. With great openness and courage, we need to question how widespread is the culture of life today among individual Christians, families, groups and communities in our Dioceses. With equal clarity and determination we must identify the steps we are called to take in order to serve life in all its truth. At the same time, we need to promote a serious and in-depth exchange about basic issues of human life with everyone, including non-believers, in intellectual circles, in the various professional spheres and at the level of people's everyday life.

96. The first and fundamental step towards this cultural transformation consists in forming consciences with regard to the incomparable and inviolable worth of every human life. It is of the greatest importance to re-establish the essential connection between life and freedom. These are inseparable goods: where one is violated, the other also ends up being violated. There is no true freedom where life is not welcomed and loved; and there is no fullness of life except in freedom. Both realities have something inherent and specific which links them inextricably:

---

23. Paul VI, Apostolic Exhortation *Evangelii Nuntiandi* (8 December 1975), 18: AAS 68 (1976), 17.
    24. Cf. *ibid.*, 20: *loc. cit.*, 18.

PART I: CHURCH TEACHING

the vocation to love. Love, as a sincere gift of self,[25] is what gives the life and freedom of the person their truest meaning.

No less critical in the formation of conscience is the recovery of the necessary link between freedom and truth. As I have frequently stated, when freedom is detached from objective truth it becomes impossible to establish personal rights on a firm rational basis; and the ground is laid for society to be at the mercy of the unrestrained will of individuals or the oppressive totalitarianism of public authority.[26]

It is therefore essential that man should acknowledge his inherent condition as a creature to whom God has granted being and life as a gift and a duty. Only by admitting his innate dependence can man live and use his freedom to the full, and at the same time respect the life and freedom of every other person. Here especially one sees that "at the heart of every culture lies the attitude man takes to the greatest mystery: the mystery of God."[27] Where God is denied and people live as though he did not exist, or his commandments are not taken into account, the dignity of the human person and the inviolability of human life also end up being rejected or compromised.

97. Closely connected with the formation of conscience is the work of education, which helps individuals to be ever more human, leads them ever more fully to the truth, instils in them growing respect for life, and trains them in right interpersonal relationships.

In particular, there is a need for education about the value of life from its very origins. It is an illusion to think that we can build a true culture of human life if we do not help the young to accept and experience sexuality and love and the whole of life according to their true meaning and in their close interconnection. Sexuality, which enriches the whole

---

25. Cf. Second Vatican Ecumenical Council, Pastoral Constitution on the Church in the Modern World *Gaudium et Spes*, 24.

26. Cf. John Paul II, Encyclical Letter *Centesimus Annus* (1 May 1991), 17: AAS 83 (1991), 814; Encyclical Letter *Veritatis Splendor* (6 August 1993), 95–101: AAS 85 (1993), 1208–1213.

27. John Paul II, Encyclical Letter *Centesimus Annus* (1 May 1991), 24: AAS 83 (1991), 822.

person, "manifests its inmost meaning in leading the person to the gift of self in love."[28] The trivialization of sexuality is among the principal factors which have led to contempt for new life. Only a true love is able to protect life. There can be no avoiding the duty to offer, especially to adolescents and young adults, an authentic education in sexuality and in love, an education which involves training in chastity as a virtue which fosters personal maturity and makes one capable of respecting the "spousal" meaning of the body.

The work of educating in the service of life involves the training of married couples in responsible procreation. In its true meaning, responsible procreation requires couples to be obedient to the Lord's call and to act as faithful interpreters of his plan. This happens when the family is generously open to new lives, and when couples maintain an attitude of openness and service to life, even if, for serious reasons and in respect for the moral law, they choose to avoid a new birth for the time being or indefinitely. The moral law obliges them in every case to control the impulse of instinct and passion, and to respect the biological laws inscribed in their person. It is precisely this respect which makes legitimate, at the service of responsible procreation, the use of natural methods of regulating fertility. From the scientific point of view, these methods are becoming more and more accurate and make it possible in practice to make choices in harmony with moral values. An honest appraisal of their effectiveness should dispel certain prejudices which are still widely held, and should convince married couples, as well as health-care and social workers, of the importance of proper training in this area. The Church is grateful to those who, with personal sacrifice and often unacknowledged dedication, devote themselves to the study and spread of these methods, as well to the promotion of education in the moral values which they presuppose.

---

28. John Paul II, Post-Synodal Apostolic Exhortation *Familiaris Consortio* (22 November 1981), 37: AAS 74 (1982), 128.

The work of education cannot avoid a consideration of suffering and death. These are a part of human existence, and it is futile, not to say misleading, to try to hide them or ignore them. On the contrary, people must be helped to understand their profound mystery in all its harsh reality. Even pain and suffering have meaning and value when they are experienced in close connection with love received and given. In this regard, I have called for the yearly celebration of the World Day of the Sick, emphasizing "the salvific nature of the offering up of suffering which, experienced in communion with Christ, belongs to the very essence of the Redemption."[29] Death itself is anything but an event without hope. It is the door which opens wide on eternity and, for those who live in Christ, an experience of participation in the mystery of his Death and Resurrection.

98. In a word, we can say that the cultural change which we are calling for demands from everyone the courage to adopt a new life-style, consisting in making practical choices—at the personal, family, social and international level—on the basis of a correct scale of values: the primacy of being over having,[30] of the person over things.[31] This renewed life-style involves a passing from indifference to concern for others, from rejection to acceptance of them. Other people are not rivals from whom we must defend ourselves, but brothers and sisters to be supported. They are to be loved for their own sakes, and they enrich us by their very presence.

In this mobilization for a new culture of life no one must feel excluded: everyone has an important role to play. Together with the family, teachers and educators have a particularly valuable contribution to make. Much will depend on them if young people, trained in true freedom, are

---

29. Letter establishing the World Day of the Sick (13 May 1992), No. 2: *Insegnamenti* XV, 1 (1992), 1410.

30. Cf. Second Vatican Ecumenical Council, Pastoral Constitution on the Church in the Modern World *Gaudium et Spes*, 35; Paul VI, Encyclical Letter *Populorum Progressio* (26 March 1967), 15: AAS 59 (1967), 265.

31. Cf. John Paul II, Letter to Families *Gratissimam sane* (2 February 1994), 13: AAS 86 (1994), 892.

to be able to preserve for themselves and make known to others new, authentic ideals of life, and if they are to grow in respect for and service to every other person, in the family and in society.

Intellectuals can also do much to build a new culture of human life. A special task falls to Catholic intellectuals, who are called to be present and active in the leading centres where culture is formed, in schools and universities, in places of scientific and technological research, of artistic creativity and of the study of man. Allowing their talents and activity to be nourished by the living force of the Gospel, they ought to place themselves at the service of a new culture of life by offering serious and well documented contributions, capable of commanding general respect and interest by reason of their merit. It was precisely for this purpose that I established the Pontifical Academy for Life, assigning it the task of "studying and providing information and training about the principal problems of law and biomedicine pertaining to the promotion of life, especially in the direct relationship they have with Christian morality and the directives of the Church's Magisterium."[32] A specific contribution will also have to come from Universities, particularly from Catholic Universities, and from Centres, Institutes and Committees of Bioethics.

An important and serious responsibility belongs to those involved in the mass media, who are called to ensure that the messages which they so effectively transmit will support the culture of life. They need to present noble models of life and make room for instances of people's positive and sometimes heroic love for others. With great respect they should also present the positive values of sexuality and human love, and not insist on what defiles and cheapens human dignity. In their interpretation of things, they should refrain from emphasizing anything that suggests or fosters feelings or attitudes of indifference, contempt or rejection in relation to life. With scrupulous concern for factual truth, they are called to combine freedom of information with respect for every person and a profound sense of humanity.

---

32. John Paul II, Motu Proprio *Vitae Mysterium* (11 February 1994), 4: AAS 86 (1994), 386–387.

PART I: CHURCH TEACHING

99. In transforming culture so that it supports life, women occupy a place, in thought and action, which is unique and decisive. It depends on them to promote a "new feminism" which rejects the temptation of imitating models of "male domination," in order to acknowledge and affirm the true genius of women in every aspect of the life of society, and overcome all discrimination, violence and exploitation.

Making my own the words of the concluding message of the Second Vatican Council, I address to women this urgent appeal: "Reconcile people with life."[33] You are called to bear witness to the meaning of genuine love, of that gift of self and of that acceptance of others which are present in a special way in the relationship of husband and wife, but which ought also to be at the heart of every other interpersonal relationship. The experience of motherhood makes you acutely aware of the other person and, at the same time, confers on you a particular task: "Motherhood involves a special communion with the mystery of life, as it develops in the woman's womb . . . This unique contact with the new human being developing within her gives rise to an attitude towards human beings not only towards her own child, but every human being, which profoundly marks the woman's personality."[34] A mother welcomes and carries in herself another human being, enabling it to grow inside her, giving it room, respecting it in its otherness. Women first learn and then teach others that human relations are authentic if they are open to accepting the other person: a person who is recognized and loved because of the dignity which comes from being a person and not from other considerations, such as usefulness, strength, intelligence, beauty or health. This is the fundamental contribution which the Church and humanity expect from women. And it is the indispensable prerequisite for an authentic cultural change.

I would now like to say a special word to women who have had an abortion. The Church is aware of the many factors which may have

---

33. *Closing Message of the Council* (8 December 1965): *To Women.*
34. John Paul II, Apostolic Letter *Mulieris Dignitatem* (15 August 1988), 18: AAS 80 (1988), 1696.

influenced your decision, and she does not doubt that in many cases it was a painful and even shattering decision. The wound in your heart may not yet have healed. Certainly what happened was and remains terribly wrong. But do not give in to discouragement and do not lose hope. Try rather to understand what happened and face it honestly. If you have not already done so, give yourselves over with humility and trust to repentance. The Father of mercies is ready to give you his forgiveness and his peace in the Sacrament of Reconciliation. To the same Father and his mercy you can with sure hope entrust your child. With the friendly and expert help and advice of other people, and as a result of your own painful experience, you can be among the most eloquent defenders of everyone's right to life. Through your commitment to life, whether by accepting the birth of other children or by welcoming and caring for those most in need of someone to be close to them, you will become promoters of a new way of looking at human life.

100. In this great endeavour to create a new culture of life we are inspired and sustained by the confidence that comes from knowing that the Gospel of life, like the Kingdom of God itself, is growing and producing abundant fruit (cf. Mk 4:26–29). There is certainly an enormous disparity between the powerful resources available to the forces promoting the "culture of death" and the means at the disposal of those working for a "culture of life and love." But we know that we can rely on the help of God, for whom nothing is impossible (cf. Mt 19:26).

Filled with this certainty, and moved by profound concern for the destiny of every man and woman, I repeat what I said to those families who carry out their challenging mission amid so many difficulties:[35] a great prayer for life is urgently needed, a prayer which will rise up throughout the world. Through special initiatives and in daily prayer, may an impassioned plea rise to God, the Creator and lover of life, from every Christian community, from every group and association, from every

---

35. Cf. John Paul II, Letter to Families *Gratissimam sane* (2 February 1994), 5: AAS 86 (1994), 872.

family and from the heart of every believer. Jesus himself has shown us by his own example that prayer and fasting are the first and most effective weapons against the forces of evil (cf. Mt 4:1–11). As he taught his disciples, some demons cannot be driven out except in this way (cf. Mk 9:29). Let us therefore discover anew the humility and the courage to pray and fast so that power from on high will break down the walls of lies and deceit: the walls which conceal from the sight of so many of our brothers and sisters the evil of practices and laws which are hostile to life. May this same power turn their hearts to resolutions and goals inspired by the civilization of life and love.

"We are writing this that our joy may be complete" (1 Jn 1:4): the Gospel of life is for the whole of human society

101. "We are writing you this that our joy may be complete" (1 Jn 1:4). The revelation of the Gospel of life is given to us as a good to be shared with all people: so that all men and women may have fellowship with us and with the Trinity (cf. 1 Jn 1:3). Our own joy would not be complete if we failed to share this Gospel with others but kept it only for ourselves.

The Gospel of life is not for believers alone: it is for everyone. The issue of life and its defence and promotion is not a concern of Christians alone. Although faith provides special light and strength, this question arises in every human conscience which seeks the truth and which cares about the future of humanity. Life certainly has a sacred and religious value, but in no way is that value a concern only of believers. The value at stake is one which every human being can grasp by the light of reason; thus it necessarily concerns everyone.

Consequently, all that we do as the "people of life and for life" should be interpreted correctly and welcomed with favour. When the Church declares that unconditional respect for the right to life of every innocent person—from conception to natural death—is one of the pillars on which every civil society stands, she "wants simply to promote a human State. A State which recognizes the defence of the fundamental rights of the human person, especially of the weakest, as its primary duty."[36]

The Gospel of life is for the whole of human society. To be actively pro-life is to contribute to the renewal of society through the promotion of the common good. It is impossible to further the common good without acknowledging and defending the right to life, upon which all the other inalienable rights of individuals are founded and from which they develop. A society lacks solid foundations when, on the one hand, it asserts values such as the dignity of the person, justice and peace, but then, on the other hand, radically acts to the contrary by allowing or tolerating a variety of ways in which human life is devalued and violated, especially where it is weak or marginalized. Only respect for life can be the foundation and guarantee of the most precious and essential goods of society, such as democracy and peace.

There can be no true democracy without a recognition of every person's dignity and without respect for his or her rights.

Nor can there be true peace unless life is defended and promoted. As Paul VI pointed out: "Every crime against life is an attack on peace, especially if it strikes at the moral conduct of people. . . . But where human rights are truly professed and publicly recognized and defended, peace becomes the joyful and operative climate of life in society."[37]

The "people of life" rejoices in being able to share its commitment with so many others. Thus may the "people for life" constantly grow in number and may a new culture of love and solidarity develop for the true good of the whole of human society.

---

36. John Paul II, Address to Participants in the Study Conference on "The Right to Life in Europe" (18 December 1987): *Insegnamenti* X, 3 (1987), 1446.

37. *Message for the 1977 World Day of Peace: AAS* 68 (1976), 711–712.

CHAPTER 13

Caritas in Veritate:
On Integral Human Development in Charity and Truth

(Excerpt)

Pope Benedict XVI

June 29, 2009

In this encyclical, which found its inspiration in Pope St. Paul VI's
Populorum Progressio, *Pope Benedict XVI furthers Paul VI's discussion
on the nature of true development. Benedict XVI emphasizes the key
relationship between rights and duties, particularly highlighting the danger
of focusing on one's own rights while neglecting one's duty to promote
the rights of others.*

❋

CHAPTER FOUR: THE DEVELOPMENT OF PEOPLE, RIGHTS AND DUTIES, AND THE ENVIRONMENT

43. "The reality of human solidarity, which is a benefit for us, also imposes a duty."[1] Many people today would claim that they owe nothing to anyone, except to themselves. They are concerned only with their rights, and they often have great difficulty in taking responsibility for their own and other people's integral development. Hence it is important to call for a renewed reflection on how *rights presuppose duties, if they are not to become mere license.*[2] Nowadays we are witnessing a grave

---

1. Paul VI, Encyclical Letter *Populorum Progressio* (26 March 1967), 17: AAS 59 (1967), 265–266.
2. Cf. John Paul II, *Message for the 2003 World Day of Peace*, 5: AAS 95 (2003), 343.

inconsistency. On the one hand, appeals are made to alleged rights, arbitrary and non-essential in nature, accompanied by the demand that they be recognized and promoted by public structures, while, on the other hand, elementary and basic rights remain unacknowledged and are violated in much of the world.[3] A link has often been noted between claims to a "right to excess," and even to transgression and vice, within affluent societies, and the lack of food, drinkable water, basic instruction and elementary health care in areas of the underdeveloped world and on the outskirts of large metropolitan centres. The link consists in this: individual rights, when detached from a framework of duties which grants them their full meaning, can run wild, leading to an escalation of demands which is effectively unlimited and indiscriminate. An over-emphasis on rights leads to a disregard for duties. Duties set a limit on rights because they point to the anthropological and ethical framework of which rights are a part, in this way ensuring that they do not become licence. Duties thereby reinforce rights and call for their defence and promotion as a task to be undertaken in the service of the common good. Otherwise, if the only basis of human rights is to be found in the deliberations of an assembly of citizens, those rights can be changed at any time, and so the duty to respect and pursue them fades from the common consciousness. Governments and international bodies can then lose sight of the objectivity and "inviolability" of rights. When this happens, the authentic development of peoples is endangered.[4] Such a way of thinking and acting compromises the authority of international bodies, especially in the eyes of those countries most in need of development. Indeed, the latter demand that the international community take up the duty of helping them to be "artisans of their own destiny,"[5] that is, to take up duties of their own. *The sharing of reciprocal duties is a more powerful incentive to action than the mere assertion of rights.*

44. The notion of rights and duties in development must also take account of the problems associated with *population growth*. This is a

---

3. Cf. *ibid.*
4. Cf. Benedict XVI, *Message for the 2007 World Day of Peace*, 13: *loc. cit.*, 781–782.
5. Paul VI, Encyclical Letter *Populorum Progressio*, 65: *loc. cit.*, 289.

PART I: CHURCH TEACHING

very important aspect of authentic development, since it concerns the inalienable values of life and the family.[6] To consider population increase as the primary cause of underdevelopment is mistaken, even from an economic point of view. Suffice it to consider, on the one hand, the significant reduction in infant mortality and the rise in average life expectancy found in economically developed countries, and on the other hand, the signs of crisis observable in societies that are registering an alarming decline in their birth rate. Due attention must obviously be given to responsible procreation, which among other things has a positive contribution to make to integral human development. The Church, in her concern for man's authentic development, urges him to have full respect for human values in the exercise of his sexuality. It cannot be reduced merely to pleasure or entertainment, nor can sex education be reduced to technical instruction aimed solely at protecting the interested parties from possible disease or the "risk" of procreation. This would be to impoverish and disregard the deeper meaning of sexuality, a meaning which needs to be acknowledged and responsibly appropriated not only by individuals but also by the community. It is irresponsible to view sexuality merely as a source of pleasure, and likewise to regulate it through strategies of mandatory birth control. In either case materialistic ideas and policies are at work, and individuals are ultimately subjected to various forms of violence. Against such policies, there is a need to defend the primary competence of the family in the area of sexuality,[7] as opposed to the State and its restrictive policies, and to ensure that parents are suitably prepared to undertake their responsibilities.

Morally responsible openness to life represents a rich social and economic resource. Populous nations have been able to emerge from poverty thanks not least to the size of their population and the talents of their people. On the other hand, formerly prosperous nations are presently passing through a phase of uncertainty and in some cases decline,

---

6. Cf. *ibid.*, 36–37: *loc. cit.*, 275–276.
7. Cf. *ibid.*, 37: *loc. cit.*, 275–276.

precisely because of their falling birth rates; this has become a crucial problem for highly affluent societies. The decline in births, falling at times beneath the so-called "replacement level," also puts a strain on social welfare systems, increases their cost, eats into savings and hence the financial resources needed for investment, reduces the availability of qualified labourers, and narrows the "brain pool" upon which nations can draw for their needs. Furthermore, smaller and at times miniscule families run the risk of impoverishing social relations, and failing to ensure effective forms of solidarity. These situations are symptomatic of scant confidence in the future and moral weariness. It is thus becoming a social and even economic necessity once more to hold up to future generations the beauty of marriage and the family, and the fact that these institutions correspond to the deepest needs and dignity of the person. In view of this, States are called to *enact policies promoting the centrality and the integrity of the family* founded on marriage between a man and a woman, the primary vital cell of society,[8] and to assume responsibility for its economic and fiscal needs, while respecting its essentially relational character.

45. Striving to meet the deepest moral needs of the person also has important and beneficial repercussions at the level of economics. *The economy needs ethics in order to function correctly*—not any ethics whatsoever, but an ethics which is people-centred. Today we hear much talk of ethics in the world of economy, finance and business. Research centres and seminars in business ethics are on the rise; the system of ethical certification is spreading throughout the developed world as part of the movement of ideas associated with the responsibilities of business towards society. Banks are proposing "ethical" accounts and investment funds. "Ethical financing" is being developed, especially through micro-credit and, more generally, micro-finance. These processes are praiseworthy and deserve much support. Their positive effects are also being felt in the less developed areas of the world. It would be advisable,

---

8. Cf. Second Vatican Ecumenical Council, Decree on the Apostolate of Lay People *Apostolicam Actuositatem*, 11.

however, to develop a sound criterion of discernment, since the adjective "ethical" can be abused. When the word is used generically, it can lend itself to any number of interpretations, even to the point where it includes decisions and choices contrary to justice and authentic human welfare.

Much in fact depends on the underlying system of morality. On this subject the Church's social doctrine can make a specific contribution, since it is based on man's creation "in the image of God" (Gen 1:27), a datum which gives rise to the inviolable dignity of the human person and the transcendent value of natural moral norms. When business ethics prescinds from these two pillars, it inevitably risks losing its distinctive nature and it falls prey to forms of exploitation; more specifically, it risks becoming subservient to existing economic and financial systems rather than correcting their dysfunctional aspects. Among other things, it risks being used to justify the financing of projects that are in reality unethical. The word "ethical," then, should not be used to make ideological distinctions, as if to suggest that initiatives not formally so designated would not be ethical. Efforts are needed—and it is essential to say this—not only to create "ethical" sectors or segments of the economy or the world of finance, but to ensure that the whole economy—the whole of finance—is ethical, not merely by virtue of an external label, but by its respect for requirements intrinsic to its very nature. The Church's social teaching is quite clear on the subject, recalling that the economy, in all its branches, constitutes a sector of human activity.[9]

46. When we consider the issues involved in the *relationship between business and ethics*, as well as the evolution currently taking place in methods of production, it would appear that the traditionally valid distinction between profit-based companies and non-profit organizations can no longer do full justice to reality, or offer practical direction for the future. In recent decades a broad intermediate area has emerged

9. Cf. Paul VI, Encyclical Letter *Populorum Progressio*, 14: *loc. cit.*, 264; John Paul II, Encyclical Letter *Centesimus Annus* (1 May 1991), 32: *AAS* 83 (1991), 832–833.

between the two types of enterprise. It is made up of traditional companies which nonetheless subscribe to social aid agreements in support of underdeveloped countries, charitable foundations associated with individual companies, groups of companies oriented towards social welfare, and the diversified world of the so-called "civil economy" and the "economy of communion." This is not merely a matter of a "third sector," but of a broad new composite reality embracing the private and public spheres, one which does not exclude profit, but instead considers it a means for achieving human and social ends. Whether such companies distribute dividends or not, whether their juridical structure corresponds to one or other of the established forms, becomes secondary in relation to their willingness to view profit as a means of achieving the goal of a more humane market and society. It is to be hoped that these new kinds of enterprise will succeed in finding a suitable juridical and fiscal structure in every country. Without prejudice to the importance and the economic and social benefits of the more traditional forms of business, they steer the system towards a clearer and more complete assumption of duties on the part of economic subjects. And not only that. *The very plurality of institutional forms of business gives rise to a market which is not only more civilized but also more competitive.*

47. The strengthening of different types of businesses, especially those capable of viewing profit as a means for achieving the goal of a more humane market and society, must also be pursued in those countries that are excluded or marginalized from the influential circles of the global economy. In these countries it is very important to move ahead with projects based on subsidiarity, suitably planned and managed, aimed at affirming rights yet also providing for the assumption of corresponding responsibilities. In *development programmes*, the principle of the *centrality of the human person*, as the subject primarily responsible for development, must be preserved. The principal concern must be to improve the actual living conditions of the people in a given region, thus enabling them to carry out those duties which their poverty does not presently allow them

to fulfil. Social concern must never be an abstract attitude. Development programmes, if they are to be adapted to individual situations, need to be flexible; and the people who benefit from them ought to be directly involved in their planning and implementation. The criteria to be applied should aspire towards incremental development in a context of solidarity—with careful monitoring of results—inasmuch as there are no universally valid solutions. Much depends on the way programmes are managed in practice. "The peoples themselves have the prime responsibility to work for their own development. But they will not bring this about in isolation."[10] These words of Paul VI are all the more timely nowadays, as our world becomes progressively more integrated. The dynamics of inclusion are hardly automatic. Solutions need to be carefully designed to correspond to people's concrete lives, based on a prudential evaluation of each situation. Alongside macro-projects, there is a place for micro-projects, and above all there is need for the active mobilization of all the subjects of civil society, both juridical and physical persons.

International cooperation requires people who can be part of the process of economic and human development through the solidarity of their presence, supervision, training and respect. From this standpoint, international organizations might question the actual effectiveness of their bureaucratic and administrative machinery, which is often excessively costly. At times it happens that those who receive aid become subordinate to the aid-givers, and the poor serve to perpetuate expensive bureaucracies which consume an excessively high percentage of funds intended for development. Hence it is to be hoped that all international agencies and non-governmental organizations will commit themselves to complete transparency, informing donors and the public of the percentage of their income allocated to programmes of cooperation, the actual content of those programmes and, finally, the detailed expenditure of the institution itself.

---

10. Paul VI, Encyclical Letter *Populorum Progressio*, 77: *loc. cit.*, 295.

48. Today the subject of development is also closely related to the duties arising from *our relationship to the natural environment*. The environment is God's gift to everyone, and in our use of it we have a responsibility towards the poor, towards future generations and towards humanity as a whole. When nature, including the human being, is viewed as the result of mere chance or evolutionary determinism, our sense of responsibility wanes. In nature, the believer recognizes the wonderful result of God's creative activity, which we may use responsibly to satisfy our legitimate needs, material or otherwise, while respecting the intrinsic balance of creation. If this vision is lost, we end up either considering nature an untouchable taboo or, on the contrary, abusing it. Neither attitude is consonant with the Christian vision of nature as the fruit of God's creation.

Nature expresses a design of love and truth. It is prior to us, and it has been given to us by God as the setting for our life. Nature speaks to us of the Creator (cf. Rom 1:20) and his love for humanity. It is destined to be "recapitulated" in Christ at the end of time (cf. Eph 1:9–10; Col 1:19–20). Thus it too is a "vocation."[11] Nature is at our disposal not as "a heap of scattered refuse,"[12] but as a gift of the Creator who has given it an inbuilt order, enabling man to draw from it the principles needed in order "to till it and keep it" (Gen 2:15). But it should also be stressed that it is contrary to authentic development to view nature as something more important than the human person. This position leads to attitudes of neo-paganism or a new pantheism—human salvation cannot come from nature alone, understood in a purely naturalistic sense. This having been said, it is also necessary to reject the opposite position, which aims at total technical dominion over nature, because the natural environment is more than raw material to be manipulated at our pleasure; it is a wondrous work of the Creator containing a "grammar" which sets forth ends and criteria for its wise use, not its reckless exploitation. Today much harm is done to development precisely as a result of these distorted

---

11. John Paul II, *Message for the 1990 World Day of Peace*, 6: AAS 82 (1990), 150.

12. Heraclitus of Ephesus (Ephesus, c. 535 B.C.–c. 475 B.C.), Fragment 22B124, in H. Diels and W. Kranz, *Die Fragmente der Vorsokratiker*, Weidmann, Berlin, 1952, 6(th) ed.

notions. Reducing nature merely to a collection of contingent data ends up doing violence to the environment and even encouraging activity that fails to respect human nature itself. Our nature, constituted not only by matter but also by spirit, and as such, endowed with transcendent meaning and aspirations, is also normative for culture. Human beings interpret and shape the natural environment through culture, which in turn is given direction by the responsible use of freedom, in accordance with the dictates of the moral law. Consequently, projects for integral human development cannot ignore coming generations, but need to be *marked by solidarity and inter-generational justice*, while taking into account a variety of contexts: ecological, juridical, economic, political and cultural.[13]

49. Questions linked to the care and preservation of the environment today need to give due consideration to *the energy problem*. The fact that some States, power groups and companies hoard non-renewable energy resources represents a grave obstacle to development in poor countries. Those countries lack the economic means either to gain access to existing sources of non-renewable energy or to finance research into new alternatives. The stockpiling of natural resources, which in many cases are found in the poor countries themselves, gives rise to exploitation and frequent conflicts between and within nations. These conflicts are often fought on the soil of those same countries, with a heavy toll of death, destruction and further decay. The international community has an urgent duty to find institutional means of regulating the exploitation of non-renewable resources, involving poor countries in the process, in order to plan together for the future.

On this front too, there is a *pressing moral need for renewed solidarity*, especially in relationships between developing countries and those that are highly industrialized.[14] The technologically advanced societies can and must lower their domestic energy consumption, either through an

---

13. Pontifical Council for Justice and Peace, *Compendium of the Social Doctrine of the Church*, 451–487.

14. Cf. John Paul II, *Message for the 1990 World Day of Peace*, 10: loc. cit., 152–153.

evolution in manufacturing methods or through greater ecological sensitivity among their citizens. It should be added that at present it is possible to achieve improved energy efficiency while at the same time encouraging research into alternative forms of energy. What is also needed, though, is a worldwide redistribution of energy resources, so that countries lacking those resources can have access to them. The fate of those countries cannot be left in the hands of whoever is first to claim the spoils, or whoever is able to prevail over the rest. Here we are dealing with major issues; if they are to be faced adequately, then everyone must responsibly recognize the impact they will have on future generations, particularly on the many young people in the poorer nations, who "ask to assume their active part in the construction of a better world."[15]

50. This responsibility is a global one, for it is concerned not just with energy but with the whole of creation, which must not be bequeathed to future generations depleted of its resources. Human beings legitimately exercise a *responsible stewardship over nature*, in order to protect it, to enjoy its fruits and to cultivate it in new ways, with the assistance of advanced technologies, so that it can worthily accommodate and feed the world's population. On this earth there is room for everyone: here the entire human family must find the resources to live with dignity, through the help of nature itself—God's gift to his children—and through hard work and creativity. At the same time we must recognize our grave duty to hand the earth on to future generations in such a condition that they too can worthily inhabit it and continue to cultivate it. This means being committed to making joint decisions "after pondering responsibly the road to be taken, decisions aimed at strengthening that *covenant between human beings and the environment*, which should mirror the creative love of God, from whom we come and towards whom we are journeying."[16] Let us hope that the international community and individual governments will succeed in countering harmful

---

15. Paul VI, Encyclical Letter *Populorum Progressio*, 65: *loc. cit.*, 289.
16. Benedict XVI, *Message for the 2008 World Day of Peace*, 7: AAS 100 (2008), 41.

ways of treating the environment. It is likewise incumbent upon the competent authorities to make every effort to ensure that the economic and social costs of using up shared environmental resources are recognized with transparency and fully borne by those who incur them, not by other peoples or future generations: the protection of the environment, of resources and of the climate obliges all international leaders to act jointly and to show a readiness to work in good faith, respecting the law and promoting solidarity with the weakest regions of the planet.[17] One of the greatest challenges facing the economy is to achieve the most efficient use—not abuse—of natural resources, based on a realization that the notion of "efficiency" is not value-free.

51. *The way humanity treats the environment influences the way it treats itself, and vice versa.* This invites contemporary society to a serious review of its life-style, which, in many parts of the world, is prone to hedonism and consumerism, regardless of their harmful consequences.[18] What is needed is an effective shift in mentality which can lead to the adoption of *new life-styles* "in which the quest for truth, beauty, goodness and communion with others for the sake of common growth are the factors which determine consumer choices, savings and investments."[19] Every violation of solidarity and civic friendship harms the environment, just as environmental deterioration in turn upsets relations in society. Nature, especially in our time, is so integrated into the dynamics of society and culture that by now it hardly constitutes an independent variable. Desertification and the decline in productivity in some agricultural areas are also the result of impoverishment and underdevelopment among their inhabitants. When incentives are offered for their economic and cultural development, nature itself is protected. Moreover, how many natural resources are squandered by wars! Peace in and among peoples would also provide greater protection for nature. The hoarding of resources, especially water, can generate serious

---

17. Cf. Benedict XVI, *Address to the General Assembly of the United Nations Organization*, New York, 18 April 2008.

18. Cf. John Paul II, *Message for the 1990 World Day of Peace*, 13: *loc. cit.*, 154–155.

19. John Paul II, Encyclical Letter *Centesimus Annus*, 36: *loc. cit.*, 838–840.

conflicts among the peoples involved. Peaceful agreement about the use of resources can protect nature and, at the same time, the well-being of the societies concerned.

The Church has a responsibility towards creation and she must assert this responsibility in the public sphere. In so doing, she must defend not only earth, water and air as gifts of creation that belong to everyone. She must above all protect mankind from self-destruction. There is need for what might be called a human ecology, correctly understood. The deterioration of nature is in fact closely connected to the culture that shapes human coexistence: *when "human ecology"*[20] *is respected within society, environmental ecology also benefits.* Just as human virtues are interrelated, such that the weakening of one places others at risk, so the ecological system is based on respect for a plan that affects both the health of society and its good relationship with nature.

In order to protect nature, it is not enough to intervene with economic incentives or deterrents; not even an apposite education is sufficient. These are important steps, but *the decisive issue is the overall moral tenor of society*. If there is a lack of respect for the right to life and to a natural death, if human conception, gestation and birth are made artificial, if human embryos are sacrificed to research, the conscience of society ends up losing the concept of human ecology and, along with it, that of environmental ecology. It is contradictory to insist that future generations respect the natural environment when our educational systems and laws do not help them to respect themselves. The book of nature is one and indivisible: it takes in not only the environment but also life, sexuality, marriage, the family, social relations: in a word, integral human development. Our duties towards the environment are linked to our duties towards the human person, considered in himself and in relation to others. It would be wrong to uphold one set of duties while trampling on the other. Herein lies a grave contradiction in our

---

20. *Ibid.*, 38: *loc. cit.*, 840–841; Benedict XVI, *Message for the 2007 World Day of Peace*, 8: *loc. cit.*, 779.

mentality and practice today: one which demeans the person, disrupts the environment and damages society.

52. Truth, and the love which it reveals, cannot be produced: they can only be received as a gift. Their ultimate source is not, and cannot be, mankind, but only God, who is himself Truth and Love. This principle is extremely important for society and for development, since neither can be a purely human product; the vocation to development on the part of individuals and peoples is not based simply on human choice, but is an intrinsic part of a plan that is prior to us and constitutes for all of us a duty to be freely accepted. That which is prior to us and constitutes us—subsistent Love and Truth—shows us what goodness is, and in what our true happiness consists. *It shows us the road to true development.*

Laudato Si':
On Care for Our Common Home

(Excerpt)

Pope Francis
May 24, 2015

Pope Francis' encyclical situates our relationship with the environment in the context of biblical revelation, highlighting that the environment is a "collective good" and that our use of the material goods of the world must always be directed to "the good of all."

✷

CHAPTER ONE: WHAT IS HAPPENING TO OUR COMMON HOME

[. . .]

IV. Decline in the Quality of Human Life and the Breakdown of Society

43. Human beings too are creatures of this world, enjoying a right to life and happiness, and endowed with unique dignity. So we cannot fail to consider the effects on people's lives of environmental deterioration, current models of development and the throwaway culture.

44. Nowadays, for example, we are conscious of the disproportionate and unruly growth of many cities, which have become unhealthy to live in, not only because of pollution caused by toxic emissions but also as

a result of urban chaos, poor transportation, and visual pollution and noise. Many cities are huge, inefficient structures, excessively wasteful of energy and water. Neighbourhoods, even those recently built, are congested, chaotic and lacking in sufficient green space. We were not meant to be inundated by cement, asphalt, glass and metal, and deprived of physical contact with nature.

45. In some places, rural and urban alike, the privatization of certain spaces has restricted people's access to places of particular beauty. In others, "ecological" neighbourhoods have been created which are closed to outsiders in order to ensure an artificial tranquillity. Frequently, we find beautiful and carefully manicured green spaces in so-called "safer" areas of cities, but not in the more hidden areas where the disposable of society live.

46. The social dimensions of global change include the effects of technological innovations on employment, social exclusion, an inequitable distribution and consumption of energy and other services, social breakdown, increased violence and a rise in new forms of social aggression, drug trafficking, growing drug use by young people, and the loss of identity. These are signs that the growth of the past two centuries has not always led to an integral development and an improvement in the quality of life. Some of these signs are also symptomatic of real social decline, the silent rupture of the bonds of integration and social cohesion.

47. Furthermore, when media and the digital world become omnipresent, their influence can stop people from learning how to live wisely, to think deeply and to love generously. In this context, the great sages of the past run the risk of going unheard amid the noise and distractions of an information overload. Efforts need to be made to help these media become sources of new cultural progress for humanity and not a threat to our deepest riches. True wisdom, as the fruit of self-examination, dialogue and generous encounter between persons, is not acquired by

a mere accumulation of data which eventually leads to overload and confusion, a sort of mental pollution. Real relationships with others, with all the challenges they entail, now tend to be replaced by a type of internet communication which enables us to choose or eliminate relationships at whim, thus giving rise to a new type of contrived emotion which has more to do with devices and displays than with other people and with nature. Today's media do enable us to communicate and to share our knowledge and affections. Yet at times they also shield us from direct contact with the pain, the fears and the joys of others and the complexity of their personal experiences. For this reason, we should be concerned that, alongside the exciting possibilities offered by these media, a deep and melancholic dissatisfaction with interpersonal relations, or a harmful sense of isolation, can also arise.

V. Global Inequality

48. The human environment and the natural environment deteriorate together; we cannot adequately combat environmental degradation unless we attend to causes related to human and social degradation. In fact, the deterioration of the environment and of society affects the most vulnerable people on the planet: "Both everyday experience and scientific research show that the gravest effects of all attacks on the environment are suffered by the poorest."[1] For example, the depletion of fishing reserves especially hurts small fishing communities without the means to replace those resources; water pollution particularly affects the poor who cannot buy bottled water; and rises in the sea level mainly affect impoverished coastal populations who have nowhere else to go. The impact of present imbalances is also seen in the premature death of many of the poor, in conflicts sparked by the shortage of resources, and in any number of other problems which are insufficiently represented on global agendas.[2]

---

1. Bolivian Bishops' Conference, Pastoral Letter on the Environment and Human Development in Bolivia *El universo, don de Dios para la vida* (23 March 2012), 17.
2. Cf. German Bishops' Conference, Commission for Social Issues, *Der Klimawandel: Brennpunkt globaler, intergenerationeller und ökologischer Gerechtigkeit* (September 2006), 28–30.

49. It needs to be said that, generally speaking, there is little in the way of clear awareness of problems which especially affect the excluded. Yet they are the majority of the planet's population, billions of people. These days, they are mentioned in international political and economic discussions, but one often has the impression that their problems are brought up as an afterthought, a question which gets added almost out of duty or in a tangential way, if not treated merely as collateral damage. Indeed, when all is said and done, they frequently remain at the bottom of the pile. This is due partly to the fact that many professionals, opinion makers, communications media and centres of power, being located in affluent urban areas, are far removed from the poor, with little direct contact with their problems. They live and reason from the comfortable position of a high level of development and a quality of life well beyond the reach of the majority of the world's population. This lack of physical contact and encounter, encouraged at times by the disintegration of our cities, can lead to a numbing of conscience and to tendentious analyses which neglect parts of reality. At times this attitude exists side by side with a "green" rhetoric. Today, however, we have to realize that a true ecological approach *always* becomes a social approach; it must integrate questions of justice in debates on the environment, so as to hear *both the cry of the earth and the cry of the poor.*

50. Instead of resolving the problems of the poor and thinking of how the world can be different, some can only propose a reduction in the birth rate. At times, developing countries face forms of international pressure which make economic assistance contingent on certain policies of "reproductive health." Yet "while it is true that an unequal distribution of the population and of available resources creates obstacles to development and a sustainable use of the environment, it must nonetheless be recognized that demographic growth is fully compatible with an integral and shared development."[3] To blame population growth

---

3. Pontifical Council for Justice and Peace, *Compendium of the Social Doctrine of the Church*, 483.

instead of extreme and selective consumerism on the part of some, is one way of refusing to face the issues. It is an attempt to legitimize the present model of distribution, where a minority believes that it has the right to consume in a way which can never be universalized, since the planet could not even contain the waste products of such consumption. Besides, we know that approximately a third of all food produced is discarded, and "whenever food is thrown out it is as if it were stolen from the table of the poor."[4] Still, attention needs to be paid to imbalances in population density, on both national and global levels, since a rise in consumption would lead to complex regional situations, as a result of the interplay between problems linked to environmental pollution, transport, waste treatment, loss of resources and quality of life.

51. Inequity affects not only individuals but entire countries; it compels us to consider an ethics of international relations. A true "ecological debt" exists, particularly between the global north and south, connected to commercial imbalances with effects on the environment, and the disproportionate use of natural resources by certain countries over long periods of time. The export of raw materials to satisfy markets in the industrialized north has caused harm locally, as for example in mercury pollution in gold mining or sulphur dioxide pollution in copper mining. There is a pressing need to calculate the use of environmental space throughout the world for depositing gas residues which have been accumulating for two centuries and have created a situation which currently affects all the countries of the world. The warming caused by huge consumption on the part of some rich countries has repercussions on the poorest areas of the world, especially Africa, where a rise in temperature, together with drought, has proved devastating for farming. There is also the damage caused by the export of solid waste and toxic liquids to developing countries, and by the pollution produced by companies which operate in less developed countries in ways they could

---

4. *Catechesis* (5 June 2013): *Insegnamenti* 1/1 (2013), 280.

never do at home, in the countries in which they raise their capital: "We note that often the businesses which operate this way are multinationals. They do here what they would never do in developed countries or the so-called first world. Generally, after ceasing their activity and withdrawing, they leave behind great human and environmental liabilities such as unemployment, abandoned towns, the depletion of natural reserves, deforestation, the impoverishment of agriculture and local stock breeding, open pits, riven hills, polluted rivers and a handful of social works which are no longer sustainable."[5]

52. The foreign debt of poor countries has become a way of controlling them, yet this is not the case where ecological debt is concerned. In different ways, developing countries, where the most important reserves of the biosphere are found, continue to fuel the development of richer countries at the cost of their own present and future. The land of the southern poor is rich and mostly unpolluted, yet access to ownership of goods and resources for meeting vital needs is inhibited by a system of commercial relations and ownership which is structurally perverse. The developed countries ought to help pay this debt by significantly limiting their consumption of non-renewable energy and by assisting poorer countries to support policies and programmes of sustainable development. The poorest areas and countries are less capable of adopting new models for reducing environmental impact because they lack the wherewithal to develop the necessary processes and to cover their costs. We must continue to be aware that, regarding climate change, there are *differentiated responsibilities*. As the United States bishops have said, greater attention must be given to "the needs of the poor, the weak and the vulnerable, in a debate often dominated by more powerful interests."[6] We need to strengthen the conviction that we are one single human family. There are no frontiers or barriers, political or social, behind which we can hide, still less is there room for the globalization of indifference.

---

5. Bishops of the Patagonia-Comahue Region (Argentina), *Christmas Message* (December 2009), 2.

6. United States Conference of Catholic Bishops, *Global Climate Change: A Plea for Dialogue, Prudence and the Common Good* (15 June 2001).

VI. Weak Responses

53. These situations have caused sister earth, along with all the abandoned of our world, to cry out, pleading that we take another course. Never have we so hurt and mistreated our common home as we have in the last two hundred years. Yet we are called to be instruments of God our Father, so that our planet might be what he desired when he created it and correspond with his plan for peace, beauty and fullness. The problem is that we still lack the culture needed to confront this crisis. We lack leadership capable of striking out on new paths and meeting the needs of the present with concern for all and without prejudice towards coming generations. The establishment of a legal framework which can set clear boundaries and ensure the protection of ecosystems has become indispensable; otherwise, the new power structures based on the techno-economic paradigm may overwhelm not only our politics but also freedom and justice.

54. It is remarkable how weak international political responses have been. The failure of global summits on the environment make it plain that our politics are subject to technology and finance. There are too many special interests, and economic interests easily end up trumping the common good and manipulating information so that their own plans will not be affected. The *Aparecida Document* urges that "the interests of economic groups which irrationally demolish sources of life should not prevail in dealing with natural resources."[7] The alliance between the economy and technology ends up sidelining anything unrelated to its immediate interests. Consequently the most one can expect is superficial rhetoric, sporadic acts of philanthropy and perfunctory expressions of concern for the environment, whereas any genuine attempt by groups within society to introduce change is viewed as a nuisance based on romantic illusions or an obstacle to be circumvented.

---

7. Fifth General Conference of the Latin American and Caribbean Bishops, *Aparecida Document* (29 June 2007), 471.

55. Some countries are gradually making significant progress, developing more effective controls and working to combat corruption. People may well have a growing ecological sensitivity but it has not succeeded in changing their harmful habits of consumption which, rather than decreasing, appear to be growing all the more. A simple example is the increasing use and power of air-conditioning. The markets, which immediately benefit from sales, stimulate ever greater demand. An outsider looking at our world would be amazed at such behaviour, which at times appears self-destructive.

56. In the meantime, economic powers continue to justify the current global system where priority tends to be given to speculation and the pursuit of financial gain, which fail to take the context into account, let alone the effects on human dignity and the natural environment. Here we see how environmental deterioration and human and ethical degradation are closely linked. Many people will deny doing anything wrong because distractions constantly dull our consciousness of just how limited and finite our world really is. As a result, "whatever is fragile, like the environment, is defenceless before the interests of a deified market, which become the only rule."[8]

57. It is foreseeable that, once certain resources have been depleted, the scene will be set for new wars, albeit under the guise of noble claims. War always does grave harm to the environment and to the cultural riches of peoples, risks which are magnified when one considers nuclear arms and biological weapons. "Despite the international agreements which prohibit chemical, bacteriological and biological warfare, the fact is that laboratory research continues to develop new offensive weapons capable of altering the balance of nature."[9] Politics must pay greater attention to foreseeing new conflicts and addressing the causes which

---

8. Apostolic Exhortation *Evangelii Gaudium* (24 November 2013), 56: AAS 105 (2013), 1043.

9. John Paul II, *Message for the 1990 World Day of Peace*, 12: AAS 82 (1990), 154.

PART I: CHURCH TEACHING

can lead to them. But powerful financial interests prove most resistant to this effort, and political planning tends to lack breadth of vision. What would induce anyone, at this stage, to hold on to power only to be remembered for their inability to take action when it was urgent and necessary to do so?

58. In some countries, there are positive examples of environmental improvement: rivers, polluted for decades, have been cleaned up; native woodlands have been restored; landscapes have been beautified thanks to environmental renewal projects; beautiful buildings have been erected; advances have been made in the production of non-polluting energy and in the improvement of public transportation. These achievements do not solve global problems, but they do show that men and women are still capable of intervening positively. For all our limitations, gestures of generosity, solidarity and care cannot but well up within us, since we were made for love.

59. At the same time we can note the rise of a false or superficial ecology which bolsters complacency and a cheerful recklessness. As often occurs in periods of deep crisis which require bold decisions, we are tempted to think that what is happening is not entirely clear. Superficially, apart from a few obvious signs of pollution and deterioration, things do not look that serious, and the planet could continue as it is for some time. Such evasiveness serves as a licence to carrying on with our present lifestyles and models of production and consumption. This is the way human beings contrive to feed their self-destructive vices: trying not to see them, trying not to acknowledge them, delaying the important decisions and pretending that nothing will happen.

VII. A Variety of Opinions

60. Finally, we need to acknowledge that different approaches and lines of thought have emerged regarding this situation and its possible solutions. At one extreme, we find those who doggedly uphold the myth

of progress and tell us that ecological problems will solve themselves simply with the application of new technology and without any need for ethical considerations or deep change. At the other extreme are those who view men and women and all their interventions as no more than a threat, jeopardizing the global ecosystem, and consequently the presence of human beings on the planet should be reduced and all forms of intervention prohibited. Viable future scenarios will have to be generated between these extremes, since there is no one path to a solution. This makes a variety of proposals possible, all capable of entering into dialogue with a view to developing comprehensive solutions.

61. On many concrete questions, the Church has no reason to offer a definitive opinion; she knows that honest debate must be encouraged among experts, while respecting divergent views. But we need only take a frank look at the facts to see that our common home is falling into serious disrepair. Hope would have us recognize that there is always a way out, that we can always redirect our steps, that we can always do something to solve our problems. Still, we can see signs that things are now reaching a breaking point, due to the rapid pace of change and degradation; these are evident in large-scale natural disasters as well as social and even financial crises, for the world's problems cannot be analyzed or explained in isolation. There are regions now at high risk and, aside from all doomsday predictions, the present world system is certainly unsustainable from a number of points of view, for we have stopped thinking about the goals of human activity. "If we scan the regions of our planet, we immediately see that humanity has disappointed God's expectations."[10]

CHAPTER TWO: THE GOSPEL OF CREATION

62. Why should this document, addressed to all people of good will, include a chapter dealing with the convictions of believers? I am well aware that in the areas of politics and philosophy there are those who

---

10. *Ibid.*, *Catechesis* (17 January 2001), 3: *Insegnamenti* 24/1 (2001), 178.

firmly reject the idea of a Creator, or consider it irrelevant, and consequently dismiss as irrational the rich contribution which religions can make towards an integral ecology and the full development of humanity. Others view religions simply as a subculture to be tolerated. Nonetheless, science and religion, with their distinctive approaches to understanding reality, can enter into an intense dialogue fruitful for both.

I. The Light Offered by Faith

63. Given the complexity of the ecological crisis and its multiple causes, we need to realize that the solutions will not emerge from just one way of interpreting and transforming reality. Respect must also be shown for the various cultural riches of different peoples, their art and poetry, their interior life and spirituality. If we are truly concerned to develop an ecology capable of remedying the damage we have done, no branch of the sciences and no form of wisdom can be left out, and that includes religion and the language particular to it. The Catholic Church is open to dialogue with philosophical thought; this has enabled her to produce various syntheses between faith and reason. The development of the Church's social teaching represents such a synthesis with regard to social issues; this teaching is called to be enriched by taking up new challenges.

64. Furthermore, although this Encyclical welcomes dialogue with everyone so that together we can seek paths of liberation, I would like from the outset to show how faith convictions can offer Christians, and some other believers as well, ample motivation to care for nature and for the most vulnerable of their brothers and sisters. If the simple fact of being human moves people to care for the environment of which they are a part, Christians in their turn "realize that their responsibility within creation, and their duty towards nature and the Creator, are an essential part of their faith."[11] It is good for humanity and the world at

---

11. John Paul II, *Message for the 1990 World Day of Peace*, 15: AAS 82 (1990), 156.

large when we believers better recognize the ecological commitments which stem from our convictions.

II. The Wisdom of the Biblical Accounts

65. Without repeating the entire theology of creation, we can ask what the great biblical narratives say about the relationship of human beings with the world. In the first creation account in the Book of Genesis, God's plan includes creating humanity. After the creation of man and woman, "God saw everything that he had made, and behold it was *very good*" (*Gen* 1:31). The Bible teaches that every man and woman is created out of love and made in God's image and likeness (cf. *Gen* 1:26). This shows us the immense dignity of each person, "who is not just something, but someone. He is capable of self-knowledge, of self-possession and of freely giving himself and entering into communion with other persons."[12] Saint John Paul II stated that the special love of the Creator for each human being "confers upon him or her an infinite dignity."[13] Those who are committed to defending human dignity can find in the Christian faith the deepest reasons for this commitment. How wonderful is the certainty that each human life is not adrift in the midst of hopeless chaos, in a world ruled by pure chance or endlessly recurring cycles! The Creator can say to each one of us: "Before I formed you in the womb, I knew you" (*Jer* 1:5). We were conceived in the heart of God, and for this reason "each of us is the result of a thought of God. Each of us is willed, each of us is loved, each of us is necessary."[14]

66. The creation accounts in the book of Genesis contain, in their own symbolic and narrative language, profound teachings about human existence and its historical reality. They suggest that human life is grounded in three fundamental and closely intertwined relationships: with God,

---

12. *Catechism of the Catholic Church*, 357.
13. *Angelus* in Osnabrück (Germany) with the disabled, 16 November 1980: *Insegnamenti* 3/2 (1980), 1232.
14. Benedict XVI, *Homily for the Solemn Inauguration of the Petrine Ministry* (24 April 2005): AAS 97 (2005), 711.

PART I: CHURCH TEACHING

with our neighbour and with the earth itself. According to the Bible, these three vital relationships have been broken, both outwardly and within us. This rupture is sin. The harmony between the Creator, humanity and creation as a whole was disrupted by our presuming to take the place of God and refusing to acknowledge our creaturely limitations. This in turn distorted our mandate to "have dominion" over the earth (cf. Gen 1:28), to "till it and keep it" (Gen 2:15). As a result, the originally harmonious relationship between human beings and nature became conflictual (cf. Gen 3:17–19). It is significant that the harmony which Saint Francis of Assisi experienced with all creatures was seen as a healing of that rupture. Saint Bonaventure held that, through universal reconciliation with every creature, Saint Francis in some way returned to the state of original innocence.[15] This is a far cry from our situation today, where sin is manifest in all its destructive power in wars, the various forms of violence and abuse, the abandonment of the most vulnerable, and attacks on nature.

67. We are not God. The earth was here before us and it has been given to us. This allows us to respond to the charge that Judaeo-Christian thinking, on the basis of the Genesis account which grants man "dominion" over the earth (cf. Gen 1:28), has encouraged the unbridled exploitation of nature by painting him as domineering and destructive by nature. This is not a correct interpretation of the Bible as understood by the Church. Although it is true that we Christians have at times incorrectly interpreted the Scriptures, nowadays we must forcefully reject the notion that our being created in God's image and given dominion over the earth justifies absolute domination over other creatures. The biblical texts are to be read in their context, with an appropriate hermeneutic, recognizing that they tell us to "till and keep" the garden of the world (cf. Gen 2:15). "Tilling" refers to cultivating, ploughing or working, while "keeping" means caring, protecting, overseeing and preserving. This implies a relationship of mutual responsibility between

---

15. Cf. Bonaventure, *The Major Legend of Saint Francis*, VIII, 1, in *Francis of Assisi: Early Documents*, vol. 2, New York-London-Manila, 2000, 586.

human beings and nature. Each community can take from the bounty of the earth whatever it needs for subsistence, but it also has the duty to protect the earth and to ensure its fruitfulness for coming generations. "The earth is the Lord's" (*Ps* 24:1); to him belongs "the earth with all that is within it" (*Dt* 10:14). Thus God rejects every claim to absolute ownership: "The land shall not be sold in perpetuity, for the land is mine; for you are strangers and sojourners with me" (*Lev* 25:23).

68. This responsibility for God's earth means that human beings, endowed with intelligence, must respect the laws of nature and the delicate equilibria existing between the creatures of this world, for "he commanded and they were created; and he established them for ever and ever; he fixed their bounds and he set a law which cannot pass away" (*Ps* 148:5b–6). The laws found in the Bible dwell on relationships, not only among individuals but also with other living beings. "You shall not see your brother's donkey or his ox fallen down by the way and withhold your help . . . If you chance to come upon a bird's nest in any tree or on the ground, with young ones or eggs and the mother sitting upon the young or upon the eggs; you shall not take the mother with the young" (*Dt* 22:4, 6). Along these same lines, rest on the seventh day is meant not only for human beings, but also so "that your ox and your donkey may have rest" (*Ex* 23:12). Clearly, the Bible has no place for a tyrannical anthropocentrism unconcerned for other creatures.

69. Together with our obligation to use the earth's goods responsibly, we are called to recognize that other living beings have a value of their own in God's eyes: "by their mere existence they bless him and give him glory,"[16] and indeed, "the Lord rejoices in all his works" (*Ps* 104:31). By virtue of our unique dignity and our gift of intelligence, we are called to respect creation and its inherent laws, for "the Lord by wisdom founded the earth" (*Prov* 3:19). In our time, the Church does not simply state that other creatures are completely subordinated to the good of human beings, as if they have no worth in themselves and can be treated as

---

16. *Catechism of the Catholic Church*, no. 2416.

we wish. The German bishops have taught that, where other creatures are concerned, "we can speak of the priority of *being* over that of *being useful*."[17] The Catechism clearly and forcefully criticizes a distorted anthropocentrism: "Each creature possesses its own particular goodness and perfection . . . Each of the various creatures, willed in its own being, reflects in its own way a ray of God's infinite wisdom and goodness. Man must therefore respect the particular goodness of every creature, to avoid any disordered use of things."[18]

70. In the story of Cain and Abel, we see how envy led Cain to commit the ultimate injustice against his brother, which in turn ruptured the relationship between Cain and God, and between Cain and the earth from which he was banished. This is seen clearly in the dramatic exchange between God and Cain. God asks: "Where is Abel your brother?" Cain answers that he does not know, and God persists: "What have you done? The voice of your brother's blood is crying to me from the ground. And now you are cursed from the ground" (Gen 4:9–11). Disregard for the duty to cultivate and maintain a proper relationship with my neighbour, for whose care and custody I am responsible, ruins my relationship with my own self, with others, with God and with the earth. When all these relationships are neglected, when justice no longer dwells in the land, the Bible tells us that life itself is endangered. We see this in the story of Noah, where God threatens to do away with humanity because of its constant failure to fulfil the requirements of justice and peace: "I have determined to make an end of all flesh; for the earth is filled with violence through them" (Gen 6:13). These ancient stories, full of symbolism, bear witness to a conviction which we today share, that everything is interconnected, and that genuine care for our own lives and our relationships with nature is inseparable from fraternity, justice and faithfulness to others.

---

17. German Bishops' Conference, *Zukunft der Schöpfung – Zukunft der Menschheit. Einklärung der Deutschen Bischofskonferenz zu Fragen der Umwelt und der Energieversorgung*, (1980), II, 2.

18. *Catechism of the Catholic Church*, no. 339.

71. Although "the wickedness of man was great in the earth" (*Gen* 6:5) and the Lord "was sorry that he had made man on the earth" (*Gen* 6:6), nonetheless, through Noah, who remained innocent and just, God decided to open a path of salvation. In this way he gave humanity the chance of a new beginning. All it takes is one good person to restore hope! The biblical tradition clearly shows that this renewal entails recovering and respecting the rhythms inscribed in nature by the hand of the Creator. We see this, for example, in the law of the Sabbath. On the seventh day, God rested from all his work. He commanded Israel to set aside each seventh day as a day of rest, a *Sabbath* (cf. *Gen* 2:2–3; *Ex* 16:23; 20:10). Similarly, every seven years, a sabbatical year was set aside for Israel, a complete rest for the land (cf. *Lev* 25:1–4), when sowing was forbidden and one reaped only what was necessary to live on and to feed one's household (cf. *Lev* 25:4–6). Finally, after seven weeks of years, which is to say forty-nine years, the Jubilee was celebrated as a year of general forgiveness and "liberty throughout the land for all its inhabitants" (cf. *Lev* 25:10). This law came about as an attempt to ensure balance and fairness in their relationships with others and with the land on which they lived and worked. At the same time, it was an acknowledgment that the gift of the earth with its fruits belongs to everyone. Those who tilled and kept the land were obliged to share its fruits, especially with the poor, with widows, orphans and foreigners in their midst: "When you reap the harvest of your land, you shall not reap your field to its very border, neither shall you gather the gleanings after the harvest. And you shall not strip your vineyard bare, neither shall you gather the fallen grapes of your vineyard; you shall leave them for the poor and for the sojourner" (*Lev* 19:9–10).

72. The Psalms frequently exhort us to praise God the Creator, "who spread out the earth on the waters, for his steadfast love endures for ever" (*Ps* 136:6). They also invite other creatures to join us in this praise: "Praise him, sun and moon, praise him, all you shining stars! Praise him, you highest heavens, and you waters above the heavens! Let them

praise the name of the Lord, for he commanded and they were created" (*Ps* 148:3–5). We do not only exist by God's mighty power; we also live with him and beside him. This is why we adore him.

73. The writings of the prophets invite us to find renewed strength in times of trial by contemplating the all-powerful God who created the universe. Yet God's infinite power does not lead us to flee his fatherly tenderness, because in him affection and strength are joined. Indeed, all sound spirituality entails both welcoming divine love and adoration, confident in the Lord because of his infinite power. In the Bible, the God who liberates and saves is the same God who created the universe, and these two divine ways of acting are intimately and inseparably connected: "Ah Lord God! It is you who made the heavens and the earth by your great power and by your outstretched arm! Nothing is too hard for you. . . . You brought your people Israel out of the land of Egypt with signs and wonders" (*Jer* 32:17, 21). "The Lord is the everlasting God, the Creator of the ends of the earth. He does not faint or grow weary; his understanding is unsearchable. He gives power to the faint, and strengthens the powerless" (*Is* 40:28b–29).

74. The experience of the Babylonian captivity provoked a spiritual crisis which led to deeper faith in God. Now his creative omnipotence was given pride of place in order to exhort the people to regain their hope in the midst of their wretched predicament. Centuries later, in another age of trial and persecution, when the Roman Empire was seeking to impose absolute dominion, the faithful would once again find consolation and hope in a growing trust in the all-powerful God: "Great and wonderful are your deeds, O Lord God the Almighty! Just and true are your ways!" (*Rev* 15:3). The God who created the universe out of nothing can also intervene in this world and overcome every form of evil. Injustice is not invincible.

75. A spirituality which forgets God as all-powerful and Creator is not acceptable. That is how we end up worshipping earthly powers,

or ourselves usurping the place of God, even to the point of claiming an unlimited right to trample his creation underfoot. The best way to restore men and women to their rightful place, putting an end to their claim to absolute dominion over the earth, is to speak once more of the figure of a Father who creates and who alone owns the world. Otherwise, human beings will always try to impose their own laws and interests on reality.

III. The Mystery of the Universe

76. In the Judaeo-Christian tradition, the word "creation" has a broader meaning than "nature," for it has to do with God's loving plan in which every creature has its own value and significance. Nature is usually seen as a system which can be studied, understood and controlled, whereas creation can only be understood as a gift from the outstretched hand of the Father of all, and as a reality illuminated by the love which calls us together into universal communion.

77. "By the word of the Lord the heavens were made" (Ps 33:6). This tells us that the world came about as the result of a decision, not from chaos or chance, and this exalts it all the more. The creating word expresses a free choice. The universe did not emerge as the result of arbitrary omnipotence, a show of force or a desire for self-assertion. Creation is of the order of love. God's love is the fundamental moving force in all created things: "For you love all things that exist, and detest none of the things that you have made; for you would not have made anything if you had hated it" (Wis 11:24). Every creature is thus the object of the Father's tenderness, who gives it its place in the world. Even the fleeting life of the least of beings is the object of his love, and in its few seconds of existence, God enfolds it with his affection. Saint Basil the Great described the Creator as "goodness without measure,"[19] while Dante

---

19. *Hom. in Hexaemeron*, I, 2, 10: PG 29, 9.

Alighieri spoke of "the love which moves the sun and the stars."[20] Consequently, we can ascend from created things "to the greatness of God and to his loving mercy."[21]

78. At the same time, Judaeo-Christian thought demythologized nature. While continuing to admire its grandeur and immensity, it no longer saw nature as divine. In doing so, it emphasizes all the more our human responsibility for nature. This rediscovery of nature can never be at the cost of the freedom and responsibility of human beings who, as part of the world, have the duty to cultivate their abilities in order to protect it and develop its potential. If we acknowledge the value and the fragility of nature and, at the same time, our God-given abilities, we can finally leave behind the modern myth of unlimited material progress. A fragile world, entrusted by God to human care, challenges us to devise intelligent ways of directing, developing and limiting our power.

79. In this universe, shaped by open and intercommunicating systems, we can discern countless forms of relationship and participation. This leads us to think of the whole as open to God's transcendence, within which it develops. Faith allows us to interpret the meaning and the mysterious beauty of what is unfolding. We are free to apply our intelligence towards things evolving positively, or towards adding new ills, new causes of suffering and real setbacks. This is what makes for the excitement and drama of human history, in which freedom, growth, salvation and love can blossom, or lead towards decadence and mutual destruction. The work of the Church seeks not only to remind everyone of the duty to care for nature, but at the same time "she must above all protect mankind from self-destruction."[22]

80. Yet God, who wishes to work with us and who counts on our cooperation, can also bring good out of the evil we have done. "The Holy

---

20. *The Divine Comedy, Paradiso,* Canto XXXIII, 145.
21. Benedict XVI, *Catechesis* (9 November 2005), 3: *Insegnamenti* 1 (2005), 768.
22. ID., Encyclical Letter *Caritas in Veritate* (29 June 2009), 51: AAS 101 (2009), 687.

Spirit can be said to possess an infinite creativity, proper to the divine mind, which knows how to loosen the knots of human affairs, including the most complex and inscrutable."[23] Creating a world in need of development, God in some way sought to limit himself in such a way that many of the things we think of as evils, dangers or sources of suffering, are in reality part of the pains of childbirth which he uses to draw us into the act of cooperation with the Creator.[24] God is intimately present to each being, without impinging on the autonomy of his creature, and this gives rise to the rightful autonomy of earthly affairs.[25] His divine presence, which ensures the subsistence and growth of each being, "continues the work of creation."[26] The Spirit of God has filled the universe with possibilities and therefore, from the very heart of things, something new can always emerge: "Nature is nothing other than a certain kind of art, namely God's art, impressed upon things, whereby those things are moved to a determinate end. It is as if a shipbuilder were able to give timbers the wherewithal to move themselves to take the form of a ship."[27]

81. Human beings, even if we postulate a process of evolution, also possess a uniqueness which cannot be fully explained by the evolution of other open systems. Each of us has his or her own personal identity and is capable of entering into dialogue with others and with God himself. Our capacity to reason, to develop arguments, to be inventive, to interpret reality and to create art, along with other not yet discovered capacities, are signs of a uniqueness which transcends the spheres of physics and biology. The sheer novelty involved in the emergence of a personal being within a material universe presupposes a direct action of God and a particular call to life and to relationship on the part of a

23. John Paul II, Catechesis (24 April 1991), 6: Insegnamenti 14 (1991), 856.

24. The Catechism explains that God wished to create a world which is "journeying towards its ultimate perfection," and that this implies the presence of imperfection and physical evil; cf. Catechism of the Catholic Church, no. 310.

25. Cf. Second Vatian Ecumenical Council, Pastoral Constitution on the Church in the Modern World Gaudium et Spes, 36.

26. Thomas Aquinas, Summa Theologiae, I, q. 104, art. 1, ad 4.

27. Ibid., In octo libros Physicorum Aristotelis expositio, Lib. II, lectio 14.

"Thou" who addresses himself to another "thou." The biblical accounts of creation invite us to see each human being as a subject who can never be reduced to the status of an object.

82. Yet it would also be mistaken to view other living beings as mere objects subjected to arbitrary human domination. When nature is viewed solely as a source of profit and gain, this has serious consequences for society. This vision of "might is right" has engendered immense inequality, injustice and acts of violence against the majority of humanity, since resources end up in the hands of the first comer or the most powerful: the winner takes all. Completely at odds with this model are the ideals of harmony, justice, fraternity and peace as proposed by Jesus. As he said of the powers of his own age: "You know that the rulers of the Gentiles lord it over them, and their great men exercise authority over them. It shall not be so among you; but whoever would be great among you must be your servant" (Mt 20:25–26).

83. The ultimate destiny of the universe is in the fullness of God, which has already been attained by the risen Christ, the measure of the maturity of all things.[28] Here we can add yet another argument for rejecting every tyrannical and irresponsible domination of human beings over other creatures. The ultimate purpose of other creatures is not to be found in us. Rather, all creatures are moving forward with us and through us towards a common point of arrival, which is God, in that transcendent fullness where the risen Christ embraces and illumines all things. Human beings, endowed with intelligence and love, and drawn by the fullness of Christ, are called to lead all creatures back to their Creator.

---

28. In this horizon we can set the contribution of Fr. Teilhard de Chardin; cf. Paul VI, *Address in a Chemical and Pharmaceutical Plant* (24 February 1966): *Insegnamenti* 4 (1966), 992–993; John Paul II, *Letter to the Reverend George Coyne* (1 June 1988): *Insegnamenti* 11/2 (1988), 1715; Benedict XVI, *Homily for the Celebration of Vespers in Aosta* (24 July 2009): *Insegnamenti* 5/2 (2009), 60.

IV. The Message of Each Creature in the Harmony of Creation

84. Our insistence that each human being is an image of God should not make us overlook the fact that each creature has its own purpose. None is superfluous. The entire material universe speaks of God's love, his boundless affection for us. Soil, water, mountains: everything is, as it were, a caress of God. The history of our friendship with God is always linked to particular places which take on an intensely personal meaning; we all remember places, and revisiting those memories does us much good. Anyone who has grown up in the hills or used to sit by the spring to drink, or played outdoors in the neighbourhood square; going back to these places is a chance to recover something of their true selves.

85. God has written a precious book, "whose letters are the multitude of created things present in the universe."[29] The Canadian bishops rightly pointed out that no creature is excluded from this manifestation of God: "From panoramic vistas to the tiniest living form, nature is a constant source of wonder and awe. It is also a continuing revelation of the divine."[30] The bishops of Japan, for their part, made a thought-provoking observation: "To sense each creature singing the hymn of its existence is to live joyfully in God's love and hope."[31] This contemplation of creation allows us to discover in each thing a teaching which God wishes to hand on to us, since "for the believer, to contemplate creation is to hear a message, to listen to a paradoxical and silent voice."[32] We can say that "alongside revelation properly so-called, contained in sacred Scripture, there is a divine manifestation in the blaze of the sun and the fall of night."[33] Paying attention to this manifestation, we learn to see ourselves in relation to all other creatures: "I express

---

29. John Paul II, *Catechesis* (30 January 2002),6: *Insegnamenti* 25/1 (2002), 140.

30. Canadian Conference of Catholic Bishops, Social Affairs Commission, Pastoral Letter *You Love All that Exists . . . All Things are Yours, God, Lover of Life*" (4 October 2003), 1.

31. Catholic Bishops' Conference of Japan, *Reverence for Life. A Message for the Twenty-First Century* (1 January 2000), 89.

32. John Paul II, *Catechesis* (26 January 2000), 5: *Insegnamenti* 23/1 (2000), 123.

33. *Ibid.*, *Catechesis* (2 August 2000), 3: *Insegnamenti* 23/2 (2000), 112.

myself in expressing the world; in my effort to decipher the sacredness of the world, I explore my own."[34]

86. The universe as a whole, in all its manifold relationships, shows forth the inexhaustible riches of God. Saint Thomas Aquinas wisely noted that multiplicity and variety "come from the intention of the first agent" who willed that "what was wanting to one in the representation of the divine goodness might be supplied by another,"[35] inasmuch as God's goodness "could not be represented fittingly by any one creature."[36] Hence we need to grasp the variety of things in their multiple relationships.[37] We understand better the importance and meaning of each creature if we contemplate it within the entirety of God's plan. As the Catechism teaches: "God wills the interdependence of creatures. The sun and the moon, the cedar and the little flower, the eagle and the sparrow: the spectacle of their countless diversities and inequalities tells us that no creature is self-sufficient. Creatures exist only in dependence on each other, to complete each other, in the service of each other."[38]

87. When we can see God reflected in all that exists, our hearts are moved to praise the Lord for all his creatures and to worship him in union with them. This sentiment finds magnificent expression in the hymn of Saint Francis of Assisi:

> Praised be you, my Lord, with all your creatures,
> especially Sir Brother Sun,
> who is the day and through whom you give us light.
> And he is beautiful and radiant with great splendour;
> and bears a likeness of you, Most High.
> Praised be you, my Lord, through Sister Moon and the stars,
> in heaven you formed them clear and precious and beautiful.

---

34. Paul Ricoeur, *Philosophie de la Volonté, t. II: Finitude et Culpabilité*, Paris, 2009, 216.
35. *Summa Theologiae*, I, q. 47, art. 1.
36. *Ibid.*
37. Cf. *ibid.*, art. 2, ad 1; art. 3.
38. *Catechism of the Catholic Church*, no. 340.

Praised be you, my Lord, through Brother Wind,
and through the air, cloudy and serene, and every kind
   of weather
through whom you give sustenance to your creatures.
Praised be you, my Lord, through Sister Water,
who is very useful and humble and precious and chaste.
Praised be you, my Lord, through Brother Fire,
through whom you light the night,
and he is beautiful and playful and robust and strong.[39]

88. The bishops of Brazil have pointed out that nature as a whole not only manifests God but is also a locus of his presence. The Spirit of life dwells in every living creature and calls us to enter into relationship with him.[40] Discovering this presence leads us to cultivate the "ecological virtues."[41] This is not to forget that there is an infinite distance between God and the things of this world, which do not possess his fullness. Otherwise, we would not be doing the creatures themselves any good either, for we would be failing to acknowledge their right and proper place. We would end up unduly demanding of them something which they, in their smallness, cannot give us.

V. A Universal Communion

89. The created things of this world are not free of ownership: "For they are yours, O Lord, who love the living" (Wis 11:26). This is the basis of our conviction that, as part of the universe, called into being by one Father, all of us are linked by unseen bonds and together form a kind of universal family, a sublime communion which fills us with a sacred, affectionate and humble respect. Here I would reiterate that "God has joined us so closely to the world around us that we can feel the

---

39. *Canticle of the Creatures*, in *Francis of Assisi: Early Documents*, New York-London-Manila, 1999, 113–114.
40. Cf. National Conference of the Bishops of Brazil, *A Igreja e a Questão Ecológica*, 1992, 53–54.
41. *Ibid.*, 61.

desertification of the soil almost as a physical ailment, and the extinction of a species as a painful disfigurement."[42]

90. This is not to put all living beings on the same level nor to deprive human beings of their unique worth and the tremendous responsibility it entails. Nor does it imply a divinization of the earth which would prevent us from working on it and protecting it in its fragility. Such notions would end up creating new imbalances which would deflect us from the reality which challenges us.[43] At times we see an obsession with denying any pre-eminence to the human person; more zeal is shown in protecting other species than in defending the dignity which all human beings share in equal measure. Certainly, we should be concerned lest other living beings be treated irresponsibly. But we should be particularly indignant at the enormous inequalities in our midst, whereby we continue to tolerate some considering themselves more worthy than others. We fail to see that some are mired in desperate and degrading poverty, with no way out, while others have not the faintest idea of what to do with their possessions, vainly showing off their supposed superiority and leaving behind them so much waste which, if it were the case everywhere, would destroy the planet. In practice, we continue to tolerate that some consider themselves more human than others, as if they had been born with greater rights.

91. A sense of deep communion with the rest of nature cannot be real if our hearts lack tenderness, compassion and concern for our fellow human beings. It is clearly inconsistent to combat trafficking in endangered species while remaining completely indifferent to human trafficking, unconcerned about the poor, or undertaking to destroy another human being deemed unwanted. This compromises the very meaning of our struggle for the sake of the environment. It is no coincidence that, in the canticle in which Saint Francis praises God for his

---

42. Apostolic Exhortation *Evangelii Gaudium* (24 November 2013), 215: AAS 105 (2013), 1109.

43. Cf. Benedict XVI, Encyclical Letter *Caritas in Veritate* (29 June 2009), 14: AAS 101 (2009), 650.

creatures, he goes on to say: "Praised be you my Lord, through those who give pardon for your love." Everything is connected. Concern for the environment thus needs to be joined to a sincere love for our fellow human beings and an unwavering commitment to resolving the problems of society.

92. Moreover, when our hearts are authentically open to universal communion, this sense of fraternity excludes nothing and no one. It follows that our indifference or cruelty towards fellow creatures of this world sooner or later affects the treatment we mete out to other human beings. We have only one heart, and the same wretchedness which leads us to mistreat an animal will not be long in showing itself in our relationships with other people. Every act of cruelty towards any creature is "contrary to human dignity."[44] We can hardly consider ourselves to be fully loving if we disregard any aspect of reality: "Peace, justice and the preservation of creation are three absolutely interconnected themes, which cannot be separated and treated individually without once again falling into reductionism."[45] Everything is related, and we human beings are united as brothers and sisters on a wonderful pilgrimage, woven together by the love God has for each of his creatures and which also unites us in fond affection with brother sun, sister moon, brother river and mother earth.

VI. The Common Destination of Goods

93. Whether believers or not, we are agreed today that the earth is essentially a shared inheritance, whose fruits are meant to benefit everyone. For believers, this becomes a question of fidelity to the Creator, since God created the world for everyone. Hence every ecological approach needs to incorporate a social perspective which takes into account the fundamental rights of the poor and the underprivileged. The principle of the subordination of private property to the universal destination of

---

44. *Catechism of the Catholic Church*, no. 2418.
45. Conference of Dominican Bishops, Pastoral Letter *Sobre la relación del hombre con la naturaleza* (21 January 1987).

goods, and thus the right of everyone to their use, is a golden rule of social conduct and "the first principle of the whole ethical and social order."[46] The Christian tradition has never recognized the right to private property as absolute or inviolable, and has stressed the social purpose of all forms of private property. Saint John Paul II forcefully reaffirmed this teaching, stating that "God gave the earth to the whole human race for the sustenance of all its members, *without excluding or favouring anyone*."[47] These are strong words. He noted that "a type of development which did not respect and promote human rights—personal and social, economic and political, including the rights of nations and of peoples—would not be really worthy of man."[48] He clearly explained that "the Church does indeed defend the legitimate right to private property, but she also teaches no less clearly that there is always a social mortgage on all private property, in order that goods may serve the general purpose that God gave them."[49] Consequently, he maintained, "it is not in accord with God's plan that this gift be used in such a way that its benefits favour only a few."[50] This calls into serious question the unjust habits of a part of humanity.[51]

94. The rich and the poor have equal dignity, for "the Lord is the maker of them all" (*Prov* 22:2). "He himself made both small and great" (*Wis* 6:7), and "he makes his sun rise on the evil and on the good" (*Mt* 5:45). This has practical consequences, such as those pointed out by the bishops of Paraguay: "Every *campesino* has a natural right to possess a reasonable allotment of land where he can establish his home, work for subsistence of his family and a secure life. This right must be guaranteed so that its exercise is not illusory but real. That means that apart

---

46. John Paul II, Encyclical Letter *Laborem Exercens* (14 September 1981), 19: AAS 73 (1981), 626.

47. Encyclical Letter *Centesimus Annus* (1 May 1991), 31: AAS 83 (1991), 831.

48. Encyclical Letter *Sollicitudo Rei Socialis* (30 December 1987), 33: AAS 80 (1988), 557.

49. *Address to Indigenous and Rural People*, Cuilapán, Mexico (29 January 1979), 6: AAS 71 (1979), 209.

50. *Homily at Mass for Farmers*, Recife, Brazil (7 July 1980): AAS 72 (1980): AAS 72 (1980), 926.

51. Cf. *Message for the 1990 World Day of Peace*, 8: AAS 82 (1990), 152.

from the ownership of property, rural people must have access to means of technical education, credit, insurance, and markets."[52]

95. The natural environment is a collective good, the patrimony of all humanity and the responsibility of everyone. If we make something our own, it is only to administer it for the good of all. If we do not, we burden our consciences with the weight of having denied the existence of others. That is why the New Zealand bishops asked what the commandment "Thou shall not kill" means when "twenty percent of the world's population consumes resources at a rate that robs the poor nations and future generations of what they need to survive."[53]

VII. The Gaze of Jesus

96. Jesus took up the biblical faith in God the Creator, emphasizing a fundamental truth: God is Father (cf. Mt 11:25). In talking with his disciples, Jesus would invite them to recognize the paternal relationship God has with all his creatures. With moving tenderness he would remind them that each one of them is important in God's eyes: "Are not five sparrows sold for two pennies? And not one of them is forgotten before God" (Lk 12:6). "Look at the birds of the air: they neither sow nor reap nor gather into barns, and yet your heavenly Father feeds them" (Mt 6:26).

97. The Lord was able to invite others to be attentive to the beauty that there is in the world because he himself was in constant touch with nature, lending it an attention full of fondness and wonder. As he made his way throughout the land, he often stopped to contemplate the beauty sown by his Father, and invited his disciples to perceive a divine message in things: "Lift up your eyes, and see how the fields are already white for harvest" (Jn 4:35). "The kingdom of God is like a grain of mustard seed

---

52. Paraguayan Bishops' Conference, Pastoral Letter *El campesino paraguayo y la tierra* (12 June 1983), 2, 4, d.

53. New Zealand Catholic Bishops' Conference, *Statement on Environmental Issues* (1 September 2006).

which a man took and sowed in his field; it is the smallest of all seeds, but once it has grown, it is the greatest of plants" (*Mt* 13:31–32).

98. Jesus lived in full harmony with creation, and others were amazed: "What sort of man is this, that even the winds and the sea obey him?" (*Mt* 8:27). His appearance was not that of an ascetic set apart from the world, nor of an enemy to the pleasant things of life. Of himself he said: "The Son of Man came eating and drinking and they say, 'Look, a glutton and a drunkard!'" (*Mt* 11:19). He was far removed from philosophies which despised the body, matter and the things of the world. Such unhealthy dualisms, nonetheless, left a mark on certain Christian thinkers in the course of history and disfigured the Gospel. Jesus worked with his hands, in daily contact with the matter created by God, to which he gave form by his craftsmanship. It is striking that most of his life was dedicated to this task in a simple life which awakened no admiration at all: "Is not this the carpenter, the son of Mary?" (*Mk* 6:3). In this way he sanctified human labour and endowed it with a special significance for our development. As Saint John Paul II taught, "by enduring the toil of work in union with Christ crucified for us, man in a way collaborates with the Son of God for the redemption of humanity."[54]

99. In the Christian understanding of the world, the destiny of all creation is bound up with the mystery of Christ, present from the beginning: "All things have been created though him and for him" (*Col* 1:16).[55] The prologue of the Gospel of John (1:1–18) reveals Christ's creative work as the Divine Word (*Logos*). But then, unexpectedly, the prologue goes on to say that this same Word "became flesh" (*Jn* 1:14). One Person of the Trinity entered into the created cosmos, throwing in his lot with it, even to the cross. From the beginning of the world, but particularly through the incarnation, the mystery of Christ is at work in a hidden

---

54. Encyclical Letter *Laborem Exercens* (14 September 1981), 27: AAS 73 (1981), 645.
55. Hence Saint Justin could speak of "seeds of the Word" in the world; cf. *II Apologia* 8, 1–2; 13, 3–6: PG 6, 457–458, 467.

manner in the natural world as a whole, without thereby impinging on its autonomy.

100. The New Testament does not only tell us of the earthly Jesus and his tangible and loving relationship with the world. It also shows him risen and glorious, present throughout creation by his universal Lordship: "For in him all the fullness of God was pleased to dwell, and through him to reconcile to himself all things, whether on earth or in heaven, making peace by the blood of his cross" (*Col* 1:19–20). This leads us to direct our gaze to the end of time, when the Son will deliver all things to the Father, so that "God may be everything to every one" (*1 Cor* 15:28). Thus, the creatures of this world no longer appear to us under merely natural guise because the risen One is mysteriously holding them to himself and directing them towards fullness as their end. The very flowers of the field and the birds which his human eyes contemplated and admired are now imbued with his radiant presence.

PART II

SCRIPTURE, SAINTS, AND SCHOLARS

CHAPTER 15

The Old Testament

Then God said, "Let us make humankind in our image, according to our likeness; and let them have dominion over the fish of the sea, and over the birds of the air, and over the cattle, and over all the wild animals of the earth, and over every creeping thing that creeps upon the earth."

So God created humankind in his image,
in the image of God he created them;
male and female he created them.

— Genesis 1:26–27

Then the LORD God formed man from the dust of the ground, and breathed into his nostrils the breath of life; and the man became a living being.

— Genesis 2:7

In his own image
God made humankind.

— Genesis 9:6

You shall not murder.

—Exodus 20:13

You shall not wrong or oppress a resident alien, for you were aliens in the land of Egypt. You shall not abuse any widow or orphan. If you do abuse them, when they cry out to me, I will surely heed their cry.

—Exodus 22:21–23

When you reap the harvest of your land, you shall not reap to the very edges of your field, or gather the gleanings of your harvest. You shall not strip your vineyard bare, or gather the fallen grapes of your vineyard; you shall leave them for the poor and the alien: I am the LORD your God.

—Leviticus 19:9–10

For the LORD your God is God of gods and Lord of lords, the great God, mighty and awesome, who is not partial and takes no bribe, who executes justice for the orphan and the widow, and who loves the strangers, providing them food and clothing. You shall also love the stranger, for you were strangers in the land of Egypt.

—Deuteronomy 10:17–19

You must not distort justice; you must not show partiality; and you must not accept bribes, for a bribe blinds the eyes of the wise and subverts the cause of those who are in the right. Justice, and only justice, you shall pursue, so that you may live and occupy the land that the LORD your God is giving you.

—Deuteronomy 16:19–20

You shall not withhold the wages of poor and needy laborers, whether other Israelites or aliens who reside in your land in one of your towns. You shall pay them their wages daily before sunset, because they are poor and their livelihood depends on them; otherwise they might cry to the LORD against you, and you would incur guilt.

— Deuteronomy 24:14–15

"As your life was precious today in my sight, so may my life be precious in the sight of the LORD, and may he rescue me from all tribulation."

— 1 Samuel 26:24

To all those who practice righteousness give alms from your possessions, and do not let your eye begrudge the gift when you make it. Do not turn your face away from anyone who is poor, and the face of God will not be turned away from you. If you have many possessions, make your gift from them in proportion; if few, do not be afraid to give according to the little you have. So you will be laying up a good treasure for yourself against the day of necessity. For almsgiving delivers from death and keeps you from going into the Darkness. Indeed, almsgiving, for all who practice it, is an excellent offering in the presence of the Most High.

— Tobit 4:6–11

What are human beings, that you make so much of them,
    that you set your mind on them,
visit them every morning,
    test them every moment?

— Job 7:17–18

When I look at your heavens, the work of your fingers,
  the moon and the stars that you have established;
what are human beings that you are mindful of them,
  mortals that you care for them?
Yet you have made them a little lower than God,
  and crowned them with glory and honor.
You have given them dominion over the works of your hands;
  you have put all things under their feet,
all sheep and oxen,
  and also the beasts of the field,
the birds of the air, and the fish of the sea,
  whatever passes along the paths of the seas.

— Psalm 8:3–8

O LORD, you will hear the desire of the meek;
  you will strengthen their heart, you will incline your ear
to do justice for the orphan and the oppressed,
  so that those from earth may strike terror no more.

— Psalm 10:17–18

On you I was cast from my birth,
  and since my mother bore me you have been my God.

— Psalm 22:10

Give the king your justice, O God,
  and your righteousness to a king's son.
May he judge your people with righteousness,
  and your poor with justice.
May the mountains yield prosperity for the people,
  and the hills, in righteousness.

May he defend the cause of the poor of the people,
　　give deliverance to the needy,
　　and crush the oppressor.

— Psalm 72:1–4

"Give justice to the weak and the orphan;
　　maintain the right of the lowly and the destitute.
Rescue the weak and the needy;
　　deliver them from the hand of the wicked."

— Psalm 82:3–4

The heavens are the LORD's heavens,
　　but the earth he has given to human beings.

— Psalm 115:16

For it was you who formed my inward parts;
　　you knit me together in my mother's womb.
I praise you, for I am fearfully and wonderfully made.
　　My frame was not hidden from you,
when I was being made in secret,
　　intricately woven in the depths of the earth.

— Psalm 139:13–15

Happy are those whose help is the God of Jacob,
　　whose hope is in the LORD their God,
who made heaven and earth,
　　the sea, and all that is in them;
who keeps faith forever;
　　who executes justice for the oppressed;
　　who gives food to the hungry.

The Lord sets the prisoners free;
> the Lord opens the eyes of the blind.
The Lord lifts up those who are bowed down;
> the Lord loves the righteous.
The Lord watches over the strangers;
> he upholds the orphan and the widow,
> but the way of the wicked he brings to ruin.

— Psalm 146:5–9

Those who oppress the poor insult their Maker,
> but those who are kind to the needy honor him.

— Proverbs 14:31

The rich and the poor have this in common:
> the Lord is the maker of them all.

— Proverbs 22:2

Speak out for those who cannot speak,
> for the rights of all the destitute.
Speak out, judge righteously,
> defend the rights of the poor and needy.

— Proverbs 31:8–9

My child, do not cheat the poor of their living,
    and do not keep needy eyes waiting.
Do not grieve the hungry,
    or anger one in need.
Do not add to the troubles of the desperate,
    or delay giving to the needy.
Do not reject a suppliant in distress,
    or turn your face away from the poor.
Do not avert your eye from the needy,
    and give no one reason to curse you;
for if in bitterness of soul some should curse you,
    their Creator will hear their prayer.

Endear yourself to the congregation;
    bow your head low to the great.
Give a hearing to the poor,
    and return their greeting politely.
Rescue the oppressed from the oppressor;
    and do not be hesitant in giving a verdict.
Be a father to orphans,
    and be like a husband to their mother;
you will then be like a son of the Most High,
    and he will love you more than does your mother.

—Sirach 4:1–10

The compassion of human beings is for their neighbors,
    but the compassion of the Lord is for every living thing.

—Sirach 18:13

He will not ignore the supplication of the orphan,
  or the widow when she pours out her complaint.
Do not the tears of the widow run down her cheek
  as she cries out against the one who causes them to fall?
The one whose service is pleasing to the Lord will be accepted,
  and his prayer will reach to the clouds.
The prayer of the humble pierces the clouds,
  and it will not rest until it reaches its goal;
it will not desist until the Most High responds
  and does justice for the righteous, and executes judgment.

—Sirach 35:17–22

  Learn to do good;
seek justice,
  rescue the oppressed,
defend the orphan,
  plead for the widow.

—Isaiah 1:17

Ah, you who make iniquitous decrees,
  who write oppressive statutes,
to turn aside the needy from justice
  and to rob the poor of my people of their right,
that widows may be your spoil,
  and that you may make the orphans your prey!
What will you do on the day of punishment,
  in the calamity that will come from far away?
To whom will you flee for help,
  and where will you leave your wealth,
so as not to crouch among the prisoners
  or fall among the slain?

—Isaiah 10:1–4

Give counsel,
 grant justice;
make your shade like night
 at the height of noon;
hide the outcasts,
 do not betray the fugitive.

—Isaiah 16:3

The LORD is a God of justice;
 blessed are all those who wait for him.

—Isaiah 30:18

Is not this the fast that I choose:
 to loose the bonds of injustice,
 to undo the thongs of the yoke,
to let the oppressed go free,
 and to break every yoke?
Is it not to share your bread with the hungry,
 and bring the homeless poor into your house;
when you see the naked, to cover them,
 and not to hide yourself from your own kin?
Then your light shall break forth like the dawn,
 and your healing shall spring up quickly;
your vindicator shall go before you,
 the glory of the Lord shall be your rear guard.
Then you shall call, and the Lord will answer;
 you shall cry for help, and he will say, Here I am.

—Isaiah 58:6–9

Before I formed you in the womb I knew you,
and before you were born I consecrated you.

—Jeremiah 1:5

They know no limits in deeds of wickedness;
    they do not judge with justice
the cause of the orphan, to make it prosper,
    and they do not defend the rights of the needy.

—Jeremiah 5:28

Deliver from the hand of the oppressor
anyone who has been robbed.

—Jeremiah 21:12

Woe to him who builds his house by unrighteousness,
    and his upper rooms by injustice;
who makes his neighbors work for nothing,
    and does not give them their wages.

—Jeremiah 22:13

Know that all lives are mine; the life of the parent as well as the life of
the child is mine.

—Ezekiel 18:4

I myself will be the shepherd of my sheep, and I will make them lie down, says the Lord God. I will seek the lost, and I will bring back the strayed, and I will bind up the injured, and I will strengthen the weak, but the fat and the strong I will destroy. I will feed them with justice.

— Ezekiel 34:15–16

Let justice roll down like waters,
    and righteousness like an ever-flowing stream.

— Amos 5:24

He has told you, O mortal, what is good;
    and what does the Lord require of you
but to do justice, and to love kindness,
    and to walk humbly with your God?

— Micah 6:8

CHAPTER 16

The New Testament

✳

"In everything do to others as you would have them do to you; for this is the law and the prophets."

—Matthew 7:12

"Let the little children come to me, and do not stop them; for it is to such as these that the kingdom of heaven belongs."

—Matthew 19:14

"When the Son of Man comes in his glory, and all the angels with him, then he will sit on the throne of his glory. All the nations will be gathered before him, and he will separate people one from another as a shepherd separates the sheep from the goats, and he will put the sheep at his right hand and the goats at the left. Then the king will say to those at his right hand, 'Come, you that are blessed by my Father, inherit the kingdom prepared for you from the foundation of the world; for I was hungry and you gave me food, I was thirsty and you gave me something to drink, I was a stranger and you welcomed me, I was naked and you gave me clothing, I was sick and you took care of me, I was in prison and you visited me.' Then the righteous will answer him, 'Lord, when was it that we saw you hungry and gave you food, or thirsty and gave you something to drink? And when was it that we saw you a stranger and welcomed you, or naked and gave you clothing? And when was it that we saw you sick or in prison and visited you?' And the king will answer them, 'Truly I tell you, just as you did it to one of the least of these who are members of my family, you did it to me.' Then he will say to those at his left hand, 'You that are accursed, depart from me into the eternal fire prepared for the devil and his angels; for I was hungry and you gave me no food, I was thirsty and you gave me nothing to drink, I was a stranger and you did not welcome me, naked and you did not give me clothing, sick and in prison and you did not visit me.' Then they also will answer, 'Lord, when was it that we saw you hungry or thirsty or a stranger or naked or sick or in prison, and did not take care of you?' Then he will answer them, 'Truly I tell you, just as you did not do it to one of the least of these, you did not do it to me.' And these will go away into eternal punishment, but the righteous into eternal life."

— Matthew 25:31–46

"The sabbath was made for humankind, and not humankind for the sabbath; so the Son of Man is lord even of the sabbath."

— Mark 2:27–28

And the crowds asked [John the Baptist], "What then should we do?" In reply he said to them, "Whoever has two coats must share with anyone who has none; and whoever has food must do likewise." Even tax collectors came to be baptized, and they asked him, "Teacher, what should we do?" He said to them, "Collect no more than the amount prescribed for you." Soldiers also asked him, "And we, what should we do?" He said to them, "Do not extort money from anyone by threats or false accusation, and be satisfied with your wages."

— Luke 3:10–14

When [Jesus] came to Nazareth, where he had been brought up, he went to the synagogue on the sabbath day, as was his custom. He stood up to read, and the scroll of the prophet Isaiah was given to him. He unrolled the scroll and found the place where it was written:

"The Spirit of the Lord is upon me,
because he has anointed me
to bring good news to the poor.
He has sent me to proclaim release to the captives
and recovery of sight to the blind,
to let the oppressed go free,
to proclaim the year of the Lord's favor."

And he rolled up the scroll, gave it back to the attendant, and sat down. The eyes of all in the synagogue were fixed on him. Then he began to say to them, "Today this scripture has been fulfilled in your hearing."

—Luke 4:16–21

"Blessed are you who are poor,
for yours is the kingdom of God.
Blessed are you who are hungry now,
for you will be filled.
Blessed are you who weep now,
for you will laugh."

—Luke 6:20–21

Just then a lawyer stood up to test Jesus. "Teacher," he said, "what must I do to inherit eternal life?" He said to him, "What is written in the law? What do you read there?" He answered, "You shall love the Lord your God with all your heart, and with all your soul, and with all your strength, and with all your mind; and your neighbor as yourself." And he said to him, "You have given the right answer; do this, and you will live."

But wanting to justify himself, he asked Jesus, "And who is my neighbor?" Jesus replied, "A man was going down from Jerusalem to Jericho, and fell into the hands of robbers, who stripped him, beat him, and went away, leaving him half dead. Now by chance a priest was going down that road; and when he saw him, he passed by on the other side. So likewise a Levite, when he came to the place and saw him, passed by on the other side. But a Samaritan while traveling came near him; and when he saw him, he was moved with pity. He went to him and bandaged his wounds, having poured oil and wine on them. Then he put him on his own animal, brought him to an inn, and took care of him. The next day he took out two denarii, gave them to the innkeeper, and said, 'Take care of him; and when I come back, I will repay you whatever more you spend.' Which of these three, do you think, was a neighbor to the man who fell into the hands of the robbers?" He said, "The one who showed him mercy." Jesus said to him, "Go and do likewise."

—Luke 10:25–37

"There was a rich man who was dressed in purple and fine linen and who feasted sumptuously every day. And at his gate lay a poor man named Lazarus, covered with sores, who longed to satisfy his hunger with what fell from the rich man's table; even the dogs would come and lick his sores. The poor man died and was carried away by the angels to be with Abraham. The rich man also died and was buried. In Hades, where he was being tormented, he looked up and saw Abraham far away with Lazarus by his side. He called out, 'Father Abraham, have mercy on me, and send Lazarus to dip the tip of his finger in water and cool my tongue; for I am in agony in these flames.' But Abraham said, 'Child, remember that during your lifetime you received your good things, and Lazarus in like manner evil things; but now he is comforted here, and you are in agony. Besides all this, between you and us a great chasm has been fixed, so that those who might want to pass from here to you cannot do so, and no one can cross from there to us.' He said, 'Then, father, I beg you to send him to my father's house—for I have five brothers—that he may warn them, so that they will not also come into this place of torment.' Abraham replied, 'They have Moses and the prophets; they should listen to them.' He said, 'No, father Abraham; but if someone goes to them from the dead, they will repent.' He said to him, 'If they do not listen to Moses and the prophets, neither will they be convinced even if someone rises from the dead.'"

—Luke 16:19–31

What has come into being in him was life, and the life was the light of all people.

—John 1:3–4

"And I, when I am lifted up from the earth, will draw all people to myself."

—John 12:32

"This is my commandment, that you love one another as I have loved you."

—John 15:12

Now the whole group of those who believed were of one heart and soul, and no one claimed private ownership of any possessions, but everything they owned was held in common. With great power the apostles gave their testimony to the resurrection of the Lord Jesus, and great grace was upon them all. There was not a needy person among them, for as many as owned lands or houses sold them and brought the proceeds of what was sold. They laid it at the apostles' feet, and it was distributed to each as any had need.

— Acts 4:32–36

[Paul said:] "I do my best always to have a clear conscience toward God and all people."

— Acts 24:16

Contribute to the needs of the saints; extend hospitality to strangers.

— Romans 12:13

Do you not know that you are God's temple and that God's Spirit dwells in you? If anyone destroys God's temple, God will destroy that person. For God's temple is holy, and you are that temple.

— 1 Corinthians 3:16–17

Indeed, the body does not consist of one member but of many. If the foot would say, "Because I am not a hand, I do not belong to the body," that would not make it any less a part of the body. And if the ear would say, "Because I am not an eye, I do not belong to the body," that would not make it any less a part of the body. If the whole body were an eye, where would the hearing be? If the whole body were hearing, where would the sense of smell be? But as it is, God arranged the members in the body, each one of them, as he chose. If all were a single member, where would the body be? As it is, there are many members, yet one body. The eye cannot say to the hand, "I have no need of you," nor again the head to the feet, "I have no need of you." On the contrary, the members of the body that seem to be weaker are indispensable, and those members of the body that we think less honorable we clothe with greater honor, and our less respectable members are treated with greater respect; whereas our more respectable members do not need this. But God has so arranged the body, giving the greater honor to the inferior member, that there may be no dissension within the body, but the members may have the same care for one another. If one member suffers, all suffer together with it; if one member is honored, all rejoice together with it.

— 1 Corinthians 12:14–26

There is no longer Jew or Greek, there is no longer slave or free, there is no longer male and female; for all of you are one in Christ Jesus.

— Galatians 3:28

I urge that supplications, prayers, intercessions, and thanksgivings be made for everyone, for kings and all who are in high positions, so that we may lead a quiet and peaceable life in all godliness and dignity. This is right and is acceptable in the sight of God our Savior, who desires everyone to be saved and to come to the knowledge of the truth.

— 1 Timothy 2:1–4

We have our hope set on the living God, who is the Savior of all people, especially of those who believe.

— 1 Timothy 4:10

Someone has testified somewhere,

> "What are human beings that you are mindful of them,
> or mortals, that you care for them?
> You have made them for a little while lower than the angels;
> you have crowned them with glory and honor,
> subjecting all things under their feet."

Now in subjecting all things to them, God left nothing outside their control. As it is, we do not yet see everything in subjection to them, but we do see Jesus, who for a little while was made lower than the angels, now crowned with glory and honor because of the suffering of death, so that by the grace of God he might taste death for everyone.

— Hebrews 2:6–9

My brothers and sisters, do you with your acts of favoritism really believe in our glorious Lord Jesus Christ? For if a person with gold rings and in fine clothes comes into your assembly, and if a poor person in dirty clothes also comes in, and if you take notice of the one wearing the fine clothes and say, "Have a seat here, please," while to the one who is poor you say, "Stand there," or, "Sit at my feet," have you not made distinctions among yourselves, and become judges with evil thoughts? Listen, my beloved brothers and sisters. Has not God chosen the poor in the world to be rich in faith and to be heirs of the kingdom that he has promised to those who love him?

— James 2:1–5

What good is it, my brothers and sisters, if you say you have faith but do not have works? Can faith save you? If a brother or sister is naked and lacks daily food, and one of you says to them, "Go in peace; keep warm and eat your fill," and yet you do not supply their bodily needs, what is the good of that? So faith by itself, if it has no works, is dead.

— James 2:14–17

Honor everyone.

— 1 Peter 2:17

His divine power has given us everything needed for life and godliness, through the knowledge of him who called us by his own glory and goodness. Thus he has given us, through these things, his precious and very great promises, so that through them you may escape from the corruption that is in the world because of lust, and may become participants of the divine nature.

— 2 Peter 1:3–4

See what love the Father has given us, that we should be called children of God; and that is what we are.

— 1 John 3:1

We know love by this, that he laid down his life for us—and we ought to lay down our lives for one another. How does God's love abide in anyone who has the world's goods and sees a brother or sister in need and yet refuses help?

— 1 John 3:16–17

We love because he first loved us. Those who say, "I love God," and hate their brothers or sisters, are liars; for those who do not love a brother or sister whom they have seen, cannot love God whom they have not seen. The commandment we have from him is this: those who love God must love their brothers and sisters also.

— 1 John 4:19–21

CHAPTER 17

The Didache

Also called "The Teaching of the Twelve Apostles," most scholars date this document to the first century AD. Along with the New Testament, it is among the earliest Christian writings. Of particular note in the context of Catholic social teaching is its unequivocal condemnation of abortion.

Give to everyone who asks, and ask nothing in return; for the Father wishes that a share of His own gifts be given to all. Blessed is the man who gives according to the commandment, for he is without blame. Woe to the man who takes. However, if the one who takes is in need, he is without blame. But should he not be in need, he shall give an account of the why and the wherefore of his taking it. And he will be put in prison and examined strictly about what he did, and 'shall not go out from there until he has paid the last cent.' But in this matter the saying also holds: 'Let your alms sweat in your hands until you know to whom you are giving.'

—Didache 1:5–6

You shall not kill an unborn child or murder a newborn infant.

—Didache 2:2

Do not hold your hands open for receiving and closed for giving. If you possess something by the labor of your hands, give it for the redemption of your sins. Do not be reluctant in giving, or murmur when you give, for you well know who He is who gives a good reward. Do not turn away from the needy, but share all with your brother and do not claim that it is your own. For, if you are sharers in immortal things, how much more in mortal.

— Didache 4:5–8

[Those who walk the way of death] are murderers of children, corrupters of the image of God; they turn away from the needy, oppress the afflicted; they are flatterers of the rich, unjust judges of the poor, and are full of all sins.

— Didache 5:2

Let no one speak with anyone who has harmed his neighbor, nor let him be heard until he repents. Offer your prayers and alms and do all things according to the Gospel of our Lord.

— Didache 15:3–4

CHAPTER 18

The Church Fathers

This group of early Christian writers, which includes great thinkers like St. Irenaeus, St. John Chrysostom, and St. Augustine, were enormously influential in shaping the theology of the Church.

✳

St. Irenaeus
(AD 130–202)

The glory of God is a human being fully alive.

— *Against Heresies*, 4.20.7

St. Clement of Alexandria
(AD 150–215)

If no one had anything, what room would be left among men for giving? . . . Riches, then, which benefit also our neighbors, are not to be thrown away. For they are possessions, inasmuch as they are possessed, and goods, inasmuch as they are useful and provided by God for the use of men; and they lie to our hand, and are put under our power, as material and instruments that are for good use to those who know the instrument. If you use it skillfully, it is skillful; if you are deficient in skill, it is affected by your lack of skill, being itself destitute of blame.

Such an instrument is wealth. Are you able to make a right use of it? Then it is subservient to righteousness. Does one make a wrong use of it? Then it is, on the other hand, a minister of wrong. For its nature is to be subservient, not to rule. That then which of itself has neither good nor evil, being blameless, ought not to be blamed; rather, any blame must lie with that which has the power of using it well and ill by reason of its possessing voluntary choice—namely, the mind and judgment of man. . . . So let no man destroy wealth, rather than the passions of the soul, which are incompatible with the better use of wealth. So that, becoming virtuous and good, he may be able to make a good use of these riches. The renunciation, then, and selling of all possessions, is to be understood as spoken of the passions of the soul.

—*Who Is the Rich Man That Shall Be Saved?*, 13, 14

St. Hippolytus of Rome
(AD 170–236)

Do you wish then to know in what manner the Word of God, who was again the Son of God, as he was of old the Word, communicated his revelations to the blessed prophets in former times? Well, as the Word shows his compassion and his denial of all respect of persons by all the saints, he enlightens them and adapts them to that which is advantageous for us, like a skillful physician, understanding the weakness of men. And the ignorant he loves to teach, and the erring he turns again to his own true way. And by those who live by faith he is easily found; and to those of pure eye and holy heart, who desire to knock at the door, he opens immediately. For he casts away none of his servants as unworthy of the divine mysteries. He does not esteem the rich man more highly than the poor, nor does he despise the poor man for his poverty. He does not disdain the barbarian, nor does he set the eunuch aside as no man. He does not hate the female on account of the woman's act of disobedience in the beginning, nor does he reject the male on account of the man's transgression. But he seeks all, and desires to save all, wishing to make all the children of God, and calling all the saints unto one perfect man. For there is also one Son (or Servant) of God, by whom we too, receiving the regeneration through the Holy Spirit, desire to come all unto one perfect and heavenly man (Eph. 4:13).

— On Christ and Antichrist, 3

Origen of Alexandria
(AD 185–254)

Both Jesus himself and his disciples desired that his followers should believe not merely in his Godhead and miracles, as if he had not also been a partaker of human nature, and had assumed the human flesh which lusts against the Spirit; but they saw also that the power which had descended into human nature, and into the midst of human miseries, and which had assumed a human soul and body, contributed through faith, along with its divine elements, to the salvation of believers, when they see that from him there began the union of the divine with the human nature, in order that the human, by communion with the divine, might rise to be divine, not in Jesus alone, but in all those who not only believe, but enter upon the life which Jesus taught, and which elevates to friendship with God and communion with him every one who lives according to the precepts of Jesus.

— Against Celsus, 3.28

"God made man, according to the image of God he made him." We must see what that image of God is and inquire diligently in the likeness of what image man is made. For the text did not say that "God made man according to the image or likeness," but "according to the image of God he made him." Therefore, what other image of God is there according to the likeness of whose image man is made, except our Savior who is "the firstborn of every creature," about whom it is written that he is "the brightness of the eternal light and the express figure of God's substance," who also says about himself: "I am in the Father, and the Father in me," and "He who has seen me has also seen the Father"? For just as one who sees an image of someone sees him whose image it is, so also one sees God through the Word of God which is the image of God. And thus what he said will be true: "He who has seen me has also seen the Father."

Man, therefore, is made according to the likeness of his image and for this reason our Savior, who is the image of God, moved with compassion for man who had been made according to his likeness, seeing him, his own image having been laid aside, to have put on the image of the evil one, he himself moved with compassion, assumed the image of man and came to him, as also the Apostle attests saying: "Since he was in the form of God, he did not think it robbery to be equal with God, but emptied himself taking the form of a servant, and in appearance found as a man, he humbled himself even to death."

All therefore, who come to him and desire to become participants in the spiritual image by their progress "are renewed daily in the inner man" according to the image of him who made them, so that they can be made "similar to the body of his glory," but each one in proportion to his own powers. The apostles transformed themselves to his likeness to such an extent that he could say of them, "I go to my Father and your Father, to my God and your God." For he had already petitioned the Father for his disciples that the original likeness might be restored in them when he says: "Father," grant "that just as you and I are one so also they may be one in us."

Let us always, therefore, contemplate that image of God that we can be transformed to his likeness. For if man, made according to the image of God, contrary to nature by beholding the image of the devil has been made like him by sin, much more by beholding the image of God, according to whose likeness he has been made by God, he will receive that form, which was given to him by nature, through the Word and his power. And let no one, seeing his image to be more with the devil than with God, despair that he can again regain the form of the image of God, because the Savior came not "to call the just, but sinners to repentance."

— *Homilies on Genesis*, Homily 1.13[1]

St. Athanasius of Alexandria
(AD 296–373)

He was made man that we might be made God; and he manifested himself by a body that we might receive the idea of the unseen Father; and he endured the insolence of men that we might inherit immortality.

— *On the Incarnation of the Word*, 54

St. Ambrose of Milan
(AD 333–397)

We are taught how fitting it is to be merciful and liberal towards the poor, and that this feeling should not be checked by the consideration of our poverty, since liberality is determined not by the amount of our possessions, but by the disposition of giving. For by the voice of the Lord that widow of whom it was said, "this poor widow has put in more than all of them" (Luke 21:3), is preferred to all. In this instance the Lord characteristically teaches all that none should be held back from giving assistance through shame at his own poverty, and that the rich should not flatter themselves that they seem to give more than the poor. For the piece of money out of a small stock is richer than treasures out of

1. Origen, *Homilies on Genesis and Exodus*, trans. Ronald E. Heine (Washington, DC: The Catholic University of America Press, 1982), 65–66.

abundance, because it is not the amount that is given but the amount that remains that is considered. No one gives more than she who has left nothing for herself.

— *Concerning Widows*, 27

St. John Chrysostom
(AD 349–407)

Not to enable the poor to share in our goods is to steal from them and deprive them of life. The goods we possess are not ours, but theirs.

— *Hom. in Lazaro*, 2, 5[2]

He tells men to receive the greatest outcasts, and punishes those that fail to do so. For, "as you did not do it to one of the least of these, you did not do it to me" (Matt. 25:45), and the converse again he affirms with respect to the same people.

Because although he may be doing no such great work, he is a man, inhabiting the same world with you, beholding the same sun, having the same soul, the same Lord, a partaker with you of the same mysteries, called to the same heaven with you; having a strong claim, his poverty, and his lack of necessary food. . . . If there comes to you a poor man wanting bread, there is no end of revilings, and reproaches, and charges of idleness, and upbraidings, and insults, and jeers; and you consider not with yourself, that you too are idle, and yet God gives you his gifts. For do not tell me that you too are doing some things, but rather point out to me if there is anything really needed that you do and are busy about. But if you tell about money-getting, and of traffic, and of the care and increase of your goods, I also would say to you, "Not these, but alms, and prayers, and the protection of the injured, and all such things, are

---

2. St. John Chrysostom, *Hom. in Lazaro* 2, 5: PG 48, 992. Quoted in *Catechism of the Catholic Church*, no. 2446 (New York: Image Books, 1995), 647.

truly works—and with respect to those, we live in thorough idleness." Yet God never told us, "Because you are idle, I do not light up the sun for you; because you do nothing of real consequence, I quench the moon, I paralyze the womb of the earth, I restrain the lakes, the fountains, the rivers, I blot out the atmosphere: I withhold the annual rains": but he gives to us all abundantly. And to some that are not merely idle, but even doing evil, he freely gives the benefit of these things.

Therefore, when you see a poor man and say, "It stops my breath that this fellow, young as he is and healthy, having nothing, would rather be fed in idleness; he is surely some slave and runaway, and has deserted his proper master": I tell you to speak these same words to yourself; or rather, permit him freely to speak them to you, and he will say with more justice, "It stops my breath that you, being healthy, are idle, and practice none of the things that God has commanded, but having run away from the commandments of your Lord, go about dwelling in wickedness, as in a strange land, in drunkenness, in gluttony, in theft, in extortion, in subverting other men's houses. . . ."

Only give, whether you are reminded to do so by yourself or by another; and do not accuse, do not smite, do not revile. For he who comes to you needs medicines, not wounds; mercy, not a sword. For tell me, if any one who had been struck with a stone, and had received a wound in his head, were to let go all others, and run unto your knees, drenched in his blood; would you indeed strike him with another stone, and add unto him another wound? I, for my part, think not; but rather, you would endeavor to cure it. Why then do you do the contrary with respect to the poor? Do you not know how much power a word has, both to raise up and to cast down? "A word," it is said, "is better than a gift" (Sir. 18:16).

Do you not consider that you are thrusting the sword into yourself, and are receiving a more grievous wound, when he, being reviled, silently withdraws, with groans and many tears? Because indeed, he is sent to you from God. Consider then, in insulting him, upon whom you are causing the insult to pass, when God indeed sends him to you, and commands you to give, but you, so far from giving, even insult him when he comes.

— Homilies on Matthew, 35.5, 7

Let no Judas then approach this table, no Simon [Magus]; no, for they both perished through greed. Let us flee then from this gulf; let us not account it enough for our salvation, if after we have stripped widows and orphans, we offer for this table a gold and jeweled cup. No; if you desire to honor the sacrifice, offer your soul, for which Christ was slain—cause that to become golden. But if your soul remains worse than lead or potter's clay while the vessel on the altar is made of gold, what is the profit?

Therefore, do not let offering only golden vessels be our aim, but to do so also from honest earnings. For these are of the sort that is more precious even than gold, these that cause no injury. For the Church is not a gold foundry nor a workshop for silver, but an assembly of angels. Thus it is souls that we require, since in fact God accepts these for the souls' sake.

That table at that time was not of silver nor that cup of gold, out of which Christ gave his disciples his own blood; but everything there was precious, and awe-inspiring, because they were full of the Spirit (Eph. 5:18).

Do you want to show honor to Christ's body? Do not neglect him when naked; do not neglect him perishing outside of cold and nakedness, while here you honor him with silken garments. For he that said, "This is my body," and by his word confirmed the fact, also said, "I was hungry and you gave me no food"; and, "as you did not do it to one of the least of these, you did not do it to me" (Matt. 25:42, 45). For this indeed needs not coverings but a pure soul; but that requires much attention.

Let us learn therefore to be strict in life, and to honor Christ as he himself desires. For to him who is honored, the honor that he desires is most pleasing, not the honor we consider best. Peter thought he was honoring Christ by forbidding him to wash his feet, but doing so was not an honor—just the contrary.

Even so do you honor him with this honor, which he ordained: spending your wealth on poor people. Because God has no need at all of golden vessels but of golden souls.

I say these things, not to forbid that such offerings be provided for the church, but to require you, together with them, to first give alms. For God indeed accepts the former, but much more the latter. For in the one the offerer alone is profited, but in the other the receiver is also. In the first, there is the danger of ostentation; in the latter, all is mercifulness and love to man.

For what is the profit when his table indeed is full of golden cups, but he perishes with hunger? First fill him, being hungered, and then abundantly decorate his table also. Do you make him a cup of gold, while you do not give him a cup of cold water? And what is the profit? Do you furnish his table with cloths bespangled with gold, while to himself you do not afford even the necessary covering? And what good comes of it? For tell me, should you see one at a loss for necessary food, and omit appeasing his hunger, while you first overlaid his table with silver, would he indeed thank you and not rather be indignant? What, again, if seeing one wrapped in rags and stiff with cold, you should neglect giving him a garment, and build golden columns, saying you were "doing it to his honor"? Would he not say that you were mocking and regard it as an insult of the most extreme kind?

Let this then be your thought with regard to Christ also, when he is going about a wanderer, and a stranger, needing a roof to cover him; and you, neglecting to receive him, deck out a pavement, and walls, and capitals of columns, and hang up silver chains by means of lamps, but himself bound in prison you will not even look upon.

— *Homilies on Matthew*, Homily 50.4

"Go," he says, "and do likewise" (Luke 10:37). And see what a parable he spoke. He did not say that a Jew did [so and so] to a Samaritan, but that a Samaritan showed all that liberality. Having then heard these things, let us not care only for "those of the family of faith" (Gal. 6:10), and neglect others. So then also you, if you see anyone in affliction, do not be curious to inquire further. His being in affliction involves a just claim on your aid. For if when you see a donkey choking you raise him up, and do not curiously inquire whose he is, much more about a man one ought not to be overcurious in inquiring whose he is. He is God's, be he unbeliever or Jew; since even if he is an unbeliever, still he needs help.

— *Homilies on Hebrews*, Homily 10.8

Do not say then, "I am but spending my own, and of my own I live delicately." It is not of your own, but of other men's. Other men's, I say, because such is your own choice: for God's will is that those things should be yours, which have been entrusted to you on behalf of your brothers. Now the things that are not your own become yours if you spend them upon others: but if you spend on yourself unsparingly, your own things become no longer yours. For since you use them cruelly, and say, "That my own things should be altogether spent on my own enjoyment is fair": therefore I call them not your own. For they are common to you and your fellow-servants; just as the sun is common, the air, the earth, and all the rest. In the case of the body, each ministration belongs both to the whole body and to each of several members; but when it is applied to one single member only, it destroys the proper function of that very member. So also it comes to pass in the case of wealth. And that what I say may be made plainer: the food of the body that is given in common to the members, should it pass into one member, even to that it turns out alien in the end. For when it cannot be digested nor afford nourishment, even to that part, I say, it turns out alien. But if it be made common, both that part and all the rest have it as their own.

So also in regard of wealth. If you enjoy it alone, you too have lost it: for you will not reap its reward. But if you possess it jointly with the rest, then will it be more your own, and then will you reap the benefit of it. Do you not see that the hands minister, and the mouth softens, and the stomach receives? Does the stomach say, "Since I have received, I ought to keep it all?" Then do not, I pray, use this language in regard to riches. For it belongs to the receiver to impart. As then it is a vice in the stomach to retain the food and not to distribute it (for it is injurious to the whole body), so it is a vice in those that are rich to keep to themselves what they have. For this destroys both themselves and others. Again, the eye receives all the light: but it does not itself alone retain it, but enlightens the entire body. For it is not its nature to keep it to itself, so long as it is an eye. Again, the nostrils are sensible of perfume; but they do not keep it all to themselves, but transmit it to the brain, and affect the stomach with a sweet savor, and by their means refresh the entire man. The feet alone walk, but they do not move only themselves away, but also transfer the whole body. In like manner, whatsoever you have been entrusted with, do not keep it to yourself alone, since you are doing harm to the whole and to yourself more than all.

And one may see this occurring not only in the case of the limbs: for the smith also, if he chose to impart of his craft to no one, ruins both himself and all other crafts. Likewise the shoemaker, the farmer, the baker, and every one of those who pursue any necessary calling; if he chose not to communicate to anyone of the results of his art, he will ruin not only the others but also himself with them. . . .

Do you impart none of your wealth unto any? Then you should not receive anything from another: in which case, the world will be turned upside down. For in everything to give and receive is the principle of numerous blessings: in seeds, in scholars, in arts. For if any one desire to keep his art to himself, he subverts both himself and the whole course of things. And the farmer, if he buries and keeps the seeds in his house, will bring about a grievous famine. So also the rich man, if he act thus in regard of his wealth, will destroy himself before the poor, heaping up the fire of hell more grievous upon his own head.

— *Homilies on First Corinthians*, Homily 10.7

St. Basil the Great
(AD 357–379)

The bread which you do not use is the bread of the hungry; the garment hanging in your wardrobe is the garment of him who is naked; the shoes that you do not wear are the shoes of the one who is barefoot; the money that you keep locked away is the money of the poor; the acts of charity that you do not perform are so many injustices that you commit.

— *Homily on the Saying of the Gospel According to Luke, "I Will Pull Down my Barns and Build Bigger Ones," and on Greed*[3]

Cattle are terrestrial and bent towards the earth. Man, a celestial growth, rises superior to them as much by the mold of his bodily conformation as by the dignity of his soul. What is the form of quadrupeds? Their head is bent towards the earth and looks towards their belly, and only pursues their belly's good. Your head, O man, is turned toward heaven; your eyes look up. Therefore, when you degrade yourself by the passions of the flesh, slave of your belly, and your lowest parts, you approach animals without reason and become like one of them. You are called

---

3. St. Basil the Great, *Homilia in illud dictum evangelii secundum Lucam*: Destruam horrea mea, et majora ædificabo: *itemque de avaritia* (Homily on the Saying of the Gospel According to Luke, "I Will Pull Down My Barns and Build Bigger Ones," and on Greed), 7. Quoted in Brandon Vogt, *Saints and Social Justice: A Guide to Changing the World* (Huntington, IN: Our Sunday Visitor, 2014), 78.

to more noble cares; "seek those things that are above, where Christ is, seated [at the right hand of God]" (Col. 3:1). Raise your soul above the earth; draw from its natural conformation the rule of your conduct; fix your conversation in heaven. Your true country is the heavenly Jerusalem; your fellow citizens and your compatriots are the first-born that are written in heaven (Heb. 12:23).

— *Hexaemeron*, Homily 9.2

The food of fish differs according to their species. Some feed on mud; others eat seaweed; others content themselves with the herbs that grow in water. But the greater part devour each other, and the smaller is food for the larger, and if one that has possessed itself of a fish weaker than itself becomes a prey to another, the conqueror and the conquered are both swallowed up in the belly of the last. And we mortals, do we act otherwise when we press our inferiors? What difference is there between the last fish and the man who, impelled by devouring greed, swallows the weak in the folds of his insatiable greed? That fellow possessed the goods of the poor; you caught him and made him a part of your abundance. You have shown yourself more unjust than the unjust, and more miserly than the miser. Look to it lest you end like the fish, by hook, by trap, or by net. Surely we too, when we have done the deeds of the wicked, shall not escape punishment at the last.

— *Hexaemeron*, Homily 7.3

Tell me, do you seek money and means from a poor man? If he had been able to make you richer, why would he have sought at your doors? Coming for assistance, he found hostility. When searching around for antidotes, he came upon poisons. It was your duty to relieve the destitution of the man, but you, seeking to drain the desert dry, increased his need. Just as if some physician, visiting the sick, instead of restoring health to them would take away even their little remnant of bodily strength, so you also would make the misfortunes of the wretched an opportunity of revenue. And, just as farmers pray for rains for the increase of their crops, so you also ask for poverty and want among men in order that your money may be productive for you. Do you not know that you are making an addition to your sins greater than the increase to your wealth, which you are planning from the interest?

— *Homily 12: A Psalm of David Against Usurers (on Psalm 14)*[4]

"The voice of the Lord in magnificence" (Ps. 28[29]:4). Magnificence is virtue extraordinarily great. He who performs great actions becomingly, such a one hears himself called magnificent. When the soul is not enslaved by the pride of the flesh, but assumes a greatness and dignity proper to it because of its awareness of its attributes received from God, in this soul is the voice of the Lord.

— *Homily 13: A Psalm of David at the Finishing of the Tabernacle*[5]

Truly, there is excessive folly and beastlike lack of reason, that he, made according to the image of the Creator, neither perceives his own constitution from the beginning, nor even wishes to understand such great dispensations which were made for his sake, at least, to learn his own dignity from them, but that he is unmindful of the fact that, throwing aside the image of the heavenly, he has taken up the image of the earthly. In order that he might not remain in sin, for his sake "The Word was made flesh, and dwelt among us" (John 1:14) and He humbled Himself to such an extent as to become "obedient to death, even to death on a cross" (Phil. 2:8). If you are not mindful of your first origin, because of the price paid for you, accept at least some idea of your dignity; look at that which was given in exchange for you and realize your own worth. You were bought with the precious blood of Christ; do not

---

4. *The Fathers of the Church: Saint Basil: Exegetic Homilies*, trans. Sister Agnes Clare Way, C.D.P. (Washington, DC: Catholic University of America Press, 1963), 183.

5. *Saint Basil: Exegetic Homilies*, 202.

become a slave of sin. Understand your own honor, in order that you may not be made like the senseless beasts.

—Homily 19: Unto the End, a Psalm for the Sons of Core on the Prosperity of the Wicked (On Psalm 48)[6]

You are obviously very far from having observed one commandment at least, and you falsely swore that you had kept it, namely, that you've loved your neighbor as yourself. For see: the Lord's commandment proves you to be utterly lacking in real love. For if what you've claimed were true, that you have kept from your youth the commandment of love, and have given to each person as much as to yourself, how has it come to you, this abundance of money? For it takes wealth to care for the needy: a little paid out for the necessity of each person you take on, and all at once everything gets parceled out, and is spent upon them. Thus, the man who loves his neighbor as himself will have acquired no more than what his neighbor has; whereas you, visibly, have acquired a lot. Where has this come from? Or is it not clear, that it comes from making your private enjoyment more important than helping other people? Therefore, however much you exceed in wealth, so much so do you fall short in love: else long since you'd have taken care to be divorced from your money, if you had loved your neighbor. But now your money sticks to you closer than the limbs of your body, and he who would separate you from it grieves you more than someone who would cut off your vital parts. For if you had clothed the naked, if you had given your bread to the hungry, if you had opened your doors to every stranger, if you'd become a father to orphans, if you had suffered together with all the powerless, what possessions would now be causing you despondency? Why should you now be upset to put aside what's left, when you'd long since have taken care to distribute these things to the needy?

— To the Rich[7]

---

6. *Saint Basil: Exegetic Homilies*, 325–326.

7. St. Basil the Great, "To the Rich," trans. Peter Gilbert, *De unione ecclesiarum*, https://bekkos.wordpress.com/st-basils-sermon-to-the-rich/.

St. Augustine of Hippo
(AD 354–430)

There is a kind of image of the Trinity in the mind itself, and the knowledge of it, which is its offspring and its word concerning itself, and love as a third, and these three are one, and one substance. Neither is the offspring less, since the mind knows itself according to the measure of its own being; nor is the love less, since it loves itself according to the measure both of its own knowledge and of its own being.

— On the Trinity, 9.12.18

Grace is the nature in which we were created, so as to possess a rational mind, by which we are enabled to understand—formed as we are in the image of God, so as to have dominion over the fish of the sea, and over the birds of the air, and over every living thing that creeps upon the earth. This, however, is not the grace that the Apostle commends to us through the faith of Jesus Christ. For it is certain that we possess this nature in common with ungodly men and unbelievers.

— On Grace and Free Will, 25

Justice being taken away, then, what are kingdoms but great robberies? For what are robberies themselves, but little kingdoms? The band itself is made up of men; it is ruled by the authority of a prince, it is knit together by the pact of the confederacy; the booty is divided by the law agreed on. If, by the admittance of abandoned men, this evil increases to such a degree that it holds places, fixes abodes, takes possession of cities, and subdues peoples, it assumes more plainly the name of a kingdom, because the reality is now manifestly conferred on it, not by the removal of covetousness, but by the addition of impunity. Indeed, that was an apt and true reply that was given to Alexander the Great by a pirate who had been seized. For when that king had asked the man what he meant by keeping hostile possession of the sea, he answered with bold pride, "What you mean by seizing the whole earth; but because I do it with a petty ship, I am called a robber, while you who does it with a great fleet are styled emperor."

— *The City of God*, 4.4

And we indeed recognize in ourselves the image of God, that is, of the supreme Trinity, an image that, though it be not equal to God, or rather, though it be very far removed from him—being neither co-eternal, nor, to say all in a word, consubstantial with him—is yet nearer to him in nature than any other of his works, and is destined to be yet restored, that it may bear a still closer resemblance. For we both are, and know that we are, and delight in our being, and our knowledge of it.

— *The City of God*, 11.26

"Let them," he says, "have dominion over the fish of the sea, and over the birds of the air, and over the cattle, and over all the wild animals of the earth, and over every creeping thing that creeps upon the earth" (Gen. 1:26). He did not intend that his rational creature, who was made in his image, should have dominion over anything but the irrational creation—not man over man, but man over the beasts. And hence the righteous men in primitive times were made shepherds of cattle rather than kings of men, God intending thus to teach us what the relative position of the creatures is, and what the desert of sin; for it is with justice, we believe, that the condition of slavery is the result of sin. And this is why we do not find the word slave in any part of Scripture until righteous Noah branded the sin of his son with this name. It is a name, therefore, introduced by sin and not by nature.

— *The City of God*, 19.15

Give then, my brothers, to the poor. Having food and covering, let us be with content that. The rich man has nothing from his riches but what the poor man begs of him—food and covering. What more have you from all that you possess? You have got food and necessary covering. Necessary I say, not useless, not superfluous. What more do you get from your riches? Tell me. Assuredly, whatever more you have is superfluous. Let your superfluities then be the poor man's necessaries. . . . He is looking to the hand that was made as he was, and you are looking to the hand that made you, and made not you only but the poor man with you. He set you both on one and the same journey; this present life you have found yourselves companions in it, walking one way: he is carrying nothing, you are loaded excessively; he is carrying nothing with him, you are carrying with you more than you need. You are loaded: give him of what you have; so shall you at once feed him, and lessen your own burden.

Give then to the poor; I beg, I advise, I charge, I command you. Give to the poor whatever you will.

— *Sermons on the New Testament*, Sermon 11.12, 13

We are even he. For if we were not he, "Just as you did it to one of the least of these who are members of my family, you did it to me," would not be true. If we were not he, "Saul, Saul, why do you persecute me?" would not be true. So then we are he, in that we are his members, in that we are his Body, in that he is our Head, in that the whole Christ is both Head and Body.

— *Sermons on the New Testament*, Sermon 83

"Our Father" . . . Here also there is an admonition to the rich and to those of noble birth so far as this world is concerned: when they have become Christians they should not comport themselves proudly toward the poor and the low of birth; since together with them they call God "Our Father"—an expression that they cannot truly and piously use unless they recognize that they themselves are brothers.

—*On the Sermon on the Mount, 2.16*

CHAPTER 19

St. Thomas Aquinas
(1225–1274)

A Dominican priest, St. Thomas Aquinas is a Doctor of the Church and is considered one of the greatest theologians in Church history.

✠

The only-begotten Son of God, wanting to make us sharers in his divinity, assumed our nature, so that he, made man, might make men gods.

—*Opusc.* 57:1–4[1]

Summa theologiae, Part 1, Question 93:

The end of the production of man

1. Is the image of God in man?

2. Is the image of God in irrational creatures?

Article 1. Whether the image of God is in man?

Objection 1. It would seem that the image of God is not in man. For it is written (Isaiah 40:18): "To whom have you likened God? or what image will you make for Him?"

---

1. St. Thomas Aquinas, *Opusc.* 57:1–4. Quoted in *Catechism of the Catholic Church*, no. 460 (New York: Image Books, 1995), 129.

Objection 2. Further, to be the image of God is the property of the First-Begotten, of whom the Apostle says (Col. 1:15): "Who is the image of the invisible God, the First-Born of every creature." Therefore the image of God is not to be found in man.

Objection 3. Further, Hilary says (De Synod., Super i can. Synod. Ancyr.) that "an image is of the same species as that which it represents"; and he also says that "an image is the undivided and united likeness of one thing adequately representing another." But there is no species common to both God and man; nor can there be a comparison of equality between God and man. Therefore there can be no image of God in man.

On the contrary, It is written (Genesis 1:26): "Let Us make man to Our own image and likeness."

I answer that, As Augustine says (QQ. 83, qu. 74): "Where an image exists, there forthwith is likeness; but where there is likeness, there is not necessarily an image." Hence it is clear that likeness is essential to an image; and that an image adds something to likeness—namely, that it is copied from something else. For an "image" is so called because it is produced as an imitation of something else; wherefore, for instance, an egg, however much like and equal to another egg, is not called an image of the other egg, because it is not copied from it.

But equality does not belong to the essence of an image; for as Augustine says (QQ. 83, qu. 74): "Where there is an image there is not necessarily equality," as we see in a person's image reflected in a glass. Yet this is of the essence of a perfect image; for in a perfect image nothing is wanting that is to be found in that of which it is a copy. Now it is manifest that in man there is some likeness to God, copied from God as from an exemplar; yet this likeness is not one of equality, for such an exemplar infinitely excels its copy. Therefore there is in man a likeness to God; not, indeed, a perfect likeness, but imperfect. And Scripture implies the same when it says that man was made "to" God's likeness; for the preposition "to" signifies a certain approach, as of something at a distance.

Reply to Objection 1. The Prophet speaks of bodily images made by man. Therefore he says pointedly: "What image will you make for Him?" But God made a spiritual image to himself in man.

Reply to Objection 2. The First-Born of creatures is the perfect Image of God, reflecting perfectly that of which he is the Image, and so he is said to be the "Image," and never "to the image." But man is said to be both "image" by reason of the likeness; and "to the image" by reason of the imperfect likeness. And since the perfect likeness to God cannot be except in an identical nature, the Image of God exists in his first-born Son; as the image of the king is in his son, who is of the same nature as himself: whereas it exists in man as in an alien nature, as the image of the king is in a silver coin, as Augustine says explains in De decem Chordis (Serm. ix, al, xcvi, De Tempore).

Reply to Objection 3. As unity means absence of division, a species is said to be the same as far as it is one. Now a thing is said to be one not only numerically, specifically, or generically, but also according to a certain analogy or proportion. In this sense a creature is one with God, or like to him; but when Hilary says "of a thing which adequately represents another," this is to be understood of a perfect image.

Article 2. Whether the image of God is to be found in irrational creatures?

Objection 1. It would seem that the image of God is to be found in irrational creatures. For Dionysius says (Div. Nom. ii): "Effects are contingent images of their causes." But God is the cause not only of rational, but also of irrational creatures. Therefore the image of God is to be found in irrational creatures.

Objection 2. Further, the more distinct a likeness is, the nearer it approaches to the nature of an image. But Dionysius says (Div. Nom. iv) that "the solar ray has a very great similitude to the Divine goodness." Therefore it is made to the image of God.

Objection 3. Further, the more perfect anything is in goodness, the more it is like God. But the whole universe is more perfect in goodness than man; for though each individual thing is good, all things together are called "very good" (Genesis 1:31). Therefore the whole universe is to the image of God, and not only man.

Objection 4. Further, Boethius (De Consol. iii) says of God: "Holding the world in His mind, and forming it into his image." Therefore the whole world is to the image of God, and not only the rational creature.

On the contrary, Augustine says (Gen. ad lit. vi, 12): "Man's excellence consists in the fact that God made him to his own image by giving him an intellectual soul, which raises him above the beasts of the field." Therefore things without intellect are not made to God's image.

I answer that, Not every likeness, not even what is copied from something else, is sufficient to make an image; for if the likeness be only generic, or existing by virtue of some common accident, this does not suffice for one thing to be the image of another. For instance, a worm, though from man it may originate, cannot be called man's image, merely because of the generic likeness. Nor, if anything is made white like something else, can we say that it is the image of that thing; for whiteness is an accident belonging to many species. But the nature of an image requires likeness in species; thus the image of the king exists in his son: or, at least, in some specific accident, and chiefly in the shape; thus, we speak of a man's image in copper. Whence Hilary says pointedly that "an image is of the same species."

Now it is manifest that specific likeness follows the ultimate difference. But some things are like to God first and most commonly because they exist; secondly, because they live; and thirdly because they know or understand; and these last, as Augustine says (QQ. 83, qu. 51), "approach so near to God in likeness, that among all creatures nothing comes nearer to him." It is clear, therefore, that intellectual creatures alone, properly speaking, are made to God's image.

Reply to Objection 1. Everything imperfect is a participation of what is perfect. Therefore even what falls short of the nature of an image, so far as it possesses any sort of likeness to God, participates in some degree in the nature of an image. So Dionysius says that effects are "contingent images of their causes"; that is, as much as they happen [*contingit*] to be so, but not absolutely.

Reply to Objection 2. Dionysius compares the solar ray to Divine goodness, as regards its causality; not as regards its natural dignity which is involved in the idea of an image.

Reply to Objection 3. The universe is more perfect in goodness than the intellectual creature as regards extension and diffusion; but intensively and collectively the likeness to the Divine goodness is found rather in the intellectual creature, which has a capacity for the highest good. Or else we may say that a part is not rightly divided against the whole, but only against another part. Wherefore, when we say that the intellectual nature alone is to the image of God, we do not mean that the universe in any part is not to God's image, but that the other parts are excluded.

Reply to Objection 4. Boethius here uses the word "image" to express the likeness which the product of an art bears to the artistic species in the mind of the artist. Thus every creature is an image of the exemplar type thereof in the Divine mind. We are not, however, using the word "image" in this sense; but as it implies a likeness in nature, that is, inasmuch as all things, as being, are like to the First Being; as living, like to the First Life; and as intelligent, like to the Supreme Wisdom.

— *Summa theologiae*, 1.93.1–2

Summa theologiae, Part 1-2, Question 91:

The various kinds of law

1. Is there an eternal law?

2. Is there a natural law?

3. Is there a human law?

4. Is there a Divine law?

5. Is there one Divine law, or several?

Article 1. Whether there is an eternal law?

Objection 1. It would seem that there is no eternal law. Because every law is imposed on someone. But there was not someone from eternity on whom a law could be imposed: since God alone was from eternity. Therefore no law is eternal.

Objection 2. Further, promulgation is essential to law. But promulgation could not be from eternity: because there was no one to whom it could be promulgated from eternity. Therefore no law can be eternal.

Objection 3. Further, a law implies order to an end. But nothing ordained to an end is eternal: for the last end alone is eternal. Therefore no law is eternal.

On the contrary, Augustine says (De Lib. Arb. i, 6): "That Law which is the Supreme Reason cannot be understood to be otherwise than unchangeable and eternal."

I answer that, As stated above (1-2.90.1.ad 2; 1-2.91.3–4), a law is nothing else but a dictate of practical reason emanating from the ruler who governs a perfect community. Now it is evident, granted that the world is ruled by Divine Providence, as was stated in 1.22.1 and 1.22.2, that the whole community of the universe is governed by Divine Reason. Wherefore the very Idea of the government of things in God the Ruler of the universe, has the nature of a law. And since the Divine Reason's conception of things is not subject to time but is eternal, according to Proverbs 8:23, therefore it is that this kind of law must be called eternal.

Reply to Objection 1. Those things that are not in themselves, exist with God, inasmuch as they are foreknown and preordained by him, according to Romans 4:17: "calls into existence the things that do not exist." Accordingly the eternal concept of the Divine law bears the character of an eternal law, in so far as it is ordained by God to the government of things foreknown by him.

Reply to Objection 2. Promulgation is made by word of mouth or in writing; and in both ways the eternal law is promulgated: because both the Divine Word and the writing of the Book of Life are eternal. But the promulgation cannot be from eternity on the part of the creature that hears or reads.

Reply to Objection 3. The law implies order to the end actively, in so far as it directs certain things to the end; but not passively—that is to say, the law itself is not ordained to the end—except accidentally, in a governor whose end is extrinsic to him, and to which end his law must needs be ordained. But the end of the Divine government is God himself, and his law is not distinct from himself. Wherefore the eternal law is not ordained to another end.

Article 2. Whether there is in us a natural law?

Objection 1. It would seem that there is no natural law in us. Because man is governed sufficiently by the eternal law: for Augustine says (De Lib. Arb. i) that "the eternal law is that by which it is right that all things should be most orderly." But nature does not abound in superfluities as neither does she fail in necessaries. Therefore no law is natural to man.

Objection 2. Further, by the law man is directed, in his acts, to the end, as stated above (1-2.90.2). But the directing of human acts to their end is not a function of nature, as is the case in irrational creatures, which act for an end solely by their natural appetite; whereas man acts for an end by his reason and will. Therefore no law is natural to man.

Objection 3. Further, the more a man is free, the less is he under the law. But man is freer than all the animals, on account of his free will, with which he is endowed above all other animals. Since therefore other animals are not subject to a natural law, neither is man subject to a natural law.

On the contrary, A gloss on Romans 2:14: "When the Gentiles, who have not the law, do by nature those things that are of the law," comments as follows: "Although they have no written law, yet they have the natural law, whereby each one knows, and is conscious of, what is good and what is evil."

I answer that, As stated above (1-2.90.1.ad 1), law, being a rule and measure, can be in a person in two ways: in one way, as in him that rules and measures; in another way, as in that which is ruled and measured, since a thing is ruled and measured, in so far as it partakes of the rule or measure. Wherefore, since all things subject to Divine providence are ruled and measured by the eternal law, as was stated above (Article 1); it is evident that all things partake somewhat of the eternal law, in so far as, namely, from its being imprinted on them, they derive their respective inclinations to their proper acts and ends. Now among all others, the rational creature is subject to Divine providence in the most excellent way, in so far as it partakes of a share of providence, by being provident both for itself and for others. Wherefore it has a share of the Eternal Reason, whereby it has a natural inclination to its proper act and end: and this participation of the eternal law in the rational creature is called the natural law. Hence the Psalmist after saying: "Offer up the sacrifice of justice," as though someone asked what the works of justice are, adds: "Many say, Who showeth us good things?" in answer to which question he says: "The light of Thy countenance, O Lord, is signed upon us" (Psalm 4:5–6): thus implying that the light of natural reason, whereby we discern what is good and what is evil, which is the function of the natural law, is nothing else than an imprint on us of the Divine light. It is therefore evident that the natural law is nothing else than the rational creature's participation of the eternal law.

Reply to Objection 1. This argument would hold, if the natural law were something different from the eternal law: whereas it is nothing but a participation thereof, as stated above.

Reply to Objection 2. Every act of reason and will in us is based on that which is according to nature, as stated above (1-2.10.1): for every act of reasoning is based on principles that are known naturally, and every act of appetite in respect of the means is derived from the natural appetite in respect of the last end. Accordingly the first direction of our acts to their end must needs be in virtue of the natural law.

Reply to Objection 3. Even irrational animals partake in their own way of the Eternal Reason, just as the rational creature does. But because the rational creature partakes thereof in an intellectual and rational manner, therefore the participation of the eternal law in the rational creature is properly called a law, since a law is something pertaining to reason, as stated above (1-2.90.1). Irrational creatures, however, do not partake thereof in a rational manner, wherefore there is no participation of the eternal law in them, except by way of similitude.

Article 3. Whether there is a human law?

Objection 1. It would seem that there is not a human law. For the natural law is a participation of the eternal law, as stated above (Article 2). Now through the eternal law "all things are most orderly," as Augustine states (De Lib. Arb. i, 6). Therefore the natural law suffices for the ordering of all human affairs. Consequently there is no need for a human law.

Objection 2. Further, a law bears the character of a measure, as stated above (1-2.90.1). But human reason is not a measure of things, but vice versa, as stated in Metaph. x, text. 5. Therefore no law can emanate from human reason.

Objection 3. Further, a measure should be most certain, as stated in Metaph. x, text. 3. But the dictates of human reason in matters of conduct are uncertain, according to Wisdom 9:14: "The thoughts of mortal men are fearful, and our counsels uncertain." Therefore no law can emanate from human reason.

On the contrary, Augustine (De Lib. Arb. i, 6) distinguishes two kinds of law, the one eternal, the other temporal, which he calls human.

I answer that, As stated above (1-2.90.1.ad 2), a law is a dictate of the practical reason. Now it is to be observed that the same procedure takes place in the practical and in the speculative reason: for each proceeds from principles to conclusions, as stated above (De Lib. Arb. i, 6). Accordingly we conclude that just as, in the speculative reason, from naturally known indemonstrable principles, we draw the conclusions of the various sciences, the knowledge of which is not imparted to us by nature, but acquired by the efforts of reason, so too it is from the precepts of the natural law, as from general and indemonstrable principles, that the human reason needs to proceed to the more particular determination of certain matters. These particular determinations, devised by human reason, are called human laws, provided the other essential conditions of law be observed, as stated above (1-2.90.2–4). Wherefore Tully says in his Rhetoric (De Invent. Rhet. ii) that "justice has its source in nature; thence certain things came into custom by reason of their utility; afterwards these things which emanated from nature and were approved by custom, were sanctioned by fear and reverence for the law."

Reply to Objection 1. The human reason cannot have a full participation of the dictate of the Divine Reason, but according to its own mode, and imperfectly. Consequently, as on the part of the speculative reason, by a natural participation of Divine Wisdom, there is in us the knowledge of certain general principles, but not proper knowledge of each single truth, such as that contained in the Divine Wisdom; so too, on the part of the practical reason, man has a natural participation of the eternal law, according to certain general principles, but not as regards the particular determinations of individual cases, which are, however, contained in the eternal law. Hence the need for human reason to proceed further to sanction them by law.

Reply to Objection 2. Human reason is not, of itself, the rule of things: but the principles impressed on it by nature, are general rules and measures of all things relating to human conduct, whereof the natural reason is the rule and measure, although it is not the measure of things that are from nature.

Reply to Objection 3. The practical reason is concerned with practical matters, which are singular and contingent: but not with necessary things, with which the speculative reason is concerned. Wherefore human laws cannot have that inerrancy that belongs to the demonstrated conclusions of sciences. Nor is it necessary for every measure to be altogether unerring and certain, but according as it is possible in its own particular genus.

Article 4. Whether there was any need for a Divine law?

Objection 1. It would seem that there was no need for a Divine law. Because, as stated above (Article 2), the natural law is a participation in us of the eternal law. But the eternal law is a Divine law, as stated above (Article 1). Therefore there was no need for a Divine law in addition to the natural law, and human laws derived therefrom.

Objection 2. Further, it is written (Sirach 15:14) that "God left man in the hand of his own counsel." Now counsel is an act of reason, as stated above (1-2.14.1). Therefore man was left to the direction of his reason. But a dictate of human reason is a human law as stated above (Article 3). Therefore there is no need for man to be governed also by a Divine law.

Objection 3. Further, human nature is more self-sufficing than irrational creatures. But irrational creatures have no Divine law besides the natural inclination impressed on them. Much less, therefore, should the rational creature have a Divine law in addition to the natural law.

On the contrary, David prayed God to set his law before him, saying (Psalm 18:33): "Set before me for a law the way of Thy justifications, O Lord."

I answer that, Besides the natural and the human law it was necessary for the directing of human conduct to have a Divine law. And this for four reasons. First, because it is by law that man is directed how to perform his proper acts in view of his last end. And indeed if man were ordained to no other end than that which is proportionate to his natural faculty, there would be no need for man to have any further direction of the part of his reason, besides the natural law and human law which is derived from it. But since man is ordained to an end of eternal happiness which is disproportionate to man's natural faculty, as stated above (1-2.5.5), therefore it was necessary that, besides the natural and the human law, man should be directed to his end by a law given by God.

Secondly, because, on account of the uncertainty of human judgment, especially on contingent and particular matters, different people form different judgments on human acts; whence also different and contrary laws result. In order, therefore, that man may know without any doubt what he ought to do and what he ought to avoid, it was necessary for man to be directed in his proper acts by a law given by God, for it is certain that such a law cannot err.

Thirdly, because man can make laws in those matters of which he is competent to judge. But man is not competent to judge of interior movements, that are hidden, but only of exterior acts which appear: and yet for the perfection of virtue it is necessary for man to conduct himself aright in both kinds of acts. Consequently human law could not sufficiently curb and direct interior acts; and it was necessary for this purpose that a Divine law should supervene.

Fourthly, because, as Augustine says (De Lib. Arb. i, 5,6), human law cannot punish or forbid all evil deeds: since while aiming at doing away with all evils, it would do away with many good things, and would hinder the advance of the common good, which is necessary for human intercourse. In order, therefore, that no evil might remain unforbidden and unpunished, it was necessary for the Divine law to supervene, whereby all sins are forbidden.

And these four causes are touched upon in Psalm 18[19]:8, where it is said: "The law of the Lord is unspotted," i.e. allowing no foulness of sin; "converting souls," because it directs not only exterior, but also interior acts; "the testimony of the Lord is faithful," because of the certainty of what is true and right; "giving wisdom to little ones," by directing man to an end supernatural and Divine.

Reply to Objection 1. By the natural law the eternal law is participated proportionately to the capacity of human nature. But to his supernatural end man needs to be directed in a yet higher way. Hence the additional law given by God, whereby man shares more perfectly in the eternal law.

Reply to Objection 2. Counsel is a kind of inquiry: hence it must proceed from some principles. Nor is it enough for it to proceed from principles imparted by nature, which are the precepts of the natural law, for the reasons given above: but there is need for certain additional principles, namely, the precepts of the Divine law.

Reply to Objection 3. Irrational creatures are not ordained to an end higher than that which is proportionate to their natural powers: consequently the comparison fails.

Article 5. Whether there is but one Divine law?

Objection 1. It would seem that there is but one Divine law. Because, where there is one king in one kingdom there is but one law. Now the whole of mankind is compared to God as to one king, according to Psalm 46:8: "God is the King of all the earth." Therefore there is but one Divine law.

Objection 2. Further, every law is directed to the end which the lawgiver intends for those for whom he makes the law. But God intends one and the same thing for all men; since according to 1 Timothy 2:4: "He will have all men to be saved, and to come to the knowledge of the truth." Therefore there is but one Divine law.

Objection 3. Further, the Divine law seems to be more akin to the eternal law, which is one, than the natural law, according as the revelation of grace is of a higher order than natural knowledge. Therefore much more is the Divine law but one.

On the contrary, The Apostle says (Hebrews 7:12): "The priesthood being translated, it is necessary that a translation also be made of the law." But the priesthood is twofold, as stated in the same passage— namely, the levitical priesthood, and the priesthood of Christ. Therefore the Divine law is twofold, namely the Old Law and the New Law.

I answer that, As stated in the 1.30.3, distinction is the cause of number. Now things may be distinguished in two ways. First, as those things that are altogether specifically different, e.g., a horse and an ox. Secondly, as perfect and imperfect in the same species, e.g., a boy and a man: and in this way the Divine law is divided into Old and New. Hence the Apostle (Galatians 3:24–25) compares the state of man under the Old Law to that of a child "under a pedagogue"; but the state under the New Law, to that of a full grown man, who is "no longer under a pedagogue."

Now the perfection and imperfection of these two laws is to be taken in connection with the three conditions pertaining to law, as stated above. For, in the first place, it belongs to law to be directed to the common good as to its end, as stated above (1-2.90.2). This good may be twofold. It may be a sensible and earthly good; and to this, man was directly ordained by the Old Law: wherefore, at the very outset of the law, the people were invited to the earthly kingdom of the Chananaeans (Exodus 3:8–17). Again it may be an intelligible and heavenly good: and to this, man is ordained by the New Law. Wherefore, at the very beginning of his preaching, Christ invited men to the kingdom of heaven, saying (Matthew 4:17): "Do penance, for the kingdom of heaven is at hand." Hence Augustine says (Contra Faust. iv) that "promises of temporal goods are contained in the Old Testament, for which reason it is called old; but the promise of eternal life belongs to the New Testament."

Secondly, it belongs to the law to direct human acts according to the order of righteousness (Article 4): wherein also the New Law surpasses the Old Law, since it directs our internal acts, according to Matthew 5:20: "Unless your justice abound more than that of the Scribes and Pharisees, you shall not enter into the kingdom of heaven." Hence the saying that "the Old Law restrains the hand, but the New Law controls the mind" (Sentent. iii, D, xl).

Thirdly, it belongs to the law to induce men to observe its commandments. This the Old Law did by the fear of punishment: but the New Law, by love, which is poured into our hearts by the grace of Christ, bestowed in the New Law, but foreshadowed in the Old. Hence Augustine says (Contra Adimant. Manich. discip. xvii) that "there is little difference [The 'little difference' refers to the Latin words 'timor' and 'amor'—'fear' and 'love.'] between the Law and the Gospel—fear and love."

Reply to Objection 1. As the father of a family issues different commands to the children and to the adults, so also the one King, God, in his one kingdom, gave one law to men, while they were yet imperfect, and another more perfect law, when, by the preceding law, they had been led to a greater capacity for Divine things.

Reply to Objection 2. The salvation of man could not be achieved otherwise than through Christ, according to Acts 4:12: "There is no other name . . . given to men, whereby we must be saved." Consequently the law that brings all to salvation could not be given until after the coming of Christ. But before his coming it was necessary to give to the people, of whom Christ was to be born, a law containing certain rudiments of righteousness unto salvation, in order to prepare them to receive him.

Reply to Objection 3. The natural law directs man by way of certain general precepts, common to both the perfect and the imperfect: wherefore it is one and the same for all. But the Divine law directs man also in certain particular matters, to which the perfect and imperfect do not stand in the same relation. Hence the necessity for the Divine law to be twofold, as already explained.

CHAPTER 20

Bartolomé de las Casas
(1484–1566)

*Born shortly before Columbus' expeditions to the New World,
Bartolomé de las Casas himself traveled to the Americas in hopes of
finding wealth and status for himself. However, after witnessing the brutal
treatment of the indigenous people, he forsook his original intentions and
spent the rest of his life as a tireless advocate of the rights of the
native people.*

A Short Account of the Destruction of the Indies[1]
1552

Not a few of the people involved in this story had become so anaesthetized to human suffering by their own greed and ambition that they had ceased to be men in any meaningful sense of the term and had become, by dint of their own wicked deeds, so totally degenerate and given over to a reprobate mind that they could not rest content with their past achievements in the realms of treachery and wickedness (when they honed to perfection the art of cruelty in order to wipe human beings from a large part of the globe), but were now pestering

---

1. All quotations in this section are from Bartolomé de Las Casas, *A Short Account of the Destruction of the Indies* (London: Penguin, 2004).

the Crown to grant them official authority and licence once again to commit their dreadful deeds, or even (if such a thing were conceivable) to devise yet worse atrocities.

— "Synopsis"

It would constitute a criminal neglect of my duty to remain silent about the enormous loss of life as well as the infinite number of human souls despatched to Hell in the course of such "conquests." . . . It is my fervent hope that, once your Highness perceives the extent of the injustices suffered by these innocent peoples and the way in which they are being destroyed and crushed underfoot, unjustly and for no other reason than to satisfy the greed and ambition of those whose purpose it is to commit such wicked atrocities, Your highness will see fit to beg and entreat His Majesty to refuse all those who seek royal licence for such evil and detestable ventures, and to put a stop once and for all to their infernal clamour in such a way that nobody will henceforth dare to make such a request nor even to mention ventures of this kind.

— "Prologue"

God made all the peoples of this area, many and varied as they are, as open and as innocent as can be imagined. The simplest people in the world—unassuming, long-suffering, unassertive, and submissive—they are without malice or guile. . . . They are also among the poorest people on the face of the earth; they own next to nothing and have no urge to acquire material possessions. . . . It was upon these gentle lambs, imbued by the Creator with all the qualities we have mentioned, that from the very first day they clapped eyes on them the Spanish fell like ravening wolves upon the fold, or like tigers and savage lions who have not eaten meat for days. The pattern established at the outset has remained unchanged to this day, and the Spaniards still do nothing save tear the natives to shreds, murder them and inflict upon them untold misery, suffering and distress, tormenting, harrying and persecuting them mercilessly.

— "Preface"

There are two main ways in which those who have travelled to this part of the world pretending to be Christians have uprooted these pitiful peoples and wiped them from the face of the earth. First, they have waged war on them: unjust, cruel, bloody and tyrannical war. Second, they have murdered anyone and everyone who has shown the slightest sign of resistance, or even of wishing to escape the torment to which they have subjected him.

— "Preface"

The reason the Christians have murdered on such a vast scale and killed anyone and everyone in their way is purely and simply greed. They have set out to line their pockets with gold and to amass private fortunes as quickly as possible so that they can then assume a status quite at odds with that into which they were born. Their insatiable greed and overweening ambition know no bounds; the land is fertile and rich, the inhabitants simple, forbearing and submissive. The Spaniards have shown not the slightest consideration for these people, treating them (and I speak from first-hand experience, having been there from the outset) not as brute animals—indeed, I would to God they had done and had shown them the consideration they afford their animals—so much as piles of dung in the middle of the road. They have had as little concern for their souls as for their bodies, all the millions that have perished having gone to their deaths with no knowledge of God and without the benefit of the Sacraments.

— "Preface"

The fifth kingdom was known as Higuey and its queen, a lady already advanced in years, went by the name of Higuanama. They strung her up and I saw with my own eyes how the Spaniards burned countless local inhabitants alive or hacked them to pieces, or devised novel ways of torturing them to death, enslaving those they took alive. Indeed, they invented so many new methods of murder that it would be quite impossible to set them all down on paper and, however hard one tried to chronicle them, one could probably never list a thousandth part of what actually took place. All I can say is that I know it to be an incontrovertible fact and do here so swear before Almighty God, that the local peoples never gave the Spanish any cause whatever for the injury and injustice that was done to them in these campaigns. On the contrary, they behaved as honourably as might the inmates of a well-run monastery, and for this they were robbed and massacred, and even those who escaped death on this occasion found themselves condemned to a lifetime of captivity and slavery. I would go further. It is my firm belief that not a single native of the island committed a capital offence, as defined in law, against the Spanish while all this time the natives themselves were being savaged and murdered. Despite the enormous provocation, very few of the natives, I hazard, were guilty of even those sins which do not lie within the ambit of human law but are properly the province of God, such as hatred and anger, or the thirst for revenge against those who committed such enormities upon them. It is my own experience of these peoples, gained over many years, that they are no more given to impetuous actions or to harbouring thoughts of retribution than are boys of ten or twelve years of age. I know beyond any shadow of a doubt that they had, from the very beginning, every right to wage war on the Europeans, while the Europeans never had just cause for waging war on the local peoples. The actions of the Europeans, throughout the New World, were without exception wicked and unjust: worse, in fact, than the blackest kind of tyranny.

— "The Kingdoms of Hispaniola"

It is of note that all these island territories began to go to the dogs once news arrived of the death of our most gracious Queen Isabella, who departed this life in 1504. Up to then, only a small number of provinces had been destroyed through unjust military action, not the whole area, and news of even this partial destruction had by and large been kept from the Queen, because, she—may her soul rest in peace—took a close personal interest in the physical and spiritual welfare of the native peoples, as those of us who lived through those years and saw examples of it with our own eyes can attest. There is one other general rule in all this, and it is that, wherever the Spaniards set foot, right throughout the Americas, they subjected the native inhabitants to the cruelties of which we have spoken, killing these poor and innocent people, tyrannizing them, and oppressing them in the most abominable fashion.

— "The Kingdoms of Hispaniola"

In 1511 the Spanish set foot in Cuba. . . . One of the leading local lords, a cacique, who went by the name of Hatuey, had fled to the island from Hispaniola with many of his people in order to escape the miseries that arose from the inhuman treatment meted out to the natives of that island by the Spanish. When he heard that the Christians had now switched their attention to Cuba, he gathered most if not all his people about him and addressed them, saying . . . "They have a God whom they worship and adore, and it is in order to get that God from us so that they can worship Him that they conquer us and kill us." He had beside him, as he spoke, a basket filled with gold jewelry and he said: "Here is the God of the Christians."

— "Cuba"

If there had been any gold in this province, the Spaniards would have finished off the local population by sending them down mines to dig it out of the earth; as it was, the only way they could realize a profit from the bodies and souls of these poor wretches for whom our Lord died on the Cross was to enslave all those whom they had not already murdered, and this they proceeded to do indiscriminately, bartering with the masters of the vessels that came in number to the region once it became known that slaves were to be had in exchange for goods.

— "The Kingdom of Yucatán"

When the Spaniards were in the very act of leaving the province, one of them demanded that the son of a local chief go with him, but the boy declined, adamant that he did not want to leave home. The Spaniard retorted: "You will come with me or I will cut off both your ears." When the boy persisted, repeating that he had no wish to leave home, the Spaniard took out his dagger and lopped off first one of his ears and then the other. When the boy insisted that he did not want to go with him, he hacked off his nose, laughing out loud as he did so as though he were doing no more than pull his hair playfully.

This was the same fiend who was later to boast to a venerable cleric, without any sign of shame or remorse, that he always laboured long and hard to make the local women pregnant so that they would fetch a higher price as slaves.

It was in this kingdom, or in one of the provinces of New Spain, that a Spaniard who was out hunting deer or rabbits realized that his dogs were hungry and, not finding anything they could hunt, took a little boy from his mother, cut his arms and legs into chunks with his knife and distributed them among his dogs. Once they had eaten up these steaks, he threw the rest of the carcass on the ground for them to fight over. These examples should suffice to give some idea of the brutality of the

Spanish throughout this territory, of how far God has given them over to a reprobate mind, and of the attitude they take towards local people created in God's image and redeemed by His blood.

— "The Kingdom of Yucatán"

If a man finds himself allotted a flock in which there is an old man or in which someone is sickly, his response is normally: "To the Devil with this old man. Why make me take him? I suppose you want me to bury him? Why should I take this sickly one? Am I to waste my substance on curing him?" Reactions like these serve to give some idea of what the Spanish think of the native people, and how closely they obey that commandment to love one's neighbour that underpins the Law and the books of the Prophets.

— "The Pearl Coast, Paria and Trinidad"

The longer men have operated in the New World and the more they have become accustomed to the carnage and butchery around them, the more brutal and the more wicked have been the crimes they commit against God and their fellow-men.

— "The Mainland in the Region Known as Florida"

For forty-two years now, these matters have been constantly before my eyes and on my mind, and I can honestly say, as God is my witness, that I have solid grounds for believing that the depredations, the harm, the destruction, the depopulation, the atrocities and massacres, the horrible cruelty and barbarism, the violence, the injustice, the plunder and the wholesale murder that all these territories have witnessed and their people suffered (and still suffer) are on such a scale that what I have here been able to relate is no more than a thousandth part of the reality of what has been taking place and continues to take place.

— "The Kingdom of New Granada"

From the very outset, the Spanish have taken no more trouble to preach the Christian faith to these peoples than if they had been dealing with dogs or other animals. Indeed, they have done their level best to prevent missionaries from preaching, presumably because they felt that the spread of the Gospel would in some way stand between them and the gold and wealth they craved. Today, the peoples of the New World are as ignorant of God as they were a hundred years ago.

— "The Kingdom of New Granada"

To date, the Crown has not shown itself strong enough to put a stop to these injustices, because everyone, young and old alike, who journeys to the New World is either openly or in secret a fortune-hunter, albeit that some are worse than others, and all such fortunes are made at the expense of the local people. That they serve their own ends while pretending to serve those of the Crown is something that not only damages the Spanish interest but also brings dishonor on the name of God and on that of the King.

— "Conclusion"

St. Peter Claver
(1580–1654)

A Spanish priest, St. Peter Claver became a missionary in New Granada
(present-day Colombia). Deeply troubled by the African slave trade,
St. Peter devoted himself to caring for the physical and spiritual needs
of the slaves, often meeting them at the ships as they were unloading and
traveling to plantations to offer spiritual counsel.

✠

Letter[1]
May 31, 1627

Yesterday, May 30, 1627, on the feast of the Most Holy Trinity, numerous blacks, brought from the rivers of Africa, disembarked from a large ship. Carrying two baskets of oranges, lemons, sweet biscuits, and I know not what else, we hurried toward them. When we approached their quarters, we thought we were entering another Guinea. We had to force our way through the crowd until we reached the sick. Large numbers of the sick were lying on the wet ground or rather in puddles of mud. To prevent excessive dampness, someone had thought of building up a mound with a mixture of tiles and broken pieces of

---

1. *Liturgy of the Hours*, Office of Readings, September 9, http://www.liturgies.net/saints/peterclaver/readings.htm.

bricks. This, then, was their couch, a very uncomfortable one not only for that reason, but especially because they were naked, without any clothing to protect them.

We laid aside our cloaks, therefore, and brought from a warehouse whatever was handy to build a platform. In that way we covered a space to which we at last transferred the sick, by forcing a passage through bands of slaves. Then we divided the sick into two groups: one group my companion approached with an interpreter, while I addressed the other group. There were two blacks, nearer death than life, already cold, whose pulse could scarcely be detected. With the help of a tile we pulled some live coals together and placed them in the middle near the dying men. Into this fire we tossed aromatics. Of these we had two wallets full, and we used them all up on this occasion. Then, using our own cloaks, for they had nothing of this sort, and to ask the owners for others would have been a waste of words, we provided for them a smoke treatment, by which they seemed to recover their warmth and the breath of life. The joy in their eyes as they looked at us was something to see.

This was how we spoke to them, not with words but with our hands and our actions. And in fact, convinced as they were that they had been brought here to be eaten, any other language would have proved utterly useless. Then we sat, or rather knelt, beside them and bathed their faces and bodies with wine. We made every effort to encourage them with friendly gestures and displayed in their presence the emotions which somehow naturally tend to hearten the sick.

After this we began an elementary instruction about baptism, that is, the wonderful effects of the sacrament on body and soul. When by their answers to our questions they showed they had sufficiently understood this, we went on to a more extensive instruction, namely, about the one God, who rewards and punishes each one according to his merit, and the rest. We asked them to make an act of contrition and to manifest their detestation of their sins. Finally, when they appeared sufficiently prepared, we declared to them the mysteries of the Trinity, the Incarnation and the Passion. Showing them Christ fastened to the cross, as he is depicted on the baptismal font on which streams of blood flow down from his wounds, we led them in reciting an act of contrition in their own language.

St. Vincent de Paul
(1581–1660)

A priest in France, St. Vincent de Paul is especially remembered for his work in reforming the clergy and his commitment to serving the poor. He also founded two religious orders, the Congregation of the Mission and the Daughters of Charity.

❉

Epistle 2546[1]
March 8, 1658

Serving the poor is to be our first preference

Even though the poor are often rough and unrefined, we must not judge them from external appearances nor from the mental gifts they seem to have received. On the contrary, if you consider the poor in the light of faith, then you will observe that they are taking the place of the Son of God who chose to be poor. Although in his passion he almost lost the appearance of a man and was considered a fool by the Gentiles and a stumbling block by the Jews, he showed them that his mission was to preach to the poor: *He sent me to preach the good news*

---

1. *Liturgy of the Hours*, Office of Readings, September 27, http://www.liturgies.net/saints/vincentdepaul/readings.htm.

to the poor. We also ought to have this same spirit and imitate Christ's actions, that is, we must take care of the poor, console them, help them, support their cause.

Since Christ willed to be born poor, he chose for himself disciples who were poor. He made himself the servant of the poor and shared their poverty. He went so far as to say that he would consider every deed which either helps or harms the poor as done for or against himself. Since God surely loves the poor, he also loves those who love the poor. For when one person holds another dear, he also includes in his affection anyone who loves or serves the one he loves. That is why we hope that God will love us for the sake of the poor. So when we visit the poor and needy, we try to be understanding where they are concerned. We sympathize with them so fully that we can echo Paul's words: *I have become all things to all men.* Therefore, we must try to be stirred by our neighbors' worries and distress. We must beg God to pour into our hearts sentiments of pity and compassion and to fill them again and again with these dispositions.

It is our duty to prefer the service of the poor to everything else and to offer such service as quickly as possible. If a needy person requires medicine or other help during prayer time, do whatever has to be done with peace of mind. Offer the deed to God as your prayer. Do not become upset or feel guilty because you interrupted your prayer to serve the poor. God is not neglected if you leave him for such service. One of God's works is merely interrupted so that another can be carried out. So when you leave prayer to serve some poor person, remember that this very service is performed for God. Charity is certainly greater than any rule. Moreover, all rules must lead to charity. Since she is a noble mistress, we must do whatever she commands. With renewed devotion, then, we must serve the poor, especially outcasts and beggars. They have been given to us as our masters and patrons.

CHAPTER 23

Bl. Frederic Ozanam
(1813–1853)

Bl. Frederic Ozanam was a husband and father who worked as a professor at the Sorbonne. With a group of friends, Bl. Frederic founded the charitable Society of St. Vincent de Paul, which is now present in 140 countries around the world.

Letter to Louis Janmot[1]
November 13, 1836

And we, dear friend, do we bear no resemblance to those saints we love, do we content ourselves with deploring the sterility of the present time, although each of us carries within his heart a seed of sanctity that the simple wishing will suffice to disclose. If we do not know how to love God as they loved Him, that should be without doubt a reproach to us, but yet our weakness is able to find some shadow of excuse, for it seems to be necessary to see in order to love and we see God only with the eyes of Faith and our Faith is so weak! Both men and the poor we see with the eyes of the flesh; they are there and we can put

---

1. *A Life in Letters*, trans. and ed. Joseph Dirvin, CM (St. Louis, MO: Society of St. Vincent de Paul, 1986), 96–97, https://via.library.depaul.edu/cgi/viewcontent.cgi?article=1000&context=ozanam_law.

finger and hand in their wounds and the scars of the crown of thorns are visible on their foreheads; and at this point incredulity no longer has place and we should fall at their feet and say with the Apostle, "Tu est Dominus et Deus meus" [My Lord and My God]. You are our masters, and we will be your servants. You are for us the sacred images of that God whom we do not see, and not knowing how to love Him otherwise shall we not love Him in your persons? Alas, if, in the Middle Ages, sick society was not able to be healed except by the immense effusion of love shown in a special way by St. Francis of Assisi, if much later new sorrows cried out to the soothing hands of St. Philip Neri, St. John of God and St. Vincent de Paul, how much charity, devotion and patience do we not need at present to heal the sufferings of these poor people, poorer than ever, because they have rejected the nourishment of the soul at the same time the bread of the body was lacking to them.

The problem that divides men in our day is no longer a problem of political structure; it is a social problem; it has to do with what is preferred, the spirit of self-interest or the spirit of sacrifice, whether society will be only a great exploitation to the profit of the strongest or a consecration of each individual for the good of all and especially for the protection of the weak. There are a great many men who have too much and who wish to have more; there are a great many others who do not have enough, who have nothing, and who are willing to take if someone gives to them. Between these two classes of men, a confrontation is coming, and this menacing confrontation will be terrible: on the one side, the power of gold, on the other, the power of despair. We must cast ourselves between these two enemy armies, if not to prevent, at least to deaden the shock. And our youth and our mediocrity does not make our role of mediators easier than our title of Christian makes us responsible. There is the possible usefulness of our Society of St. Vincent de Paul.

CHAPTER 24

St. Damien of Molokai
(1840–1889)

A missionary priest from Belgium, St. Damien was sent to Hawaii, and served on the island of Molokai. Deeply moved by the suffering of the lepers who were forced into quarantine on the Kalaupapa Peninsula, St. Damien committed to live and work among them for the rest of his life. After ten years serving the people in both their spiritual and physical needs, St. Damien contracted the disease, which would eventually take his life.

Writings from Three Letters[1]
August 1873; November 25, 1873; and November 9, 1887

I have accepted this disease as my particular cross.

[August 1873]

D ivine Providence, having compassion on the unfortunate, has thought fit to look upon your unworthy servant to care for the spiritual needs of a well-known leprosy hospital that our Government had to establish to preserve the whole archipelago from disease. Thus, it is in my role as pastor of an unusual parish of eight hundred lepers,

---

1. *Liturgy of the Hours*, Office of Readings, May 10, http://www.liturgies.net/saints/damienofmolokai/readings.htm.

nearly half of whom are now Catholics, that I take the liberty to write to you these lines.

Here I am in the midst of my dear lepers. They are so frightful to see, it is true, but they have souls redeemed at the price of the Precious Blood of our Divine Saviour. He also in his divine charity consoled lepers. If I can not cure them as he did, at least I can console them and by the holy ministry which in his goodness he has entrusted to me, I hope that many among them, purified from the leprosy of the soul, will present themselves before his tribunal prepared to enter the communion of the blessed.

My chapel, which was too big the first weeks I was here, has now become too small. Three weeks in a row I have had to ask some of the older Christians to stand outside along the windows in order to give their places to the new-comers or to the fallen away who have returned or to the catechumens of whom there are always some.

Besides Sunday, there are a good number who come regularly to Mass and evening rosary everyday of the week. A good number receive communion every Sunday. Besides the consolations that the heart of a priest finds in the church, there is also much good to do by visiting homes, going from one hut to another, almost all of them filled with poor unfortunates who can hardly drag themselves around as often their hands and feet have been eaten away by this horrible disease. They are condemned to breathe foul air. Ordinarily they listen with great attention to the word of salvation which I share with each one according to their disposition.

[November 25, 1873]

Even though I am not a leper, I make myself a leper with the lepers; when I preach, I always use the expression, "We, lepers." Thus may I gain all for Christ as St. Paul.

[November 9, 1887]

As you know, it has been already quite a while that Divine Providence chose me to become a victim of this repugnant disease of ours. I hope to remain eternally grateful for this grace. It seems to me that this disease will shorten and narrow the way that will lead me to our dear homeland. In that hope I accepted this disease as my particular cross; I try to bear it as did Simon of Cyrene, following in the footsteps of our Divine Master. Please assist me with your good prayers, so as to obtain for me the strength of perseverance, until I reach the summit of Calvary.

Letter[2]

November 23, 1873

Leprosy, so far as is known, is incurable; it seems to begin by a corruption of the blood. Discolored patches appear on the skin, especially on the cheeks, and the parts affected lose their feeling. After a time, this discoloration covers the whole body; then ulcers begin to open, chiefly at the extremities. The flesh is eaten away and gives out a fetid odor; even the breath of the leper becomes so foul that the air around is poisoned with it. I have had great difficulty in getting accustomed to such an atmosphere. One day at the Sunday Mass, I found myself so stifled that I thought I must leave the altar to breathe a little of the outer air, but I restrained myself, thinking of our Lord when He commanded them to open the grave of Lazarus, notwithstanding Martha's words, *jam faetet*. Now my sense of smell does not cause me so much inconvenience and I enter the huts of the lepers without difficulty. Sometimes, indeed, I still feel some repugnance when I have to hear the confessions of those near their end, whose wounds are full of maggots. Often, also, I scarce know how to administer extreme unction, when both hands and feet are nothing but raw wounds.

---

2. Quoted in Bartle Teeling, "Father Damien," *The American Catholic Quarterly Review* 15 (January to October, 1890): 724.

This may give you some idea of my daily work. Picture to yourself a collection of huts with eight hundred lepers. No doctor; in fact, as there is no cure, there seems no place for a doctor's skill. A white man, who is a leper, and your humble servant do all the doctoring work.

Every morning, then, after my Mass, which is always followed by an instruction, I go to visit the sick, half of whom are Catholics. On entering each hut, I begin by offering to hear their confessions. Those who refuse this spiritual help, are not, therefore, refused temporal assistance, which is given to all without distinction. Consequently, every one, with the exception of a few bigoted heretics, look on me as a Father. As for me, I make myself a leper with the lepers, to gain all to Jesus Christ. That is why, in preaching, I say We, lepers, not My brethren, as in Europe. You may judge by the following fact, what a power the missionary has. Last Saturday, some of the younger people, discontented with their lot and thinking themselves ill-treated by the government, determined on an attempt at revolt. All except two were Calvinists, or Mormons. Well, I only had to present myself and say a word or two, and all the heads were bowed, and all was over. I have baptized more than a hundred persons since my arrival. I have also buried a large number. The average of deaths is about one every day. Many are so destitute that there is nothing to defray their burial expenses. They are simply wrapped in a blanket. As far as my duties allow me time, I make coffins myself for these people.

CHAPTER 25

Servant of God Dorothy Day
(1897–1980)

*An American journalist and social activist, Dorothy Day came into
the Catholic Church in 1927. In 1932, with Peter Maurin, she co-founded
the Catholic Worker Movement, which is committed to spreading
Catholic social teaching and to practicing the spiritual and corporal works
of mercy.*

C.W. States Stand on Strikes[1]

July 1936

Let us be honest. Let us say that fundamentally, the stand we are
taking is not on the ground of wages and hours and conditions of
labor, but on the fundamental truth that men should be treated not as
chattels, but as human beings, as "temples of the Holy Ghost." When
Christ took on our human nature—when He became Man, "He dignified and ennobled human nature." He said, "The Kingdom of Heaven
is within you." When men are striking, they are following an impulse,
often blind, often uninformed, but a good impulse—one could even say
an inspiration of the Holy Spirit. They are trying to uphold their rights
to be treated not as slaves, but as men. They are fighting for a share in

---

1. Dorothy Day, "C.W. States Stand on Strikes," *The Catholic Worker*, July 1936, pp. 1, 2,
https://www.catholicworker.org/dorothyday/articles/940.html.

the management for their right to be considered partners in the enterprise in which they are engaged. They are fighting against the idea of their labor as a commodity, to be bought and sold.

Camden Strike

Let us concede that the conditions at the Victor RCA plant down in Camden, where a strike started last month, and which is said to involve 13,000 men, are not bad conditions, and that the wages and hours are not bad. There probably is a company union which is supposed to take care of such conditions and complaints, but they perpetuate the enslavement of the worker.

Let us concede that the conditions of the seamen are not so atrocious as *The Daily Worker* contends. (It is no use talking about the steward's department on passenger ships which has unbearable hours and conditions of labor.) Let us get down to the fundamental point that the seamen are striking for—the right to be considered partners, sharers in responsibility—the right to be treated as men and not as chattels.

Change the Social Order

Is it not a cause worth fighting for? Is it not a cause which demands all the courage, the integrity, of the men involved? **Let us be frank and make this our issue.**

Let us be honest and confess that it is the social order which we wish to change. The workers are never going to be satisfied, not matter how much pay they get—no matter what their hours are.

This, of course, is the contention of the ship owners, of the employers and industrialists the world over. They know that strikes are going to go on, no matter what concessions are made along these lines. They, too, will not face the fundamental issues involved.

Seamen's Strike

During the seamen's strike in the spring and the months after when the men were staying at the Catholic Worker House on Mott street— there were about fifty who came and found jobs and went away to have their places taken by others—we had an opportunity to talk to many of them. There was many a round table discussion over the preparation of vegetables and the washing of dishes and the mailing out of the paper (for the men joined in our work while they were with us). They have written to us after they left, and they have returned to see us when they came back into port.

One night we were talking with a Communist, a young fellow from Iowa, born of a Catholic father and a Methodist mother. It was hard to talk to him—we were both convinced we were right, we were both animated by truth, but he refused to concede the spiritual. Philosophically we differed. But a great many truths came out in these arguments.

Communist Arguments

He used to stand in the middle of the kitchen floor, a dish towel in his hands and suspend all operations while he talked. Tennessee, Yank, Ryan and the others went on working, laughing at his earnestness and his inability to co-ordinate work and discussion.

He used to take refuge in anti-clericalism, in attacks on our refusal to face facts, in what he liked to label our sentimentality. Often he would be driven to name-calling because he felt himself defeated in argument and there was no other refuge for him.

But there were many things we agreed on.

Fake Tactics

He was telling us one night how he caused a disturbance on board ship over the constant mess of stew they had been served. Overtime work, crowded quarters, uncomfortable mattresses, the menu, all these were the issues seized upon as a chance for disturbance, a miniature strike. He had been spending his days at sea figuring out ways to forward the revolution, and on this occasion it was stew.

We asked him whether he really thought that a cause worth fighting for to the shedding of blood. We asked him whether the other seamen who were fundamentally sane, did not object to these obstructionist tactics of the Communist. If they did not hinder their own cause by this tactic?

He maintained that if they would not join in it was because they were cowardly and selfish.

We maintained that it was because they knew it was not the cause for which they were fighting.

Recognition of Sacrifice

We pointed out that there on Mott street they were sleeping six in an apartment, between blankets, no sheets, that the food was insufficient and the washing facilities most primitive. They had no showers, no hot water to wash out their clothes (and they were always washing out their clothes. A cleaner lot of men would be hard to find). They had to walk ten blocks to get to a public bath.

We pointed out the fact that if the men were running the ship themselves, they would put up with any sacrifice, do without food, submit to crowded quarters, take a minimum of pay, if only they were recognized as men, masters of their own destinies.

And that is why we are working towards a workers republic, he said triumphantly.

Functional Classes

We made him admit that some men were capable of leadership and others weren't, that some men were trained to hold certain positions and had to hold them. We brought out Tawney's ideas of functional classes as opposed to acquisitive classes.

But the worker had no chance of improving himself so that he had a chance to become an officer, he claimed. Or if he had, he was still in the position of being a flunkey, a hireling of the masters. There were always the masters. There was always the profit system, the idea of labor being sold as a commodity, whether it was the labor of the captain or the crew.

It was, we conceded, the whole social system which was out of joint. And it was to reconstruct the social order, that we were throwing ourselves in with the workers, whether in factories, or shipyards or on the sea.

Co-operative Ideal

The co-operative movement is a good one because it offers an opportunity to rebuild within the shell of the old with a new philosophy, which is a philosophy so old that it seems like new. And in the co-operative movement there is a chance for a real united front and for a peaceful and ethical accomplishment of our aims. But where there is no chance at co-operative enterprise right now, in factories, on ships, what then?

The Pope Says

The popes have hit the nail on the head.

"No man may outrage with impunity that human dignity which God Himself treats with reverence" [Pope Leo XIII].

"Religion teaches the rich man and the employer that their work people are not their slaves; that they must respect in every man his dignity as a man and as a Christian; that labor is an honorable employment; and that it is shameful and inhuman to treat men like chattels to make money by, or to look upon them merely as so much muscle or physical power" [Pope Leo XIII].

"Enlightened Self Interest"

These are fundamental principles which the A.F. of L. [American Federation of Labor] has neglected to bring out. They have based their appeal on enlightened self interest, a phrase reeking with selfishness and containing a warning and a threat. A warning to the workers of the world that they are working for themselves alone, and not as members one of another. One can see how it has worked out in this country. What percentage of the workers are organized? A fraction only of the laboring men of the country. And how has the highly organized worker cared for his poorer brother? There has grown up an aristocracy of labor, so that it has been an irksome fact that bricklayers and printers receive more than farmers or editors in the necessary goods of this world—in goods which we should strive for in order that we may have those God-given means to develop to the full and achieve the Kingdom of Heaven.

Recognition of Last End

We are not losing sight of the fact that our end is spiritual. We are not losing sight of the fact that these better conditions of labor are means to an end. But the labor movement has lost sight of this fact. The leaders have forgotten such a thing as the philosophy of labor. They have not given to the worker a philosophy of labor, and they have betrayed him.

And the inarticulate rank and file throughout the world is rising up in rebellion, and are being labeled Communist for so doing—for refusing to accept the authority of such leaders, which they very rightly do not consider their authority. They know better than their leaders what it is they are looking for. But they allow themselves to be misled and deceived.

Positive Not Negative

We have so positive a program that we need all our energy, we have to bend all our forces, material and spiritual, to this end, to promulgate it. Let us uphold our positive program of changing the social order.

But let us too, examine the Communist means to the end which they claim they are working for, a true brotherhood of man. We, none of us, can have any objection to the ideal of the brotherhood of man. We do not talk about a classless society, because we acknowledge functional classes as opposed to acquisitive classes.

We agree with this end, but we do not agree on the means to attain it.

Brotherhood of Man

The Communist says that all men are our brothers except the capitalist, so we will kill him off. They do not actually believe in the dignity of man as a human being, because they try to set off one or another class of men and say "they are not our brothers and never will be. So let us liquidate them," and then to point their argument, they say with scorn, "Do you ever think to convert J.P. Morgan or Rockefeller or Charlie Schwab?"

They are protesting against man's brutality to man, and at the same time they perpetuate it. It is like having one more war to end all wars. We disagree with this technique of class war, without which the Communist says the brotherhood of man cannot be achieved.

Nothing will be achieved until the worker rises up in arms and forcibly takes the position that is his, the Communist says. Your movement which trusts to powerful means, radical though it may seem, is doomed to failure.

Victorious Failure

We admit that we may seem to fail, but we recall to our readers the ostensible failure of Christ when he died upon the Cross, forsaken by all his followers. Out of this failure a new world sprang up. We recall to our readers the folly of the cross which St. Paul talks about.

When we participate in strikes, when we go out on picket lines and distribute leaflets, when we speak at strike meetings—we are there because we are reaching the workers when they are massed together for action. We are taking advantage of a situation. We may not agree that to strike was the wise thing to do at that particular time. We believe that the work of organization must be thorough before any strike action occurs, unless indeed the strike is a spontaneous one which is the outcome of unbearable conditions.

We Oppose Violence

We oppose all use of violence as un-Christian. We do not believe in persuading scabs with clubs. They are workers, too, and the reason there are scabs is because the work of organization has been neglected. We oppose the misuse of private property while we uphold the right of private property. The Holy Father says that "as many as possible of the workers should become owners" [Pope Leo XIII], and how else in many cases except by developing the cooperative ideal?

We Repeat Our Stand

We repeat for the benefit of our readers, this assurance; while we are upholding cooperatives as part of the Christian social order, we are upholding at the same time, unions as organizations of workers wherein they can be indoctrinated and taught to rebuild the social order. While we stress the back-to-the-land movement so that the worker may be "deproletarianized," we are not going to leave the city to the Communist.

Month by month, in every struggle, in every strike, on every picket line, we shall do our best to join with the worker in his struggle for recognition as a man and not as a chattel. We reiterate the slogan of the old I.W.W.'s [Industrial Workers of the World], "An injury to one is an injury to all." St. Paul says when the health of one member of the Mystical Body suffers, the health of the whole body is lowered.

We are all members, one of another, in the Mystical Body of Christ, so let us work together for Christian solidarity.

On Pilgrimage[2]

April 1948

Whenever I groan within myself and think how hard it is to keep writing about love in these times of tension and strife which may at any moment become for us all a time of terror, I think to myself, "What else is the world interested in? What else do we all want, each one of us, except to love and be loved, in our families, in our work, in all

---

2. Dorothy Day, "On Pilgrimage," *The Catholic Worker*, April 1948, 1, 2, 11, https://www.catholicworker.org/dorothyday/articles/467.html.

our relationships. God is Love. Love casts out fear. Even the most ardent revolutionist, seeking to change the world, to overturn the tables of the money changers, is trying to make a world where it is easier for people to love, to stand in that relationship with each other of love. We want with all our hearts to love, to be loved. And not just in the family but to look upon all as our mothers, sisters, brothers, children. It is when we love the most intensely and most humanly, that we can recognize how tepid is our love for others. The keenness and intensity of love brings with it suffering, of course, but joy too because it is a foretaste of heaven. I often think in relation to my love for little Beckie, Susie and Eric: "That is the way I must love every child and want to serve them, cherish them and protect them." Even that relationship which is set off from other loves by that slight change in phraseology (instead of "Loving," one is "in love") the very change in terminology, denoting a living in love, a dwelling in love at all times, being bathed in love, so that every waking thought, word, deed and suffering is permeated by that love, yes, that relationship above all should give us not only a taste of the love of God for us, but the kind of love we should have for all.

When you love people, you see all the good in them, all the Christ in them. God sees Christ, His Son, in us and loves us. And so we should see Christ in others, and nothing else, and love them. There can never be enough of it. There can never be enough thinking about it. St. John of the Cross said that where there was no love, put love and you would take out love. This sounds rather clumsy, and I would like to get the exact quotation and translation if some of our readers would send it in to me. The principle certainly works. I've seen my friend Sister Peter Claver with that warm friendliness of hers which is partly natural (she is half Jew and half Irish), but which is intensified and made enduring by grace, come into a place which is cold with tension and conflict, and warm the house with her love.

And this is not easy. Everyone will try to kill that love in you, even your nearest and dearest; at least, they will try to prune it. "Don't you know this, that and the other thing, about this person? He or she did this. If you don't want to hear it, you must hear. It is for your good to hear it. It is my duty to tell you, and it is your duty to take recognition of it. You must stop loving, modify your loving, show your disapproval. You cannot possibly love if you pretend you do, you are a hypocrite and the truth is not in you. You are contributing to the delinquency of that person by your sentimental blindness. It is such people as you who add to the sum total of confusion and wickedness and soft appeasement and compromise and the policy of expediency in this world. You are to blame for communism, for industrial capitalism, and finally for hell on earth."

The antagonism often rises to a crescendo of vituperation, an intensification of opposition on all sides. You are quite borne down by it. And the only Christian answer is love, to the very end, to the laying down of your life.

On Pilgrimage[3]

November 1948

There is a character in *The Plague*, by Albert Camus, who says that he is tired of hearing about men dying for an idea. He would like to hear about a man dying for love for a change. He goes on to say that men have forgotten how to love, that all they seem to be thinking of these days is learning how to kill. Man, he says, seems to have lost the capacity for love.

What is God but Love? What is a religion without love? We read of the saints dying for love, and we wonder what they mean. There was a silly verse I used to hear long ago: "Men have died from time to time, and worms have eaten them, but not for love." It comes from *As You*

---

3. Dorothy Day, "On Pilgrimage," *The Catholic Worker*, November 1948, https://www. catholicworker.org/dorothyday/articles/485.html

Like It. And nowadays in this time of war and preparing for war, we would agree, except for the saints. Yes, they have died for love of God. But Camus's character would say, "I mean for love of man." Our Lord did that, but most people no longer believe in Him. It is hard to talk to people about God if they do not believe in Him. So one can talk and write of love. People want to believe in that even when they are all but convinced that it is an illusion. (It would be better still to love rather than to write about it. It would be more convincing.)

In the Old and New Testaments there are various ways in which the relationship of God and men [is] mentioned. There is the shepherd and his sheep. "The Lord is my shepherd." "I am the Good Shepherd." The animal and the man. There is the servant and the master, there is the son and the father, and there is the bride and the bridegroom. "Behold, the bridegroom cometh." The Song of Songs, the Canticle of Canticles, is all about love. "Let Him kiss me with the kisses of His mouth."

It is hard to believe in this love. In a book by Hugh of St. Victor, which I read once on the way from St. Paul to Chicago, there is a conversation between the soul and God about this love. The soul is petulant and wants to know what kind of a love is that which loves everyone indiscriminately, the thief and the Samaritan, the wife and the mother and the harlot? The soul complains that it wishes a particular love, a love for herself alone. And God replies fondly that, after all, since no two people are alike in this world, He has indeed a particular fondness for each one of us, an exclusive love to satisfy each one alone.

It is hard to believe in this love because it is a tremendous love. "It is a terrible thing to fall into the hands of the living God." If we do once catch a glimpse of it, we are afraid of it. Once we recognize that we are sons of God, that the seed of divine life has been planted in us at baptism, we are overcome by that obligation placed upon us of growing in the love of God. And what we do not do voluntarily, He will do for us.

Father Roy, our dear Josephite friend who worked with us at Easton and who has been these past two years in a hospital in Montreal, learning what it is to be loved, used to tell a story of a leper he met at a hospital up on the Gaspé peninsula. The leper complained to him, How could he believe in the love of God?

Father Roy proceeded to tell his favorite story. First of all, there is dirt, the humus from which all things spring, and the flower says to the dirt, "How would you like to grow and wave in the breeze and praise God?" And the dirt says "Yes," and that necessitates its losing its own self as dirt and becoming something else. Then the chicken comes along and says to the flower, "How would you like to be a chicken and walk around like I do and praise God?" And the flower assures the chicken that it would like it indeed. But then it has to cease to be a flower. And the man comes to the chicken and says to it, "How would you like to be a man and praise God?" And of course the chicken would like it too, but it has to undergo a painful death to be assimilated to the man, in order to praise God.

When Father Roy told this story, he said with awe, "And the leper looked at me, and a light dawned in his eyes, and he clasped my hands and gasped, 'Father!' And then we both cried together."

Father Roy is a childlike man, and the Russian leper up in the Canadian peninsula was a simple sufferer, and he saw the point that Father Roy was trying to make, and he began to believe in this love and to see some reason for his sufferings. He began to comprehend the heights and the depths and the strange mystery of this love. But it still takes the eyes of faith to see it.

The love of God and man becomes the love of equals, as the love of the bride and the bridegroom is the love of equals, and not the love of the sheep for the shepherd, or the servant for the master, or the son for the father. We may stand at times in the relationship of servant, and at other times in that of son, as far as our feelings go and in our present state. But the relationship we hope to attain to is that of the love of the Canticle of Canticles. If we cannot deny the self in us, kill the self-love, as He has commanded, and put on the Christ life, then God will do it for us. We must become like Him. Love must go through these purgations.

Unfortunately, when we speak of the human love of man and woman, most people, though they hope against hope, still regard it as an illusion, a great and glowing experience, a magic which comes into their lives for the sake of the procreation of the race. They assume and accept the fact that it will die, that it will not last, and in their vain clutching at it, they will put off one partner and look for it in another, and so the sad game goes on, with our movie stars going from the fifth to the sixth bride and swearing the selfsame promises to each.

The Best Years of Our Lives had a sad and cynical ending. While one young couple plighted their troth, exchanged their promises, another young couple disregarded promises already made and fell into each other's arms to try to regain, to recapture love once more. Illusive love!

Vladimir Solovyov writes in *The Meaning of Love* about the need to study this problem, to seek the growth of this love, so that the force of love may be set loose in the world today to combat the terrible force of hate and violence that we have unloosed. Father D'Arcy deals with the problem in *The Mind and Heart of Love*. De Rougemont, in *Love in the Western World*, writes also about this work of love. These books may be hard reading for those who seem to learn of love by reading best-sellers and seeing the prize movies. But the very fact that all best-sellers and prize movies deal with this very theme of love should make the man of today turn to such books as these and get down to a study of what is most vital in our lives.

That most people in America look upon love as an illusion would seem to be evidenced by the many divorces we see today—and the sensuality of despair that exists all around us. But all these divorces may too be an evidence about love. They hear very little of it in this war-torn world, and they are all seeking it. Pascal said of love, "You would not seek me if you had not already found me." Just so much faith is there, at any rate. A faith in love, a seeking for love. It is something, then, to build on, amongst the mass of people who have lost God, who do not know in what they believe, though they believe in and seek for love.

And where are the teachers to teach of this love, of the stages of this love, the purgations of this love, the sufferings entailed by this love, the stages through which natural love must pass to reach the supernatural?

We would all like to hear of men laying down their lives for love for their fellows, and we do not want to hear of it in the heroic tones of a statesman or a prince of the church. We all know that such phrases used in wartime mean nothing. Men are taught to kill, not to lay down their lives if they can possibly help it. Of course we do not talk of brothers in wartime. We talk of the enemy, and we forget the Beatitudes and the commandment to love our enemy, do good to them that persecute us. "A new commandment I give you, that you love one another as I have loved you." One said that who did lay down His life for all men.

Youth demands the heroic, Claudel said, and youth likes to dream of heroic deeds and of firing squads, of martyrs and of high adventure. But bread means life too; and money, which buys bread, for which we work, also means life. Sharing and community living mean laying down your life for your fellows also, and it was of these things that Father Perrin, S.J., the workman priest in Germany, wrote in his moving book.

We have repeated so many times that those who have two cloaks should follow the early Fathers, who said, "The coat that hangs in your closet belongs to the poor." And those who have a ten-room house can well share it with those who have none and who are forced to live in a municipal lodging house. How many large houses could be made into several apartments to take in others? Much hospitality could be given to relieve the grave suffering today. But people are afraid. They do not know where it all will end. They have all gone far enough in generosity to know that an ordeal is ahead, that the person taken in will turn into "the friend of the family," most likely, or "the man who came to dinner." No use starting something that you cannot finish, they say. Once bitten is twice shy. We have all had our experiences of ingratitude, of nursing a viper in our bosom, as the saying goes. So we forget about pruning in the natural order in order to attain much fruit. We don't want to pay the cost of love. We do not want to exercise our capacity to love.

There are many stories one could tell about Catholic Worker life, but it is always better to wait until years have passed so that they become more impersonal, less apt to be identified with this one or that. There is the story of the sorcerer's apprentice who took over the kitchen this last month at the farm. There is the story of a "friend of the family" who tried to stab a neighbor and was evicted by the neighbors. Too bad we cannot write these stories for the edification and instruction of those who are starting new houses of hospitality today.

There is a story now, however, about a reader of the paper—and this happened long enough ago so that we can tell it—who adopted a young girl and educated her, and the young girl proved to be a great joy and a comfort. Now she has entered a contemplative order to spend her life in prayer and work. The same reader then took in another young woman, who brought home a fatherless baby, and when that was forgiven her, went out and brought in still another, and there was apt to be a third, and our friend wrote and begged us for advice and help as to what to do. Was she contributing to the delinquency of this girl by forgiving seventy times seven, and was she perhaps going to have seventy times seven children to take care of?

It is good to think of the prophet Hosea, whom I have mentioned before in writing on love. He was commanded by God to take a harlot to wife, and she had many children by other men. He was a dignified, respected teacher of his people, and he was shamed and humiliated by the wife of his bosom. Yet he was to go down in history as exemplifying the love of God for His adulterous people.

Love must be tried and tested and proved. It must be tried as though by fire, and fire burns. "It is a dreadful thing to fall into the hands of the living God."

In times of catastrophe we are all willing to share. In an earthquake, hurricane, war, or plague, people begin to love one another. Of course, the wife must consider her husband, but it is not so necessary for the husband to consider the wife. As head of the household, it is his job to lead the wife in hospitality, and if he is willing to support others in need, he should induce his wife to go along with him. He should share all but his intimate love with others, and that is for her alone. If he should withdraw that tenderness, that embrace, then he would be guilty indeed.

What kind of a love was that of Scobie, the Major in the current bestseller of Graham Greene, the love which had turned to indifference, if not to loathing at times, and which the author felt to be redeemed by the pity and compassion of Scobie for his nagging wife? How to love truly a woman after the illusion has passed and that woman becomes a climbing, snobbish, petty, self-conscious inferior, and not an equal, with whom there is no longer any possibility of the love of equals, which is the love of the Canticle of Canticles?

Here are some excerpts from Solovyov that perhaps are pertinent:

> It is well known to everyone that in love there inevitably exists a special idealization of the beloved object, which presents itself to the lover in an entirely different light from that in which outsiders

see it. I speak here of light not merely in a metaphorical sense; it is a matter here not only of a special moral and intellectual estimate, but moreover of a special sensuous reception; the lover actually sees, visually receives what others do not. And if for him too this light of love quickly fades away, yet does it follow from this that it was false, that it was only a subjective illusion?

. . . The true significance of love consists not in the simple experience of this feeling but what is accomplished by means of it, in the work of love.

For love it is not enough to feel for itself the unconditional significance of the beloved object, but it is necessary effectively to impart or communicate this significance to this object. . . .

. . . Each man comprises in himself the image of God. Theoretically and in the abstract, this Divine image is known to us in mind and through mind, but in love it is known in the concrete and in life. And if this revelation of the ideal nature, ordinarily concealed by its material manifestation, is not confined in love to an inward feeling, but at times becomes noticeable also in the sphere of external feelings, then so much greater is the significance we are bound to acknowledge for love as being from the very first the visible restoration of the Divine image in the world of matter. . . .

A woman wants compassion, not pity, and Major Scobie did not work very hard at communicating the significance of his love to his wife. Even two of the characters in *The Best Years of Our Lives* had gone a bit farther along the path of love when they told their daughter, who was falling in love with a married man, "How often have we hated one another!" In other words, what a purgation, what a working out we have been through together!

(I am consciously and purposely writing with these allusions so that those who are not able to read Solovyov but who do go to the movies will also know what I am writing about.)

True love is delicate and kind, full of gentle perception and understanding, full of beauty and grace, full of joy unutterable. Eye hath not seen, nor ear heard, what God hath prepared for those who love Him.

And there should be some flavor of this in all our love for others. We are all one. We are one flesh in the Mystical Body, as man and woman are said to be one flesh in marriage. With such a love one would see all things new; we would begin to see people as they really are, as God sees them.

We may be living in a desert when it comes to such perceptions now, and that desert may stretch out before us for years. But a thousand years are as one day in the sight of God, and soon we will know as we are known. Until then, we will have glimpses of brotherhood in play, in suffering, in serving, and we will begin to train for that community, that communion, that Father Perrin talked so much about in his story of the workman priest in Germany.

This last month there was an article by John Cogley in America about his experiences in the Chicago House of Hospitality. He writes of it as in the dim and distant past, and tells of the "mushroom growth" of such houses back in the thirties. In the present there are a few still struggling along, he writes, and a few farms existing in dire poverty.

Yes, the problems have become intensified; a great many have left the running. Where there were thirty-two houses of hospitality and farms, there are now eleven. But in those eleven we are still trying to work out a theory of love, a study of the problem of love so that the revolution of love, instead of that of hate, may come about, and we will have a new heaven and a new earth wherein justice dwelleth.

POEM FOR FALL

All around are the irregular fields.
Irregular because woodlots space the scene.
The fields are colorful with red and purple cabbages, pale
carrots, green turnips, feathery dill, and dark red beets.
The harvest is not yet in, and far in the hundred-acre field are
the bent figures of a dozen workers dressed in denim.
The trees—the oak, the maple, the elm and sassafras—
Are decked out brilliantly,
Dying gloriously
With joy,
With thankfulness.

Hope springs in my heart like a refreshing fountain.
This is the season of hope,
This, the month when we pray for the dead.
And I, whom "the certainty of dying afflicteth,
Am consoled by the promise of future immortality."
"Life is changed, not taken away."
Life is still there.

And as I walk these wagon tracks between fields,
Through the bright November air, sharp with impending frost,
But with the caress of the sun still on it,
Still as only November days can be still, expectant, breathless,
It is easy to think on death and life and their embrace.

For it is long since that my dying has begun.
So long that one gets used to it.
And long since, and yet how short a time
That I began to live.
The life increases with my dying.

That life becomes the more abundant life.
Life that is the beginning of our heaven here and now.

Some fields are bare and brown amid the green,
And striding through the harrowed field
Comes the sower.
His arm swings with long rhythms;
He strides freely.
He flings the seed.
Overhead wheel the swallows,
Swooping and dancing in the sun.
Another field far distant
Already shows its cover crop
Of tender rye,
And as I watch, I think of St. Paul's words:

But some man will say:
"How do the dead rise again?
Or with what manner of body shall they come?"

Senseless man! That which thou sowest is not quickened,
Except it die first.

And that which thou sowest,
Thou sowest not the body that shall be,
But bare grain,
As of wheat, or of some of the rest.
But God giveth it a body as He will,
And to every seed its proper body.
All flesh is not the same flesh;
But one is the flesh of man,
Another of beasts,
Another of birds,

Another of fishes.
And there are bodies celestial
And bodies terrestrial;
But one is the glory of the celestial
And another of the terrestrial.
One is the glory of the sun,
Another the glory of the moon,
And another the glory of the stars.
For star differeth from star in glory.
So also is the resurrection of the dead.

It is sown in corruption;
It shall rise in incorruption.
It is sown in dishonor;
It shall rise in glory.
It is sown in weakness;
It shall rise in power.

It is sown a natural body;
It shall rise a spiritual body.

Behold, I tell you a mystery.
We shall all indeed rise again.

Deo gratias.

Fall Appeal[4]

October 1964

To help the poor! This is a great and fearful work. It is through the poor that we achieve our salvation; Jesus Christ Himself has said it in His picture of the Last Judgment. It is through the poor that we can exercise faith and learn to love Him. It is a great relief to read the lives of such saints as St. Vincent de Paul when doing this kind of work. An article some years ago said that he had contact with refugees, convicts, thieves, assassins and bandits, as well as with professional beggars, swindlers, prostitutes. "He saw quite clearly, and sometimes said, that many of these poor people were filthy, physically repulsive and suffering from loathsome diseases, that sometimes they were dishonest, drunken, hypocritical and ungrateful; but to use his own phrase, that is only one side of the medal. Turn it, and with the eyes of faith you see that each is stamped with the image of God and is a brother of Jesus Christ." . . . "The poor are your masters, he said, and thank God you are allowed to serve them." We too see in ourselves our measure of sin and decay of mind and body, but the more we can look at the good side of the coin, the better off we are ourselves, finding Christ. Our faith will grow through such an exercise of love.

It is a joyful experience, to serve the poor, and to be poor ourselves.

---

4. Dorothy Day, "Fall Appeal," *The Catholic Worker*, October 1964, https://www. catholicworker.org/dorothyday/articles/819.html.

CHAPTER 26

Bl. Pier Giorgio Frassati
(1901–1925)

Bl. Pier Giorgio Frassati was born into a wealthy and established family in Italy. Though his parents were not religious, he came to a deep love of the Catholic faith and the poor. Without the knowledge of his family, Pier Giorgio visited the poor and the sick, distributing money, food, and medicine. Upon his death from polio at the age of twenty-four, his family was shocked to see thousands of people line the streets to pay their respects to the man who had served them.

Notes for a Speech about Charity[1]

Friends, it is not with you that I should talk about one of the most interesting problems of our daily life. You who belong to the FUCI [Italian Catholic Federation of University Students] do not need to listen to things re-hashed in poor words which you have already heard so many times. However, given the gravity of the subject I do not believe it is useless to repeat what has already been said.

Every one of you knows that the foundation of our religion is Charity. Without it all our religion would crumble, because we would not truly be Catholics as long as we did not fulfill, or rather conform our life to,

---

1. *Pier Giorgio Frassati: Letters to His Friends and Family*, ed. Fr. Timothy E. Deeter and Christine M. Wohar (Staten Island, NY: St. Paul's, 2009), 239–241.

the two commandments in which the essence of the Catholic Faith lies: to love God and to love our neighbor as ourselves. And here is the explicit proof that the Catholic Faith is based on real Love and not, as so many would like, in order to quiet their conscience, to base the religion of Christ on violence.

With violence hatred is sown and then its evil fruits are harvested. With Charity Peace is sown among men, but not the peace of the world, True Peace which only faith in Jesus Christ can give binding us together in brotherly love.

I know this way is steep and difficult and full of thorns, whereas the other at first sight would seem more beautiful and easier and more satisfying, but if we could plunge the depths of those who unfortunately follow the perverse ways of the world, we would see that there is never in them the serenity had by those who have faced thousands of difficulties and have renounced material pleasures in order to follow the laws of God.

Today, after a terrible war [World War I] has deluged the whole world bringing material and moral ruin, we have a strict duty to cooperate generously in the moral regeneration of society worldwide so that a radiant dawn may break in which all nations recognize Jesus Christ as King not only in words but in all their people's lives, as the Florentine Republic did in the Middle Ages. But to bring this great plan to fulfillment, this most beautiful plan, we need to work generously and one of the most appropriate tasks is that offered by the Conferences of St. Vincent.

I don't know if you are aware what these institutions are that were so marvelously conceived by St. Vincent de Paul.

It is a simple institution suitable for students because it does not involve commitment apart from being in a particular place one day a week and then visiting two or three families every week. You will see, in just a little time, how much good we can do to those we visit and how much good we can do to ourselves.

The members who visit these families are, I would say, unworthy instruments of Divine Providence. As we grow closer to the poor little by little we gain their confidence and can advise them in the most terrible moments of this earthly pilgrimage. We can give them the comforting words of faith and we often succeed, not by our own merit, in putting on the right path people who have strayed not out of malice.

I think I can say that the Conference of St. Vincent with its visits to the poor serves to curb our passions, it gives us increasing incentives to get on the right road by which we are all trying to reach the great harbor.

Seeing daily the faith with which families often bear the most atrocious sufferings, the constant sacrifices they make and that they do all this for the love of God often makes us ask this question: I, who have had so many things from God, have always been so neglectful, so bad, while they, who have not been privileged like me, are infinitely better than me. Then we resolve in our conscience to follow the way of the Cross from then onward, the only way that leads to Eternal Salvation.

Now there are many conferences in the city of Turin and among those there is one for university students, which however is composed primarily of people who are on the verge of ending their student careers and beginning the life of adults.

Now we direct to you a warm appeal that you might want to swell the ranks of our members which are now very meager and so that each of you can contribute in your own way to relieve those who suffer.

Come with enthusiasm to this conference, come and every sacrifice of yours will certainly be compensated in Heaven because Jesus Christ has promised that all we do for the poor for Love of Him He will consider it as having been done to Himself. You don't want to refuse this Love to

Jesus Who, because of infinite love for Humanity, wanted to be in the Sacrament of the Eucharist, as our Consoler and as Bread of the Soul.

To be members one is not required to pay membership dues, it is enough to have good will and nothing else. It is true that at the end of the meeting there is a collection, but everybody is free to put whatever he wants.

CHAPTER 27

St. Teresa of Kolkata
(1910–1997)

*St. Teresa of Kolkata (aka Mother Teresa) was born in what is now
North Macedonia. She joined the Sisters of Loreto and became
a missionary in India, working as a teacher at convent schools. In 1946,
she received a "call within the call," and heard Jesus beckoning her
to a life totally committed to the poorest of the poor. She went to live in
the slums of Kolkata and founded the Missionaries of Charity,
a religious order now present in over 130 countries. She received the
Nobel Peace Prize in 1979.*

National Prayer Breakfast Message[1]

*Make us worthy, Lord, to serve our fellow man throughout the world who
live and die in poverty and hunger. Give them through our hands this day
their daily bread, and by our understanding love, give peace and joy.*

Jesus came to give us the good news that God loves us, and that He
wants us to love one another as he loves each one of us. And to
make it easy for us to love one another, Jesus said, "Whatever you do
to the least, you do it to me." "If you give a glass of water, you give it
to me." "If you receive a little child in my name, you receive me." So,
whatever you do to the least, you do it to me.

---

1. "On February 3, 1994, Mother Teresa was invited to speak at the National Prayer Breakfast sponsored by the U.S. Senate and House of Representatives. President Bill Clinton and his wife Hillary along with Vice President Al Gore and his wife Tipper were also in attendance. The room got very quiet as she spoke about the violence of abortion, but soon applause erupted and became nearly unanimous, with four notable exceptions" (Marcellino D'Ambrosio, Crossroads Initiative). This is a lightly edited transcript of her address and so retains certain repetitions, omitted words, and imprecise phrasings. Mother Teresa of Kolkata, "National Prayer Breakfast Address," American Rhetoric, https://www.americanrhetoric.com/speeches/mother teresanationalprayerbreakfast.htm.

And where does this love begin? In our own family.

How does it begin? By praying together.

The family that prays together, stays together. And if you stay together, you will love each other as God loves each one of you. So teach your children to pray, and pray with them; and you will have the joy and the peace and the unity of Christ's own love living in you.

As we have gathered together here, I think it will be beautiful if you begin with a prayer that expresses very well what Jesus wants us to do for the least. St. Francis of Assisi understood very well these words of Jesus and in his life very well expressed by prayer. And this prayer, which we say every day after Holy Communion, always surprises me very much, because it is very fitting for each one of us. And [I] always wonder whether 800 years ago, when St. Francis lived, they had the same difficulties that we have today. I think that some of you already have this prayer of peace—so we will pray it together.

Let us pray.

"Lord, make me a channel of your peace"—

Do you have the prayer book? [to audience].

We will say it together?

[audience in unison, though Mother Teresa's initial words are slightly different than those recited from the prayer book]

Lord, make me a channel of Your peace,
where there is hatred, let me sow love;
where there is injury, pardon;
where there is doubt, faith;
where there is despair, hope;

where there is darkness, light;
where there is sadness, joy.

O, Divine Master, grant that I may not so much seek
to be consoled as to console;
to be understood as to understand;
to be loved as to love.
For it is in giving that we receive;
it is in pardoning that we are pardoned;
it is in dying that we are born again to Eternal Life.

Let us thank God for the opportunity He has given us today to have come here to pray together. We have come here especially to pray for peace, for joy, and for love. We are reminded that Jesus came to bring the good news to the poor. He had told us what is that good news when He said: my "Peace I leave with you, My peace I give unto you." He came not to give the peace of the world, which is only that we don't bother each other. He came to give the peace of heart which comes from loving, from doing good to others.

And God loved the world so much that He gave His Son—it was a giving. God gave His son to the Virgin Mary, and what did she do with Him? As soon as Jesus came into Mary's life, immediately she went in haste to give that good news. And as she came into the house of her cousin, Elizabeth, Scripture tells us that the unborn child—the child in the womb of Elizabeth—leapt with joy. While still in the womb of Mary, Jesus brought peace to John the Baptist who leapt for joy in the womb of Elizabeth. The unborn was the first one to proclaim the coming of Christ.

And as if that were not enough, as if it were not enough that God the Son should become one of us and bring peace and joy while still in the womb of Mary, Jesus also died on the Cross to show that greater love. He died for you and for me, and for that leper, and for that man dying of hunger, and that naked person lying in the street, not only of [Kolkata], but of Africa, and all over the world.

Our Sisters serve these poor people in 105 countries throughout the world. Jesus insisted that we love one another as He loves each one of us. Jesus gave His life to love us and He tells us that we also have to give whatever it takes to do good to one another. And in the Gospel Jesus says very clearly: "Love as I have loved you."

Jesus died on the Cross because that is what it took for Him to do good to us—to save us from our selfishness and sin. He gave up everything to do the Father's will, to show us that we too must willing—must be willing to give up everything to do God's will—to love one another as He loves each one of us.

If we are not willing to give whatever it takes to do good to one another, sin is still in us. That is why we too must give to each other until it hurts. It is not enough to say—for us to say: "I love God." But I also have to love my neighbor. St. John says that you are a liar if you say you love God and you don't love your neighbor. How can you love God whom you do not see, if you do not love your neighbor whom you see whom you touch, with whom you live? And so it is very important for us to realize that love, to be true, has to hurt. I must be willing to give whatever it takes not to harm other people and, in fact, to do good to them. This requires that I be willing to give until it hurts. Otherwise, there is no true love in me; and I bring injustice, not peace, to those around me.

It hurt Jesus to love us. We have been created in His image for greater things, to love and to be loved. We must "put on Christ," as Scripture tells us. And so, we have been created to love as He loves us. Jesus makes Himself the hungry one, the naked one, the homeless one, the unwanted one, and He says, "You did it to Me." On the last day He will say to those on His right, "Whatever you did to the least of these, you did to Me." And He will also say to those on His left, "Whatever you neglected to do for the least of these, you neglected to do it for Me."

When He was dying on the Cross, Jesus said, "I thirst." Jesus is thirsting for our love, and this is the thirst of everyone, poor and rich alike. We all thirst for love of others, that they go out of their way to avoid harming us and to do good to us. This is the meaning of true love, to give until it hurts.

I can never forget the experience I had in visiting a home where they kept all these old parents of sons and daughters who had just put them into an institution and forgotten them. Maybe. I saw that in that home these old people had everything—good food, comfortable place, television, everything, but everyone was looking toward the door. And I did not see a single one with a smile on the face. I turned to the Sister and I asked: "Why do these people, who have every—every comfort here, they are there looking toward the door? Why are they not smiling? I am so used to seeing the smiles on our people, even the dying ones smile." And Sister said: "This is the way it is nearly everyday. They are expecting—they are hoping that a son or a daughter will come to visit them. They are hurt because they are forgotten."

And see, this neglect to love brings spiritual poverty. Maybe in our own family we have somebody who is feeling lonely, who is feeling sick, who is feeling worried. Are we there? Are we willing to give until it hurts in order to be with our family, or do we put our interests first? These are the questions we must ask ourselves, especially as we begin this year of the family. We must remember that love begins at home. And we must also remember that: The future of humanity passes through the family.

I was surprised in the West to see so many young boys and girls given to drugs. And I tried to find out why. Why is it like that, when those in the West have so many more things than those in the East? And the answer was: because there is no one in the family to receive them. Our children depend on us for everything—their health, their nutrition, their security, their coming to know and love God. For all of this, they look to us with trust, hope, and expectation. But often father and mother are so busy they have no time for their children, or perhaps they are not even married or have given up on their marriage. So their children go to the streets and get involved in drugs or other things. We are talking of love of the child, which is where love and peace must begin—there, in our own family.

But I feel that the greatest destroyer of peace today is abortion, because Jesus said, "If you receive a little child, you receive me." So, every abortion is the denial of receiving Jesus—is the neglect of receiving Jesus.

It is really a war against the child, a direct killing of the innocent child, murder by the mother herself. And if we accept that a mother can kill even her own child, how can we tell other people not to kill one another? How do we persuade a woman not to have an abortion? As always, we must persuade her with love and we remind ourselves that love means to be willing to give until it hurts.

Jesus gave even His life to love us. So, the mother who is thinking of abortion should be helped to love—that is, to give until it hurts her plans, her free time, to respect the life of her child. For the child is the greatest gift of God to the family because they have been created to love and be loved.

The father of that child, however, must also give until it hurts.

By abortion, the mother does not learn to love, but kills even her own child to solve her problems. And, by abortion, the father is told that he does not have to take any responsibility at all for the child he has brought into the world. That—So that father is likely to put other women into the same trouble. So, abortion just leads to more abortion. Any country that accepts abortion is not teaching its people to love one another, but to use any violence to get what they want. This is why the greatest destroyer of love and peace is abortion.

The beautiful gift God has given our congregation is to fight abortion by adoption. We have given already—We have given already from one house in [Kolkata], over 3,000 children in adoption. And I can't tell you what joy, what love, what peace those children have brought into those families. It has been a real gift of God for them and for us. I remember one of the little ones got very sick, so I sent for the father and the mother and I asked them: "Please give me back the sick child. I will give you a healthy one." And the father looked at me and said, "Mother Teresa, take my life first—then take the child." So beautiful to see it. So much love, so much joy that little one has brought into that family. So pray for us that we continue this beautiful gift. And also I offer you, since our Sisters are here, anybody who doesn't want the child, please give it to me. I—I want the child.

I will tell you something beautiful. As I already told you, the abortion by adoption—by care of the mother and adoption for her baby. We have saved thousands of lives. We have sent word to the clinics, to the hospitals and police stations: "Please don't destroy the child. We will take the child." So we always have someone tell the mothers in trouble: "Come, we will take—take care of you. We will get a home for your child." And we have a tremendous demand from couples who cannot have a child. But I never give a child to a couple who have done something not to have a child. Jesus said, "Anyone who receives a child in my name, receives me." By adopting a child, these couples receive Jesus but, by aborting a child, a couple refuses to receive Jesus.

Please don't kill the child. I want the child. Please give me the child. I am willing to accept any child who would be aborted and to give that child to [a] married couple who will love the child and be loved by the child.

I know that couples have to plan their family and for that there is natural family planning. The way to plan the family is natural family planning, not contraception. In destroying the power of giving life, of loving, through contraception, a husband or wife is doing something to self. This turns the attention to self, and so it destroys the gifts of love in him and her.

In loving, the husband and wife must turn the attention to each other, as happen[s] in natural family planning, and not to self, as happens in contraception. Once that living love is destroyed by contraception, abortion follows very easily. That's why I never give a child to a family that has used contraception—because if the mother has destroyed the power of loving, how will she love my child?

I also know that there are great problems in the world—that many spouses do not love each other enough to practice [natural family planning]. We cannot solve [all] the problems in the world, but let us never bring in the worst problem of all—to destroy love, to destroy life.

The poor are very great people. They can teach us so many beautiful things. Once, one of them came to thank us for teaching her natural family planning and said: "You people who have practiced chastity, you are the best people to teach us natural family planning because it is nothing more than self-control out of love for each other." And what this poor person said is very true. These poor people maybe have nothing to eat, maybe—maybe they have not a home to live in, but they can still be great people when they are spiritually rich and love one another as God loves each one of them.

When I pick up a person from the streets, hungry, I give him a plate of rice, a piece of bread. But a person who is shut out, who feels unwanted, unloved, terrified, the person who has been thrown out of society—that spiritual poverty is much harder to be overcome. And abortion, which often follows from contraception, brings a people to be spiritually poor, and that is the worst poverty and the most difficult to overcome.

Those who are materially poor can be very wonderful people. One evening we went out and we picked up four people from the street. And one of them was in a most terrible condition. I told the Sisters: "You take care of the other three; I will take care of the one who looks are worse." So I did for her all that my love can do. I put her in bed, and there was such a beautiful smile on her face. She took hold of my hand, as she said one word only: "Thank you." And she died.

I couldn't help but examine my conscience before her. And I asked: "What would I say if I were in her place?" And my answer was very simple. I would have tried to draw a little attention to myself. I would have said: "I am hungry. I am dying. I am cold. I am in pain." But she gave me much more: She gave me her grateful love. She died with a big smile on her face.

Then there was the man we picked up from the drain, half eaten with worms. And after we had brought him to the home, he only said, "I have lived like an animal in the street, but I am going to die as an angel, loved and cared." Then, after we had removed all the worms from his body, all he said, with a big smile: "Sister, I am going home to God." And he died. I[t] was—was so wonderful to see the greatness of that man who could speak like that without blaming anybody, without comparing anything, like an angel. This is the greatness of people who are spiritually rich even when they are materially poor.

We are not social workers. We may be doing social work in the eyes of some people, but we must be contemplatives in the heart of the world. For we must bring that presence of God into your family. For the family that prays together, stays together. There is so much hatred, so much misery, and we with our prayer, with our sacrifice, are beginning at home. Love begins at home, and it is not how much we do, but how much love we put into what we do.

If we are contemplatives in the heart of the world with all its problem[s], these problems can never . . . discourage us. We must always remember that God tells us in Scripture: "Even if a mother could forget the child in her womb"—something impossible, but even if she could forget—"I will never forget you."

And so, here I am talking with you. I want you to find the poor here, right in your own home first. And begin love there. Be that good news to your own people first. And find out about your next-door neighbor. Do you know who they are?

I had the most extraordinary experience of love of neighbor with a Hindu family. A gentleman came to our house and said: "Mother Teresa, there is a family who have not eaten for so long. Do something." So I took some rice and went there immediately. And I saw the children, their eyes shining with hunger. I don't know if you have ever seen hunger. But I have seen it very often. And the mother of the family took the rice I gave her and went out. When she came back, I asked her: "Where did you go? What did you do?" And she gave me a very simple answer: "They are hungry also."

What struck me was that she knew. And who [were they]? A Muslim family. And she knew that they were hungry. And I did not bring any more rice that evening because I wanted them, Hindus and family— and Muslim family, to enjoy the joy of loving each others. She just left her own children, who were hungry; her first thought was her neighbor. But there were those children, radiating joy, sharing the joy and peace of their mother because she had the love to give until it hurts. And you see this is where love begins—at home in the family.

So, as the example of this family shows, God will never forget us, and there is something you and I can always do. We can keep the joy of loving Jesus in our hearts, and share that joy with all we come in contact with. Let us make that one point—that no child will be unwanted, unloved, uncared for, or killed and thrown away. And give until it hurts—with a smile.

As you know, we have homes—a number of homes here in the United States, where people need tender love and care. This is the joy of sharing. Come and share. We have the young people suffering with AIDS. They need that tender love and care. But such beautiful—I've never yet seen a young man or anybody . . . displeased or angry or frightened, really going home to God. Such a beautiful smile, always. So let us pray that we have the gift of sharing the joy with others and loving until it hurts.

Because I talk so much of giving with a smile, once a professor from the United States asked me: "Are you married?" And I said: "Yes, and I find it sometimes very difficult to smile at my spouse, Jesus, because He can be—He can be very demanding sometimes." This is really something true. And [this] is where love comes in: when it is demanding, and yet we can give it with joy.

One of the most demanding things for me is travelling everywhere—and with publicity. I have said to Jesus that if I don't go to heaven for anything else, I will be going to heaven for all the travelling with all the publicity, because it has purified me and sacrificed me and made me really ready to go home to God.

If we remember that God loves us, and that we can love others as He loves us, then America can become a sign of peace for the whole world, be a sign of joy. From here, a sign of care for the weakest [of] the weak, the unborn child, must go out to the world. If you become a burning light of justice and peace in the world, then really you will be true to what the founders—founders of this country stood for.

Let us love one another as God loves each one of us.

And where does this love begin? In our own home.

How does it begin? By praying together.

Pray for us that we continue God's work with great love. The sisters, the brothers, and the fathers, lay missionaries of Charity, and coworkers: We are all one heart full of love, that we may bring that joy of loving everywhere we go.

And my—my prayer for you is that through this love for one another, for this peace and joy in the family, that you may grow in holiness. Holiness is not the luxury of the few; it is a simply duty, for you and for me, because Jesus has very clearly said, "Be ye holy as the father in heaven is holy." So let us pray for each other that we grow in love for each other, and through this love become holy, as Jesus wants us to be, for he died out of love for us.

One day, I met a lady who was dying of cancer in a most terrible condition. And I told her, I say, "You know, this terrible pain is only the kiss of Jesus, a sign that you have come so close to Jesus on the cross that he can kiss you." And she joined her hands together and said, "Mother Teresa, please tell Jesus to stop kissing me."

So pray for us that we continue God's work with great love. And I will pray for you—for all your—all your families.

And also I want to thank the families who have been so generous in giving their daughters to us to—to consecrate their life to Jesus by the vow of poverty, chastity, obedience, and by giving wholehearted, free service to the poorest of the poor. This is our fourth vow in our congregation. And we have a novitiate in San Francisco where we have many beautiful vocations who are wanting to give their whole life to Jesus in the service of the poorest of the poor.

So, once more, I thank you for giving your children to God. And pray for us that we continue God's work with great love.

God bless you all.

CHAPTER 28

St. Óscar Romero
(1917–1980)

St. Óscar Romero was appointed Archbishop of San Salvador in 1977.
Though initially hesitant to become involved in political matters,
his witnessing of cruel injustice against the poor and their defenders
led him to become an outspoken critic of those in power.
As a consequence of his defense of the basic rights of those under
his care, he was assassinated during Mass in 1980.

The Creator[1]

How wonderful it is, sisters and brothers, to feel governed by God, placed under God's sovereignty! That is what the Holy Bible means when it says that there is no power that does not come from God and that authority must be obeyed because it comes from God (Rom. 13:1). But the Bible also says that the human sovereign, the one who commands, must not command anything apart from what God wants; moreover, it says that authority is to be respected only because it reflects God's sacred power. When human authority contravenes God's law and violates the rights, the freedom, and the dignity of human beings, then it is time to cry out as Saint Peter did in the Bible, "We must obey God rather than men" (Acts 5:29). All power comes from God, and therefore

---

1. Óscar Romero, *The Scandal of Redemption: When God Liberates the Poor, Saves Sinners, and Heals Nations* (Walden, NY: Plough, 2018), 18–23.

rulers cannot use their authority capriciously but only according to the Lord's will. God's providence aims to govern the nations, and the rulers are only his ministers, servants of God like all the rest of his creatures.

The Bible says that he is a just God (Wis. 12:13–18): "You do not judge unjustly." "Your power is the source of justice." Consider the richness of this concept of justice. Justice is the manifestation of power. A power is not true power unless it is just. God himself, who can do what he wills, does not abuse power; indeed, he cannot abuse it because he is just; he is justice par excellence. God's power is illuminated by his infinite justice. "You judge with moderation." This is the eternal serenity of God; he does not get impatient. He is the God who holds the reins of all peoples and all human beings, and that is why his justice is restrained; it is justice that is serene and holy. Still another title that comes from today's readings is "merciful God." "Your universal sovereignty makes you spare all." "You govern us with great indulgence because you can do whatever you want." . . . Dear sisters and brothers, this is our God. Let us not forget him; let us respect him, realizing that he is the source of all the joy and the confidence of our faith. May the God that Jesus Christ reveals to us as Father, as providence, as goodness, always capture our hearts so that we will serve him not out of fear but out of love. Only when we see the God of our Lord Jesus Christ illuminating our dawns, our seas, and our volcanoes will we understand that God has created a world out of love to give it to his children, with whom he wants to enter into the communion of family. In this way we understand how the earth groans beneath the weight of sin (Rom. 8:22) because humanity has not understood that the whole of creation exists for the happiness of all human beings and not for us to be comfortably settled here on earth. There is no anonymous person among those of us who are here. All of you have your own individual histories, even the humblest of persons, even the smallest child who has come to this Mass, even the poorest and sickest folks listening by radio, all those people about whom nobody will talk in the history books. God has loved each of you singularly, as an unrepeatable phenomenon. God has not made human beings in a mold. . . . It was not my parents who gave me being; they were simply instruments or means that God used to give me life. . . . Even prior to the months of my gestation, I existed in the mind of God as a project which, if brought to fulfillment, would make of me a saint because a saint is nothing else than the full realization of a life according to the design of God.

The whole history of Israel is the story of humanity's return to God after breaking away. The whole marvelous book of Exodus tells how the people left slavery in Egypt and journeyed toward the Promised Land; it is a symbol of pilgrimage, of return, of the search for reconciliation. . . . The people had no certainty about the future; they lived believing in the land God had promised them, though they didn't know where it was. They seemed crazy but they weren't crazy; they were people of faith: "God has promised it! He will make it happen!" . . . There is a wonderful relationship here with our own situation in El Salvador, where the land is being fought over. Let us not forget that the land is closely tied to the blessings and promises of God. . . . Not having land is a consequence of sin. When Adam left paradise, he was a man without land as the result of sin. Now Israel, pardoned by God, has returned to the land and can eat of the fruits and the grains of the earth. God gives his blessings in the form of land. The land contains much of God, and therefore it groans when the unjust monopolize it and leave no space for others. Agrarian reform is a theological necessity. A country's land cannot remain in the hands of just a few; it must be given to all so that all can share in the blessings God gives through the land. . . . There will be no true reconciliation between our people and God as long as there is no just distribution, as long as the goods of our Salvadoran land do not bring benefits and happiness to all Salvadorans. Let us look this morning, sisters and brothers, on this church which extends far beyond the tiny geographical speck which is El Salvador. We feel that we are sisters and brothers with all the peoples of Central America, of this continent of North America, of Canada, of Europe. And we are all called to follow this light. What is marvelous to consider is that in this convocation of peoples God—the God of nations—respects the freedom, the customs, and the unique way of being of each people. The reading from Isaiah tells us, "The riches of the sea shall be emptied before you, and the wealth of nations shall be brought to you" (Isa. 60:5). This kingdom of God certainly has no need of our material goods, but we recognize that God is the origin of our coffee crops, our sugar cane, our cotton fields, all our wealth, and all the wealth of the world, and he has a right to all of these things. So we generously offer these things to God, recognizing that he owns them all, just as the magi placed gold, frankincense, and myrrh by the Christ Child's crib. Everything that the world produces is God's. The true wealth of the church as God's kingdom is the realization that all the differences among the world's peoples come from God. God has created in this world a kingdom rich like no other because all the marvels of the earth are his. Everything produced by human cultures belongs to God. It is God who promotes and guides all the wealth and progress of the peoples. Under the sign of bread and wine the priests of all latitudes of the world tell the Lord that we are offering him, in this bread and in this wine, the work of human hands. When we say "the work of human hands," we understand this to be the work of all the latitudes of the world. We offer it all to God because without God human labors and human progress have no meaning. We all contribute to this kingdom of God.

Last Homily[2]

March 24, 1980

Because of what Jorgito has written in today's editorial in El Independiente, I have some understanding of his filial emotions on the anniversary of his mother's death. In particular, I can glimpse her noble spirit, how she placed all of her refined education, her graciousness, at the service of a cause that is so important today: our people's true liberation.

My dear brothers and sisters, I think we should not only pray this evening for the eternal rest of our dear Doña Sarita, but above all we should take up her message, which every Christian ought to give intense life to. Many do not understand, and they think Christianity should not get involved in such things. But, to the contrary, you have just heard Christ's Gospel, that one must not love oneself so much as to avoid getting involved in the risks of life which history demands of us, that those who would avoid the danger will lose their life, while those who out of love for Christ give themselves to the service of others will live, like the grain of wheat that dies, but only apparently. If it did not die, it would remain alone. The harvest comes about because it dies, allows itself to be sacrificed in the earth and destroyed. Only by destroying itself does it produce the harvest.

From her place in eternity, Doña Sarita wonderfully confirms the message of the following passage from Vatican II, which I have chosen on her behalf. It says:

> We do not know when the earth and humanity will be consummated, nor do we know how the universe will be transformed. This

---

2. "As archbishop of San Salvador, Óscar Romero advocated for the poor and worked for peace amid an escalating civil war. For this reason, he was assassinated as he concluded his homily on March 24, 1980." "This is the homily Óscar Romero was delivering when he was killed," *America*, trans. James R. Brockman, SJ, https://www.americamagazine.org/faith/2018/10/12/homily-oscar-romero-was-delivering-when-he-was-killed.

world's present state, deformed by sin, is to pass away. But God teaches us that He is preparing a new dwelling place and a new earth where justice dwells and whose blessedness will fulfill and surpass all the longings for peace which spring up in the human heart. Then, when death has been overcome, God's children will arise in Christ. What was sown as something weak and corrupt will be clothed with incorruptibility. Charity and its fruits will endure, and all the creatures that God created with human beings in mind will be free of the bondage of futility.

We are warned that it profits one nothing to gain the whole world and lose oneself. Nevertheless, the expectation of a new earth must not weaken but rather stimulate our concern for perfecting this earth, where the body of the new human family grows, a body that even now is able in some way to foreshadow that new age. And so, to the extent that temporal progress can contribute to the better ordering of human society, it is of serious concern for the kingdom of God, even though temporal progress must be carefully distinguished from the growth of Christ's kingdom.

For after we have spread the benefits of human dignity, brotherhood and freedom across the earth in the Lord's Spirit and following his command, we shall rediscover all those good effects of our nature and of our efforts, but clean of every stain, brightened and transfigured. Then Christ will hand over to the Father "an eternal and universal kingdom: a kingdom of truth and life, a kingdom of holiness and grace, a kingdom of justice, love and peace" [Preface from the Mass of Christ the King]. "On this earth that kingdom is already present in mystery. When the Lord returns, its perfection will be accomplished."

[*Gaudium et Spes*, No. 39]

This is the hope that inspires us Christians. We know that every effort to better a society, especially one that is so enmeshed in injustice and in sin, is an effort that God blesses, that God desires, that God demands of us. And when one finds generous people, like Sarita, and her thought incarnated in Jorgito and in all those who work for these ideals—one must try to purify them, of course, Christianize them, clothe them with the hope of what lies beyond. That makes them stronger, giving us the assurance that all that we work at on earth, if we nourish it in a Christian hope, will never be a failure. We'll find it in a purer form in that kingdom where our merit will be in what we have worked at here on earth.

I think that to aspire is not without purpose at a time of hope and struggle, on this anniversary. We remember with gratitude that generous woman who was able to sympathize with the concerns of her husband and of her son and of all who work for a better world, and who added her own part, her grain of wheat, in her suffering. Beyond a doubt, this will guarantee that her heavenly reward will be in proportion to that sacrifice and understanding, which many lack at this moment in El Salvador.

I beg you all, dear brothers and sisters, let us look at these matters at this moment in our history with this hope, with this spirit of giving, of sacrifice, and let us do what we can. We can all do something, at least have a sense of understanding. The holy woman we remember today could not do many things directly perhaps, but she could encourage those who can work, could sympathize with their struggle, and above all could pray. Even after her death, she sends a message from eternity that it is worthwhile to labor, because all those longings for justice, peace and well-being that we experience on earth become realized for us if we enlighten them with Christian hope. We know that no one can go on forever, but those who have put into their work a sense of very great faith, of love for God, of hope among human beings, find it all results in the splendors of a crown that is the sure reward of all who labor thus, spreading truth, justice, love and kindness on the earth. It does not remain here, but, purified by God's Spirit, is harvested for us and given us for our reward.

This holy Mass, the Eucharist, is itself an act of faith. With Christian faith we know that at this moment the wheaten host is changed into the body of the Lord who offered himself for the world's redemption and in that chalice the wine is transformed into the blood that was the price of salvation. May this body immolated and this blood sacrificed for humans nourish us also, so that we may give our body and our blood to suffering and to pain—like Christ, not for self, but to impart notions of justice and peace to our people.

Let us, then, join together intimately in faith and hope at this moment of prayer for Doña Sarita and for ourselves.

[At this moment the fatal shot struck Archbishop Romero, and he fell mortally wounded.]